39.99

CASANOVA

AVARITIA

MATT FRACTION
GABRIEL BÁ

colors by Cris Peter
letters by Dustin Harbin

book design

Drew Gill & Gabriel Bá

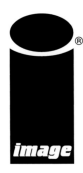

IMAGE COMICS, INC.
Robert Kirkman – Chief Operating Officer
Erik Larsen – Chief Financial Officer
Todd McFarlane – President
Marc Silvestri – Chief Executive Officer
Jim Valentino – Vice-President

Eric Stephenson – Publisher
Ron Richards – Director of Business Development
Jennifer de Guzman – Director of Trade Book Sales
Kat Salazar – Director of PR & Marketing
Corey Murphy – Director of Retail Sales
Jeremy Sullivan – Director of Digital Sales
Emilio Bautista – Sales Assistant
Branwyn Bigglestone – Senior Accounts Manager
Emily Miller – Accounts Manager
Jessica Ambriz – Administrative Assistant
David Brothers – Content Manager
Jonathan Chan – Production Manager
Drew Gill – Art Director
Meredith Wallace – Print Manager
Addison Duke – Production Artist
Vincent Kukua – Production Artist
Tricia Ramos – Production Assistant
IMAGECOMICS.COM

CASANOVA, THE COMPLETE EDITION VOLUME 3: AVARITIA. First printing. April 2015. Published by Image Comics, Inc. Office of publication: 2001 Center Street, Sixth Floor, Berkeley, CA 94704. Contains material originally published in magazine form as CASANOVA: AVARITIA #1-4. Printed in Canada. For international rights, contact: foreignlicensing@imagecomics.com. ISBN: 978-1-63215-191-9

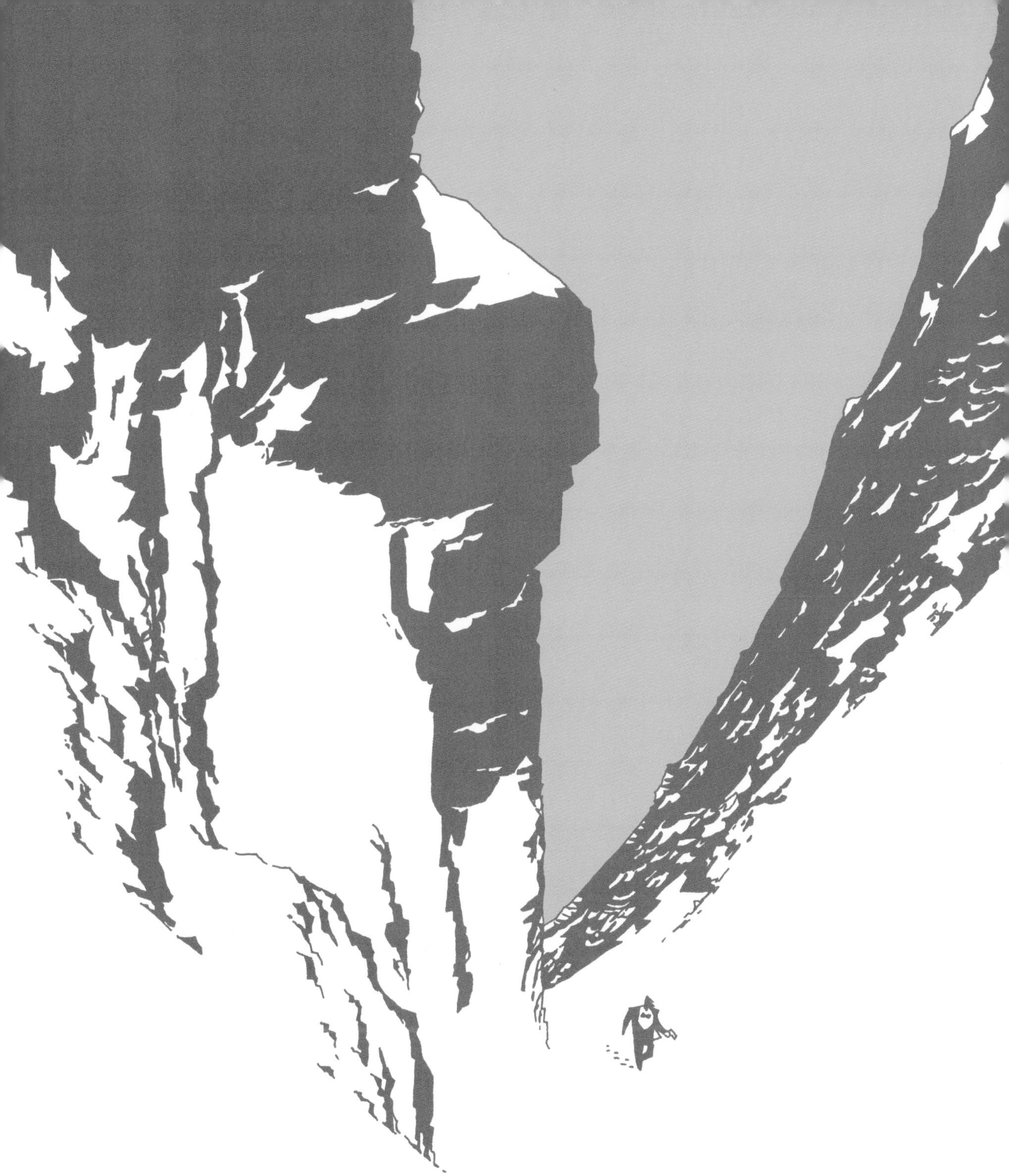

Matt Fraction:

For Bill King and Martha Maricoat Dunigan
who taught me everything

Gabriel Bá:

For Jean Giraud Moebius and Katsuhiro Otomo

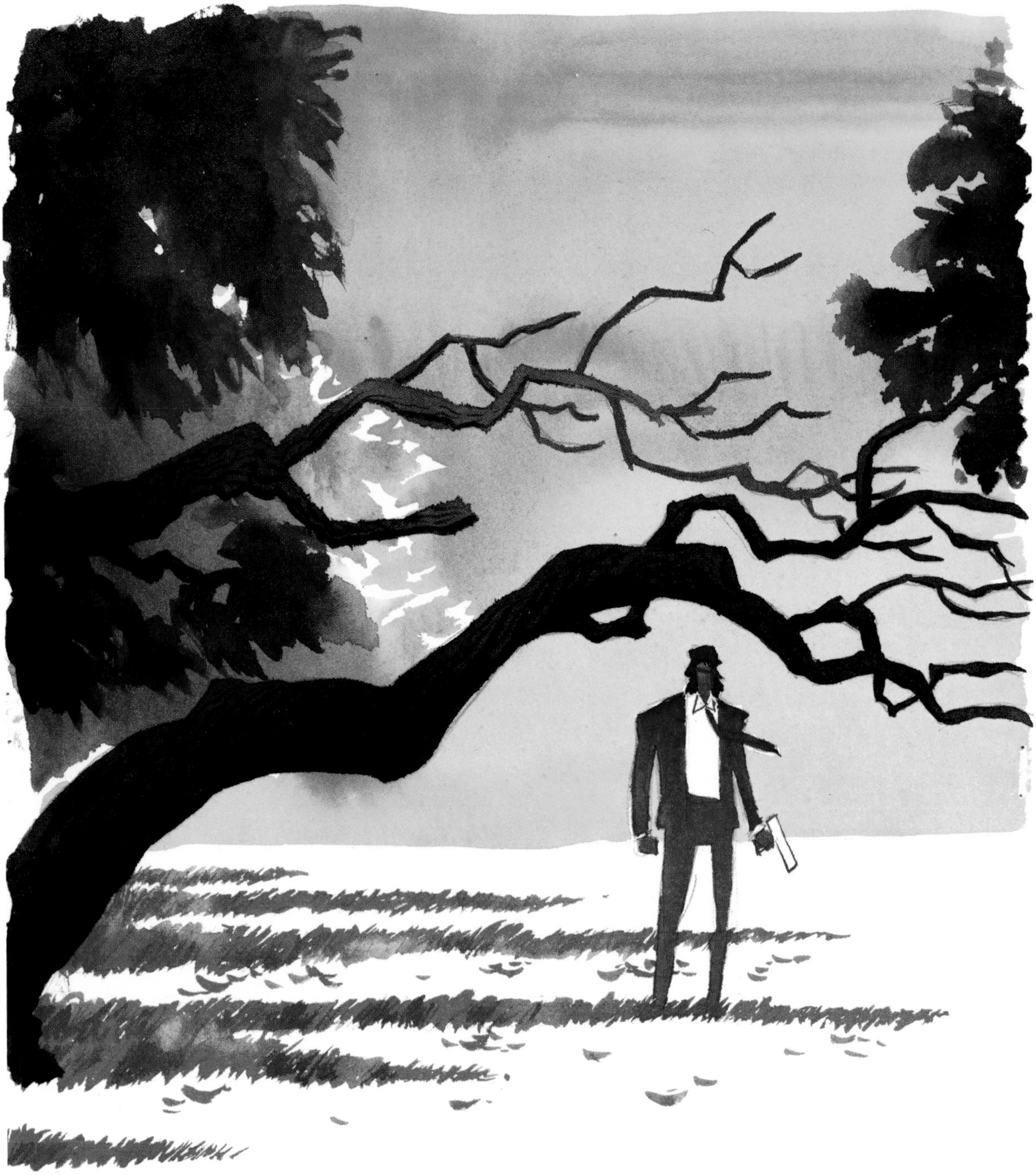

"Time forks perpetually into
countless futures. In one of them
I am your enemy."

Jorge Luis Borges
The Garden Of Forking Paths (1958)

"...(A)lways remember what
Jean-Luc Godard said:
'It's not where you take things from—
it's where you take them to.'"

Jim Jarmusch (2004)

"... I (...) intend to sound an urgent
word of warning relative to rather
obvious pre-nova conditions."

William S. Burroughs (1963)

"Everybody has a plan until they get
punched in the mouth."

Mike Tyson (date unknown)

W.A.S.T.E.-FREE WILDERNESS

WHAT IF IT'S NEVER ENOUGH

HARM REDUCTION

RELAXED IN PERSON

BACKMATTER

1. THE WIZARD BUYS A HAT

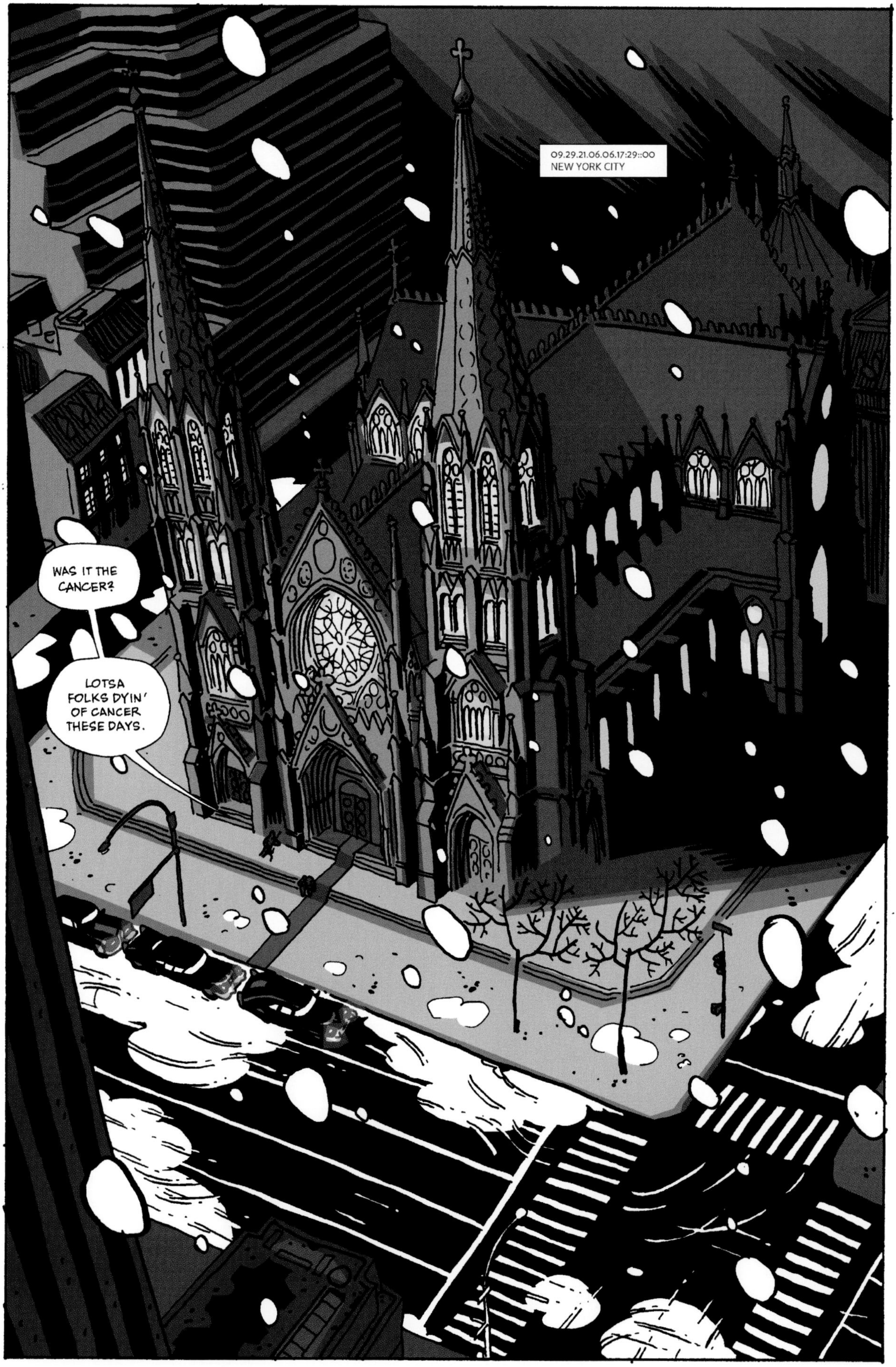
09.29.21.06.06.17:29::00
NEW YORK CITY
WAS IT THE CANCER?
LOTSA FOLKS DYIN' OF CANCER THESE DAYS.

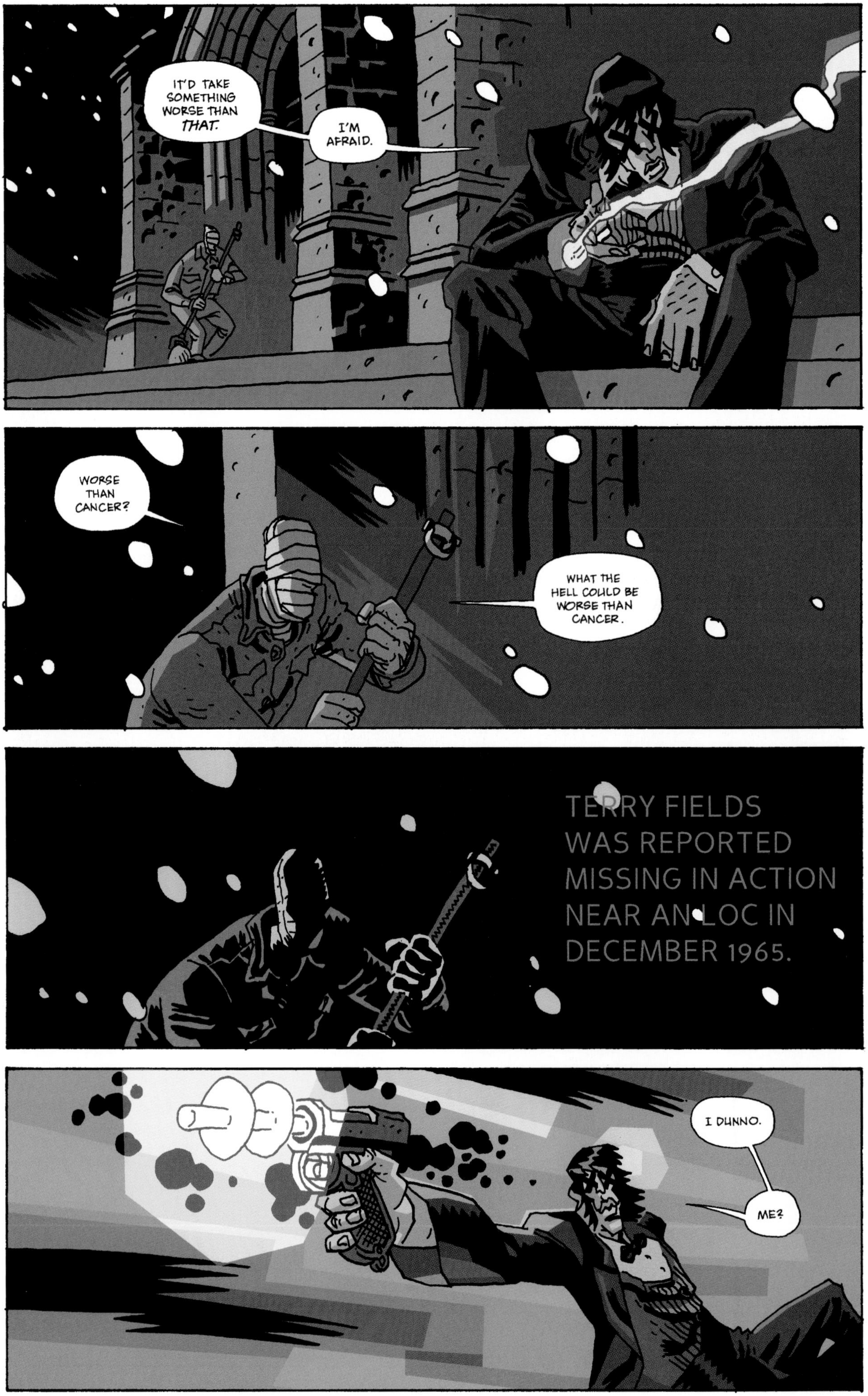
IT'D TAKE SOMETHING WORSE THAN THAT.
I'M AFRAID.
WORSE THAN CANCER?
WHAT THE HELL COULD BE WORSE THAN CANCER.
TERRY FIELDS WAS REPORTED MISSING IN ACTION NEAR AN LOC IN DECEMBER 1965.
I DUNNO.
ME?

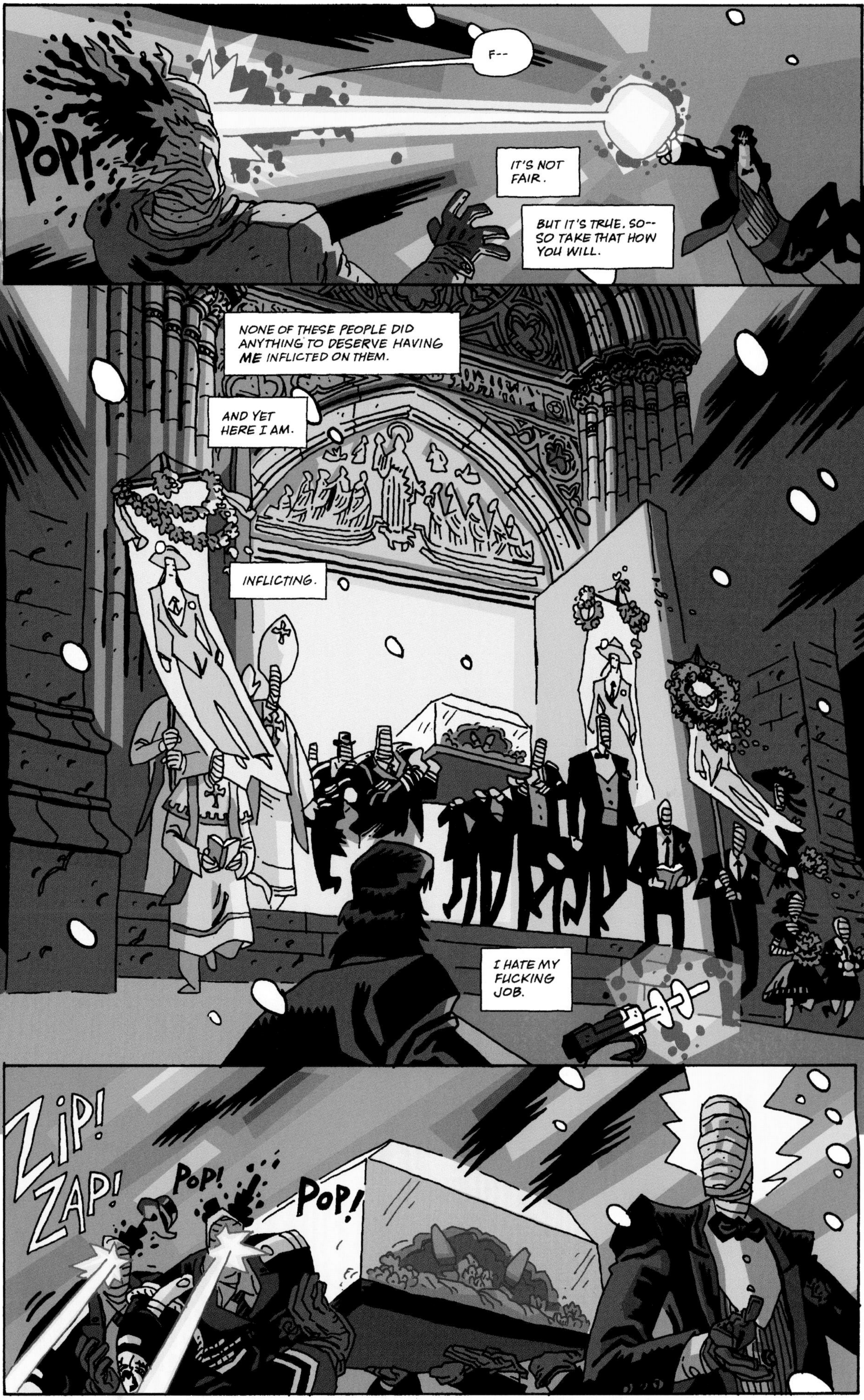
POP!
F--
IT'S NOT FAIR.
BUT IT'S TRUE. SO-- SO TAKE THAT HOW YOU WILL.
NONE OF THESE PEOPLE DID ANYTHING TO DESERVE HAVING ME INFLICTED ON THEM.
AND YET HERE I AM.
INFLICTING.
I HATE MY FUCKING JOB.
ZIP!
ZAP!
POP!
POP!

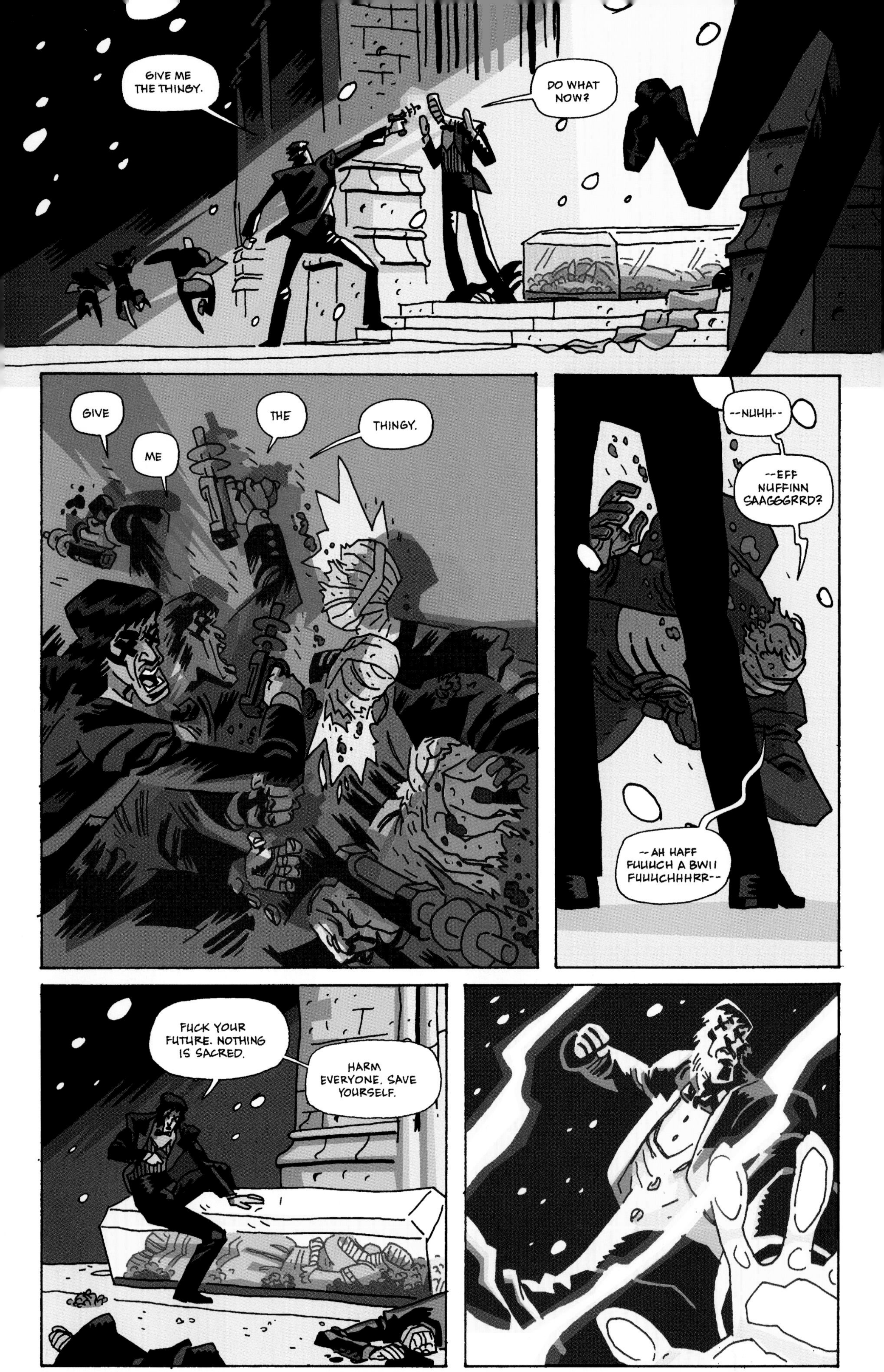
GIVE ME THE THINGY.
DO WHAT NOW?
GIVE
ME
THE
THINGY.
--NUHH--
--EFF NUFFINN SAAGGGRRD?
--AH HAFF FUUUCH A BWII FUUUCHHHRR--
FUCK YOUR FUTURE. NOTHING IS SACRED.
HARM EVERYONE. SAVE YOURSELF.

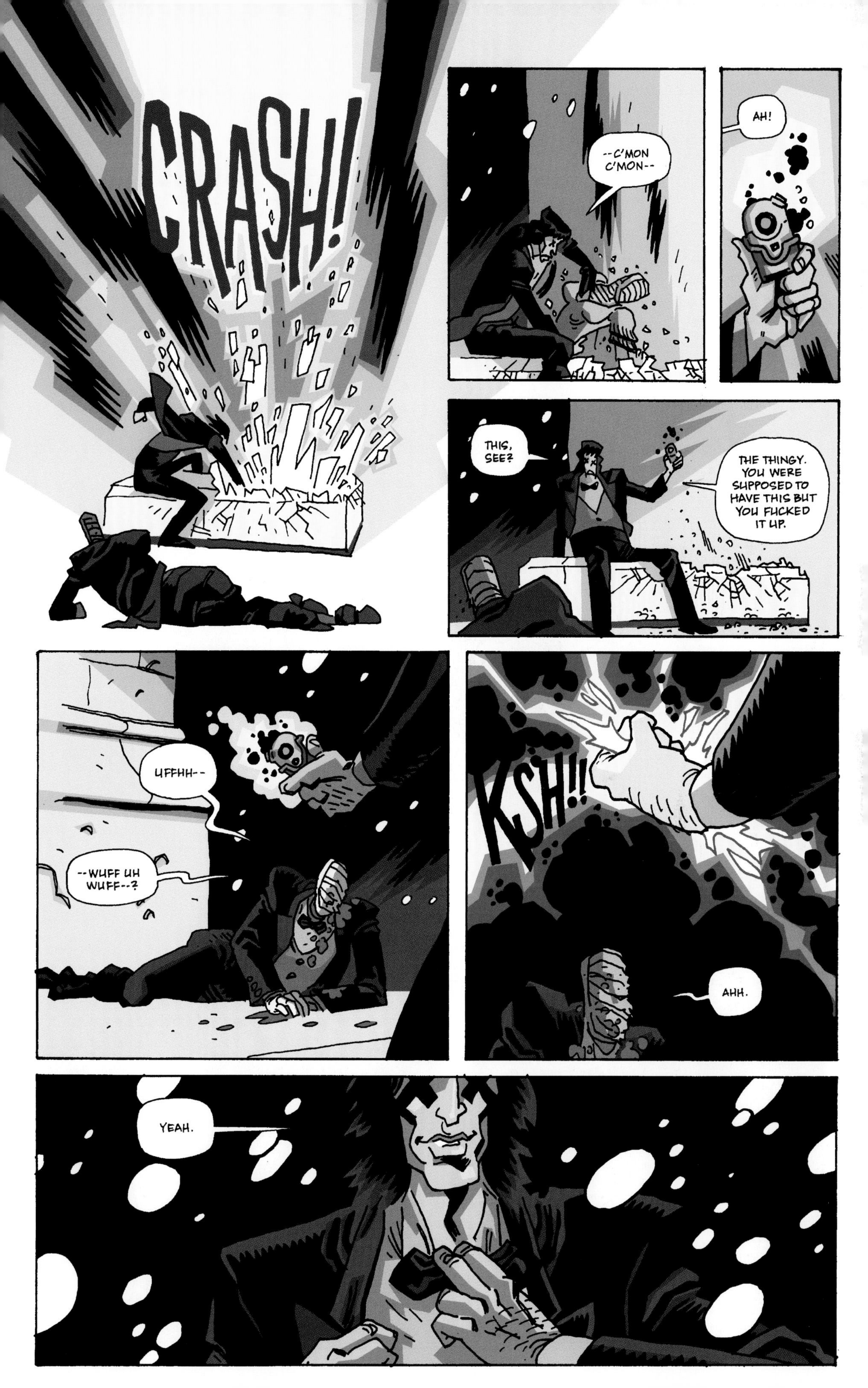
CRASH!
--C'MON C'MON--
AH!
THIS, SEE?
THE THINGY. YOU WERE SUPPOSED TO HAVE THIS BUT YOU FUCKED IT UP.
UFFHH--
--WUFF UH WUFF--?
KSH!!
AHH.
YEAH.

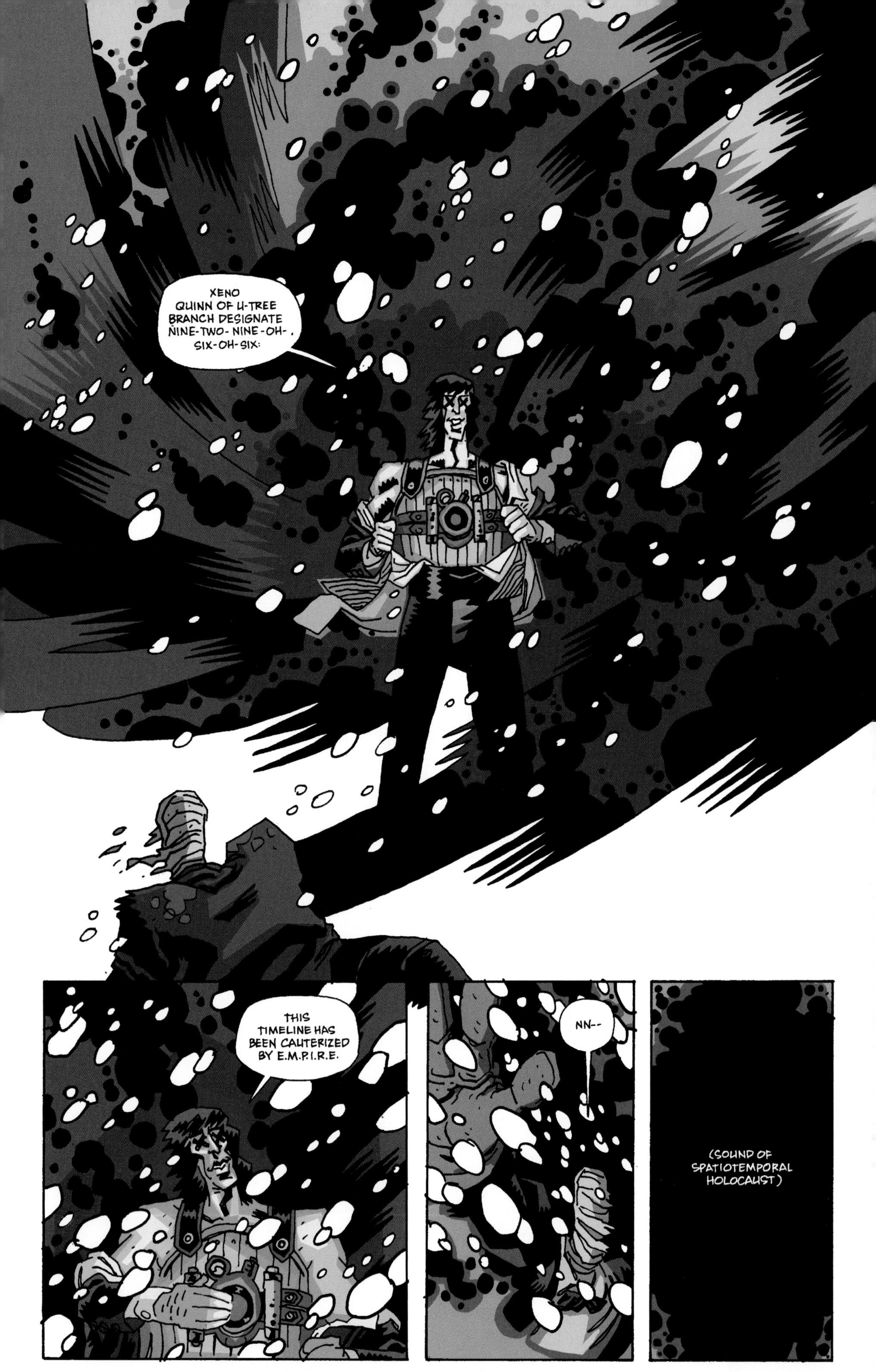
XENO QUINN OF U-TREE BRANCH DESIGNATE ÑINE-TWO- NINE-OH-, SIX-OH-SIX:
THIS TIMELINE HAS BEEN CAUTERIZED BY E.M.P.I.R.E.
NN--
(SOUND OF SPATIOTEMPORAL HOLOCAUST)

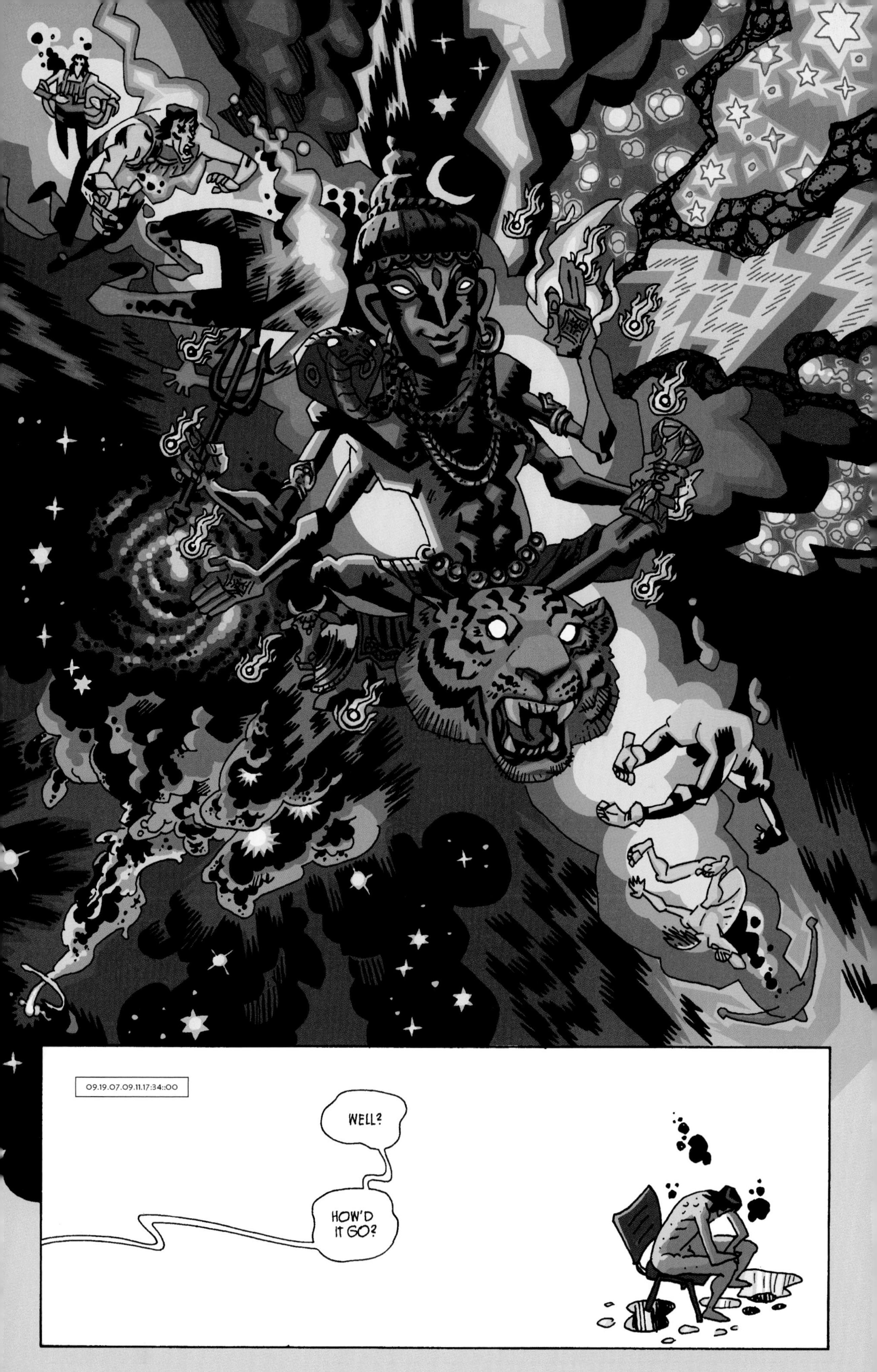
09.19.07.09.11.17:34::00
WELL?
HOW'D IT GO?

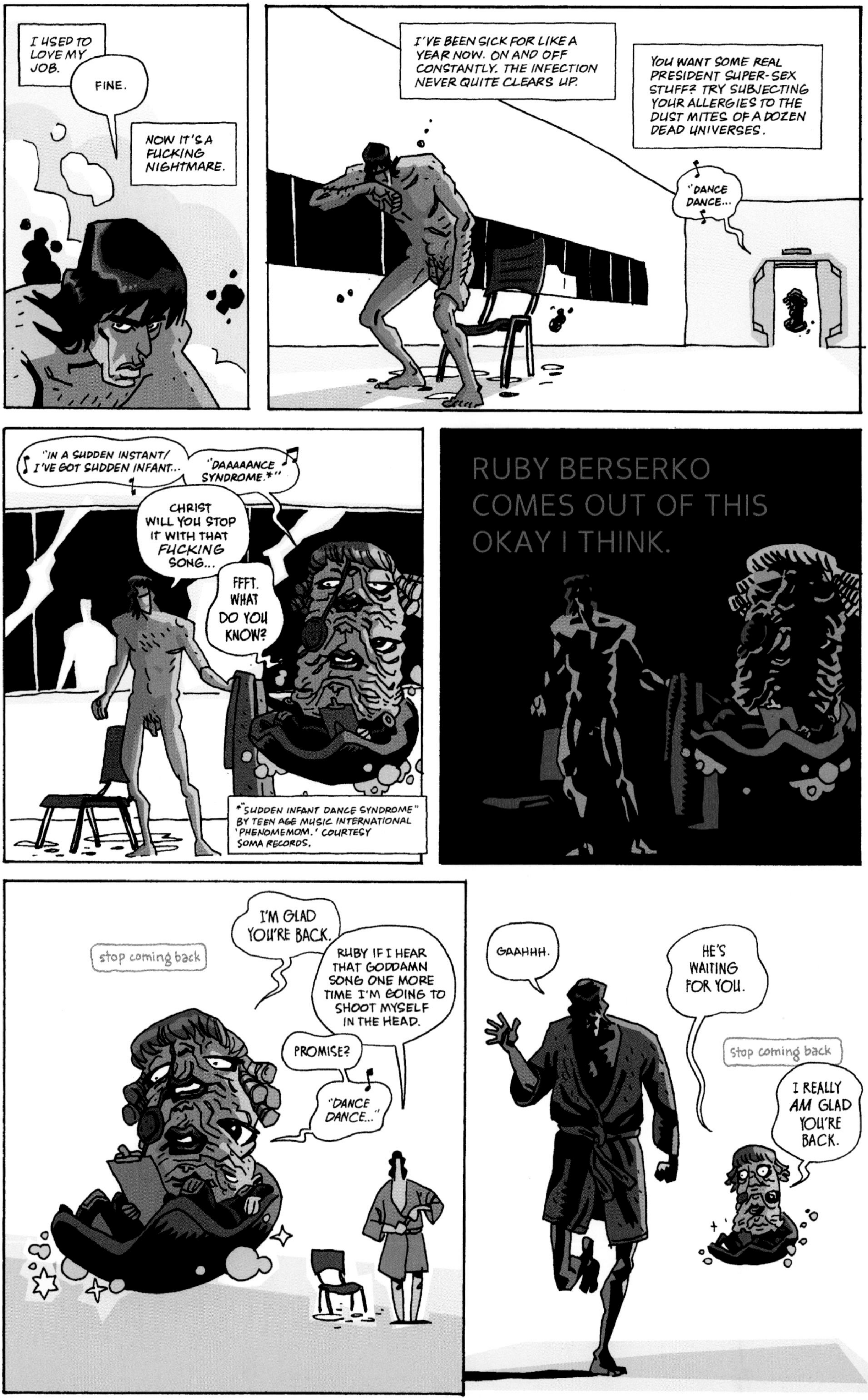
I USED TO LOVE MY JOB.
FINE.
NOW IT'S A FUCKING NIGHTMARE.
I'VE BEEN SICK FOR LIKE A YEAR NOW. ON AND OFF CONSTANTLY. THE INFECTION NEVER QUITE CLEARS UP.
YOU WANT SOME REAL PRESIDENT SUPER-SEX STUFF? TRY SUBJECTING YOUR ALLERGIES TO THE DUST MITES OF A DOZEN DEAD UNIVERSES.
"DANCE DANCE...
"IN A SUDDEN INSTANT/ I'VE GOT SUDDEN INFANT...
"DAAAAANCE SYNDROME.*"
CHRIST WILL YOU STOP IT WITH THAT FUCKING SONG...
FFFT. WHAT DO YOU KNOW?
*"SUDDEN INFANT DANCE SYNDROME" BY TEEN AGE MUSIC INTERNATIONAL 'PHENOMEMOM.' COURTESY SOMA RECORDS.
RUBY BERSERKO COMES OUT OF THIS OKAY I THINK.
I'M GLAD YOU'RE BACK.
stop coming back
RUBY IF I HEAR THAT GODDAMN SONG ONE MORE TIME I'M GOING TO SHOOT MYSELF IN THE HEAD.
PROMISE?
"DANCE DANCE..."
GAAHHH.
HE'S WAITING FOR YOU.
stop coming back
I REALLY AM GLAD YOU'RE BACK.

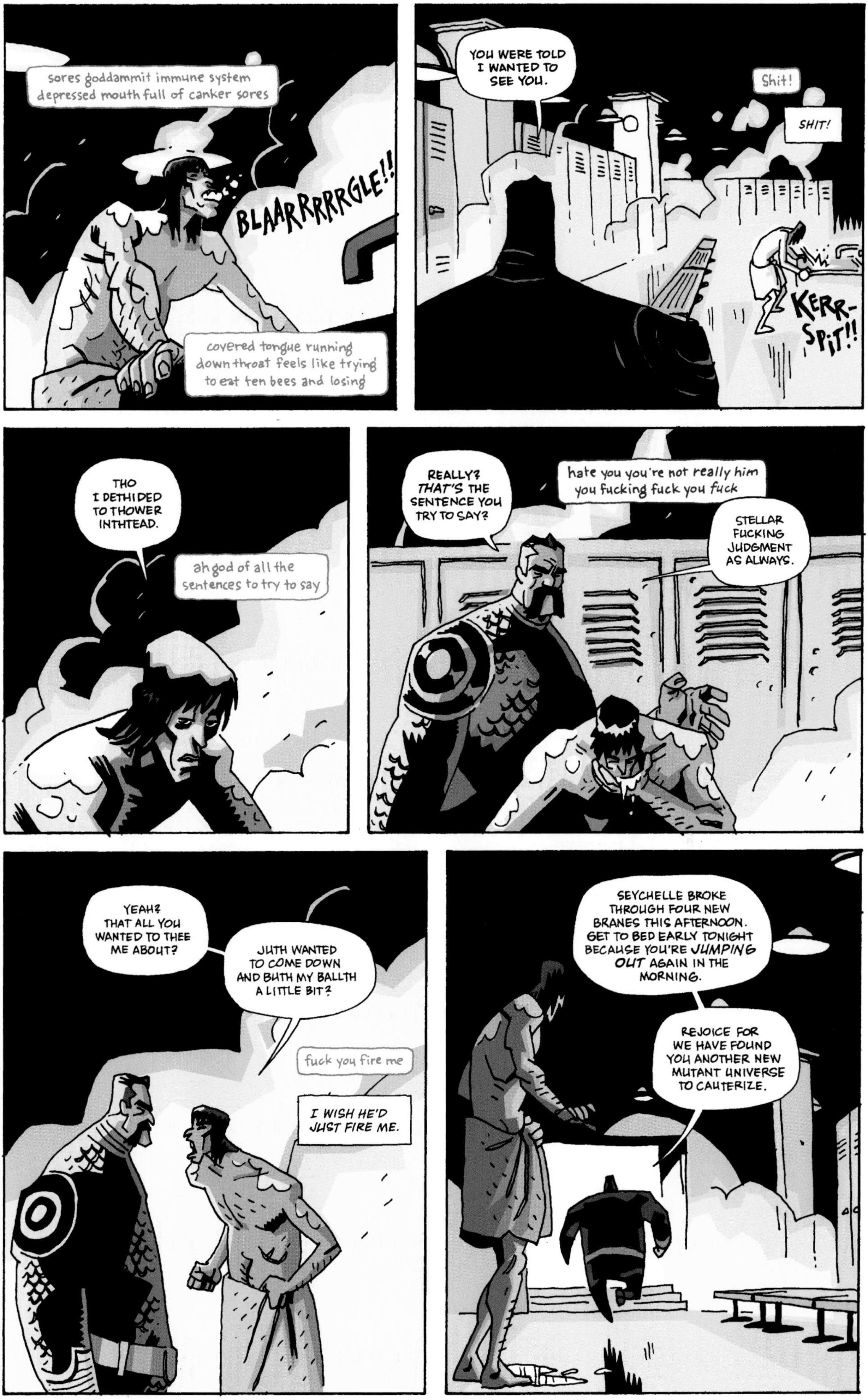
sores goddammit immune system depressed mouth full of canker sores
BLAARRRRRGLE!!
covered tongue running down throat feels like trying to eat ten bees and losing
YOU WERE TOLD I WANTED TO SEE YOU.
Shit!
SHIT!
KERR-SPIT!!
THO I DETHIDED TO THOWER INTHTEAD.
ah god of all the sentences to try to say
REALLY? THAT'S THE SENTENCE YOU TRY TO SAY?
hate you you're not really him you fucking fuck you fuck
STELLAR FUCKING JUDGMENT AS ALWAYS.
YEAH? THAT ALL YOU WANTED TO THEE ME ABOUT?
JUTH WANTED TO COME DOWN AND BUTH MY BALLTH A LITTLE BIT?
fuck you fire me
I WISH HE'D JUST FIRE ME.
SEYCHELLE BROKE THROUGH FOUR NEW BRANES THIS AFTERNOON. GET TO BED EARLY TONIGHT BECAUSE YOU'RE JUMPING OUT AGAIN IN THE MORNING.
REJOICE FOR WE HAVE FOUND YOU ANOTHER NEW MUTANT UNIVERSE TO CAUTERIZE.

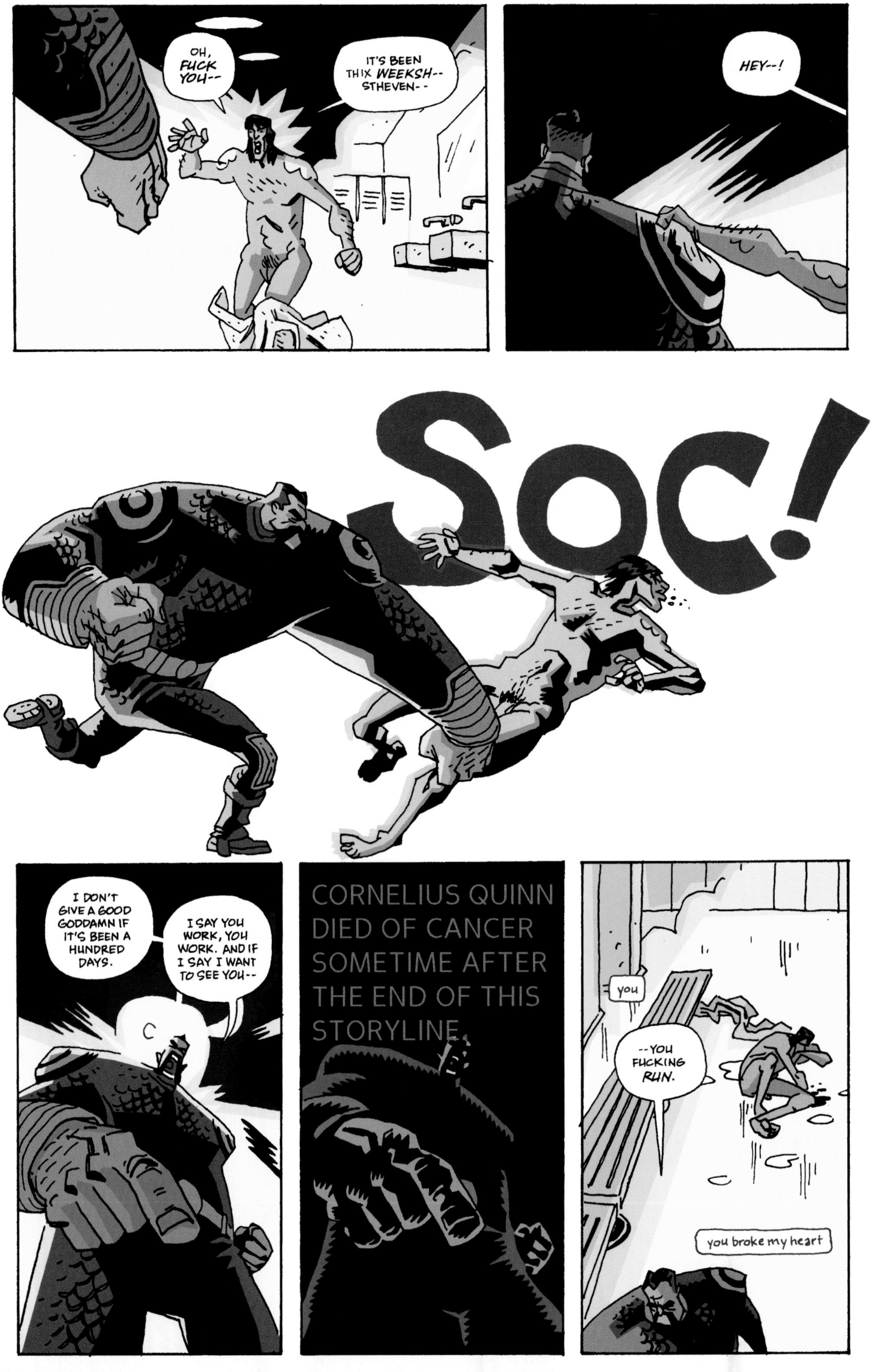
OH, FUCK YOU--
IT'S BEEN THIX WEEKSH-- STHEVEN--
HEY--!
SOC!
I DON'T GIVE A GOOD GODDAMN IF IT'S BEEN A HUNDRED DAYS.
I SAY YOU WORK, YOU WORK. AND IF I SAY I WANT TO SEE YOU--
CORNELIUS QUINN DIED OF CANCER SOMETIME AFTER THE END OF THIS STORYLINE.
you
--YOU FUCKING RUN.
you broke my heart

IT'S BEEN THREE YEARS, FOUR MONTHS, THREE WEEKS, AND ONE DAY. ...

I HATE MY LIFE.

I'M TRAPPED.

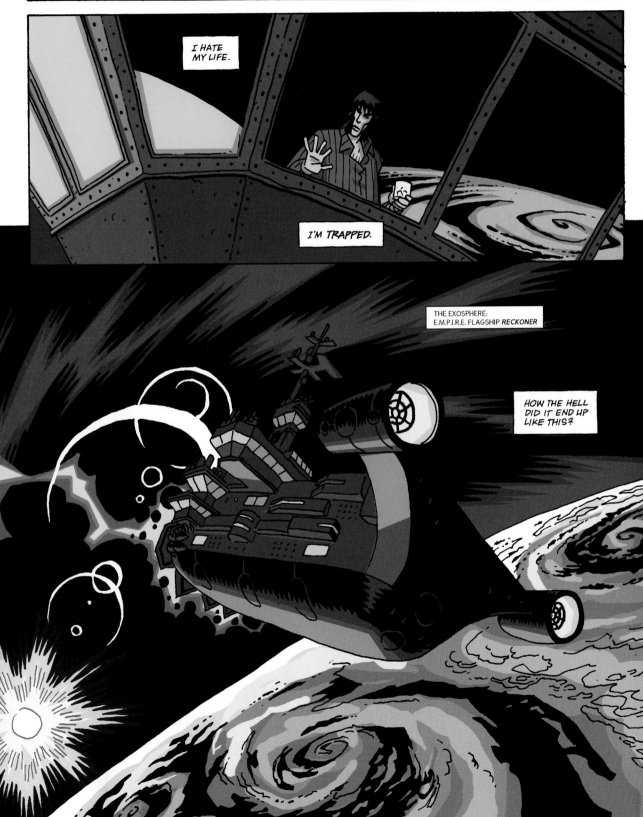

THE EXOSPHERE: E.M.P.I.R.E. FLAGSHIP *RECKONER*

HOW THE HELL DID IT END UP LIKE THIS?

2. I'M IN LOVE WITH MY CAR

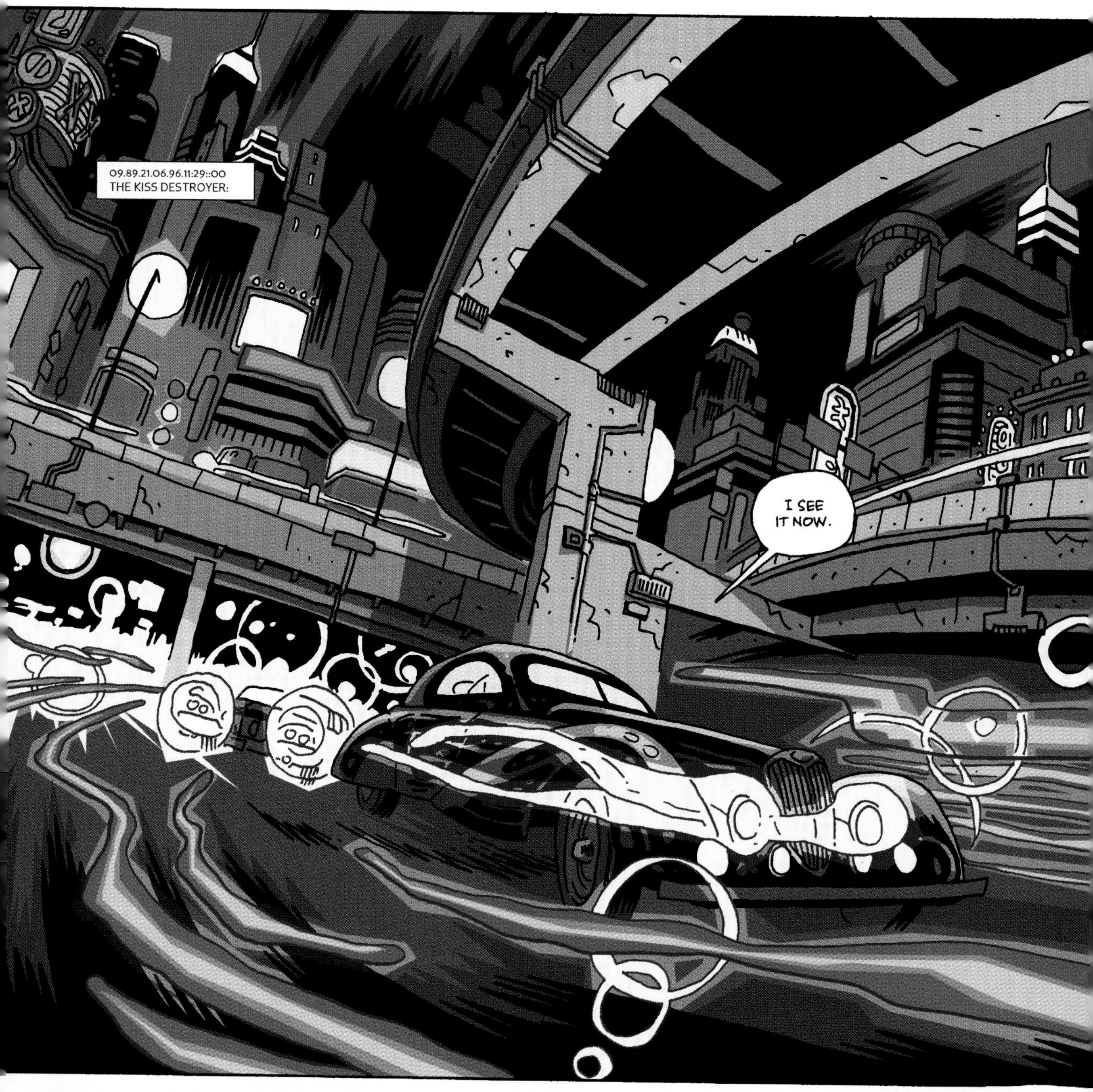
09.89.21.06.96.11:29::00
THE KISS DESTROYER:
I SEE IT NOW.

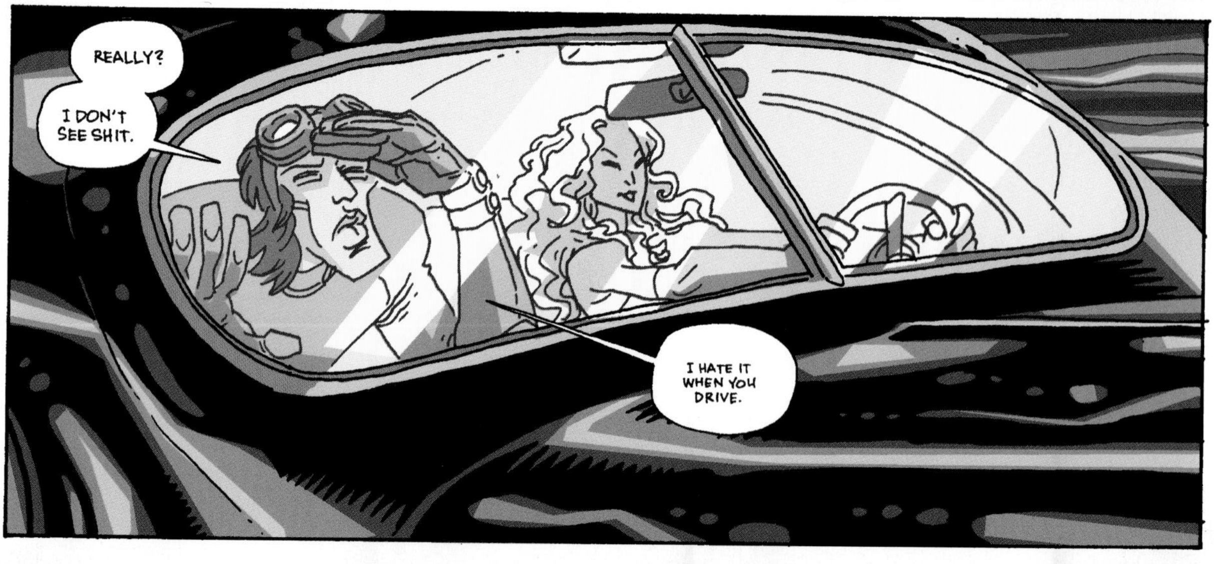
REALLY?
I DON'T SEE SHIT.
I HATE IT WHEN YOU DRIVE.

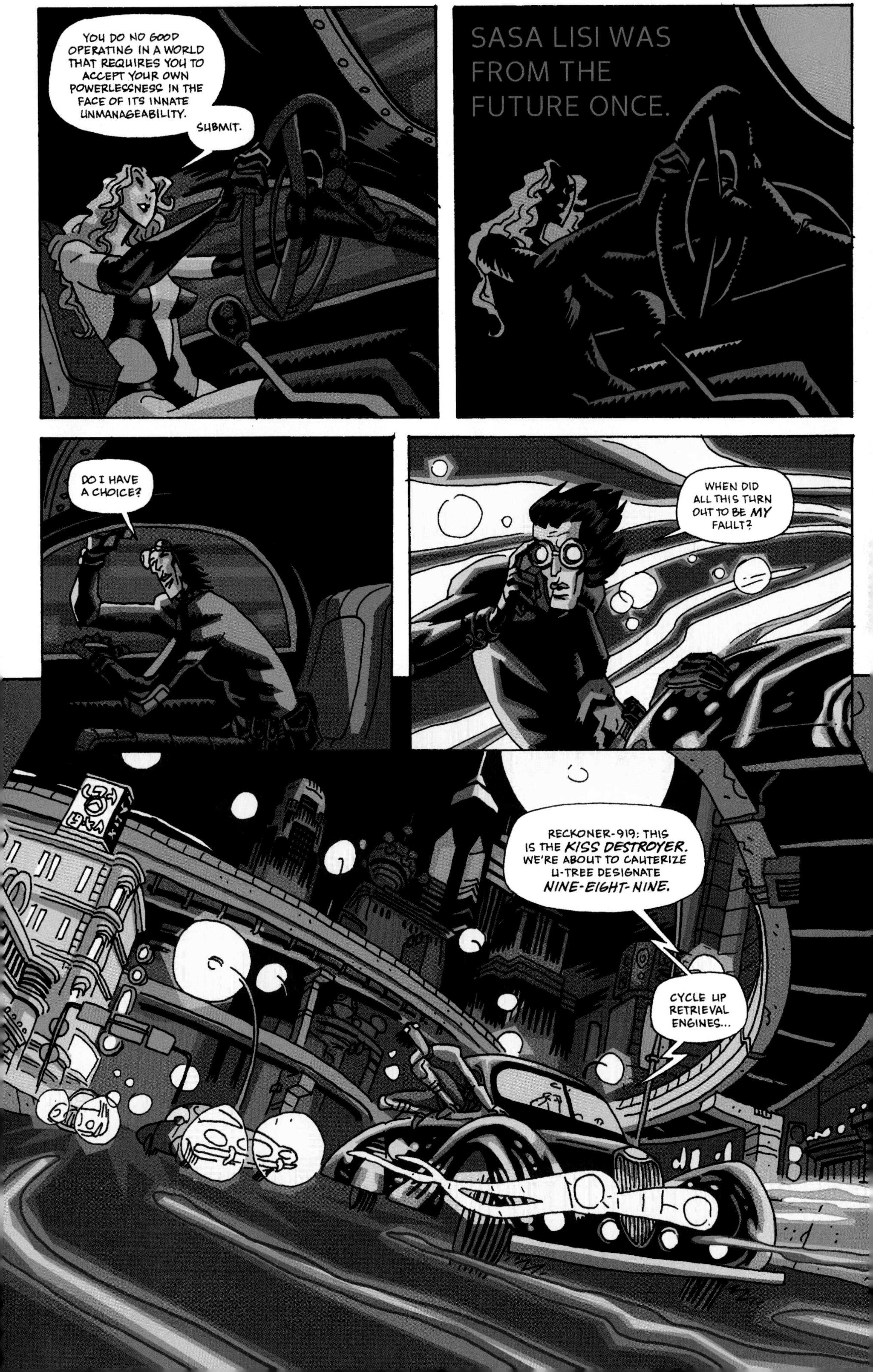
YOU DO NO GOOD OPERATING IN A WORLD THAT REQUIRES YOU TO ACCEPT YOUR OWN POWERLESSNESS IN THE FACE OF ITS INNATE UNMANAGEABILITY.
SUBMIT.
SASA LISI WAS FROM THE FUTURE ONCE.
DO I HAVE A CHOICE?
WHEN DID ALL THIS TURN OUT TO BE MY FAULT?
RECKONER-919: THIS IS THE KISS DESTROYER. WE'RE ABOUT TO CAUTERIZE U-TREE DESIGNATE NINE-EIGHT-NINE.
CYCLE UP RETRIEVAL ENGINES...

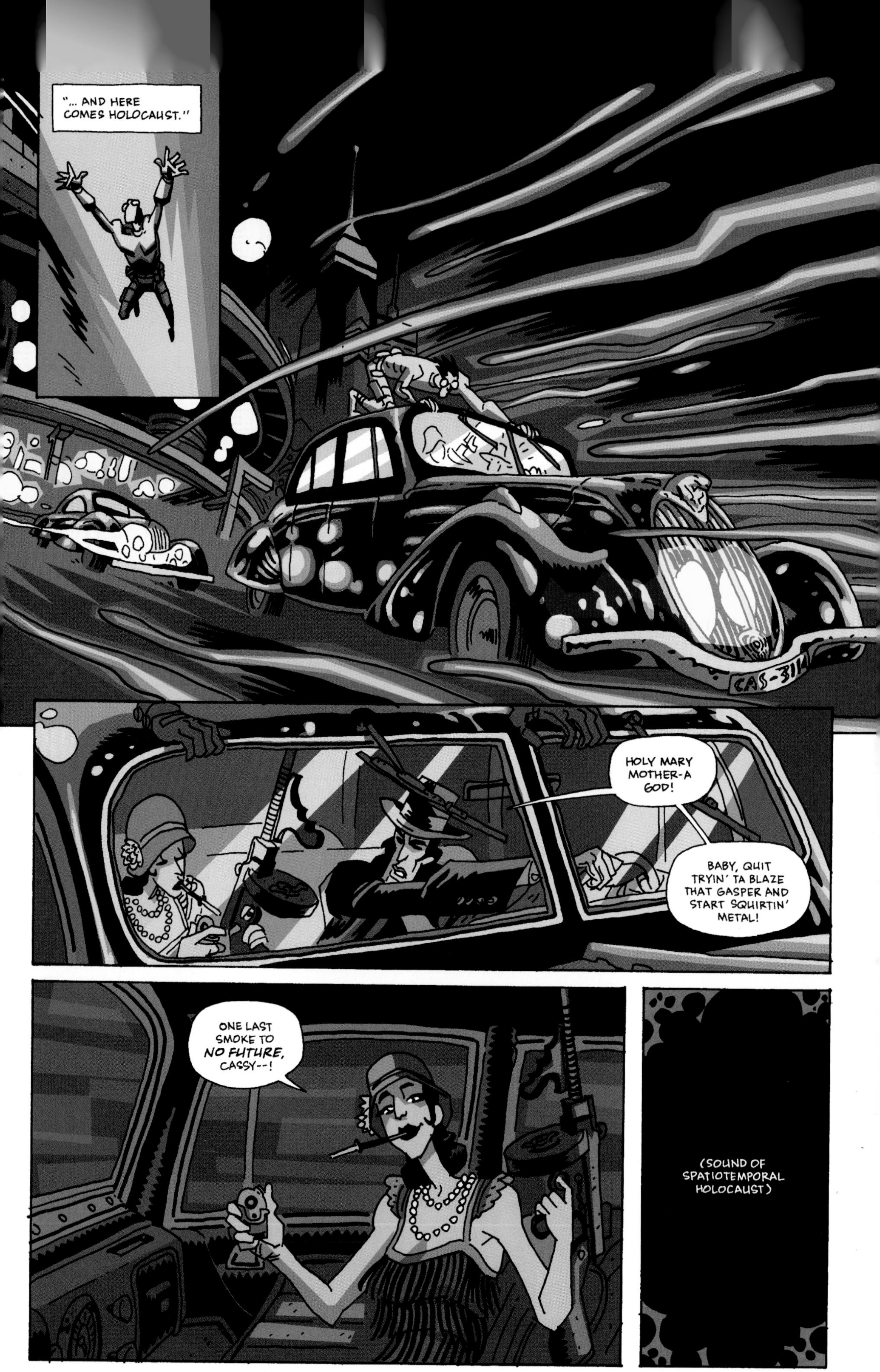
"... AND HERE COMES HOLOCAUST."
CAS-3114
HOLY MARY MOTHER-A GOD!
BABY, QUIT TRYIN' TA BLAZE THAT GASPER AND START SQUIRTIN' METAL!
ONE LAST SMOKE TO *NO FUTURE*, CASSY--!
(SOUND OF SPATIOTEMPORAL HOLOCAUST)

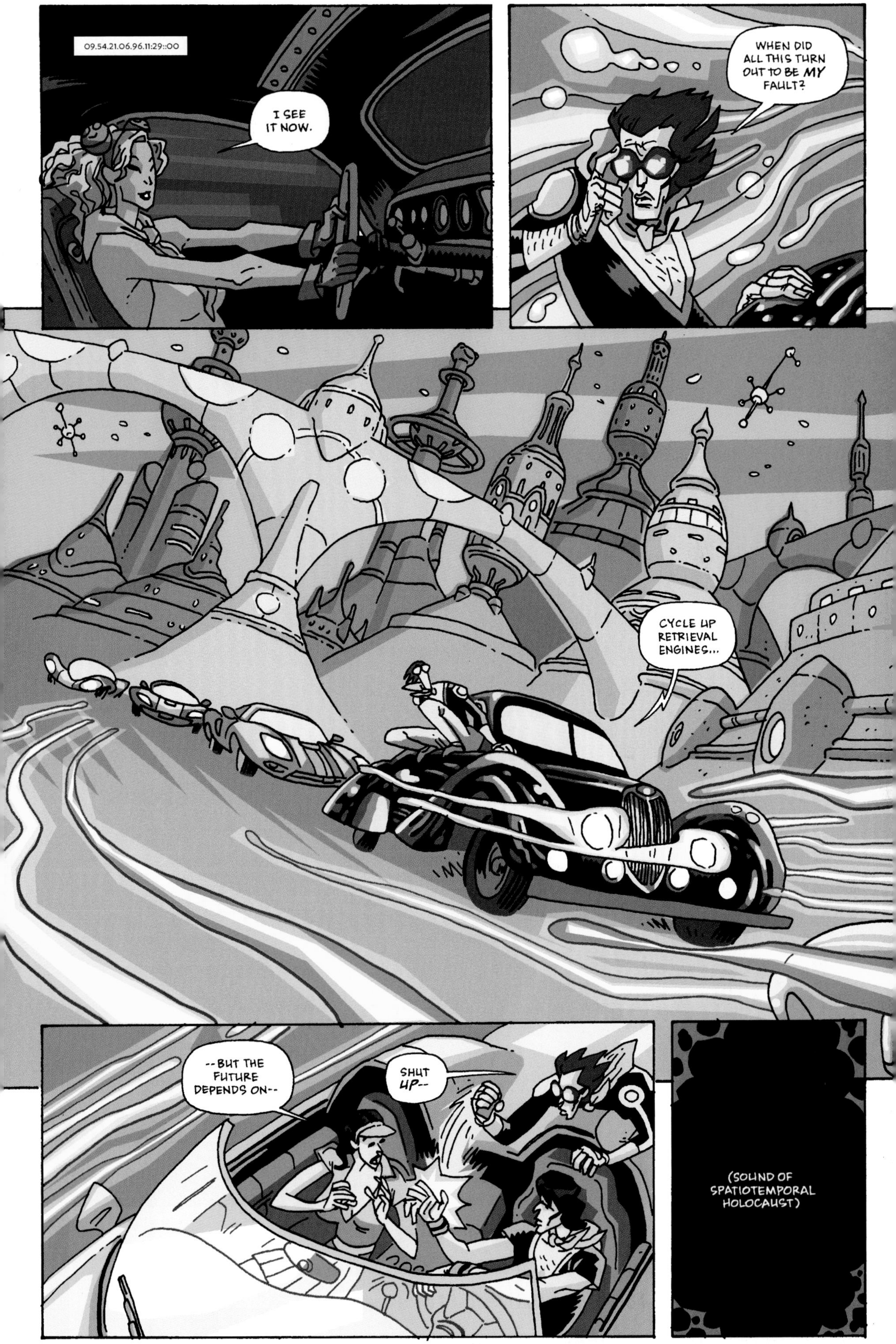
09.54.21.06.96.11:29::00
I SEE IT NOW.
WHEN DID ALL THIS TURN OUT TO BE MY FAULT?
CYCLE UP RETRIEVAL ENGINES...
--BUT THE FUTURE DEPENDS ON--
SHUT UP--
(SOUND OF SPATIOTEMPORAL HOLOCAUST)

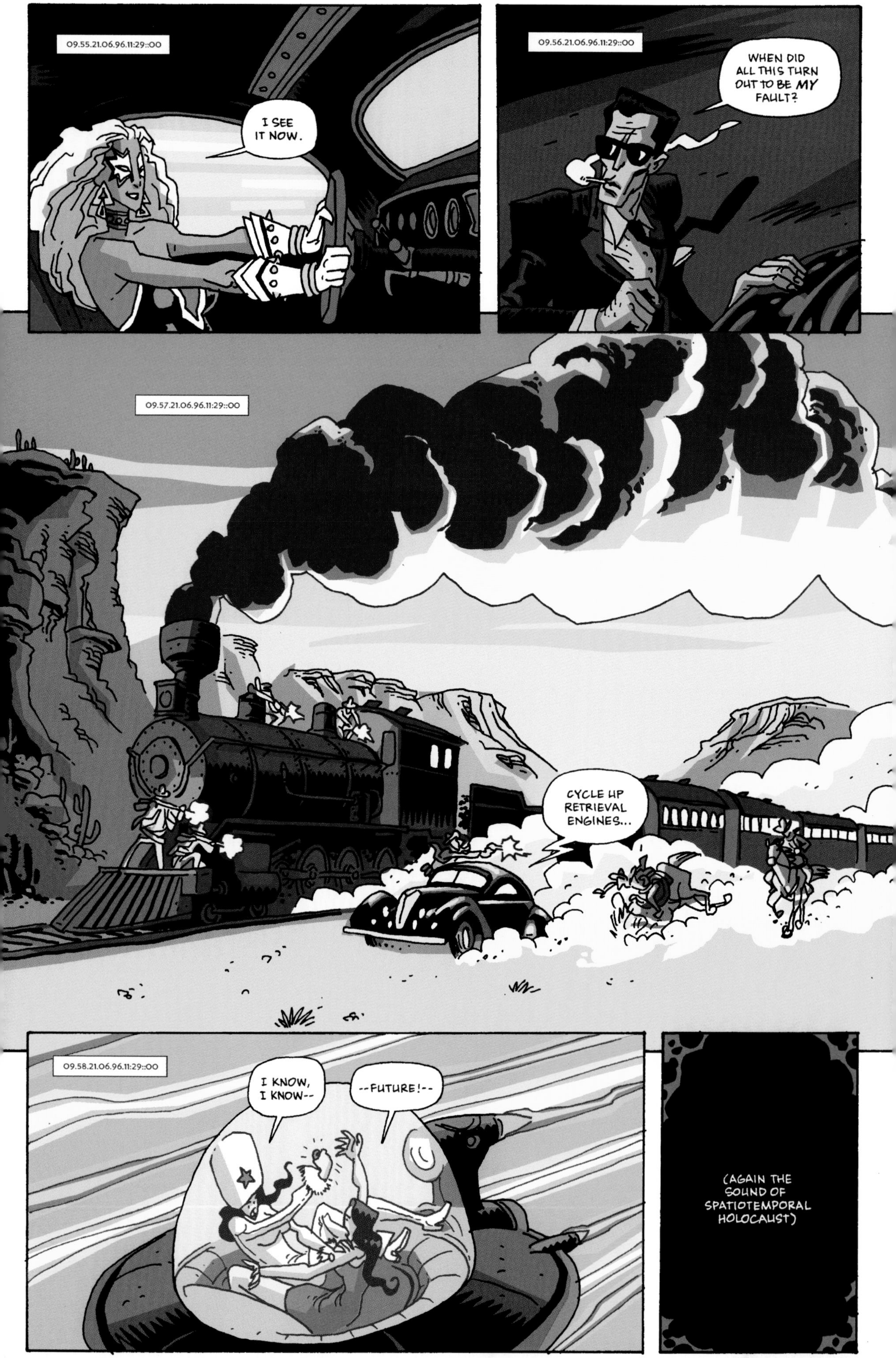
09.55.21.06.96.11:29::00
I SEE IT NOW.
09.56.21.06.96.11:29::00
WHEN DID ALL THIS TURN OUT TO BE MY FAULT?
09.57.21.06.96.11:29::00
CYCLE UP RETRIEVAL ENGINES...
09.58.21.06.96.11:29::00
I KNOW, I KNOW--
--FUTURE!--
(AGAIN THE SOUND OF SPATIOTEMPORAL HOLOCAUST)

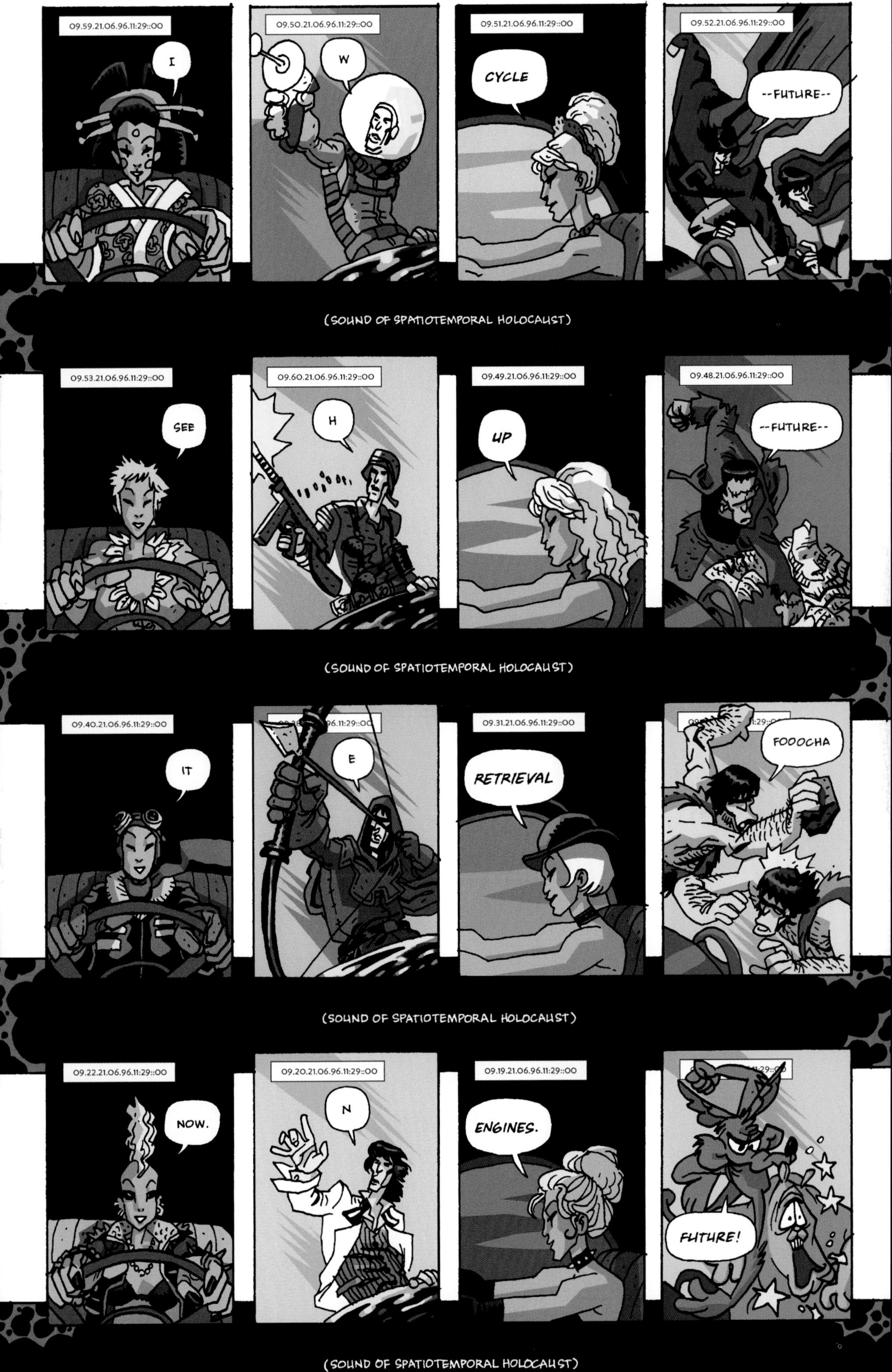

09.59.21.06.96.11:29::00
I
09.50.21.06.96.11:29::00
W
09.51.21.06.96.11:29::00
CYCLE
09.52.21.06.96.11:29::00
--FUTURE--
(SOUND OF SPATIOTEMPORAL HOLOCAUST)
09.53.21.06.96.11:29::00
SEE
09.60.21.06.96.11:29::00
H
09.49.21.06.96.11:29::00
UP
09.48.21.06.96.11:29::00
--FUTURE--
(SOUND OF SPATIOTEMPORAL HOLOCAUST)
09.40.21.06.96.11:29::00
IT
E
09.31.21.06.96.11:29::00
RETRIEVAL
FOOOCHA
(SOUND OF SPATIOTEMPORAL HOLOCAUST)
09.22.21.06.96.11:29::00
NOW.
09.20.21.06.96.11:29::00
N
09.19.21.06.96.11:29::00
ENGINES.
FUTURE!
(SOUND OF SPATIOTEMPORAL HOLOCAUST)

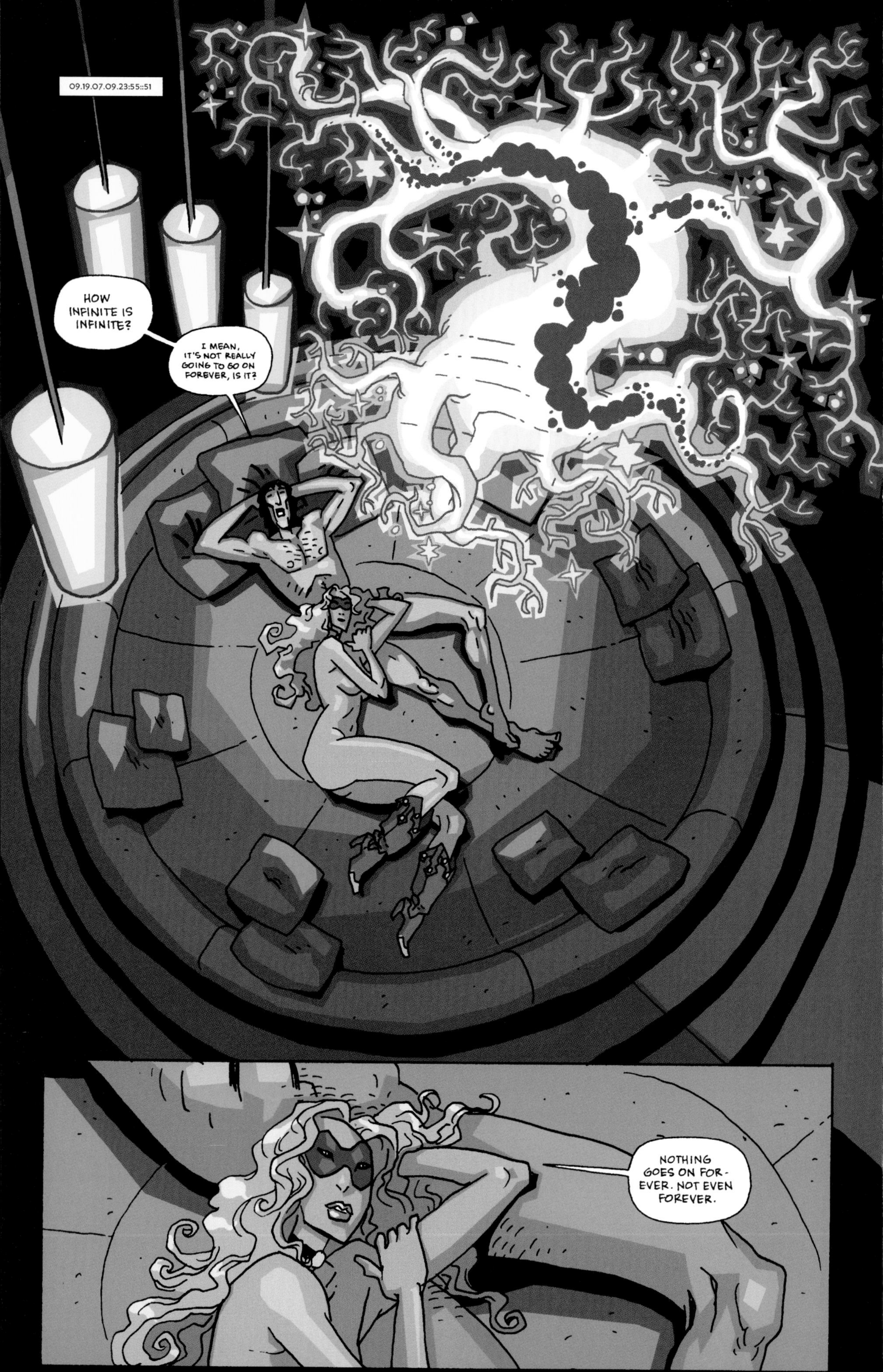
09.19.07.09.23:55::51
HOW INFINITE IS INFINITE?
I MEAN, IT'S NOT REALLY GOING TO GO ON FOREVER, IS IT?
NOTHING GOES ON FOR-EVER. NOT EVEN FOREVER.

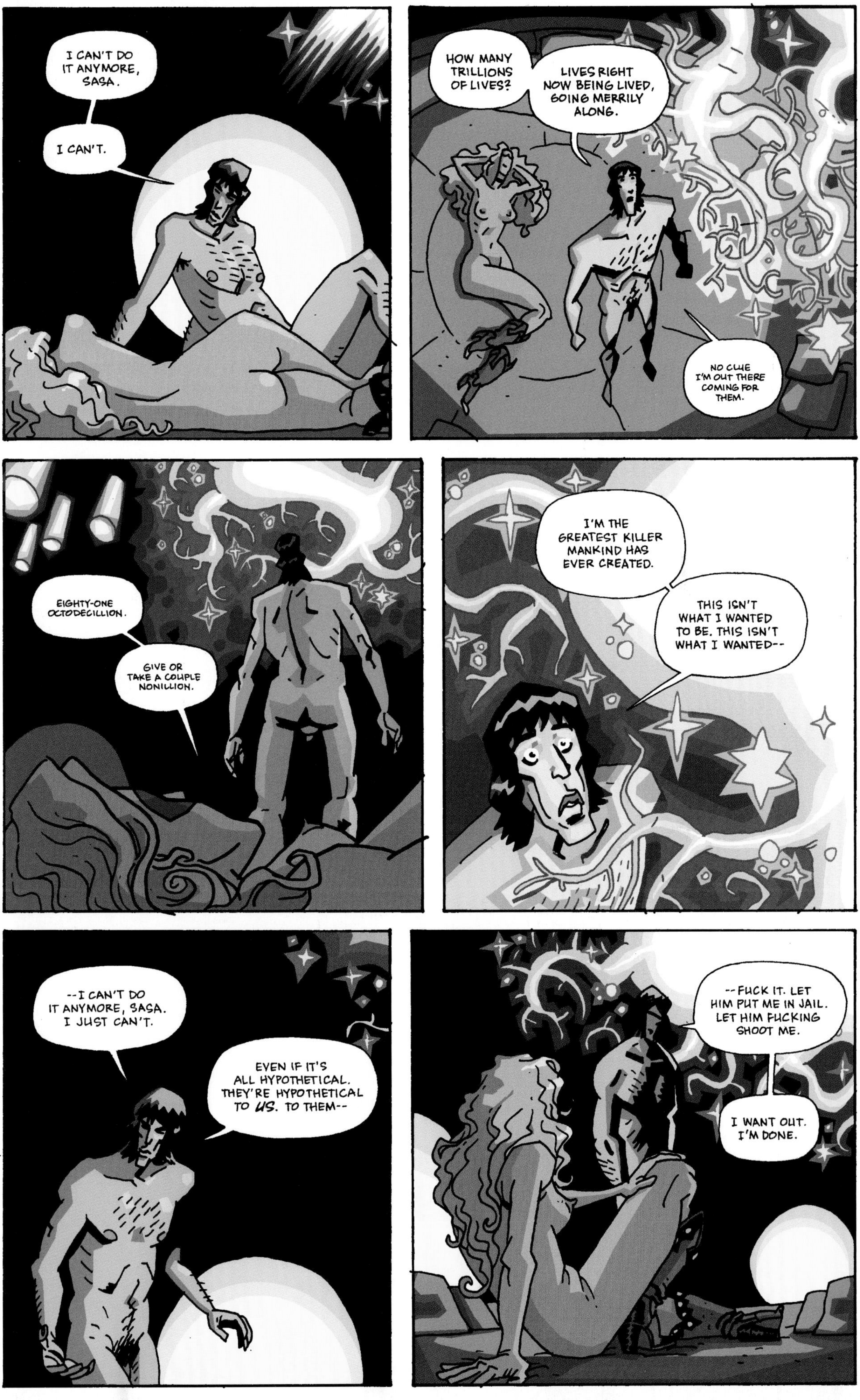
I CAN'T DO IT ANYMORE, SASA.
I CAN'T.
HOW MANY TRILLIONS OF LIVES?
LIVES RIGHT NOW BEING LIVED, GOING MERRILY ALONG.
NO CLUE I'M OUT THERE COMING FOR THEM.
EIGHTY-ONE OCTODECILLION.
GIVE OR TAKE A COUPLE NONILLION.
I'M THE GREATEST KILLER MANKIND HAS EVER CREATED.
THIS ISN'T WHAT I WANTED TO BE. THIS ISN'T WHAT I WANTED--
--I CAN'T DO IT ANYMORE, SASA. I JUST CAN'T.
EVEN IF IT'S ALL HYPOTHETICAL. THEY'RE HYPOTHETICAL TO *US*. TO THEM--
--FUCK IT. LET HIM PUT ME IN JAIL. LET HIM FUCKING SHOOT ME.
I WANT OUT. I'M DONE.

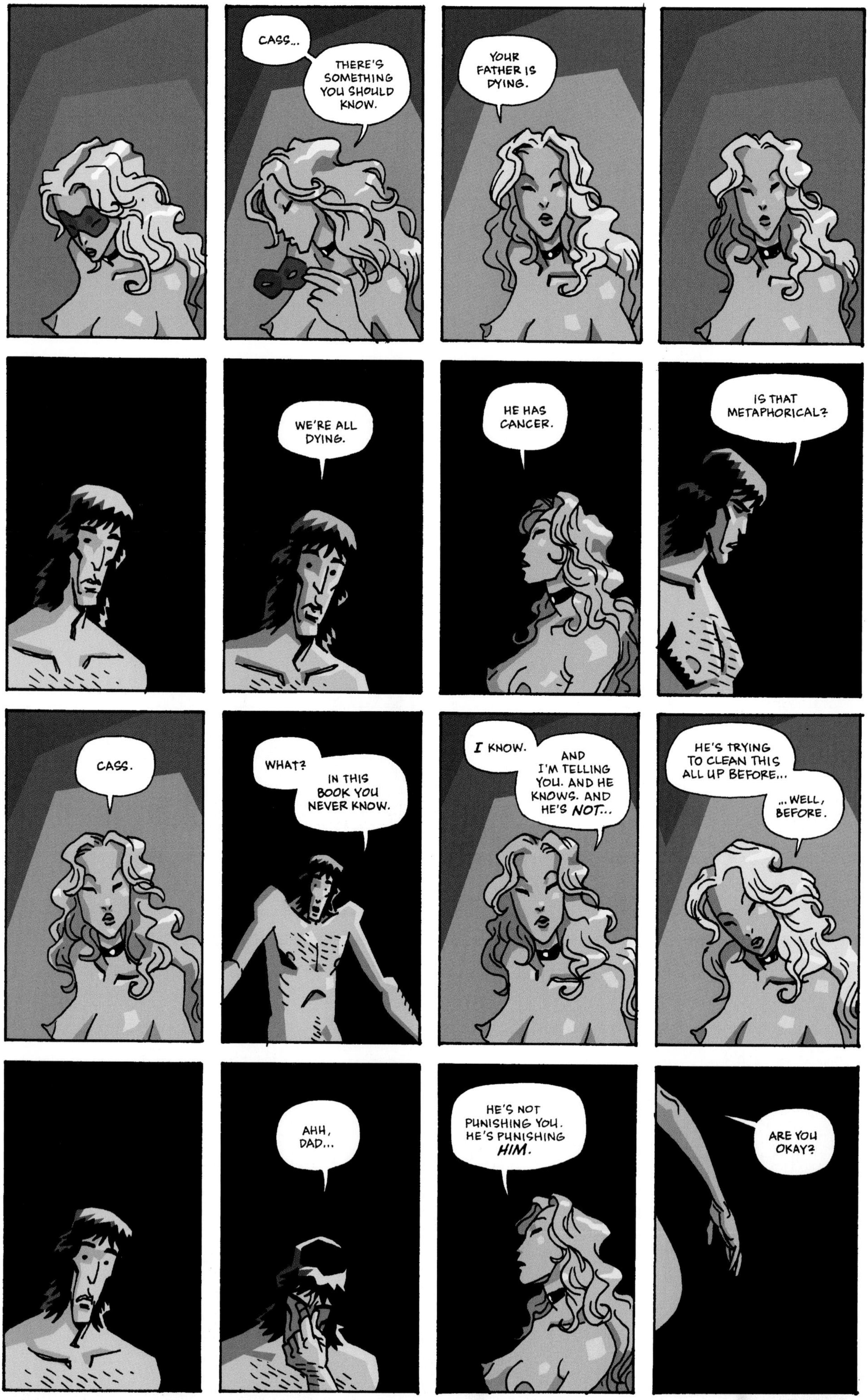
CASS...
THERE'S SOMETHING YOU SHOULD KNOW.
YOUR FATHER IS DYING.
WE'RE ALL DYING.
HE HAS CANCER.
IS THAT METAPHORICAL?
CASS.
WHAT?
IN THIS BOOK YOU NEVER KNOW.
I KNOW.
AND I'M TELLING YOU. AND HE KNOWS. AND HE'S NOT...
HE'S TRYING TO CLEAN THIS ALL UP BEFORE...
...WELL, BEFORE.
AHH, DAD...
HE'S NOT PUNISHING YOU. HE'S PUNISHING HIM.
ARE YOU OKAY?

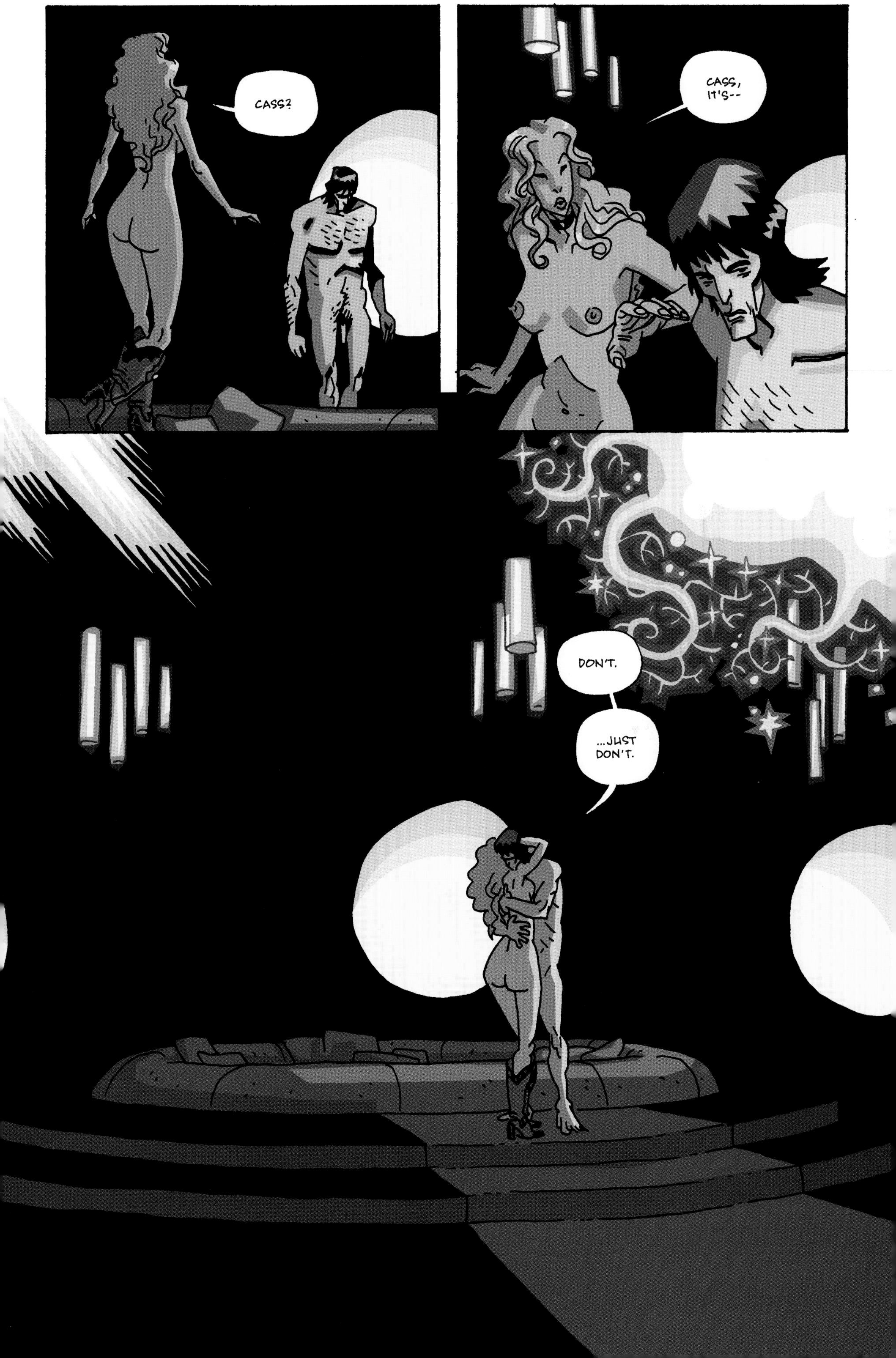
CASS?
CASS, IT'S--
DON'T.
...JUST DON'T.

3. EVERYTHING IS OVER

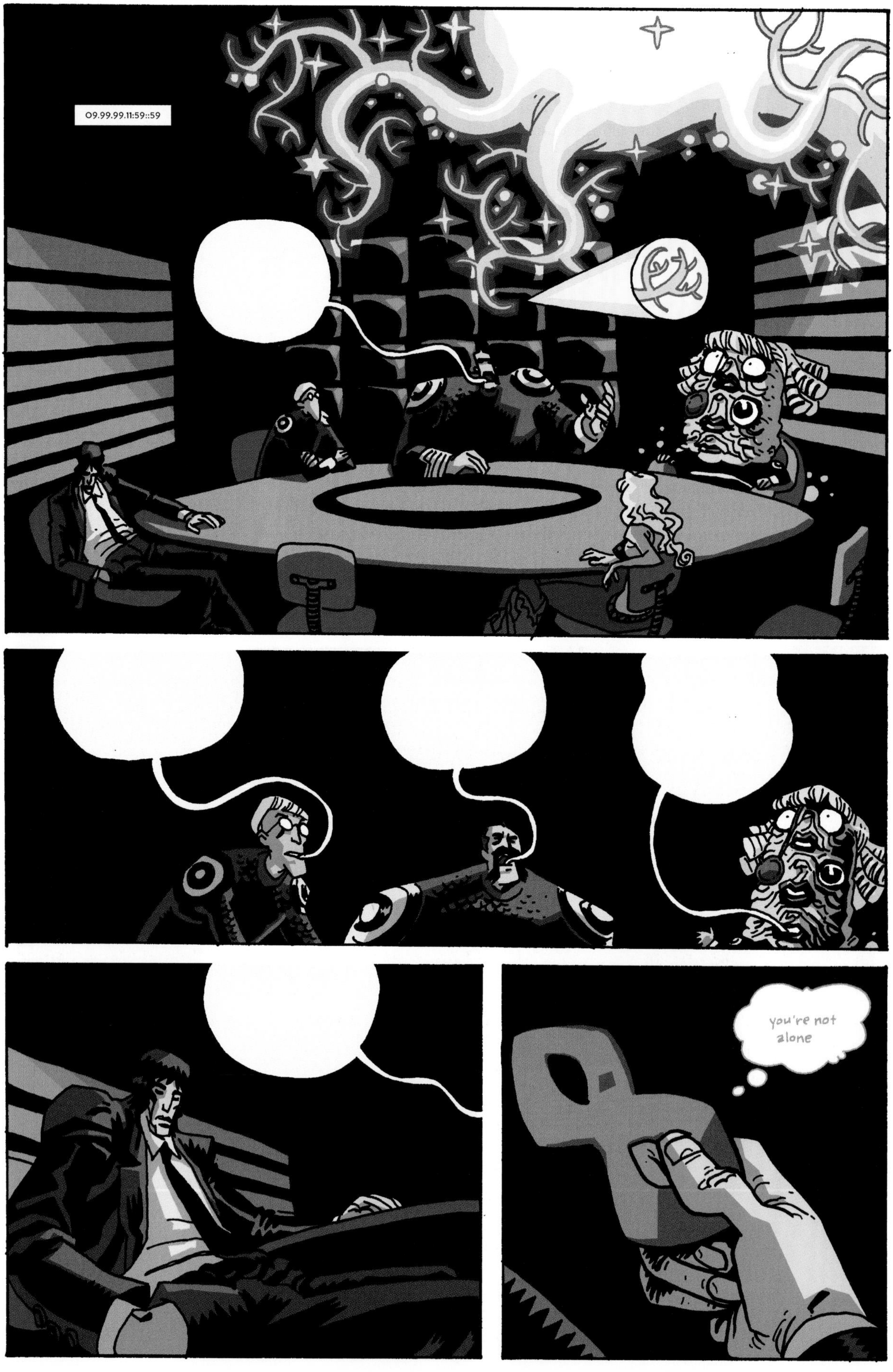
09.99.99.11:59::59
you're not alone

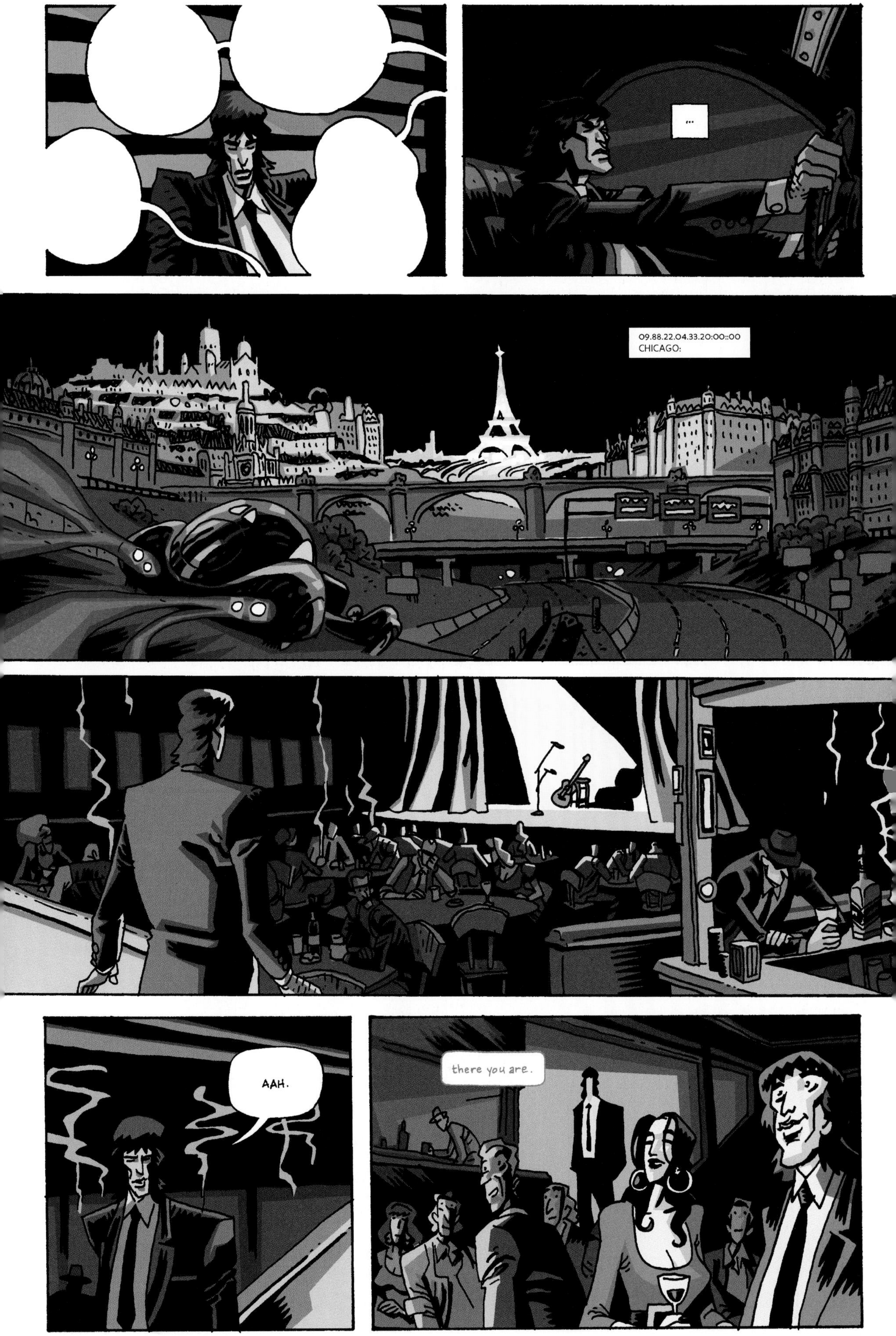
...
09.88.22.04.33.20:00::00
CHICAGO:
AAH.
there you are.

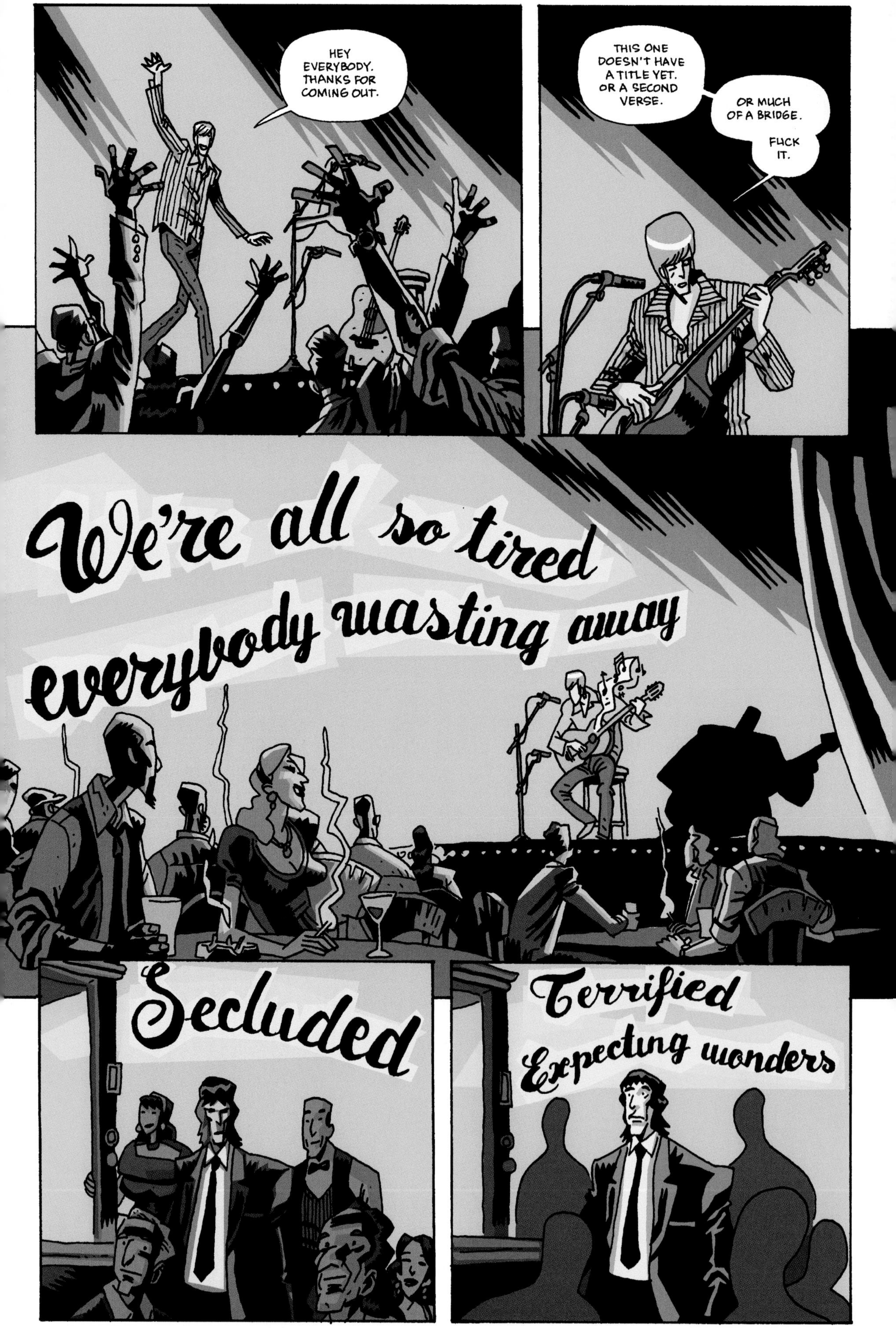
HEY EVERYBODY. THANKS FOR COMING OUT.
THIS ONE DOESN'T HAVE A TITLE YET. OR A SECOND VERSE.
OR MUCH OF A BRIDGE.
FUCK IT.
We're all so tired
everybody wasting away
Secluded
Terrified
Expecting wonders

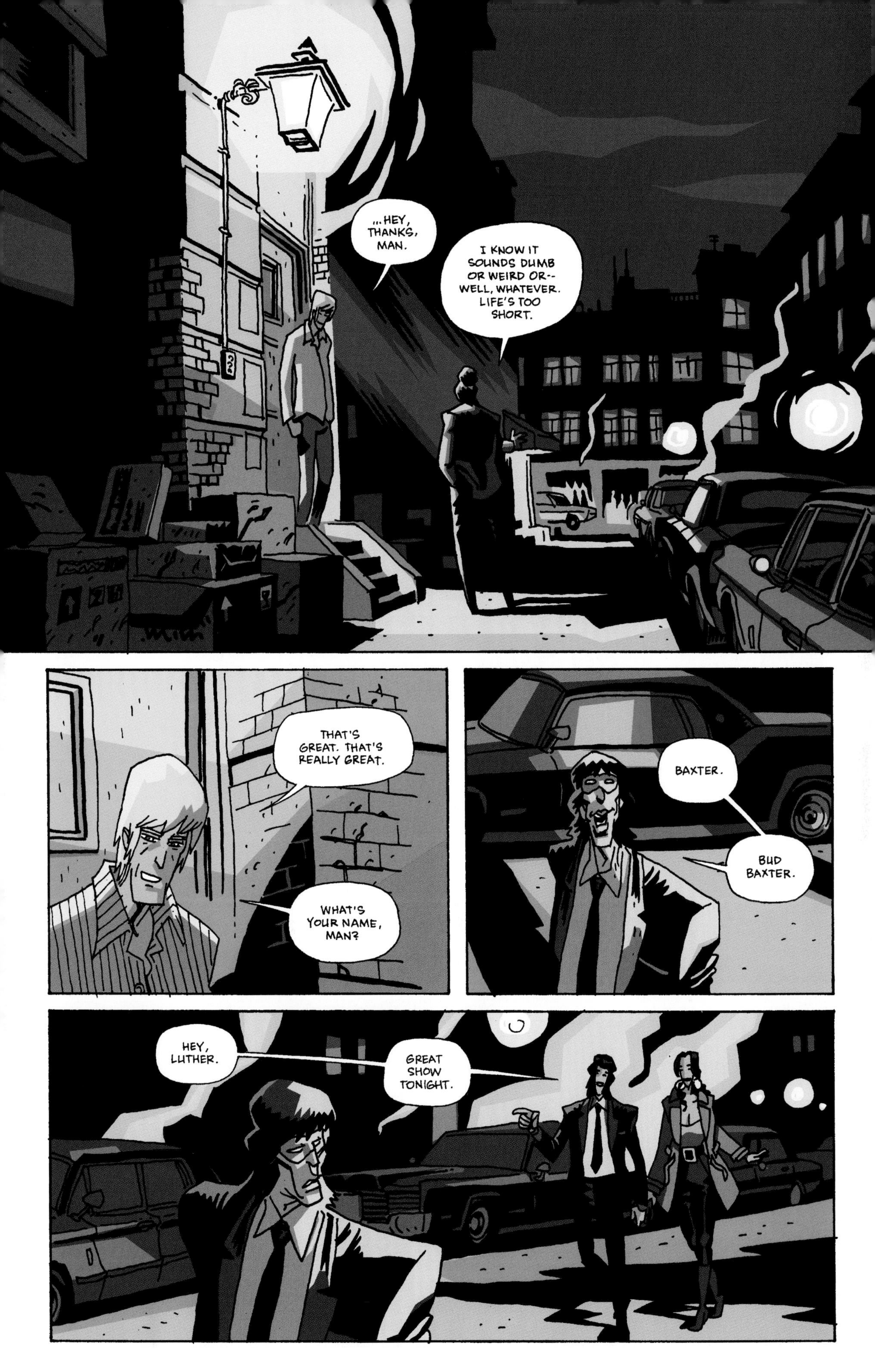
...HEY, THANKS, MAN.
I KNOW IT SOUNDS DUMB OR WEIRD OR-- WELL, WHATEVER. LIFE'S TOO SHORT.
THAT'S GREAT. THAT'S REALLY GREAT.
WHAT'S YOUR NAME, MAN?
BAXTER.
BUD BAXTER.
HEY, LUTHER.
GREAT SHOW TONIGHT.

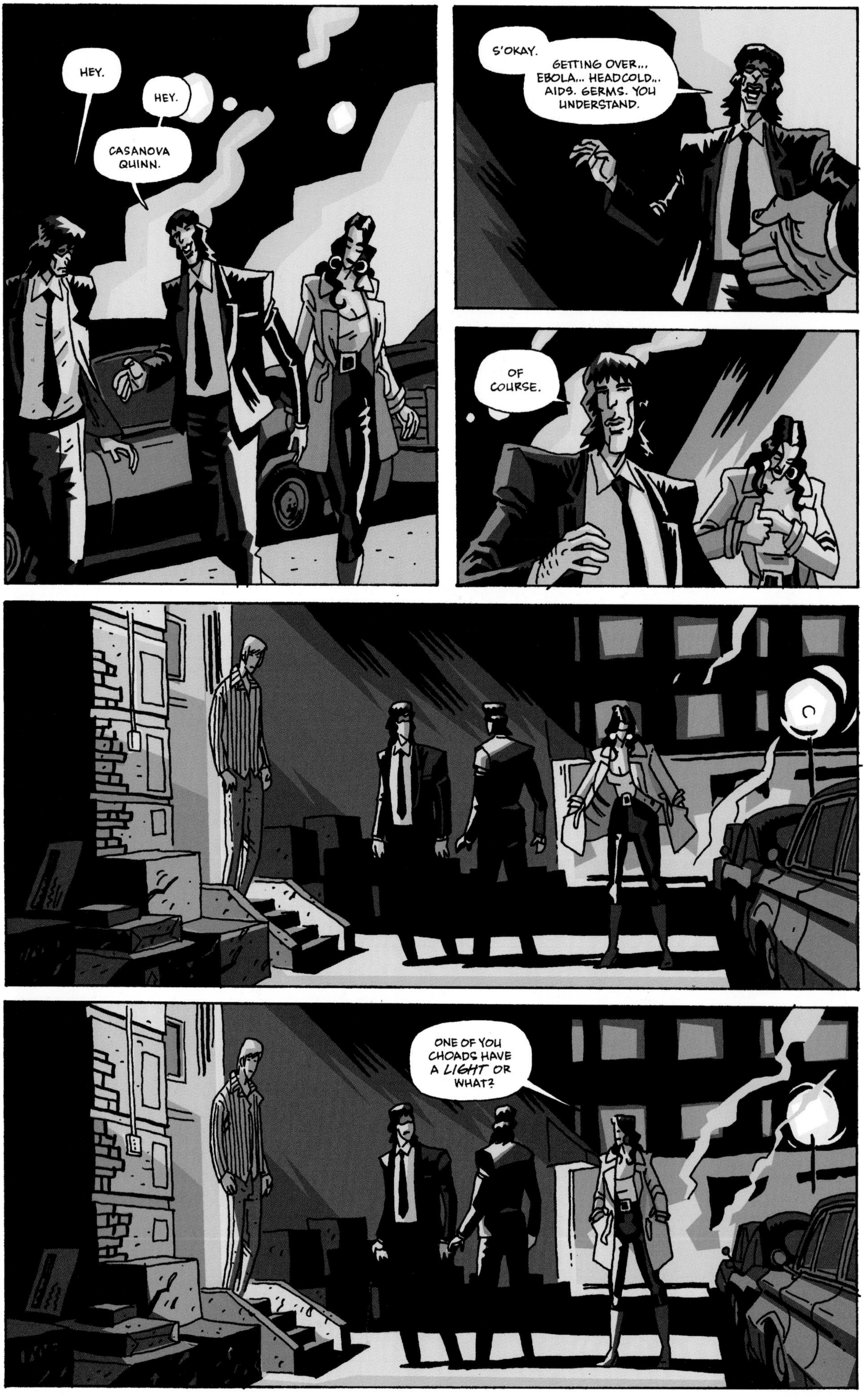
HEY.
HEY.
CASANOVA QUINN.
S'OKAY.
GETTING OVER... EBOLA... HEADCOLD... AIDS. GERMS. YOU UNDERSTAND.
OF COURSE.
ONE OF YOU CHOADS HAVE A *LIGHT* OR WHAT?

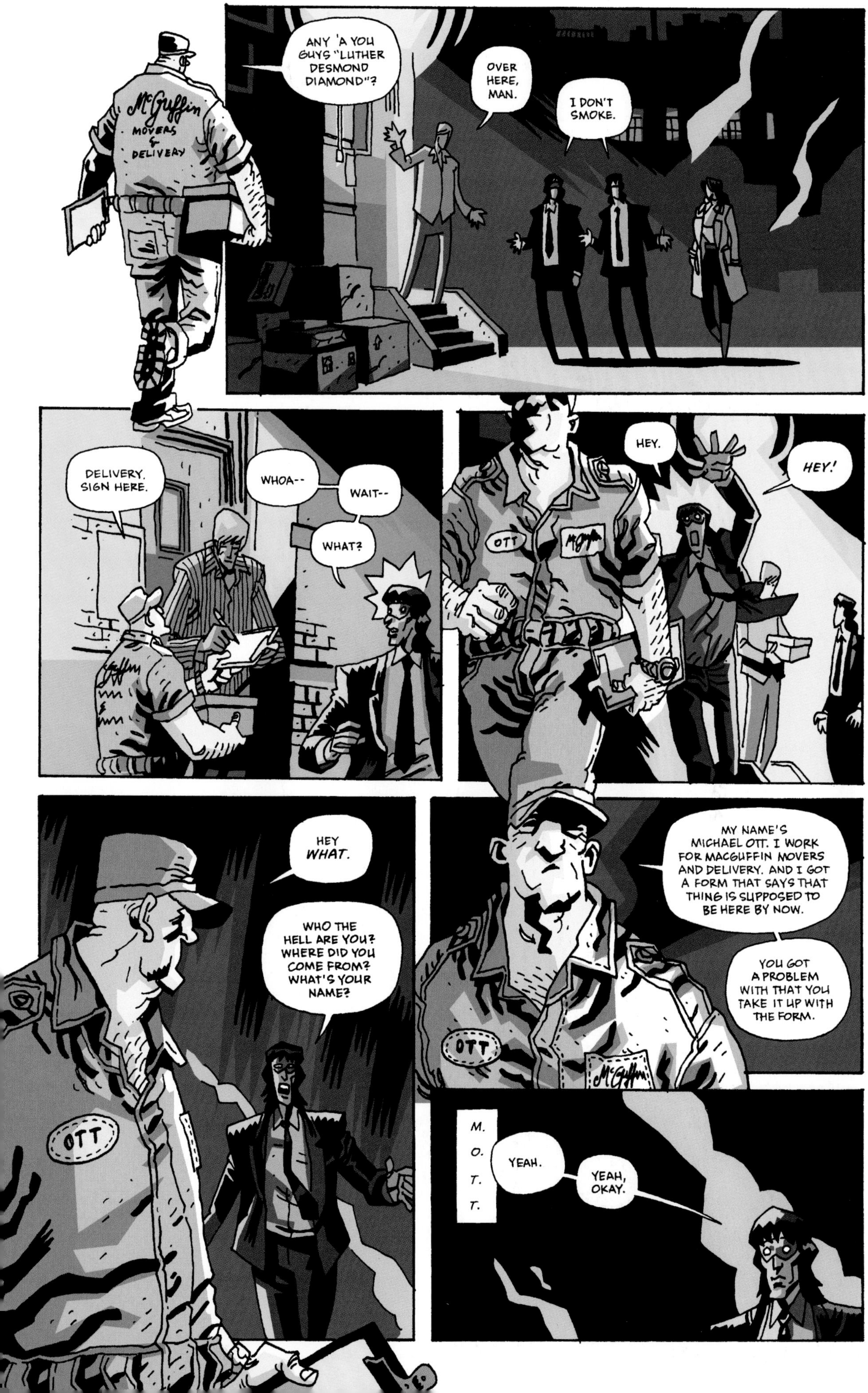

ANY 'A YOU GUYS "LUTHER DESMOND DIAMOND"?
OVER HERE, MAN.
I DON'T SMOKE.
McGuffin MOVERS & DELIVERY
DELIVERY. SIGN HERE.
WHOA--
WAIT--
WHAT?
HEY.
HEY!
OTT
HEY WHAT.
WHO THE HELL ARE YOU? WHERE DID YOU COME FROM? WHAT'S YOUR NAME?
OTT
MY NAME'S MICHAEL OTT. I WORK FOR MACGUFFIN MOVERS AND DELIVERY. AND I GOT A FORM THAT SAYS THAT THING IS SUPPOSED TO BE HERE BY NOW.
YOU GOT A PROBLEM WITH THAT YOU TAKE IT UP WITH THE FORM.
OTT
M. O. T. T.
YEAH.
YEAH, OKAY.

SO, LOOK, I NEED TO GO DO MY SECOND SET BUT LATER, YOU GUYS SHOULD COME BY THE HOTEL AND HANG OUT...

I'M STAYING UNDER MY ALIAS OF "NEWMAN XENO."

M.O.T.T.

GET IT?

...WHAT?

MY ROCK STAR ALIAS.

"NEWMAN XENO." NEW MAN. XENO, ALIEN. MR. X. Y'KNOW.

IT'S FUN?

WHAT?

WHAT'S IN THE BOX, EARTHMAN?

OH. UH...

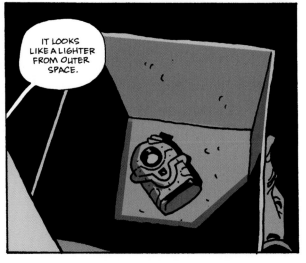

IT LOOKS LIKE A LIGHTER FROM OUTER SPACE.

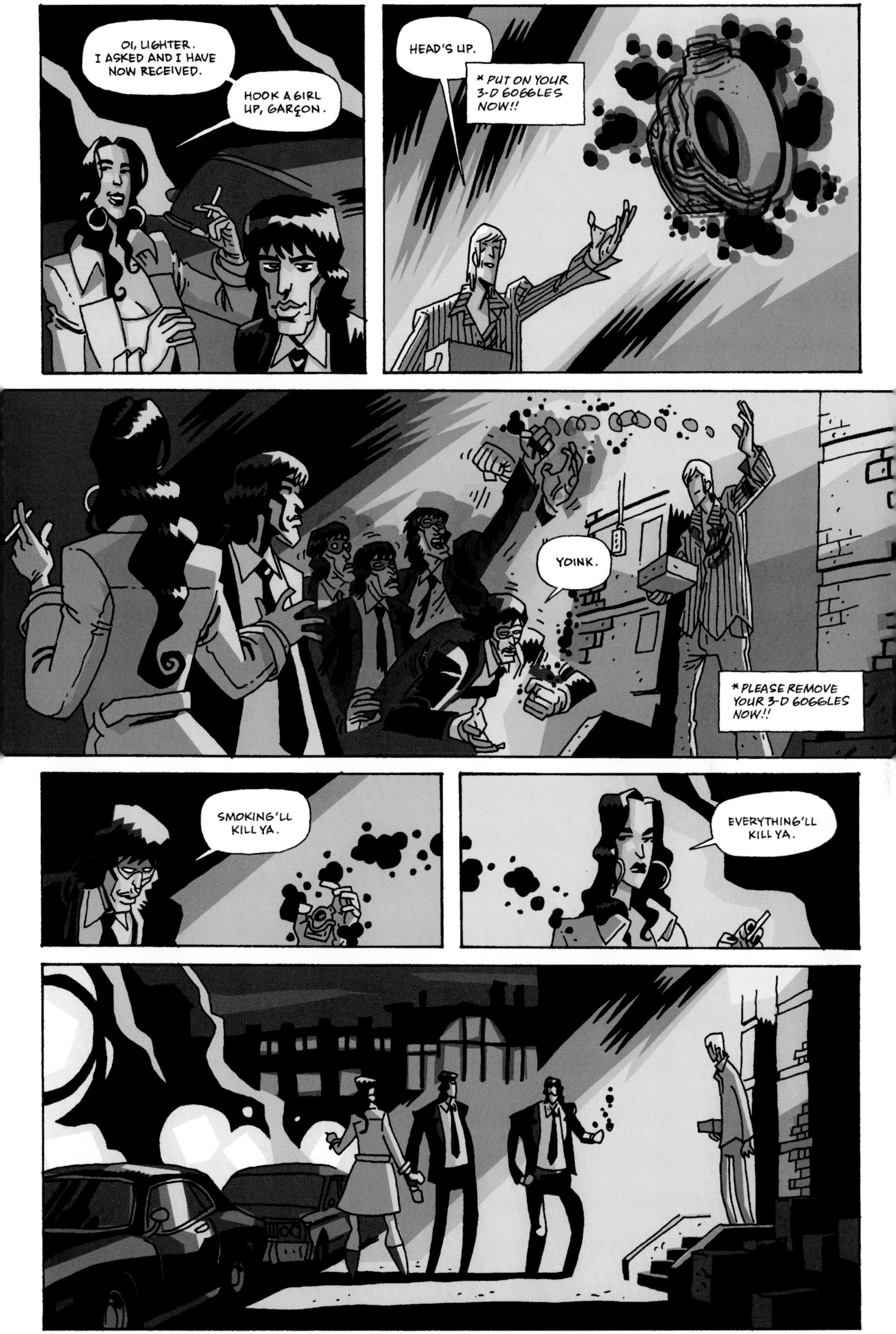

OI, LIGHTER. I ASKED AND I HAVE NOW RECEIVED.
HOOK A GIRL UP, GARÇON.
HEAD'S UP.
* PUT ON YOUR 3-D GOGGLES NOW!!
YOINK.
* PLEASE REMOVE YOUR 3-D GOGGLES NOW!!
SMOKING'LL KILL YA.
EVERYTHING'LL KILL YA.

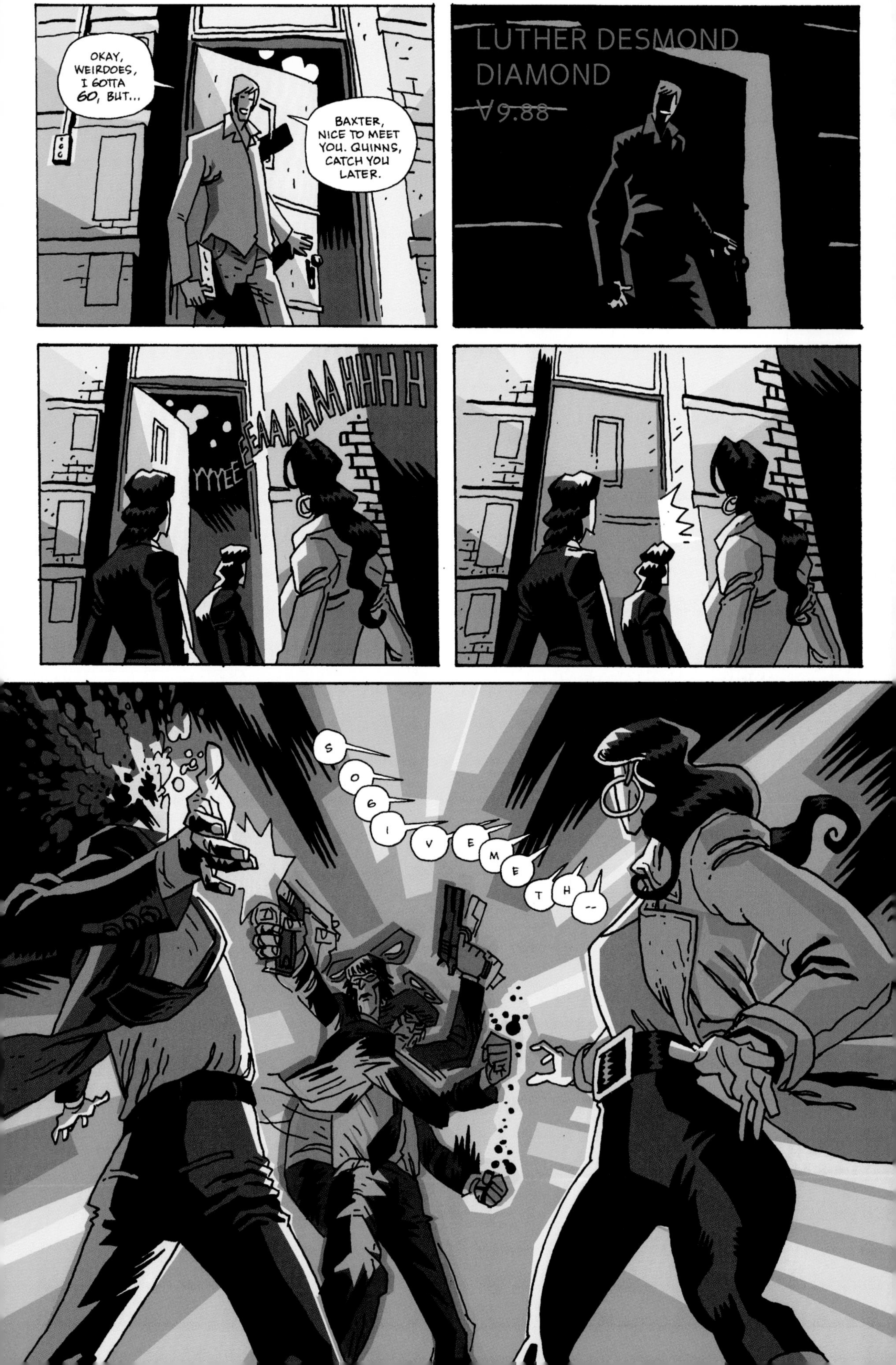
OKAY, WEIRDOES, I GOTTA GO, BUT...
BAXTER, NICE TO MEET YOU. QUINNS, CATCH YOU LATER.
LUTHER DESMOND DIAMOND
∀9.88
YYYEEEEAAAAAAAHHHHH
S O G I V E M E T H--

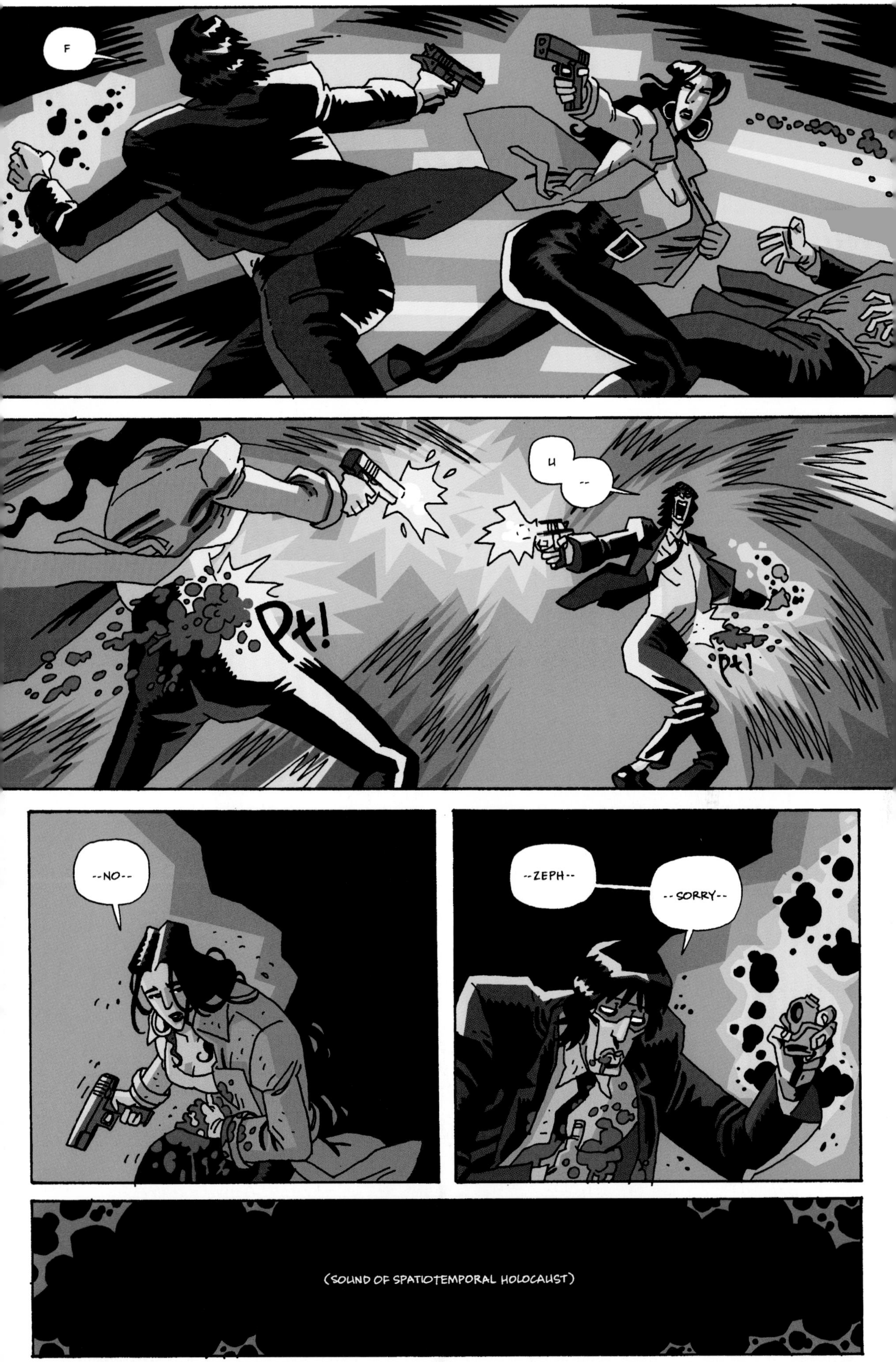
F
U
--
Pt!
Pt!
--NO--
--ZEPH--
--SORRY--
(SOUND OF SPATIOTEMPORAL HOLOCAUST)

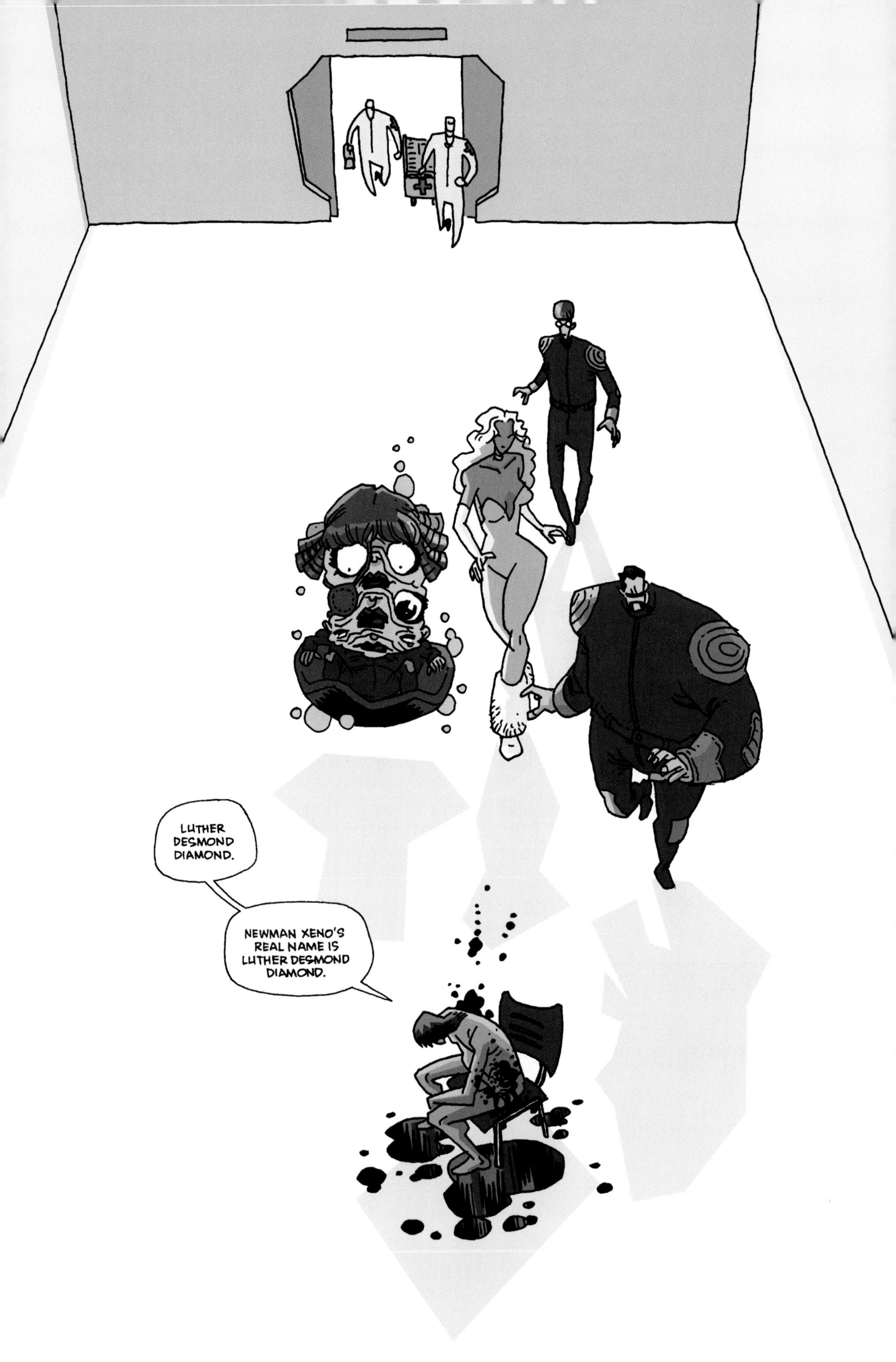
LUTHER DESMOND DIAMOND.
NEWMAN XENO'S REAL NAME IS LUTHER DESMOND DIAMOND.

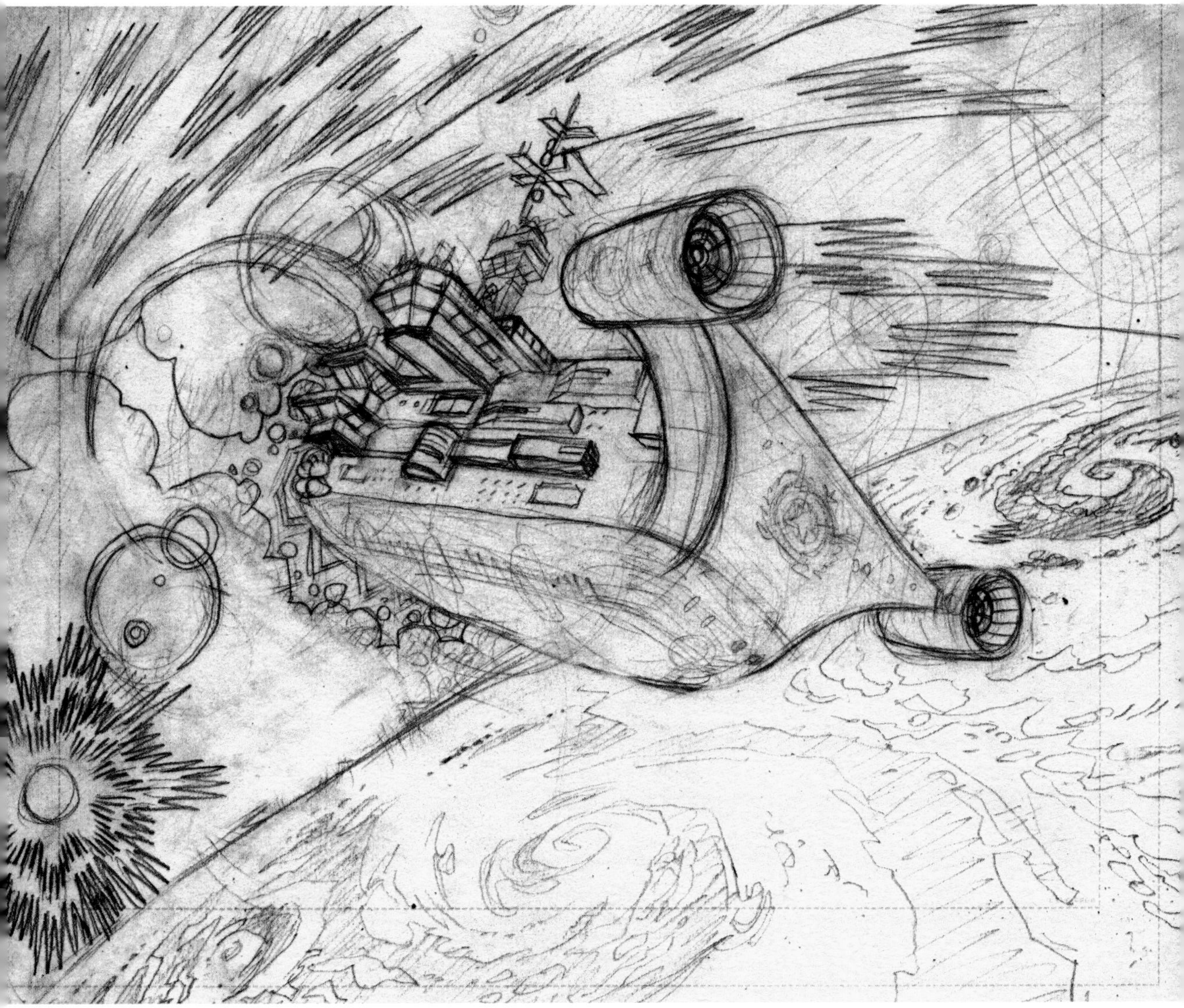

4. 'TIL I DIE

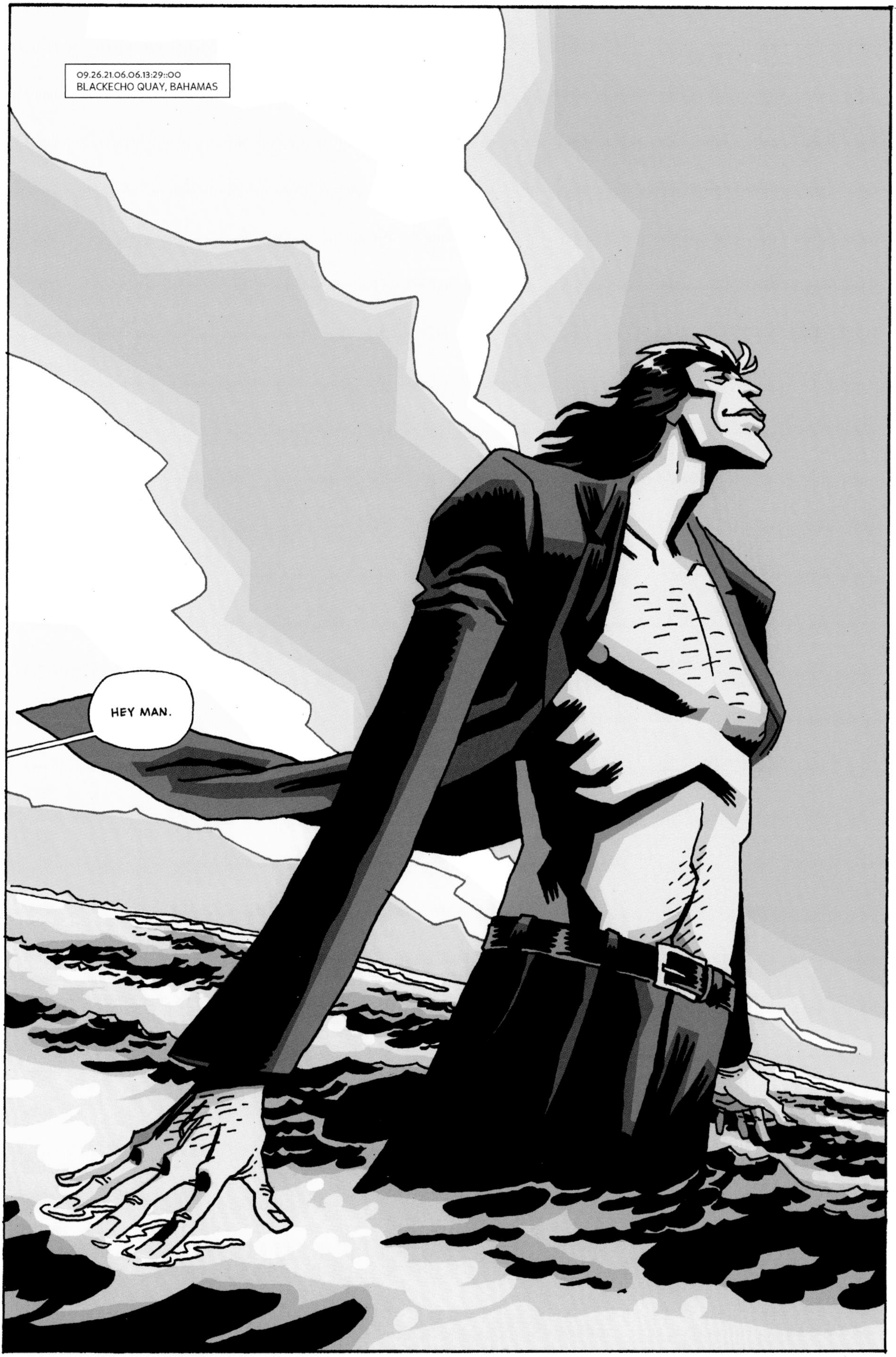
09.26.21.06.06.13:29::00
BLACKECHO QUAY, BAHAMAS
HEY MAN.

YOU'RE KIND OF COMPLICATING MY THING, MAN.
WHAT THE HELL ARE YOU DOING HERE?
NOT TO BE A COCK BUT IF YOU KNEW HOW MUCH MONEY IT COST ME TO BUY A WHOLE ISLAND JUST SO I COULD MAKE MY MUSIC ALONE...
...WHAT ARE YOU, PRESS? A FAN?
LUTHER DESMOND DIAMOND v9.26
OI, FUCKO! I SAID --
--I--
KER SPLASH
THIS IS IT.
THIS IS THE JOB NOW.

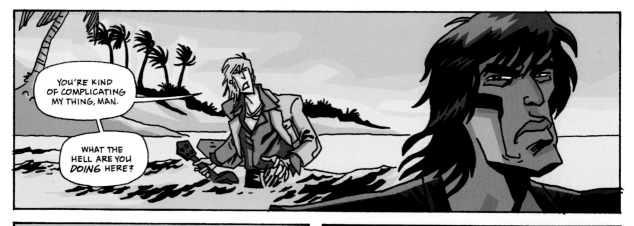

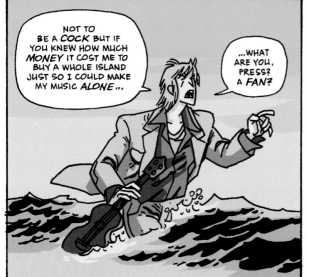

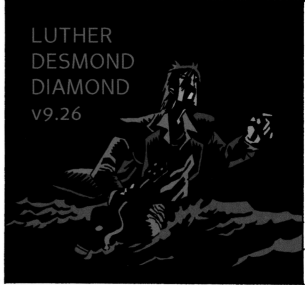

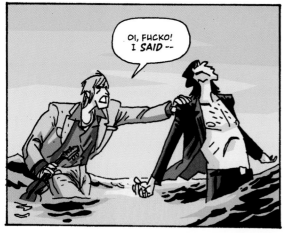

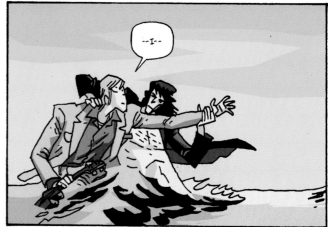

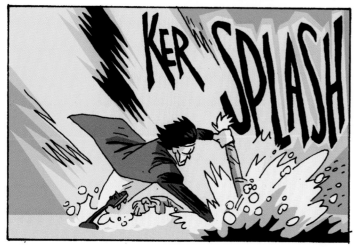

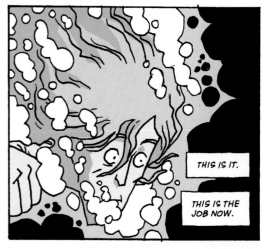

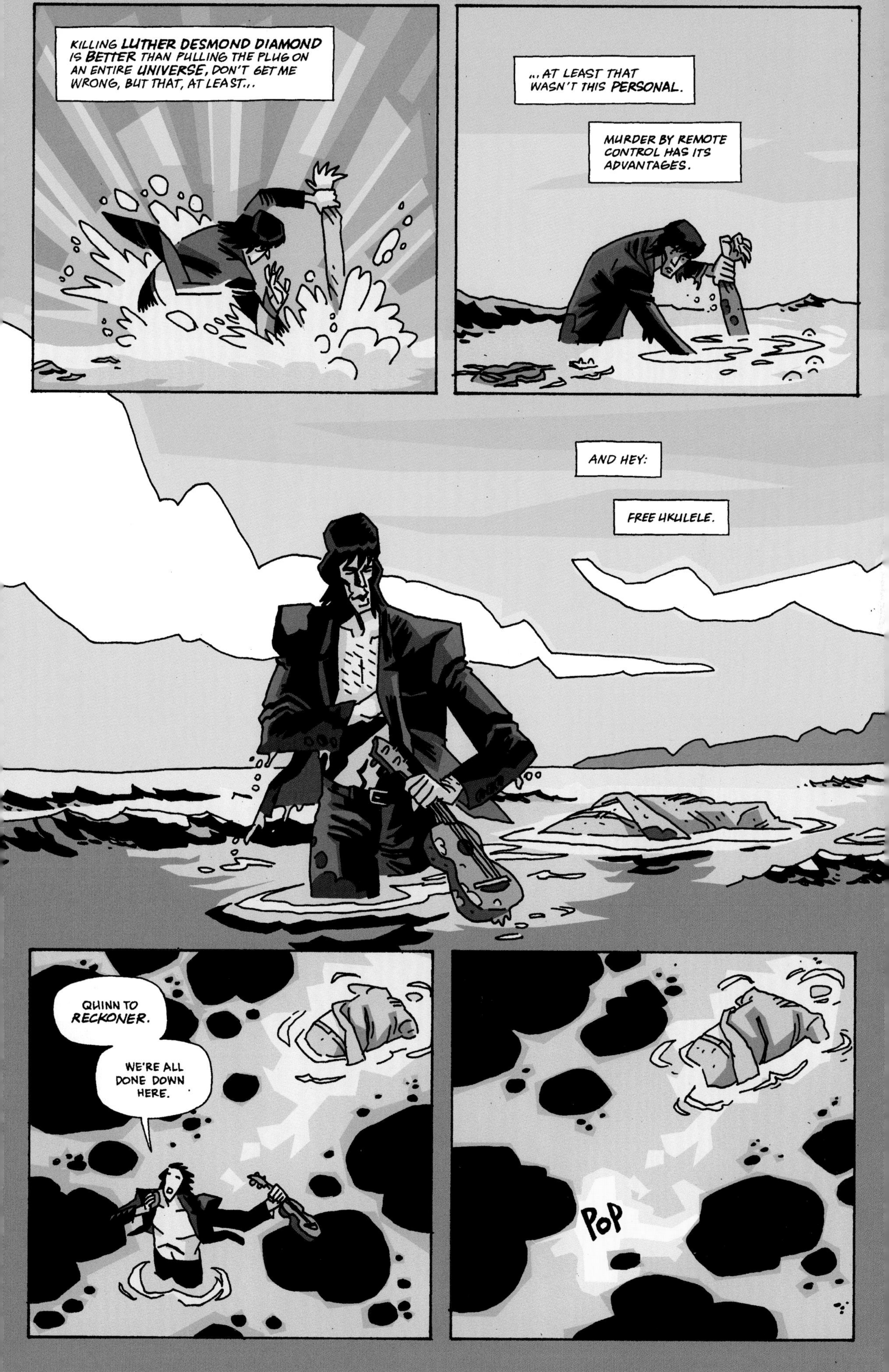
KILLING LUTHER DESMOND DIAMOND IS BETTER THAN PULLING THE PLUG ON AN ENTIRE UNIVERSE, DON'T GET ME WRONG, BUT THAT, AT LEAST...
...AT LEAST THAT WASN'T THIS PERSONAL.
MURDER BY REMOTE CONTROL HAS ITS ADVANTAGES.
AND HEY:
FREE UKULELE.
QUINN TO RECKONER.
WE'RE ALL DONE DOWN HERE.
POP

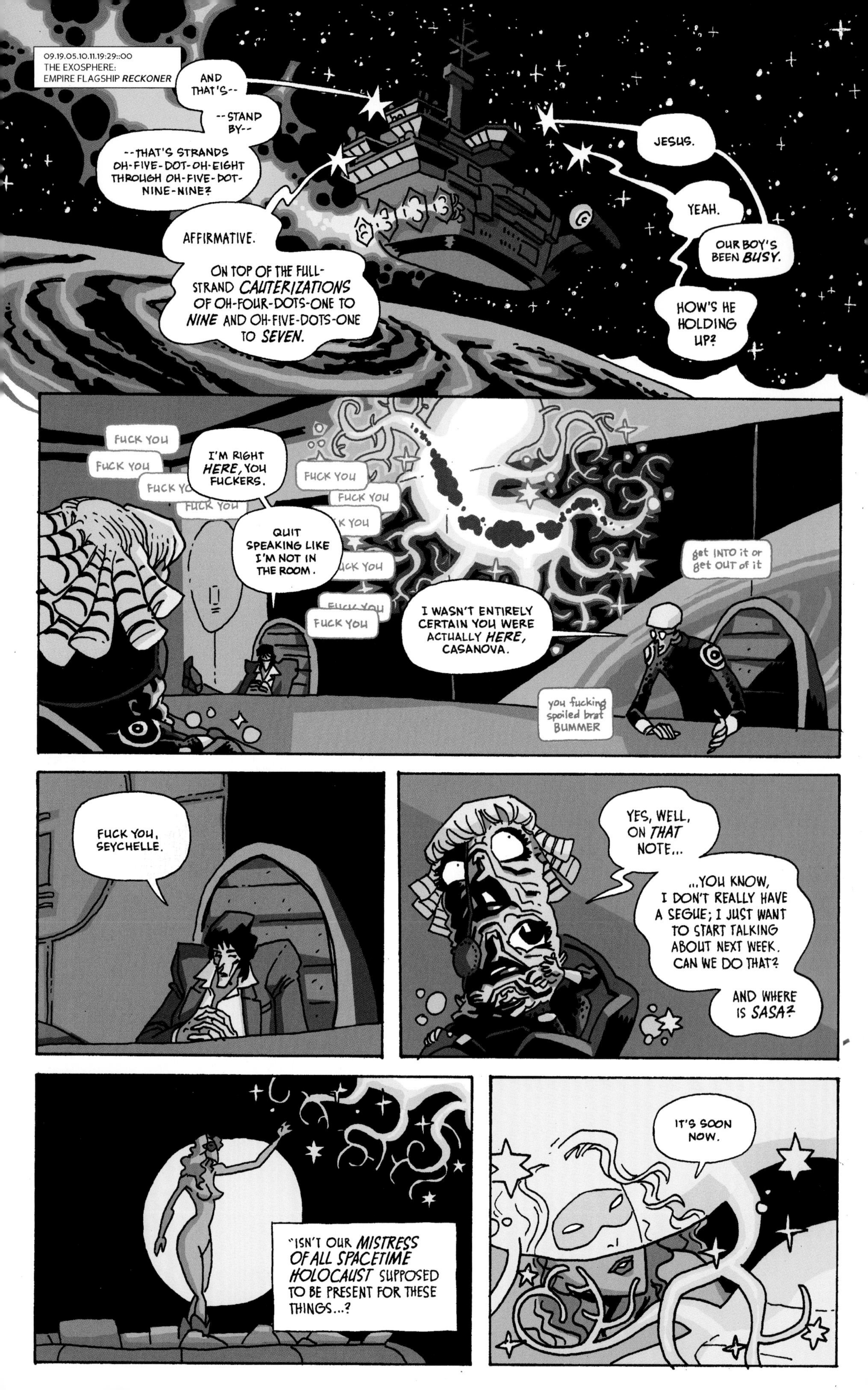
09.19.05.10.11.19:29::00
THE EXOSPHERE:
EMPIRE FLAGSHIP RECKONER
AND THAT'S--
--STAND BY--
--THAT'S STRANDS OH-FIVE-DOT-OH-EIGHT THROUGH OH-FIVE-DOT-NINE-NINE?
AFFIRMATIVE.
ON TOP OF THE FULL-STRAND CAUTERIZATIONS OF OH-FOUR-DOTS-ONE TO NINE AND OH-FIVE-DOTS-ONE TO SEVEN.
JESUS.
YEAH.
OUR BOY'S BEEN BUSY.
HOW'S HE HOLDING UP?
FUCK YOU
FUCK YOU
FUCK YOU
FUCK YOU
I'M RIGHT HERE, YOU FUCKERS.
QUIT SPEAKING LIKE I'M NOT IN THE ROOM.
FUCK YOU
FUCK YOU
FUCK YOU
FUCK YOU
FUCK YOU
get INTO it or get OUT of it
I WASN'T ENTIRELY CERTAIN YOU WERE ACTUALLY HERE, CASANOVA.
you fucking spoiled brat BUMMER
FUCK YOU, SEYCHELLE.
YES, WELL, ON THAT NOTE...
...YOU KNOW, I DON'T REALLY HAVE A SEGUE; I JUST WANT TO START TALKING ABOUT NEXT WEEK. CAN WE DO THAT?
AND WHERE IS SASA?
"ISN'T OUR MISTRESS OF ALL SPACETIME HOLOCAUST SUPPOSED TO BE PRESENT FOR THESE THINGS...?
IT'S SOON NOW.

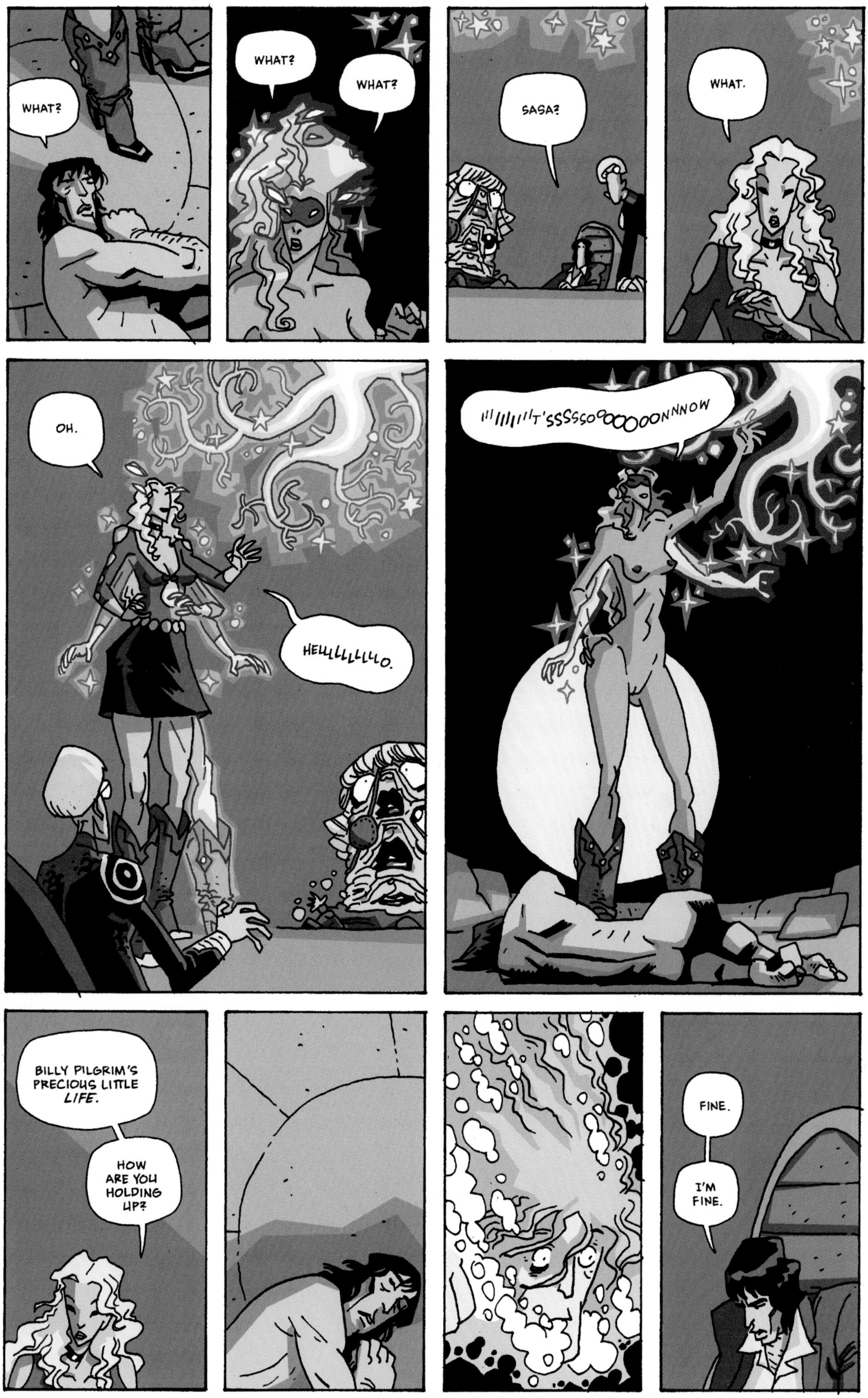

WHAT?
WHAT?
WHAT?
SASA?
WHAT.
OH.
HELLLLLLLLLO.
IIIIIIIIIT'SSSSSOOOOOOONNNOW
BILLY PILGRIM'S PRECIOUS LITTLE *LIFE*.
HOW ARE YOU HOLDING UP?
FINE.
I'M FINE.

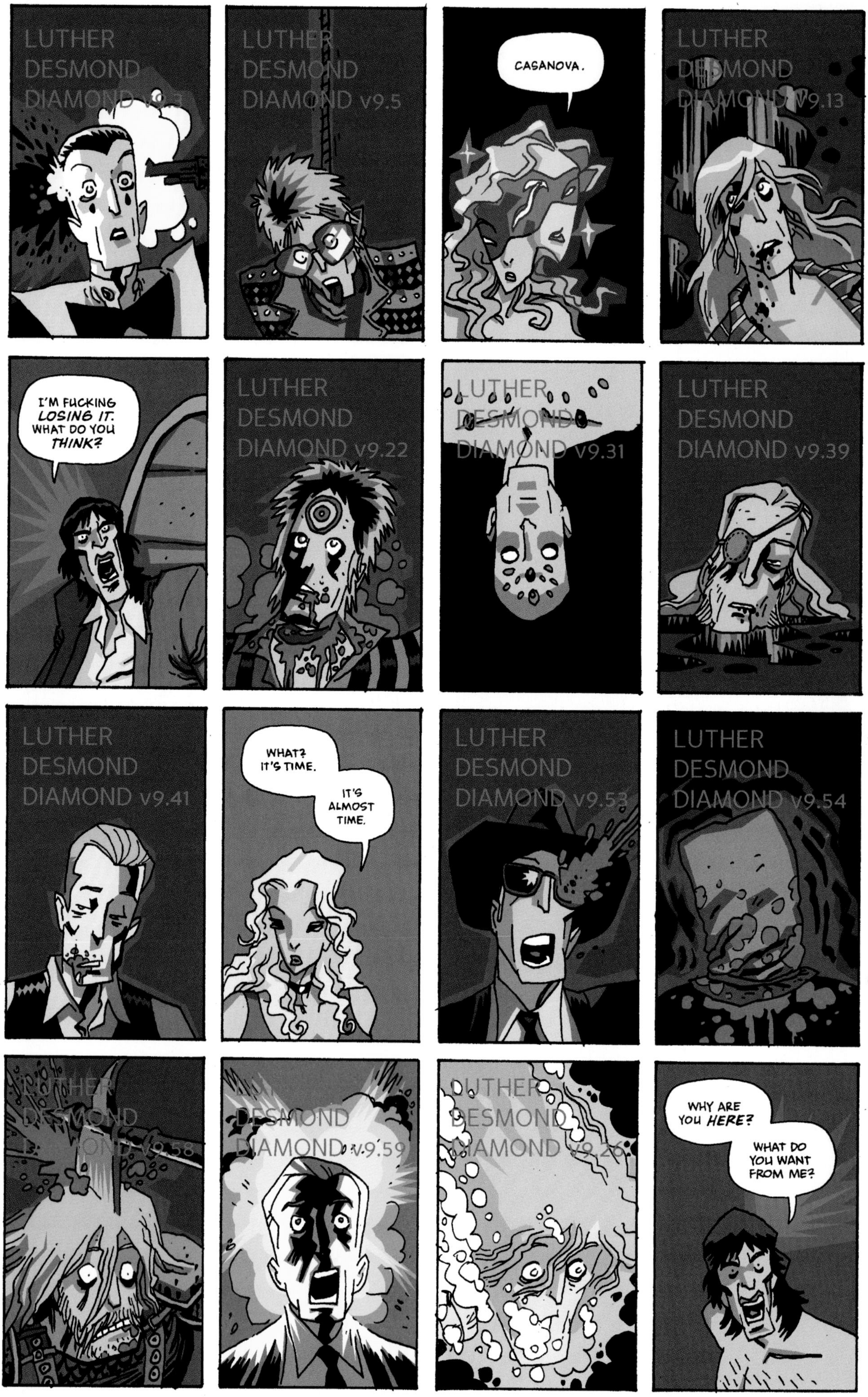

LUTHER DESMOND DIAMOND
LUTHER DESMOND DIAMOND v9.5
CASANOVA.
LUTHER DESMOND DIAMOND v9.13
I'M FUCKING *LOSING IT.* WHAT DO YOU *THINK?*
LUTHER DESMOND DIAMOND v9.22
LUTHER DESMOND DIAMOND v9.31
LUTHER DESMOND DIAMOND v9.39
LUTHER DESMOND DIAMOND v9.41
WHAT? IT'S TIME.
IT'S ALMOST TIME.
LUTHER DESMOND DIAMOND v9.53
LUTHER DESMOND DIAMOND v9.54
LUTHER DESMOND v9.58
DESMOND DIAMOND v9.59
LUTHER DESMOND DIAMOND v9.26
WHY ARE YOU *HERE?*
WHAT DO YOU WANT FROM ME?

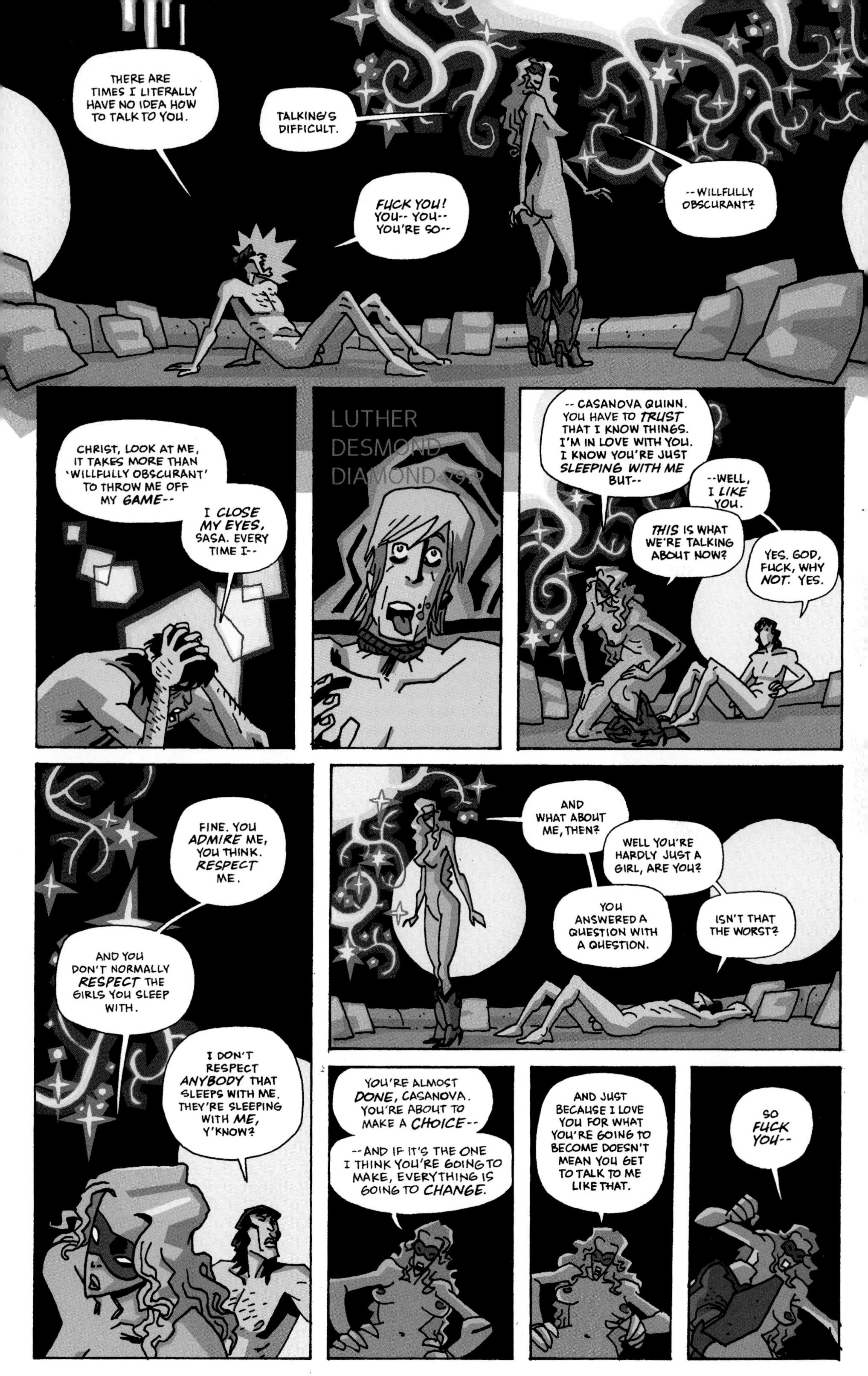
THERE ARE TIMES I LITERALLY HAVE NO IDEA HOW TO TALK TO YOU.
TALKING'S DIFFICULT.
FUCK YOU! YOU-- YOU-- YOU'RE SO--
--WILLFULLY OBSCURANT?
CHRIST, LOOK AT ME, IT TAKES MORE THAN 'WILLFULLY OBSCURANT' TO THROW ME OFF MY GAME--
I CLOSE MY EYES, SASA. EVERY TIME I--
LUTHER DESMOND DIAMOND
-- CASANOVA QUINN. YOU HAVE TO TRUST THAT I KNOW THINGS. I'M IN LOVE WITH YOU. I KNOW YOU'RE JUST SLEEPING WITH ME BUT--
--WELL, I LIKE YOU.
THIS IS WHAT WE'RE TALKING ABOUT NOW?
YES. GOD, FUCK, WHY NOT. YES.
FINE. YOU ADMIRE ME, YOU THINK. RESPECT ME.
AND YOU DON'T NORMALLY RESPECT THE GIRLS YOU SLEEP WITH.
I DON'T RESPECT ANYBODY THAT SLEEPS WITH ME. THEY'RE SLEEPING WITH ME, Y'KNOW?
AND WHAT ABOUT ME, THEN?
WELL YOU'RE HARDLY JUST A GIRL, ARE YOU?
YOU ANSWERED A QUESTION WITH A QUESTION.
ISN'T THAT THE WORST?
YOU'RE ALMOST DONE, CASANOVA. YOU'RE ABOUT TO MAKE A CHOICE--
--AND IF IT'S THE ONE I THINK YOU'RE GOING TO MAKE, EVERYTHING IS GOING TO CHANGE.
AND JUST BECAUSE I LOVE YOU FOR WHAT YOU'RE GOING TO BECOME DOESN'T MEAN YOU GET TO TALK TO ME LIKE THAT.
SO FUCK YOU--

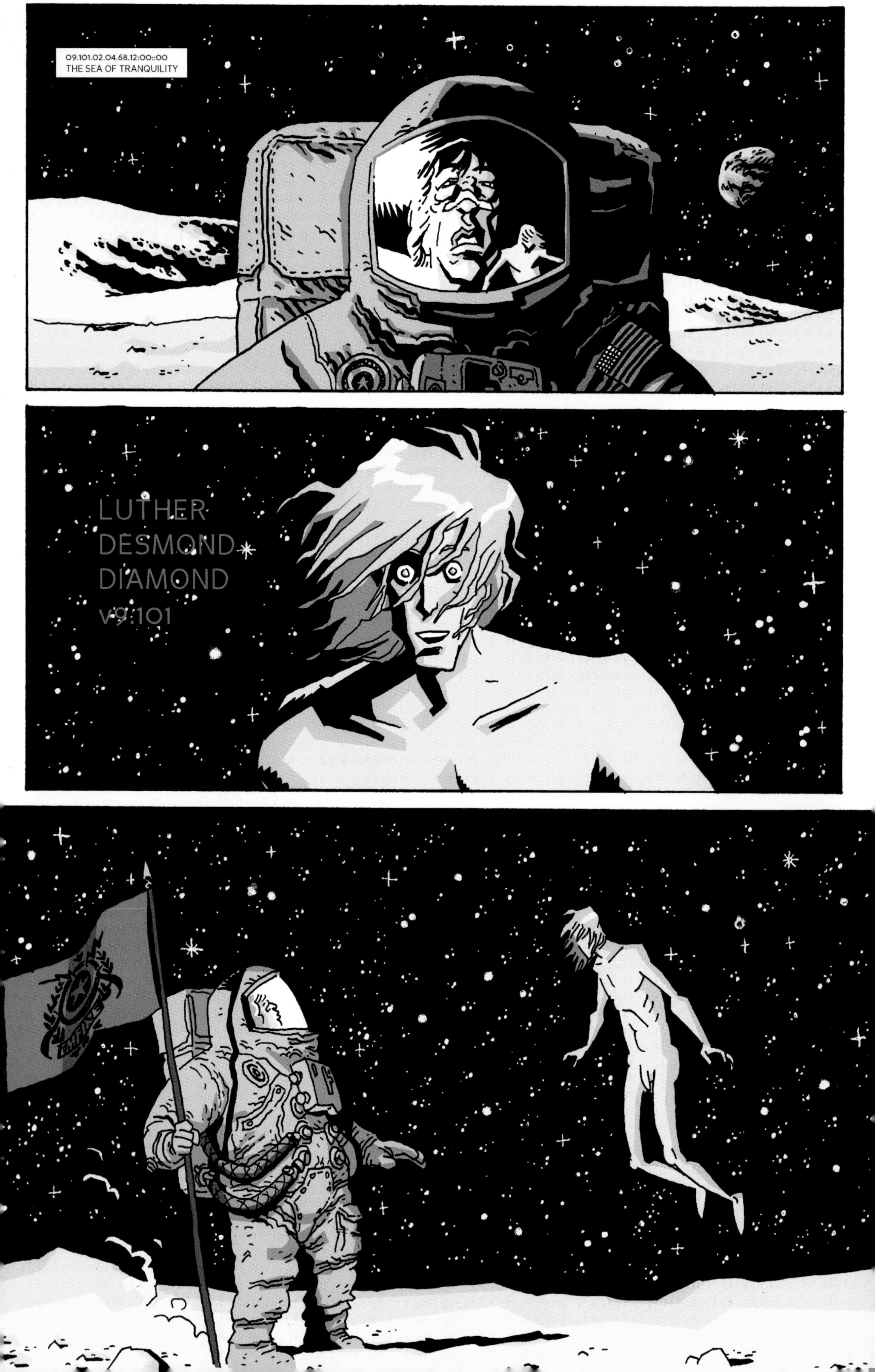
09.101.02.04.68.12:00::00
THE SEA OF TRANQUILITY
LUTHER
DESMOND
DIAMOND
v9:101

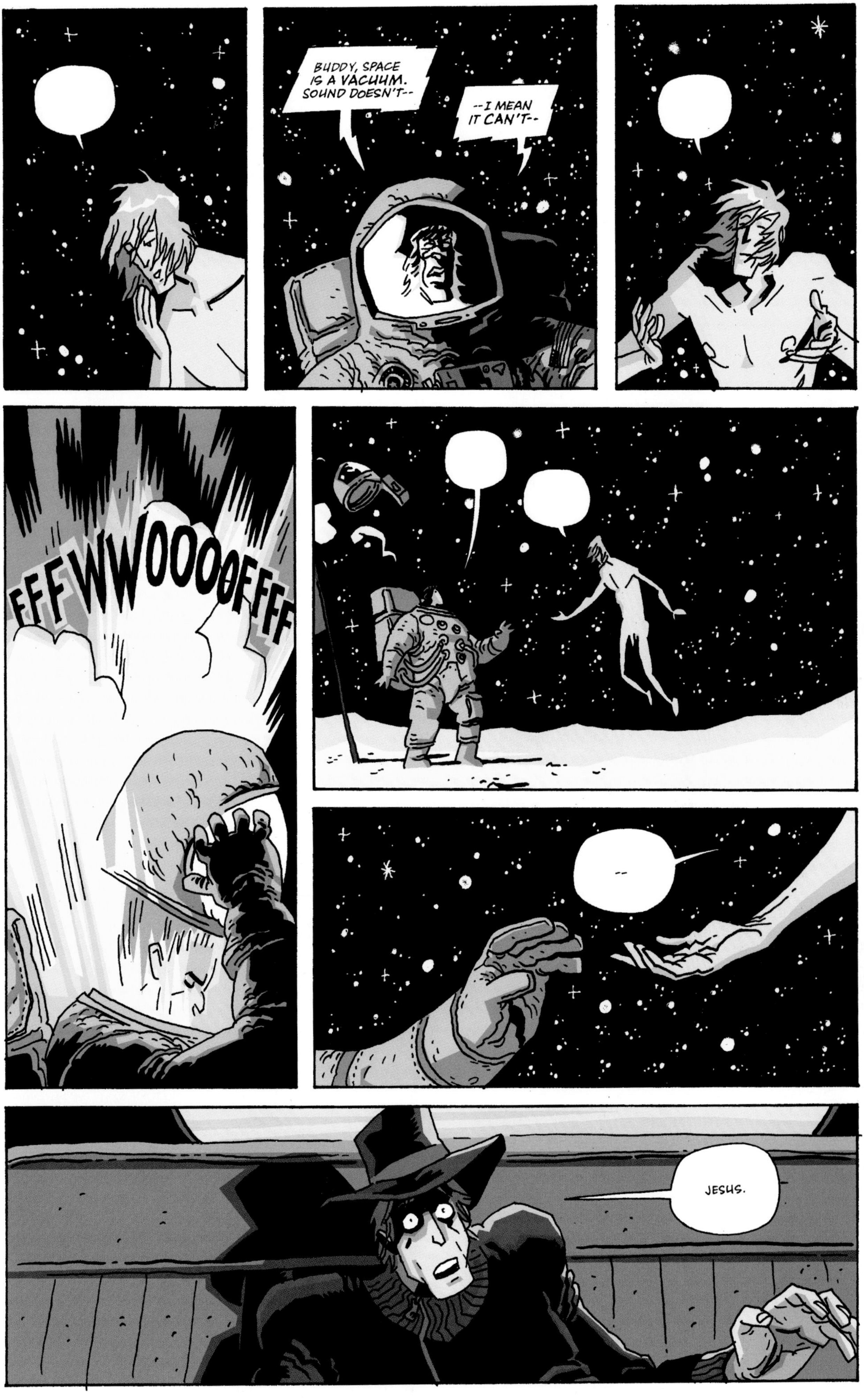
BUDDY, SPACE IS A VACUUM. SOUND DOESN'T--
--I MEAN IT CAN'T--
FFFWWOOOOFFFF
--
JESUS.

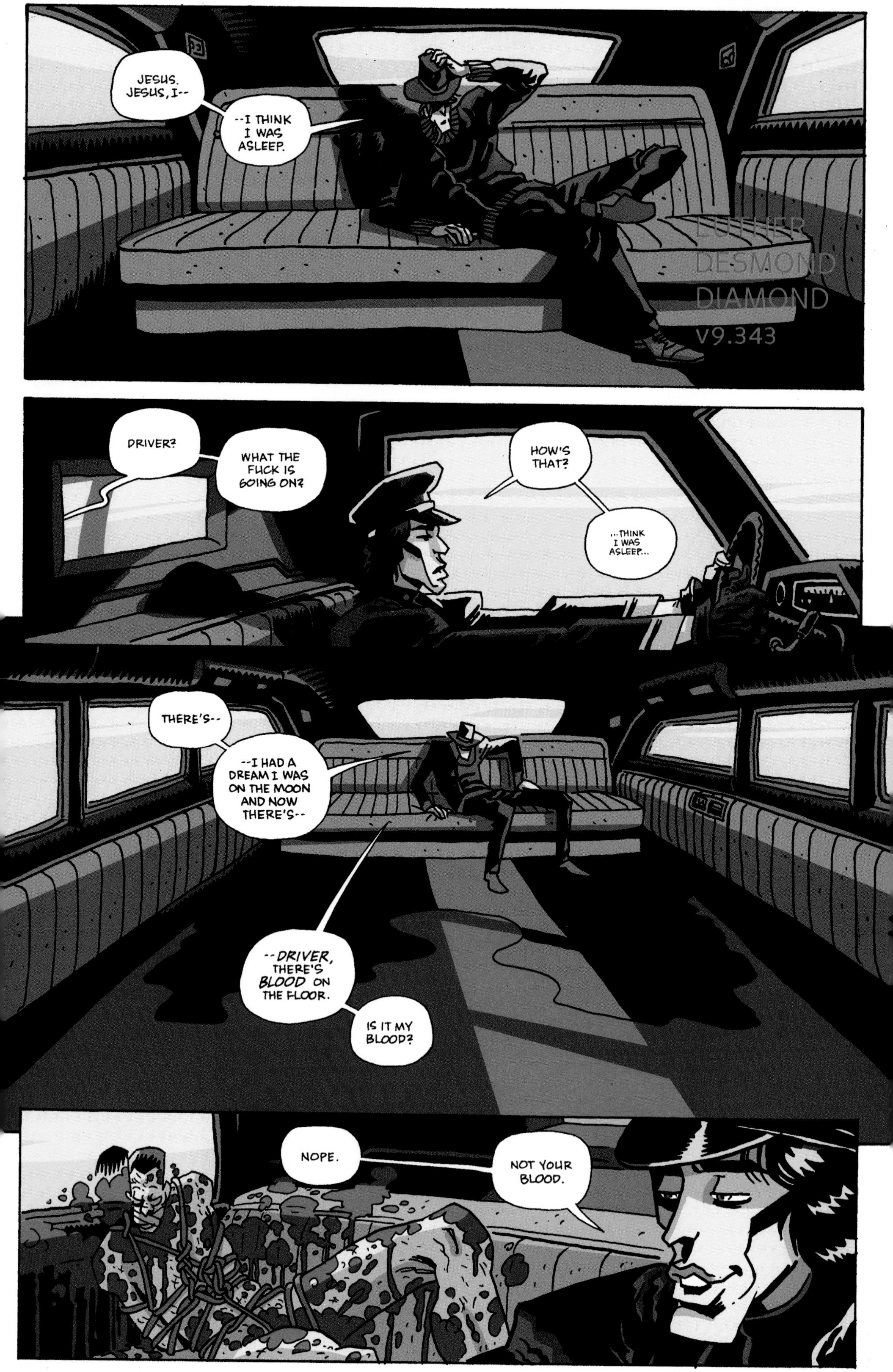
JESUS. JESUS, I--
--I THINK I WAS ASLEEP.
LUTHER DESMOND DIAMOND V9.343
DRIVER?
WHAT THE FUCK IS GOING ON?
HOW'S THAT?
...THINK I WAS ASLEEP...
THERE'S--
--I HAD A DREAM I WAS ON THE MOON AND NOW THERE'S--
--DRIVER, THERE'S BLOOD ON THE FLOOR.
IS IT MY BLOOD?
NOPE.
NOT YOUR BLOOD.

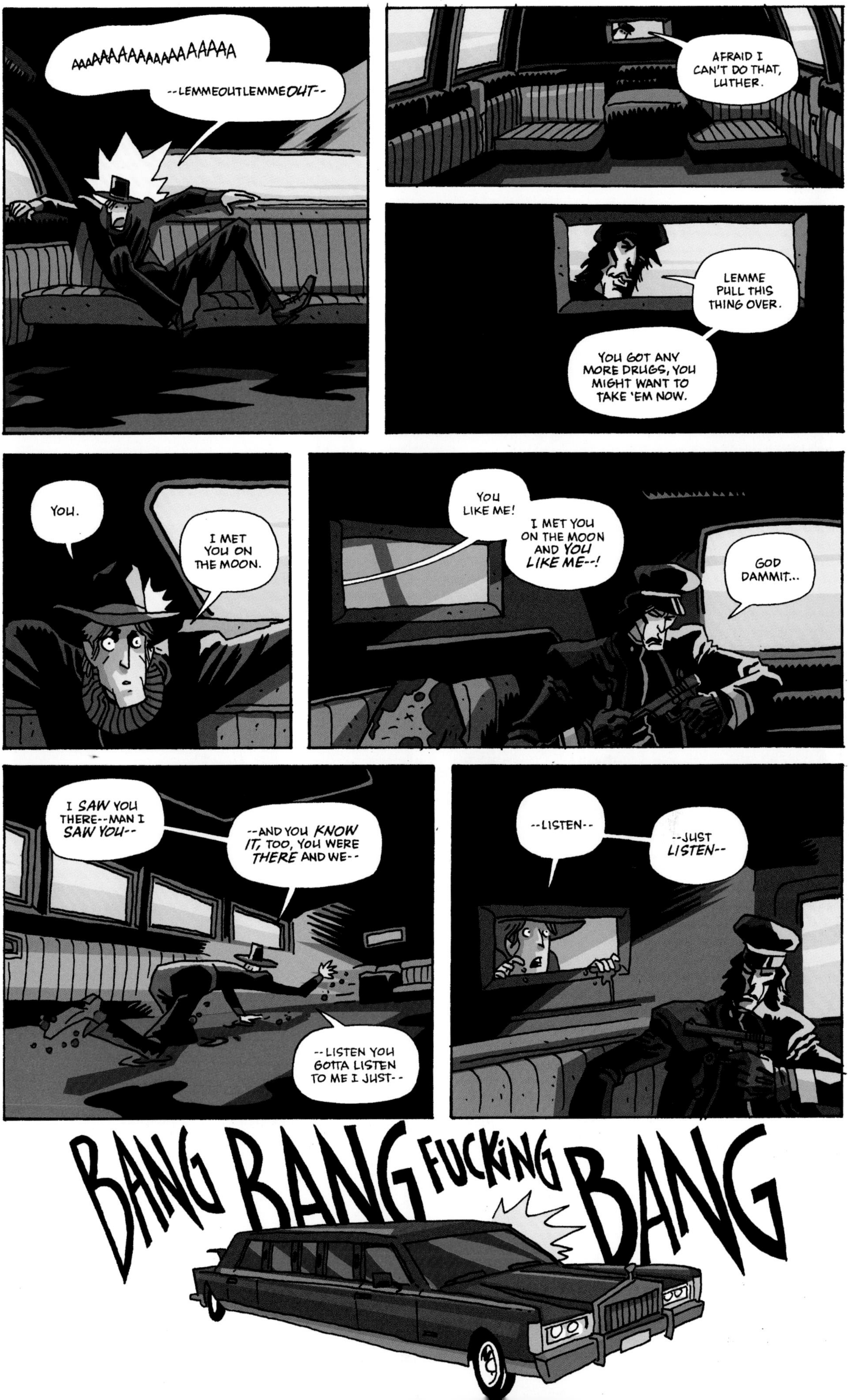
AAAAAAAAAAAAAAAAA
--LEMMEOUTLEMMEOUT--
AFRAID I CAN'T DO THAT, LUTHER.
LEMME PULL THIS THING OVER.
YOU GOT ANY MORE DRUGS, YOU MIGHT WANT TO TAKE 'EM NOW.
YOU.
I MET YOU ON THE MOON.
YOU LIKE ME!
I MET YOU ON THE MOON AND YOU LIKE ME--!
GOD DAMMIT...
I SAW YOU THERE--MAN I SAW YOU--
--AND YOU KNOW IT, TOO, YOU WERE THERE AND WE--
--LISTEN YOU GOTTA LISTEN TO ME I JUST--
--LISTEN--
--JUST LISTEN--
BANG BANG FUCKING BANG

5. MAN ON THE MOON

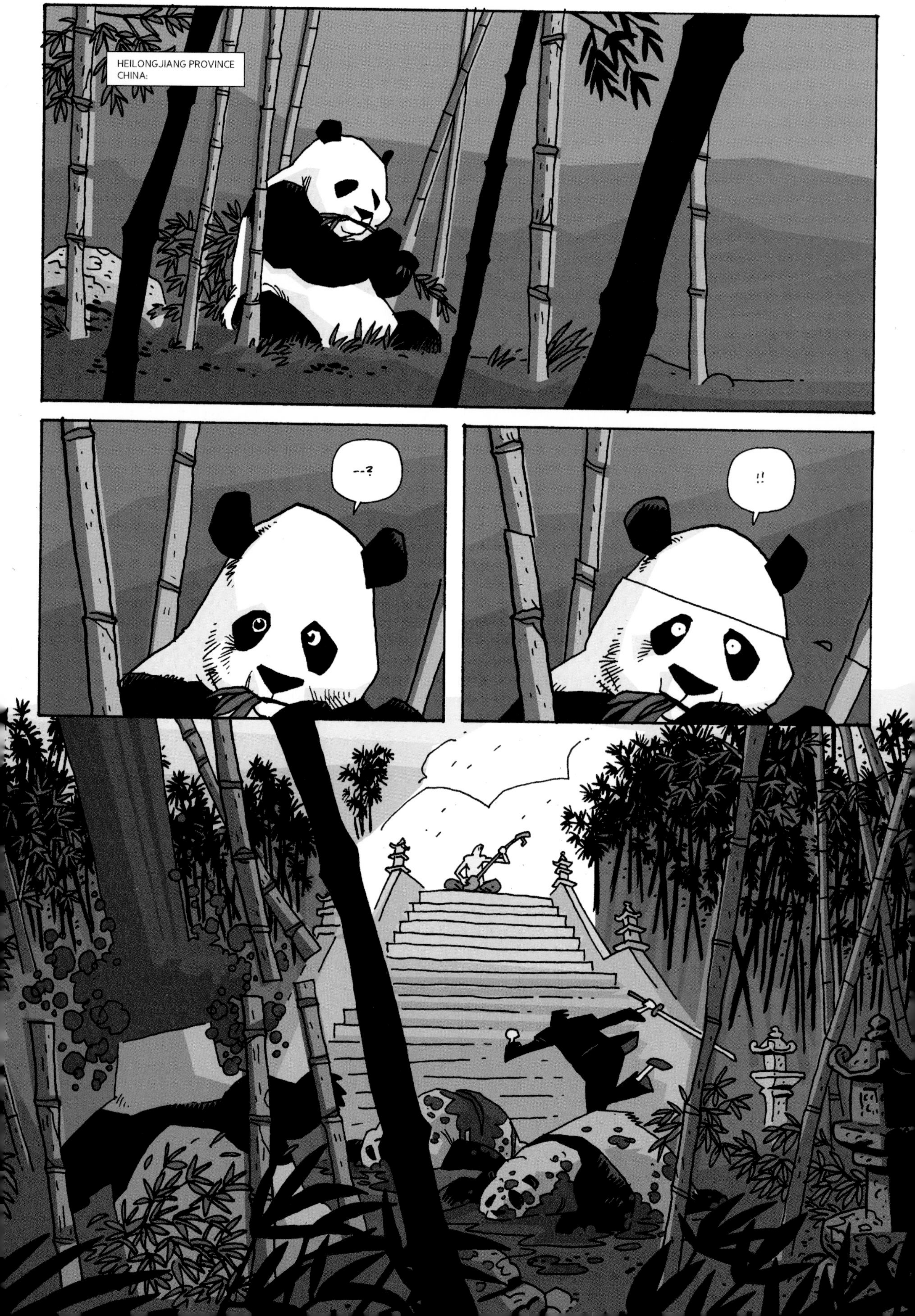
HEILONGJIANG PROVINCE
CHINA:
--?
!!

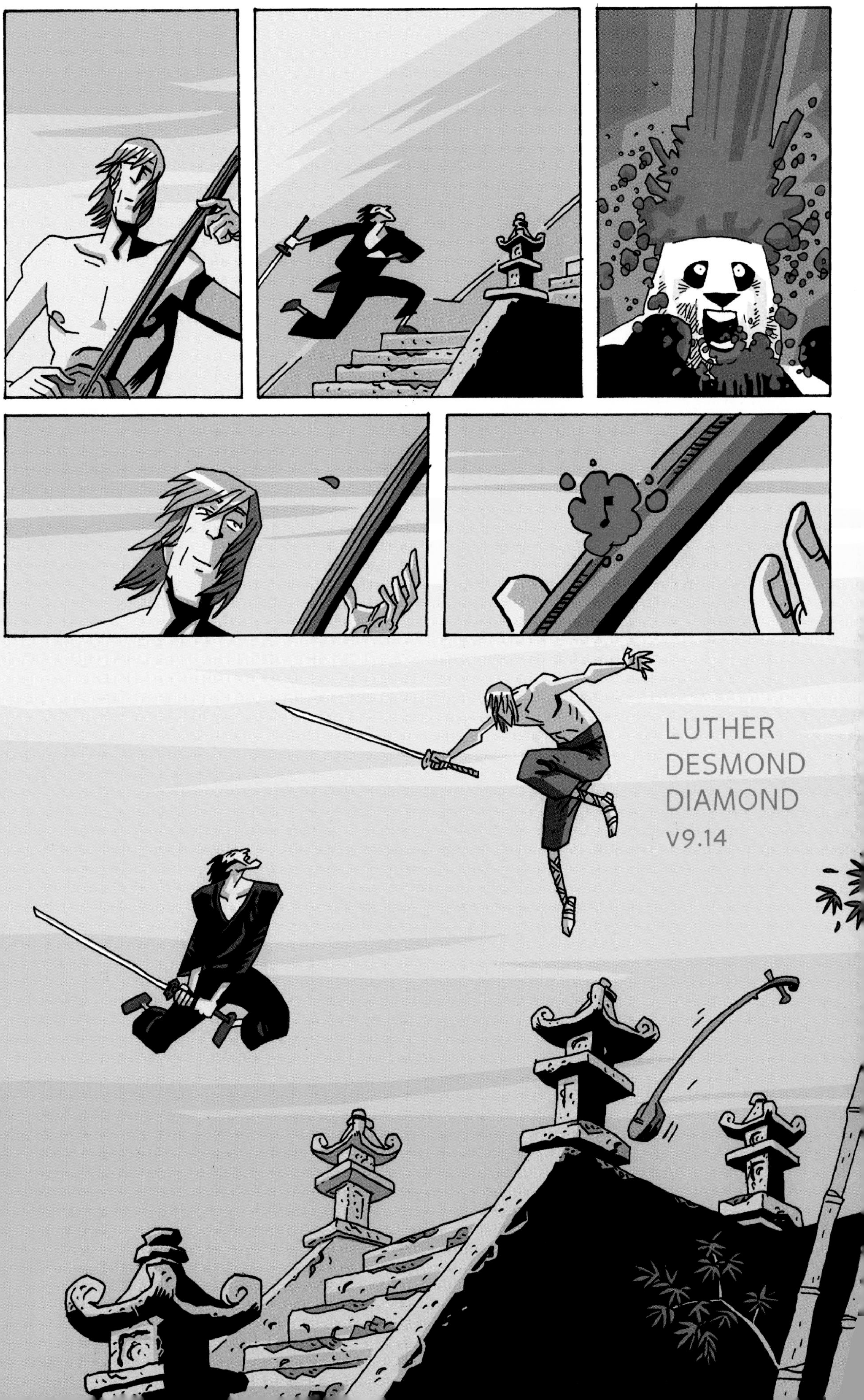
LUTHER
DESMOND
DIAMOND
v9.14

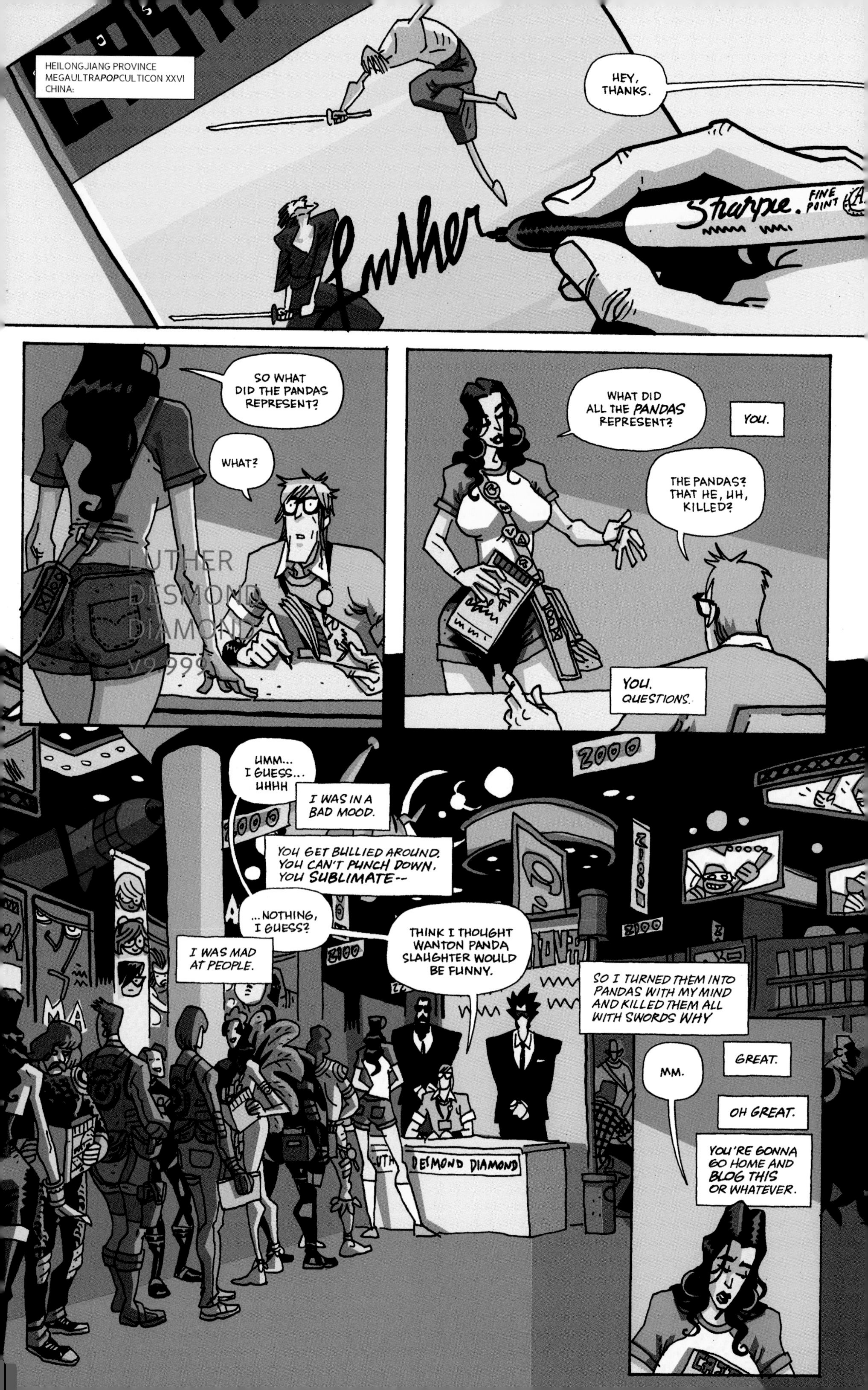

HEILONGJIANG PROVINCE
MEGAULTRAPOPCULTICON XXVI
CHINA:
HEY, THANKS.
Luther
Sharpie. FINE POINT
SO WHAT DID THE PANDAS REPRESENT?
WHAT?
LUTHER
DESMOND
DIAMOND
v9.999
WHAT DID ALL THE PANDAS REPRESENT?
YOU.
THE PANDAS? THAT HE, UH, KILLED?
YOU. QUESTIONS.
UMM... I GUESS... UHHH
I WAS IN A BAD MOOD.
YOU GET BULLIED AROUND. YOU CAN'T PUNCH DOWN. YOU SUBLIMATE--
...NOTHING, I GUESS?
I WAS MAD AT PEOPLE.
THINK I THOUGHT WANTON PANDA SLAUGHTER WOULD BE FUNNY.
SO I TURNED THEM INTO PANDAS WITH MY MIND AND KILLED THEM ALL WITH SWORDS WHY
DESMOND DIAMOND
MM.
GREAT.
OH GREAT.
YOU'RE GONNA GO HOME AND BLOG THIS OR WHATEVER.

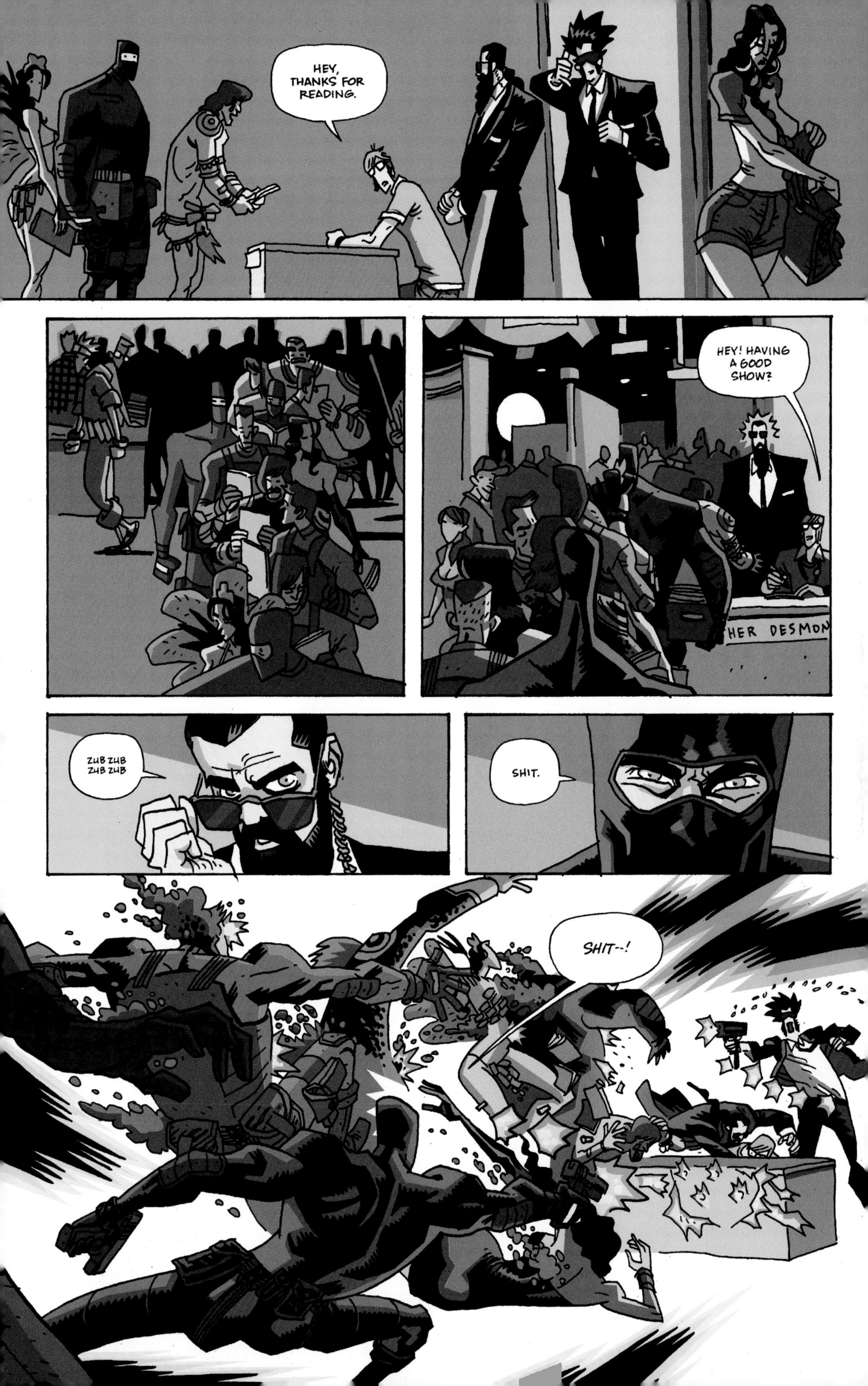
HEY, THANKS FOR READING.
HEY! HAVING A GOOD SHOW?
HER DESMON
ZUB ZUB ZUB ZUB
SHIT.
SHIT--!

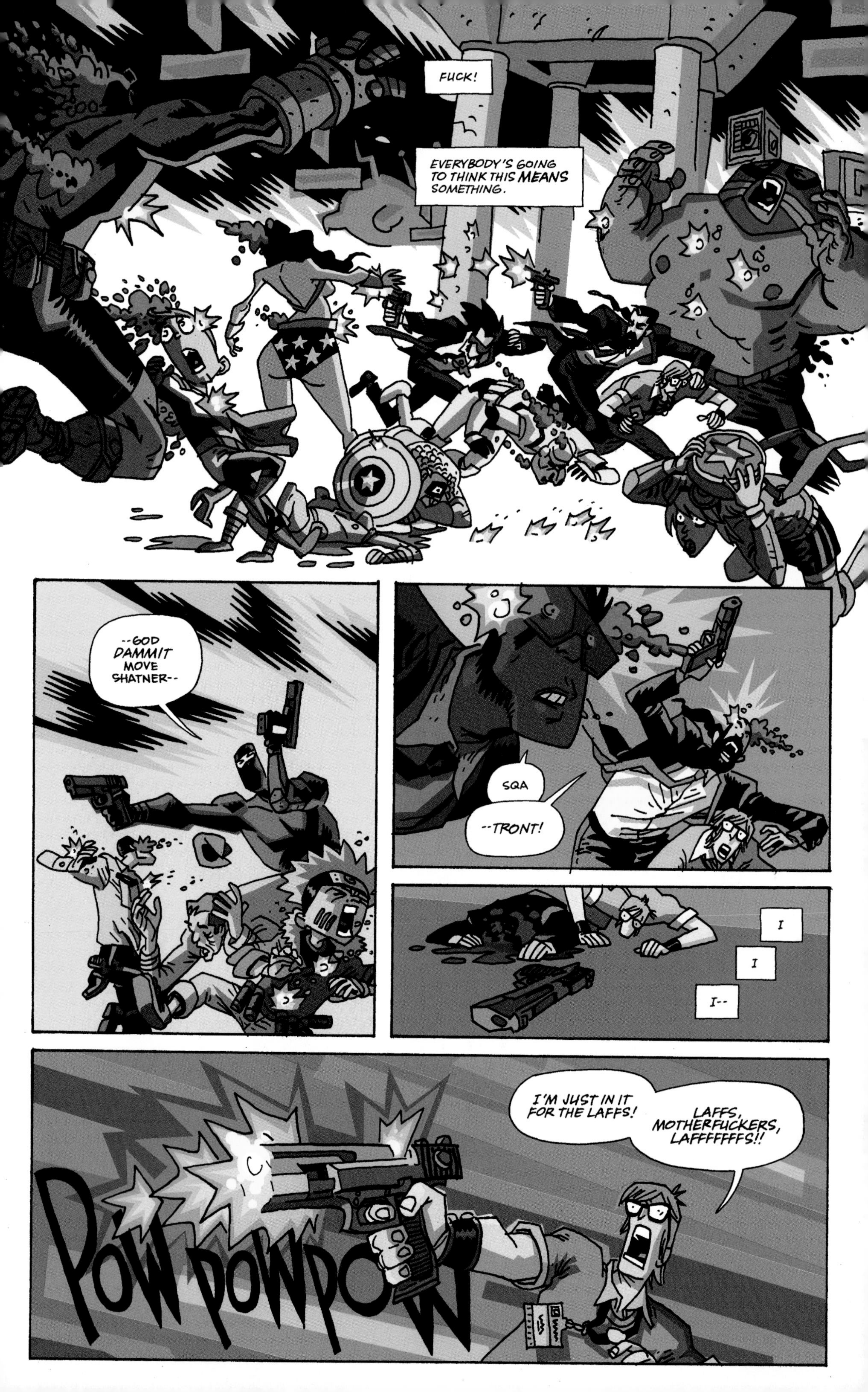

FUCK!
EVERYBODY'S GOING TO THINK THIS MEANS SOMETHING.
--GOD DAMMIT MOVE SHATNER--
SQA
--TRONT!
I
I
I--
I'M JUST IN IT FOR THE LAFFS!
LAFFS, MOTHERFUCKERS, LAFFFFFFFS!!
POW POW POW

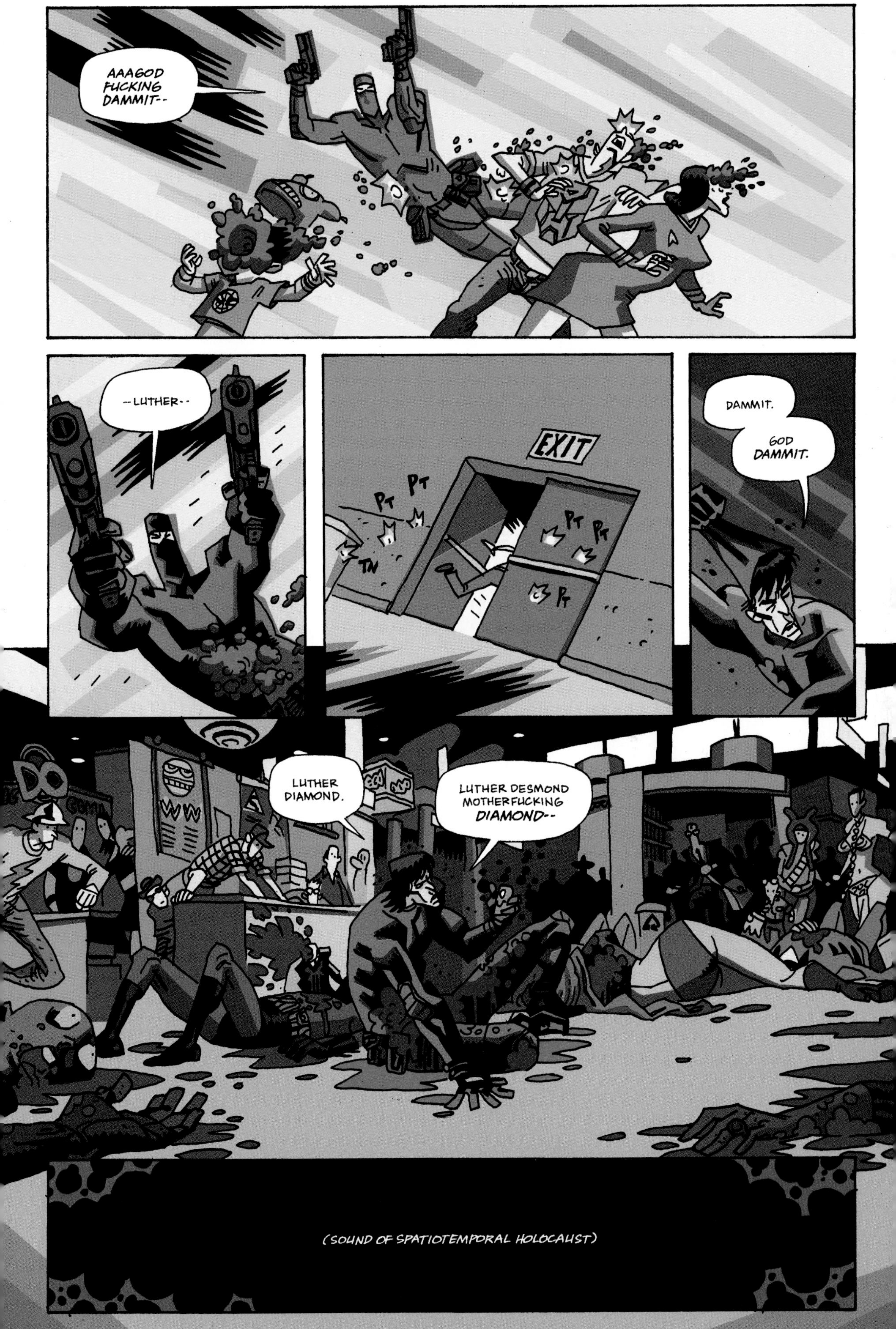
AAAGOD FUCKING DAMMIT--
--LUTHER--
EXIT
DAMMIT.
GOD DAMMIT.
LUTHER DIAMOND.
LUTHER DESMOND MOTHERFUCKING DIAMOND--
(SOUND OF SPATIOTEMPORAL HOLOCAUST)

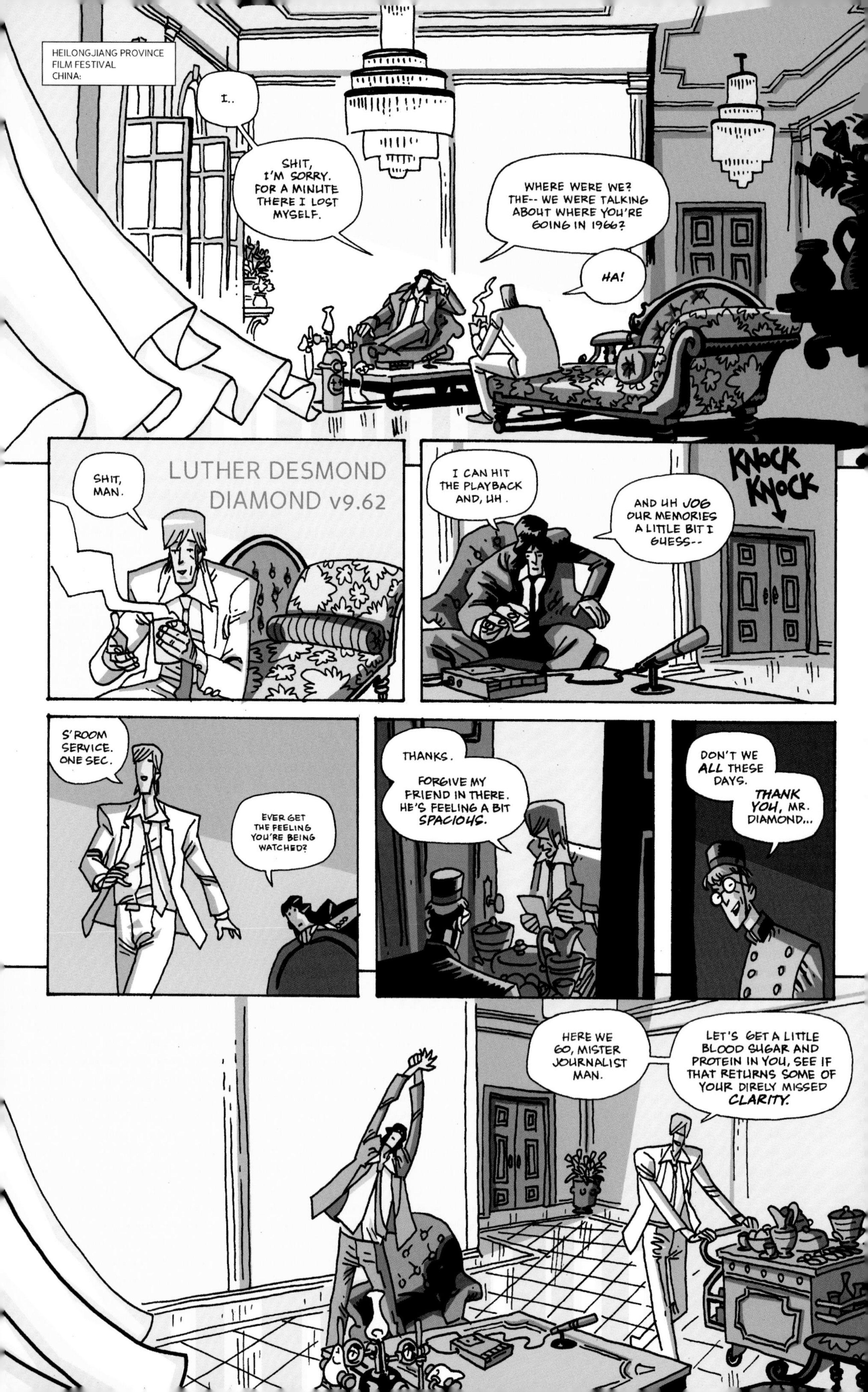
HEILONGJIANG PROVINCE FILM FESTIVAL CHINA:
I..
SHIT, I'M SORRY. FOR A MINUTE THERE I LOST MYSELF.
WHERE WERE WE? THE-- WE WERE TALKING ABOUT WHERE YOU'RE GOING IN 1966?
HA!
SHIT, MAN.
LUTHER DESMOND DIAMOND v9.62
I CAN HIT THE PLAYBACK AND, UH.
AND UH JOG OUR MEMORIES A LITTLE BIT I GUESS--
KNOCK KNOCK
S'ROOM SERVICE. ONE SEC.
EVER GET THE FEELING YOU'RE BEING WATCHED?
THANKS.
FORGIVE MY FRIEND IN THERE. HE'S FEELING A BIT SPACIOUS.
DON'T WE ALL THESE DAYS.
THANK YOU, MR. DIAMOND...
HERE WE GO, MISTER JOURNALIST MAN.
LET'S GET A LITTLE BLOOD SUGAR AND PROTEIN IN YOU, SEE IF THAT RETURNS SOME OF YOUR DIRELY MISSED CLARITY.

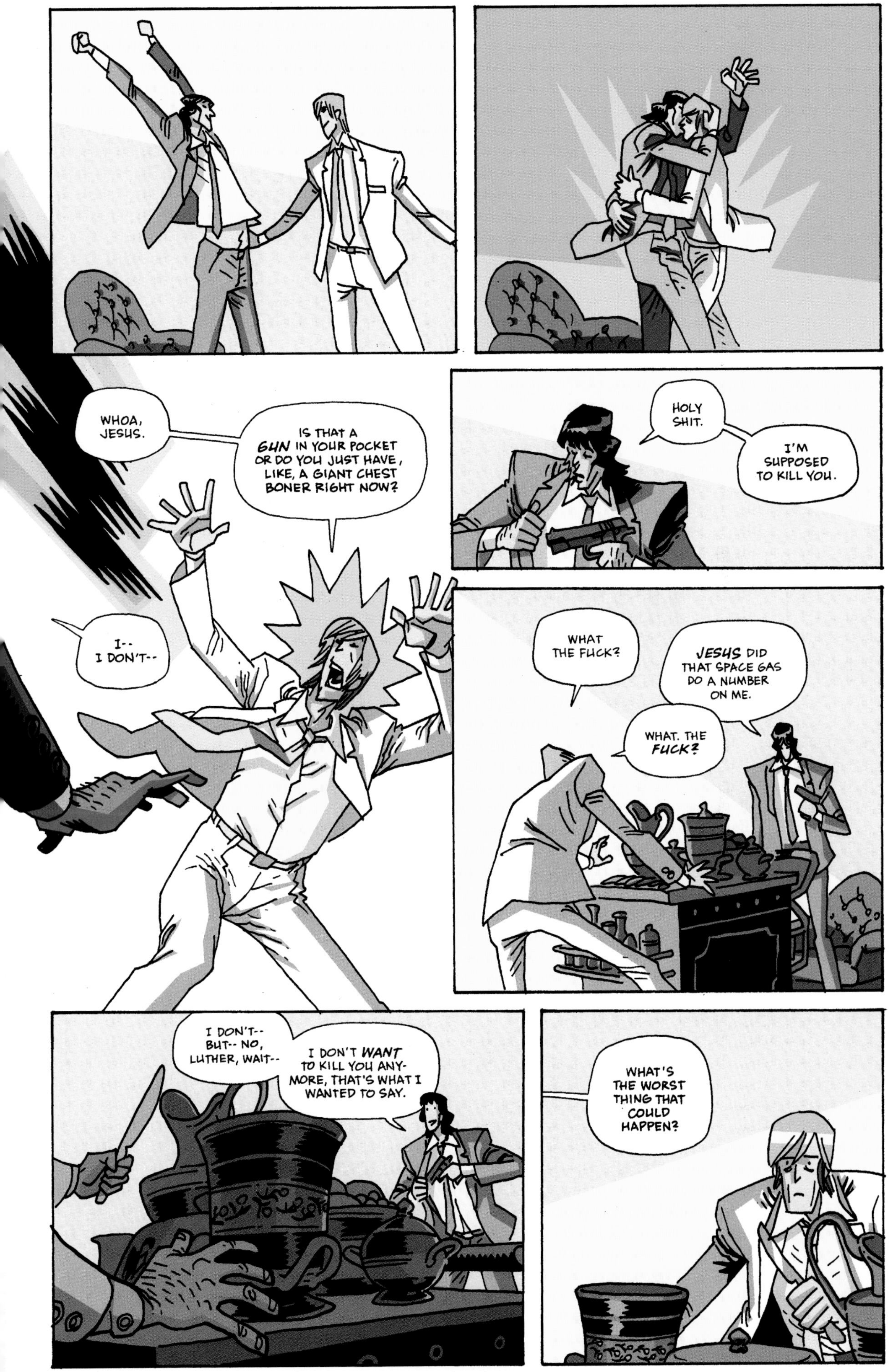
WHOA, JESUS.
IS THAT A GUN IN YOUR POCKET OR DO YOU JUST HAVE, LIKE, A GIANT CHEST BONER RIGHT NOW?
I-- I DON'T--
HOLY SHIT.
I'M SUPPOSED TO KILL YOU.
WHAT THE FUCK?
JESUS DID THAT SPACE GAS DO A NUMBER ON ME.
WHAT. THE FUCK?
I DON'T-- BUT-- NO, LUTHER, WAIT--
I DON'T WANT TO KILL YOU ANY-MORE, THAT'S WHAT I WANTED TO SAY.
WHAT'S THE WORST THING THAT COULD HAPPEN?

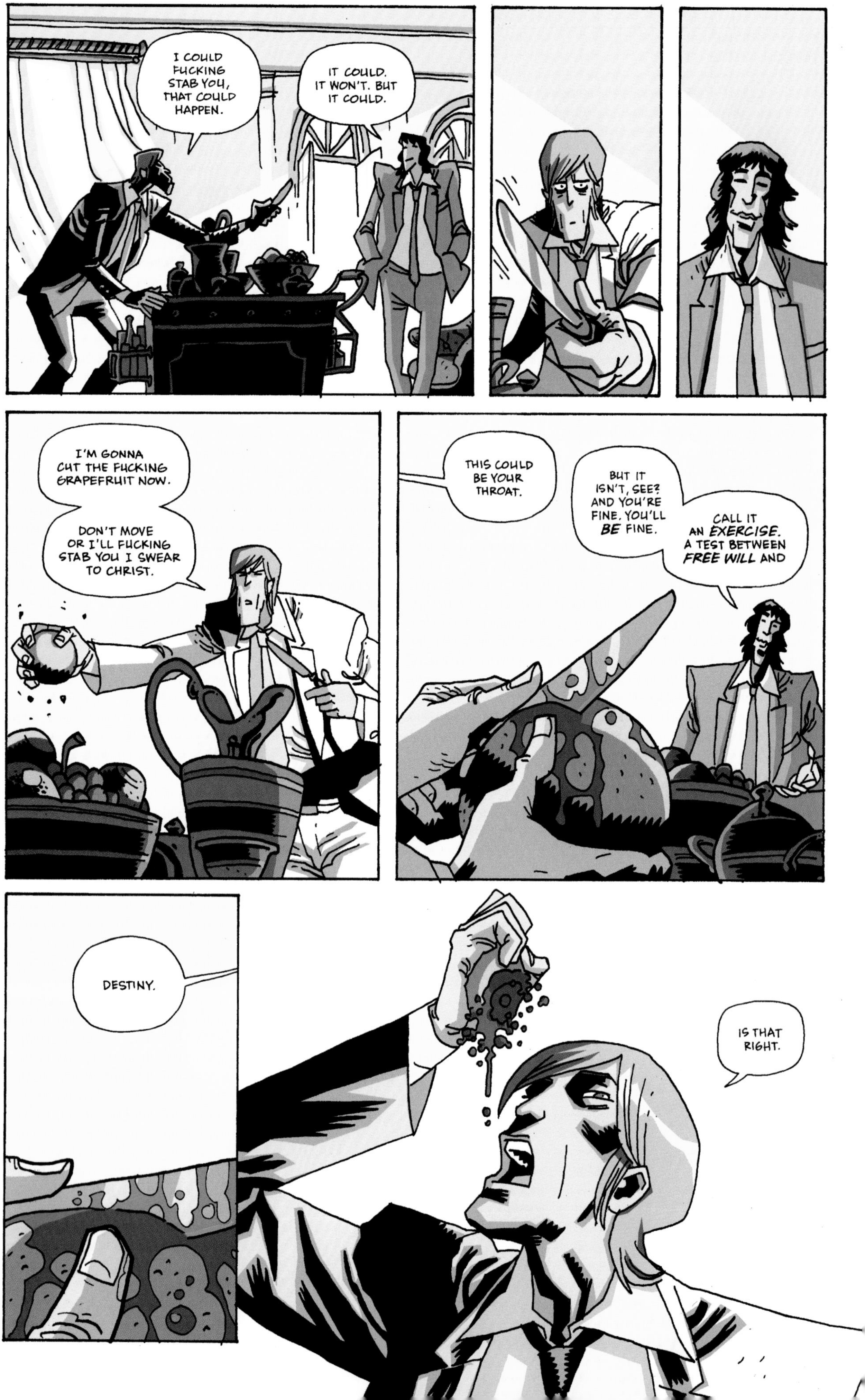
I COULD FUCKING STAB YOU, THAT COULD HAPPEN.
IT COULD. IT WON'T. BUT IT COULD.
I'M GONNA CUT THE FUCKING GRAPEFRUIT NOW.
DON'T MOVE OR I'LL FUCKING STAB YOU I SWEAR TO CHRIST.
THIS COULD BE YOUR THROAT.
BUT IT ISN'T, SEE? AND YOU'RE FINE. YOU'LL BE FINE.
CALL IT AN EXERCISE. A TEST BETWEEN FREE WILL AND
DESTINY.
IS THAT RIGHT.

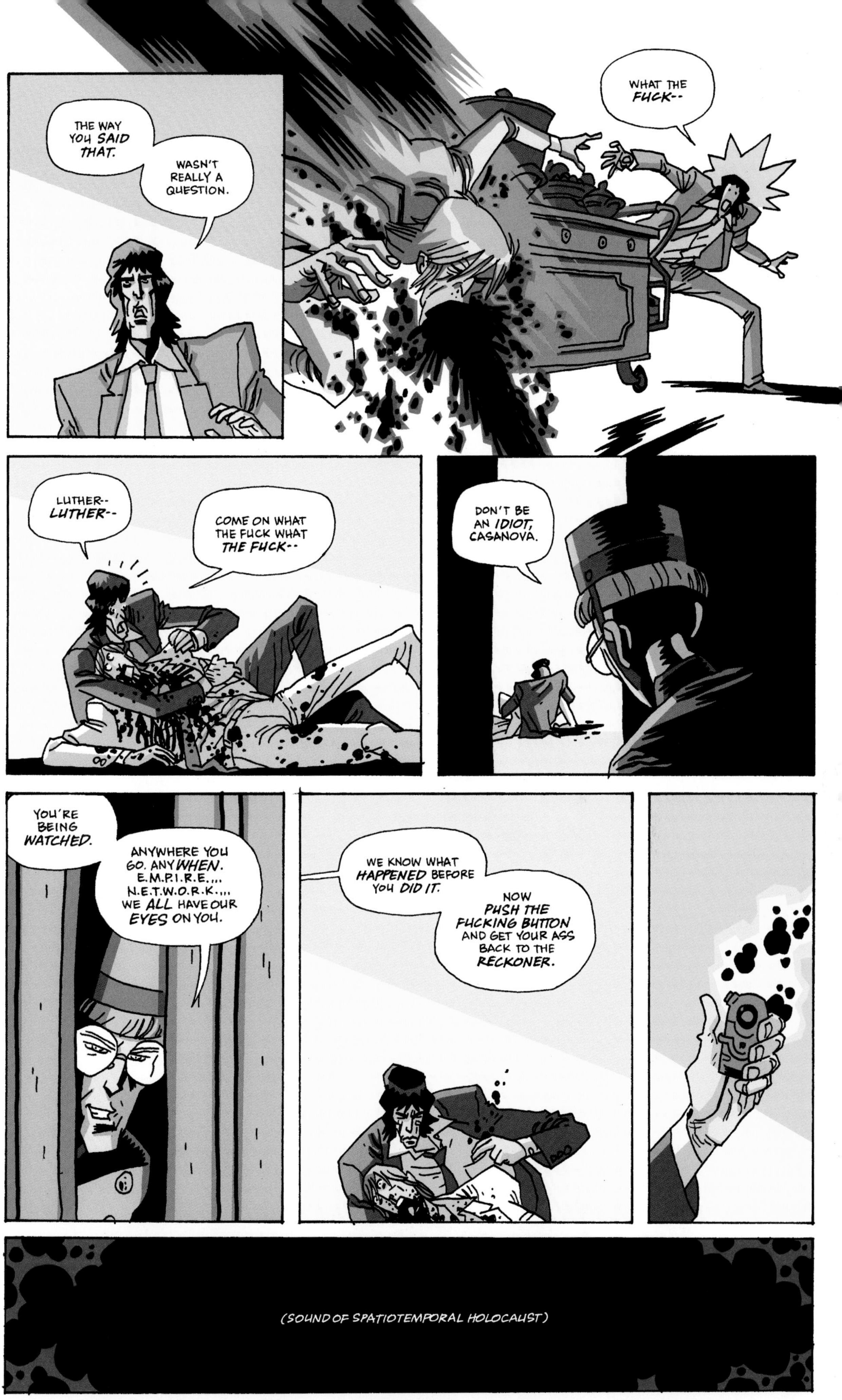
THE WAY YOU SAID THAT.
WASN'T REALLY A QUESTION.
WHAT THE FUCK--
LUTHER-- LUTHER--
COME ON WHAT THE FUCK WHAT THE FUCK--
DON'T BE AN IDIOT, CASANOVA.
YOU'RE BEING WATCHED.
ANYWHERE YOU GO. ANYWHEN. E.M.P.I.R.E.... N.E.T.W.O.R.K.... WE ALL HAVE OUR EYES ON YOU.
WE KNOW WHAT HAPPENED BEFORE YOU DID IT.
NOW PUSH THE FUCKING BUTTON AND GET YOUR ASS BACK TO THE RECKONER.
(SOUND OF SPATIOTEMPORAL HOLOCAUST)

6. NIGHT IS OVER

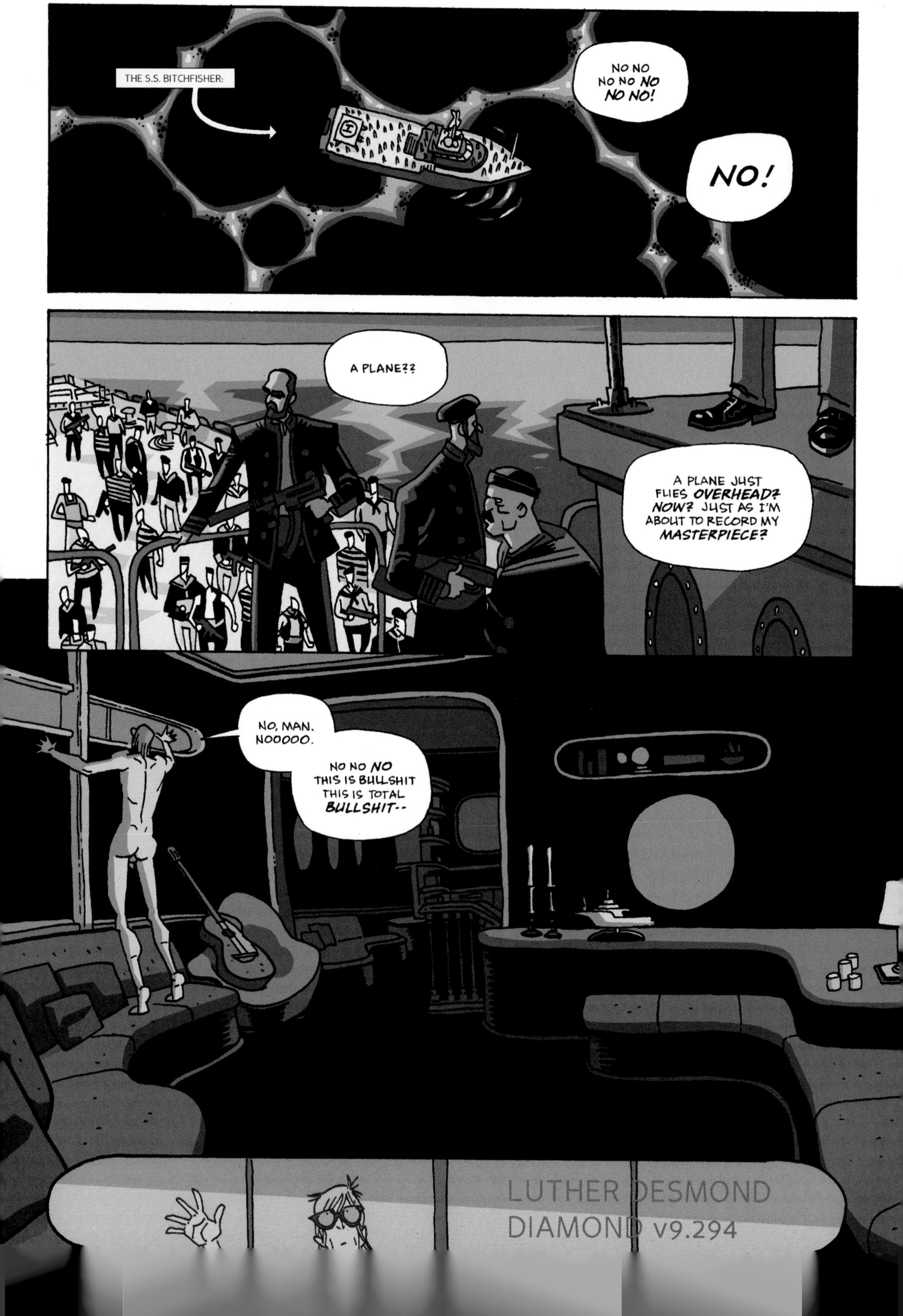
THE S.S. BITCHFISHER:
NO NO NO NO NO NO NO!
NO!
A PLANE??
A PLANE JUST FLIES OVERHEAD? NOW? JUST AS I'M ABOUT TO RECORD MY MASTERPIECE?
NO, MAN. NOOOOO.
NO NO NO THIS IS BULLSHIT THIS IS TOTAL BULLSHIT--
LUTHER DESMOND DIAMOND v9.294

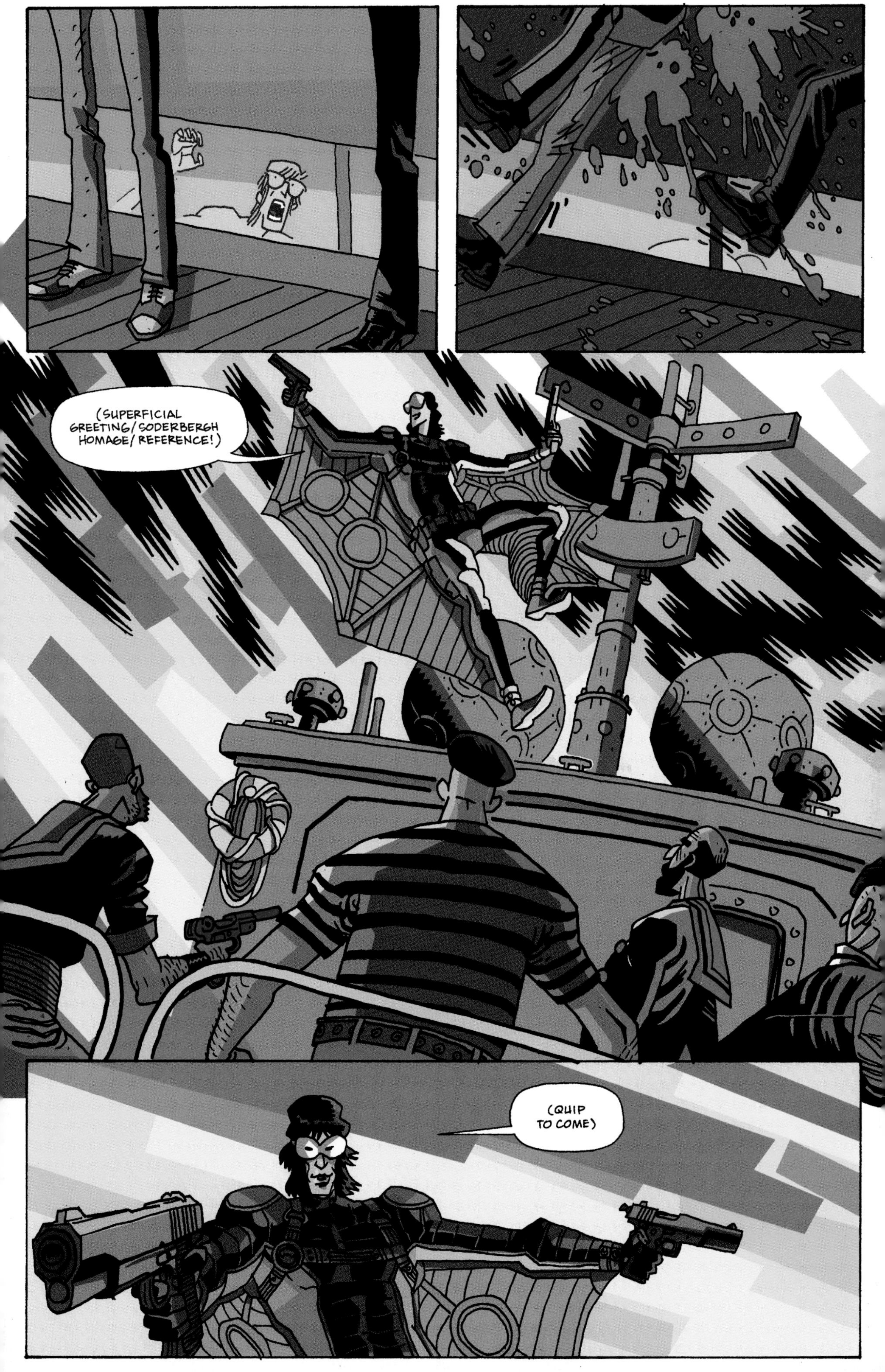
(SUPERFICIAL GREETING/ SODERBERGH HOMAGE/ REFERENCE!)
(QUIP TO COME)

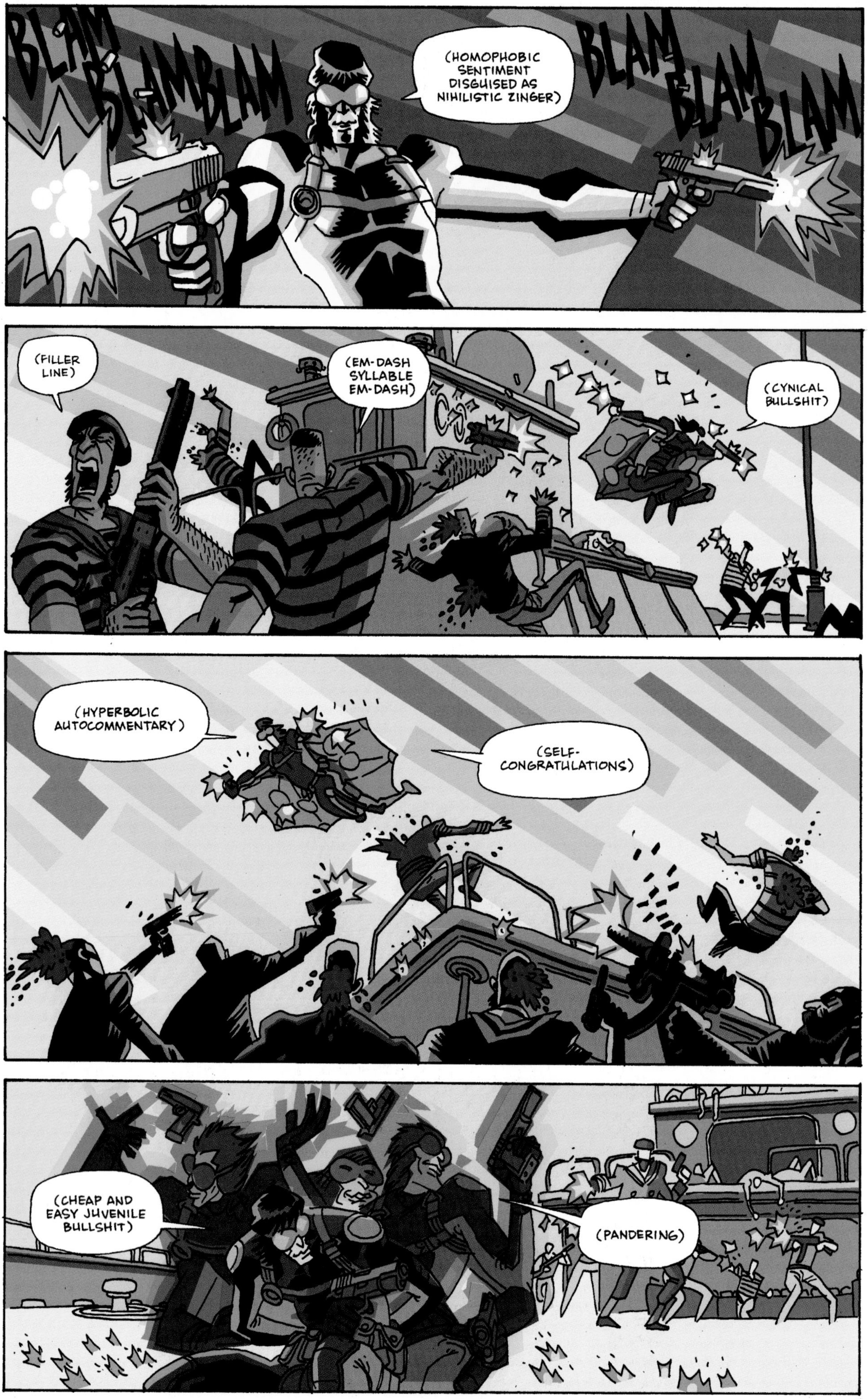
BLAM BLAMBLAM
(HOMOPHOBIC SENTIMENT DISGUISED AS NIHILISTIC ZINGER)
BLAM BLAM BLAM
(FILLER LINE)
(EM-DASH SYLLABLE EM-DASH)
(CYNICAL BULLSHIT)
(HYPERBOLIC AUTOCOMMENTARY)
(SELF-CONGRATULATIONS)
(CHEAP AND EASY JUVENILE BULLSHIT)
(PANDERING)

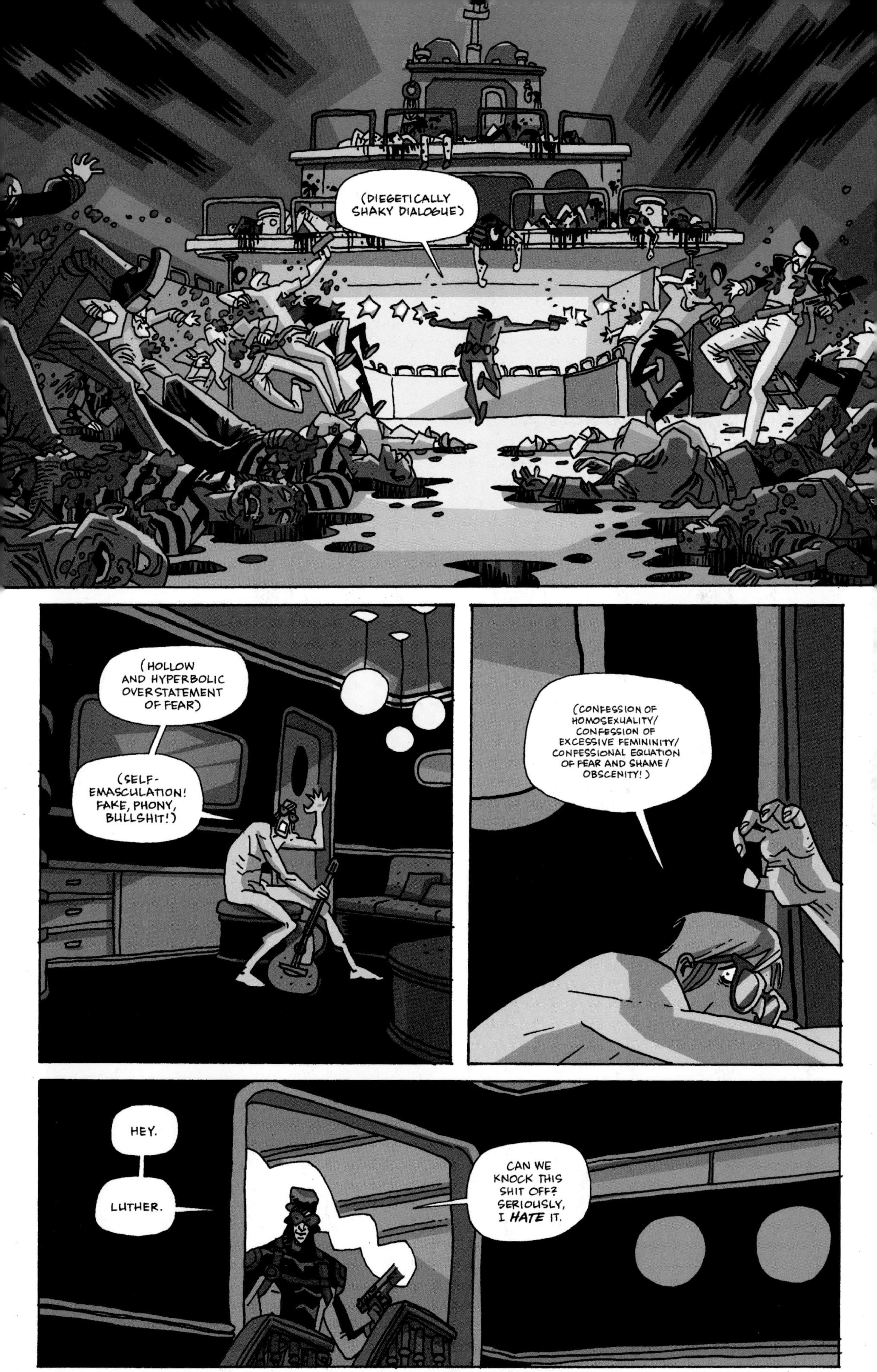

(DIEGETICALLY SHAKY DIALOGUE)
(HOLLOW AND HYPERBOLIC OVERSTATEMENT OF FEAR)
(SELF-EMASCULATION! FAKE, PHONY, BULLSHIT!)
(CONFESSION OF HOMOSEXUALITY/ CONFESSION OF EXCESSIVE FEMININITY/ CONFESSIONAL EQUATION OF FEAR AND SHAME/ OBSCENITY!)
HEY.
LUTHER.
CAN WE KNOCK THIS SHIT OFF? SERIOUSLY, I HATE IT.

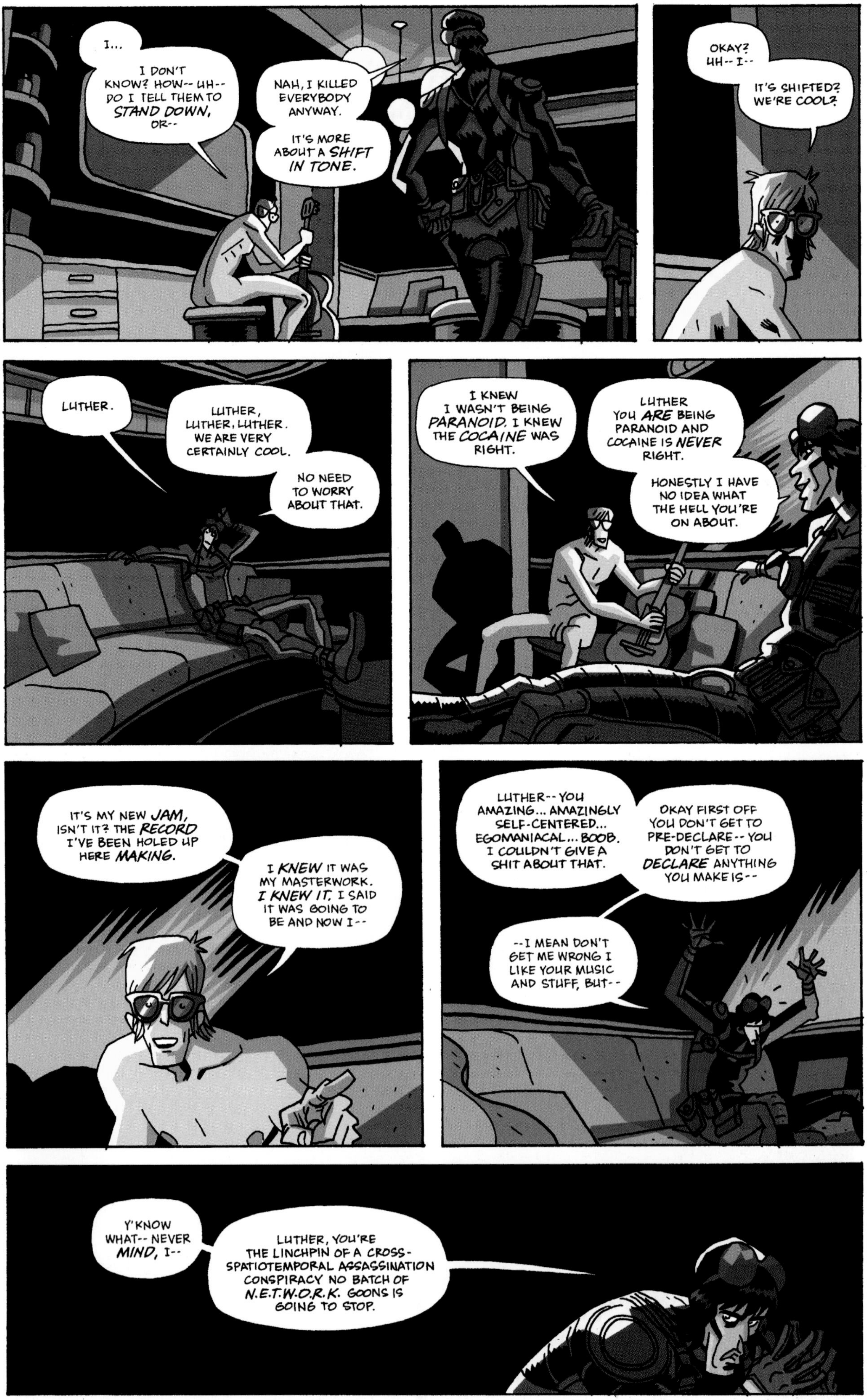
I...
I DON'T KNOW? HOW-- UH-- DO I TELL THEM TO STAND DOWN, OR--
NAH, I KILLED EVERYBODY ANYWAY.
IT'S MORE ABOUT A SHIFT IN TONE.
OKAY? UH-- I--
IT'S SHIFTED? WE'RE COOL?
LUTHER.
LUTHER, LUTHER, LUTHER. WE ARE VERY CERTAINLY COOL.
NO NEED TO WORRY ABOUT THAT.
I KNEW I WASN'T BEING PARANOID. I KNEW THE COCAINE WAS RIGHT.
LUTHER YOU ARE BEING PARANOID AND COCAINE IS NEVER RIGHT.
HONESTLY I HAVE NO IDEA WHAT THE HELL YOU'RE ON ABOUT.
IT'S MY NEW JAM, ISN'T IT? THE RECORD I'VE BEEN HOLED UP HERE MAKING.
I KNEW IT WAS MY MASTERWORK. I KNEW IT. I SAID IT WAS GOING TO BE AND NOW I--
LUTHER-- YOU AMAZING... AMAZINGLY SELF-CENTERED... EGOMANIACAL... BOOB. I COULDN'T GIVE A SHIT ABOUT THAT.
OKAY FIRST OFF YOU DON'T GET TO PRE-DECLARE-- YOU DON'T GET TO DECLARE ANYTHING YOU MAKE IS--
--I MEAN DON'T GET ME WRONG I LIKE YOUR MUSIC AND STUFF, BUT--
Y'KNOW WHAT-- NEVER MIND, I--
LUTHER, YOU'RE THE LINCHPIN OF A CROSS-SPATIOTEMPORAL ASSASSINATION CONSPIRACY NO BATCH OF N.E.T.W.O.R.K. GOONS IS GOING TO STOP.

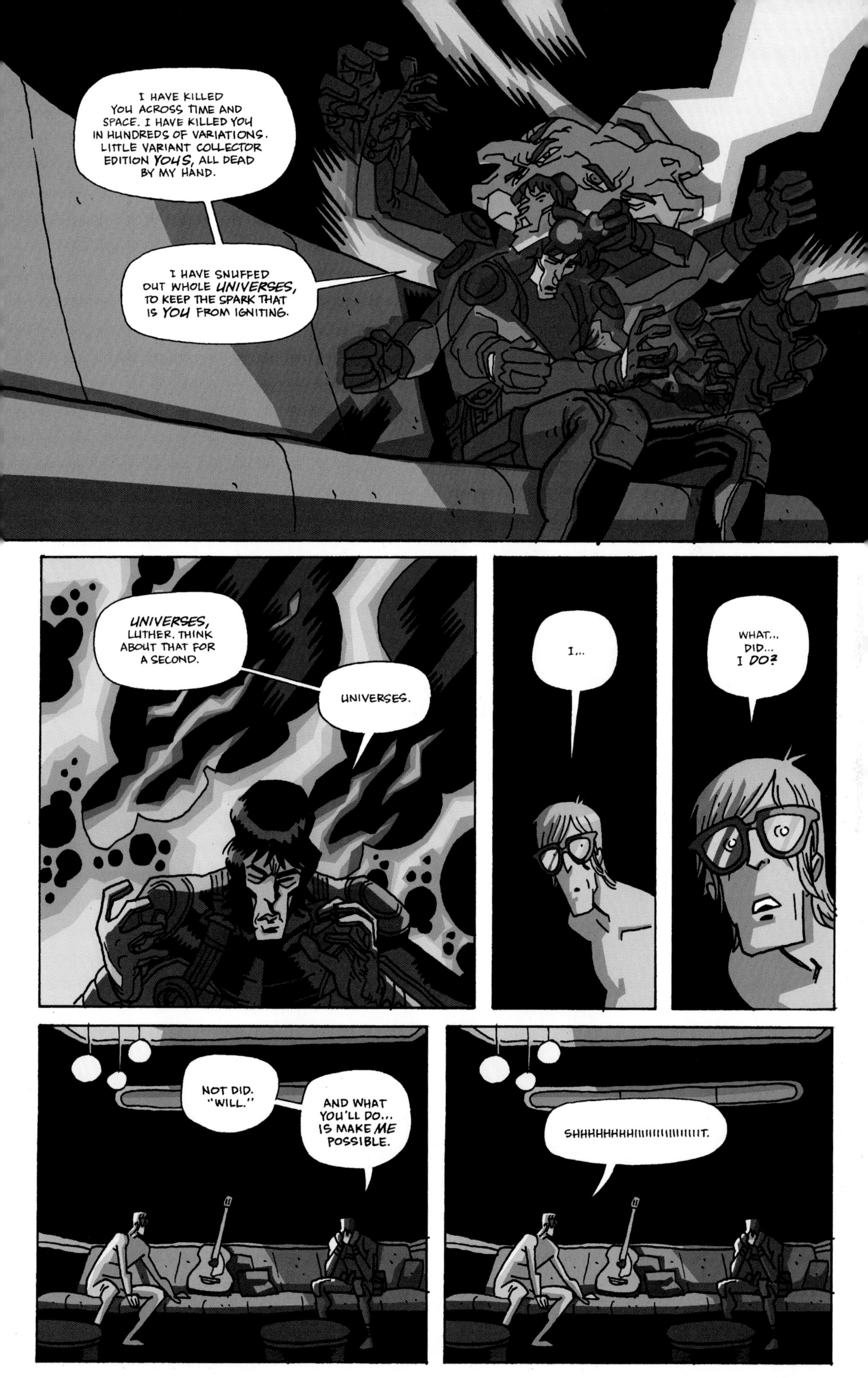
I HAVE KILLED YOU ACROSS TIME AND SPACE. I HAVE KILLED YOU IN HUNDREDS OF VARIATIONS. LITTLE VARIANT COLLECTOR EDITION *YOUS*, ALL DEAD BY MY HAND.
I HAVE SNUFFED OUT WHOLE *UNIVERSES*, TO KEEP THE SPARK THAT IS *YOU* FROM IGNITING.
UNIVERSES, LUTHER. THINK ABOUT THAT FOR A SECOND.
UNIVERSES.
I...
WHAT... DID... I *DO?*
NOT DID. "WILL."
AND WHAT YOU'LL DO... IS MAKE *ME* POSSIBLE.
SHHHHHHHHIIIIIIIIIIIIIIIIIT.

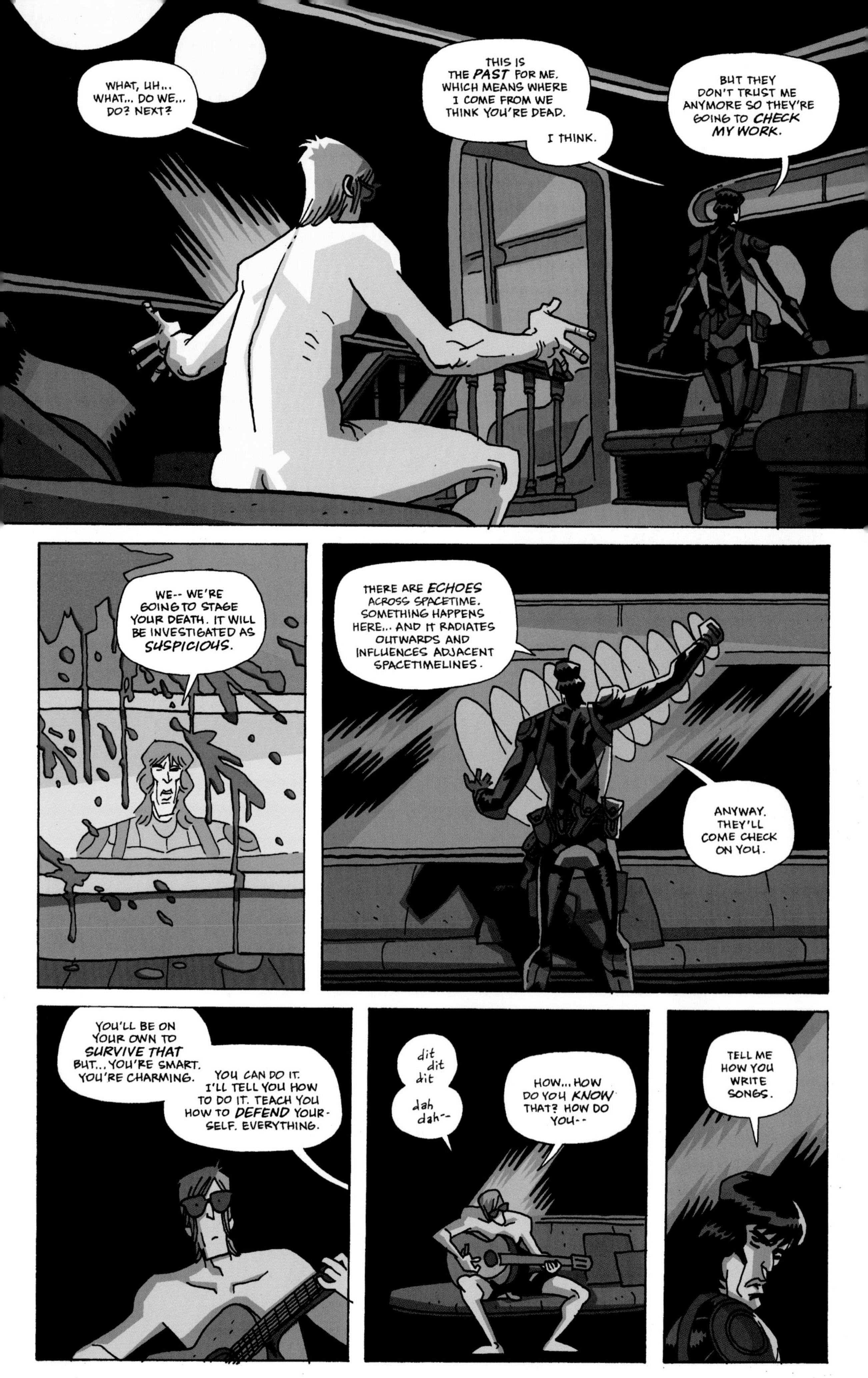
WHAT, UH... WHAT... DO WE... DO? NEXT?
THIS IS THE PAST FOR ME. WHICH MEANS WHERE I COME FROM WE THINK YOU'RE DEAD.
I THINK.
BUT THEY DON'T TRUST ME ANYMORE SO THEY'RE GOING TO CHECK MY WORK.
WE-- WE'RE GOING TO STAGE YOUR DEATH. IT WILL BE INVESTIGATED AS SUSPICIOUS.
THERE ARE ECHOES ACROSS SPACETIME. SOMETHING HAPPENS HERE... AND IT RADIATES OUTWARDS AND INFLUENCES ADJACENT SPACETIMELINES.
ANYWAY. THEY'LL COME CHECK ON YOU.
YOU'LL BE ON YOUR OWN TO SURVIVE THAT BUT... YOU'RE SMART. YOU'RE CHARMING.
YOU CAN DO IT. I'LL TELL YOU HOW TO DO IT. TEACH YOU HOW TO DEFEND YOURSELF. EVERYTHING.
dit dit dit
dah dah--
HOW... HOW DO YOU KNOW THAT? HOW DO YOU--
TELL ME HOW YOU WRITE SONGS.

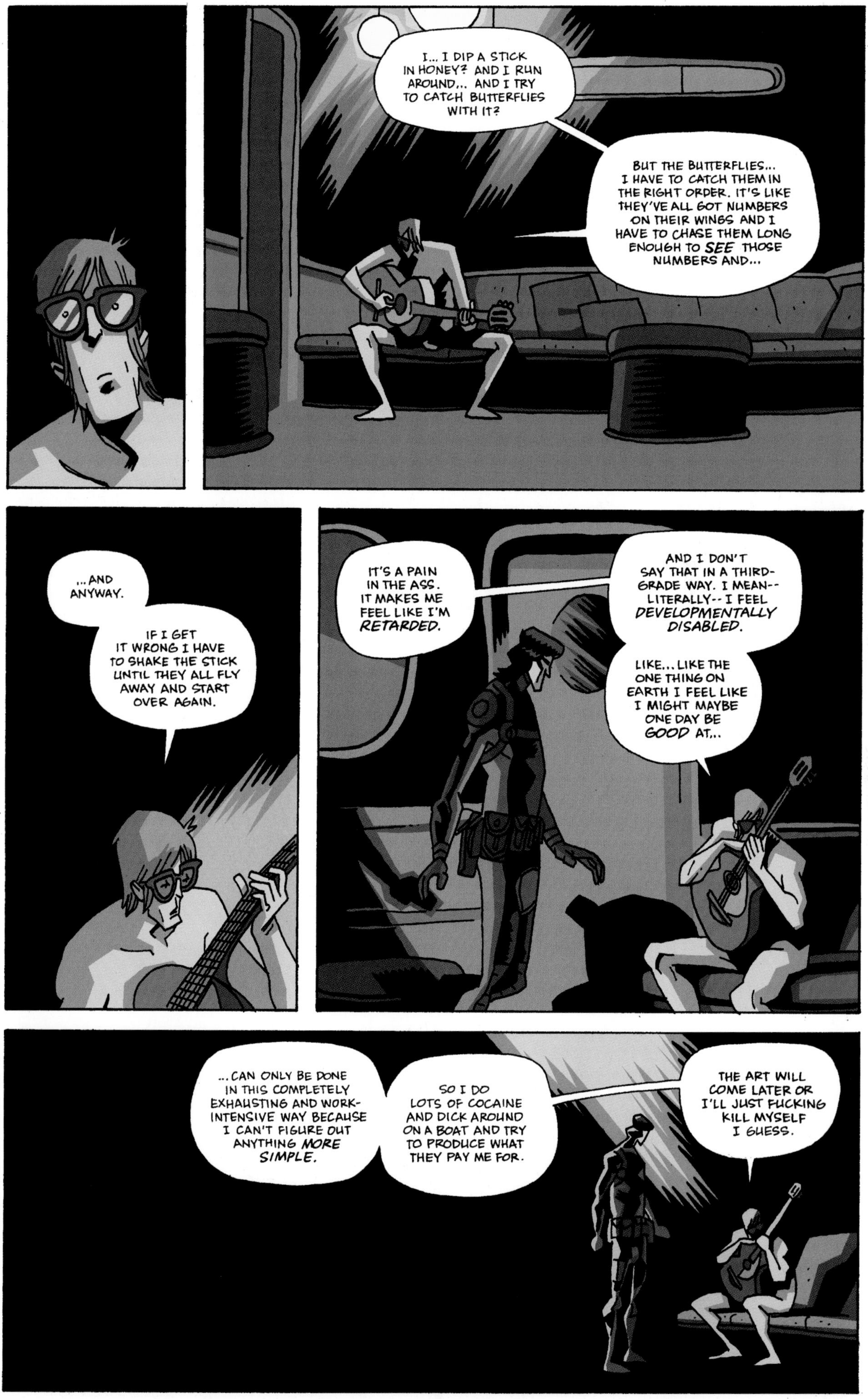
I... I DIP A STICK IN HONEY? AND I RUN AROUND... AND I TRY TO CATCH BUTTERFLIES WITH IT?
BUT THE BUTTERFLIES... I HAVE TO CATCH THEM IN THE RIGHT ORDER. IT'S LIKE THEY'VE ALL GOT NUMBERS ON THEIR WINGS AND I HAVE TO CHASE THEM LONG ENOUGH TO *SEE* THOSE NUMBERS AND...
...AND ANYWAY.
IF I GET IT WRONG I HAVE TO SHAKE THE STICK UNTIL THEY ALL FLY AWAY AND START OVER AGAIN.
IT'S A PAIN IN THE ASS. IT MAKES ME FEEL LIKE I'M *RETARDED*.
AND I DON'T SAY THAT IN A THIRD-GRADE WAY. I MEAN-- LITERALLY-- I FEEL *DEVELOPMENTALLY DISABLED*.
LIKE... LIKE THE ONE THING ON EARTH I FEEL LIKE I MIGHT MAYBE ONE DAY BE *GOOD* AT...
...CAN ONLY BE DONE IN THIS COMPLETELY EXHAUSTING AND WORK-INTENSIVE WAY BECAUSE I CAN'T FIGURE OUT ANYTHING *MORE SIMPLE*.
SO I DO LOTS OF COCAINE AND DICK AROUND ON A BOAT AND TRY TO PRODUCE WHAT THEY PAY ME FOR.
THE ART WILL COME LATER OR I'LL JUST FUCKING KILL MYSELF I GUESS.

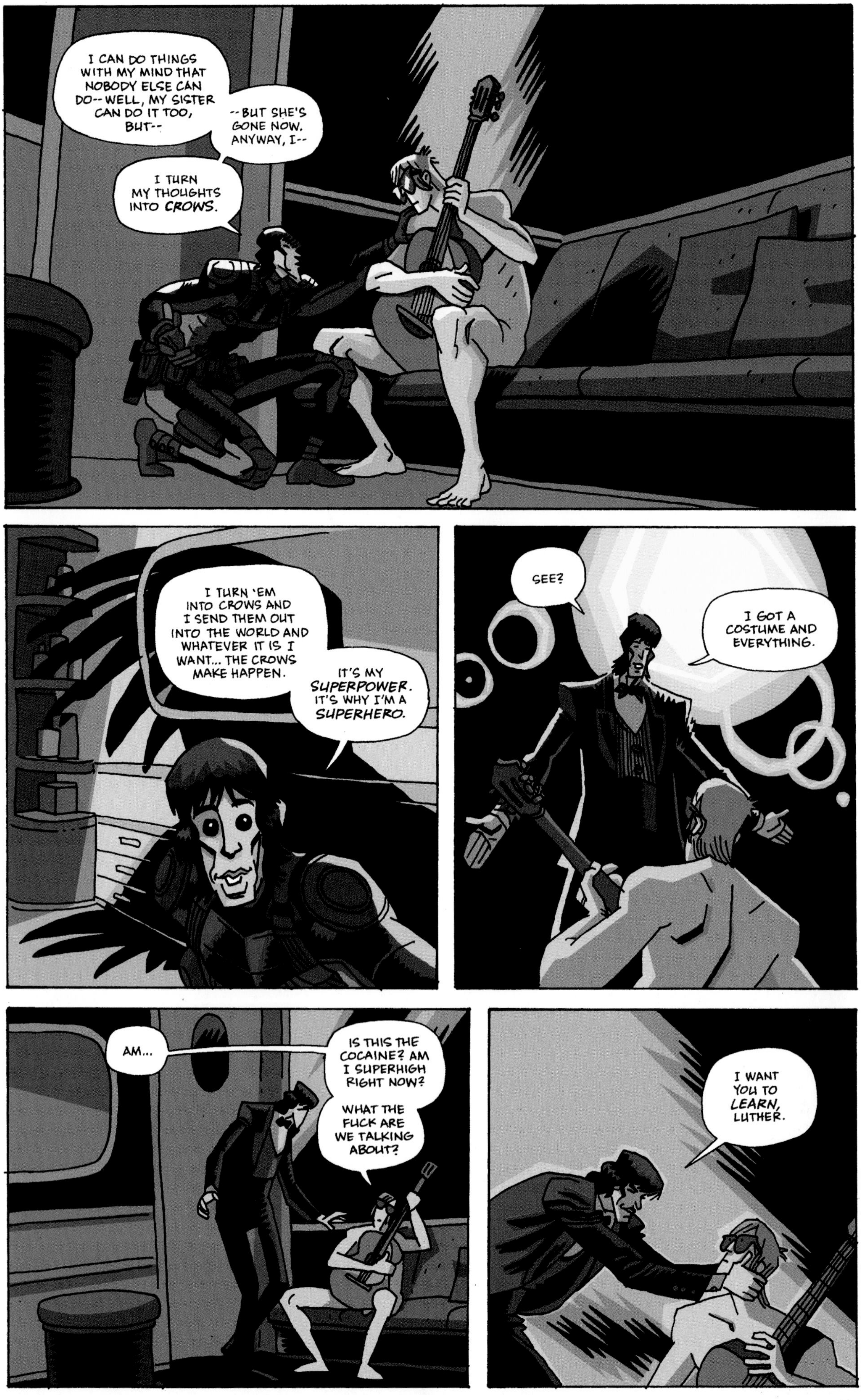
I CAN DO THINGS WITH MY MIND THAT NOBODY ELSE CAN DO-- WELL, MY SISTER CAN DO IT TOO, BUT--
--BUT SHE'S GONE NOW. ANYWAY, I--
I TURN MY THOUGHTS INTO CROWS.
I TURN 'EM INTO CROWS AND I SEND THEM OUT INTO THE WORLD AND WHATEVER IT IS I WANT... THE CROWS MAKE HAPPEN.
IT'S MY SUPERPOWER. IT'S WHY I'M A SUPERHERO.
SEE?
I GOT A COSTUME AND EVERYTHING.
AM...
IS THIS THE COCAINE? AM I SUPERHIGH RIGHT NOW?
WHAT THE FUCK ARE WE TALKING ABOUT?
I WANT YOU TO LEARN, LUTHER.

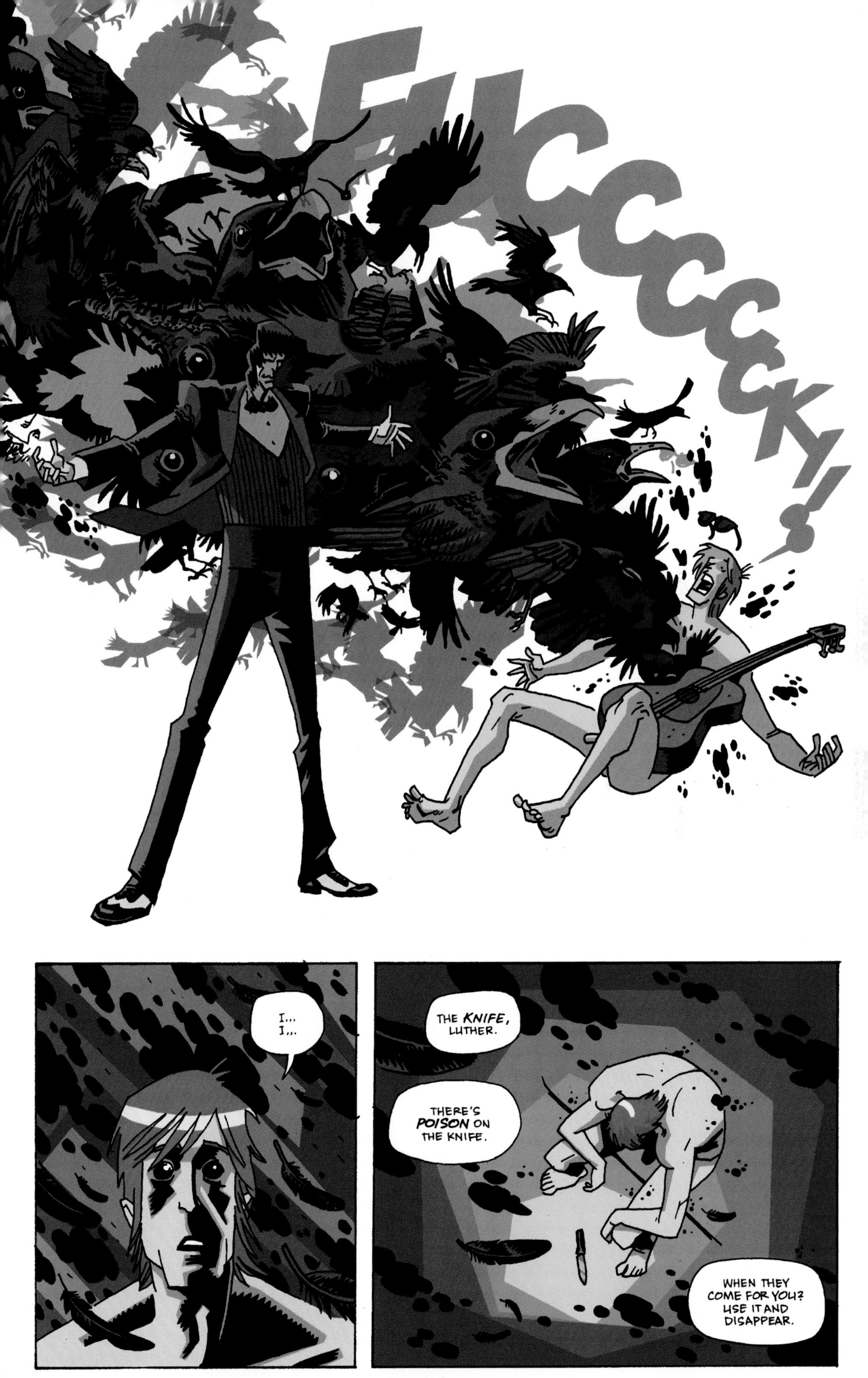
FUCCCCCKY!!
I... I...
THE *KNIFE*, LUTHER.
THERE'S *POISON* ON THE KNIFE.
WHEN THEY COME FOR YOU? USE IT AND DISAPPEAR.

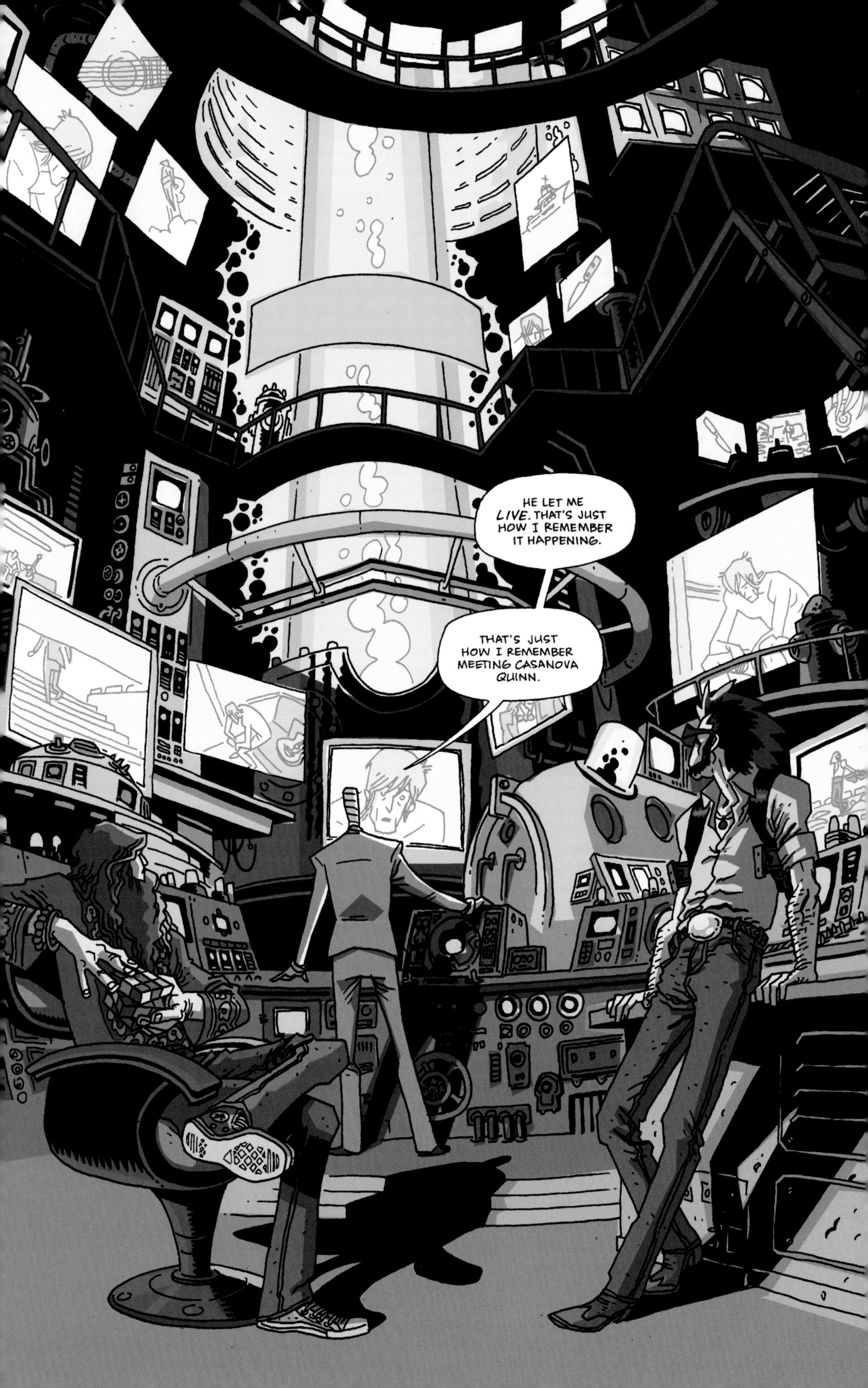
HE LET ME LIVE. THAT'S JUST HOW I REMEMBER IT HAPPENING.
THAT'S JUST HOW I REMEMBER MEETING CASANOVA QUINN.

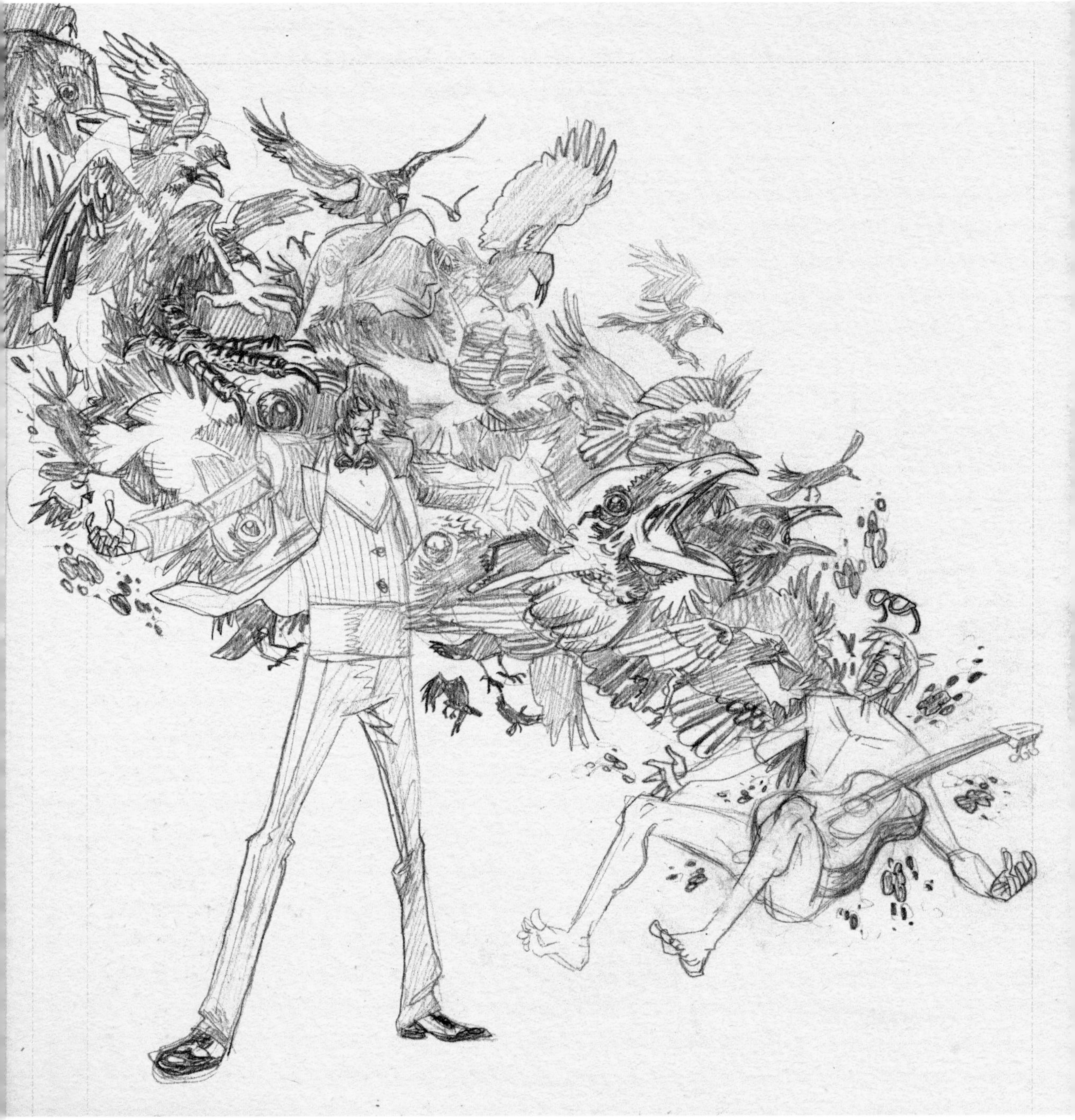

W.A.S.T.E.-FREE WILDERNESS

WHAT IF IT'S NEVER ENOUGH

HARM REDUCTION

RELAXED IN PERSON

BACKMATTER

7. THE WIDTH OF A CIRCLE

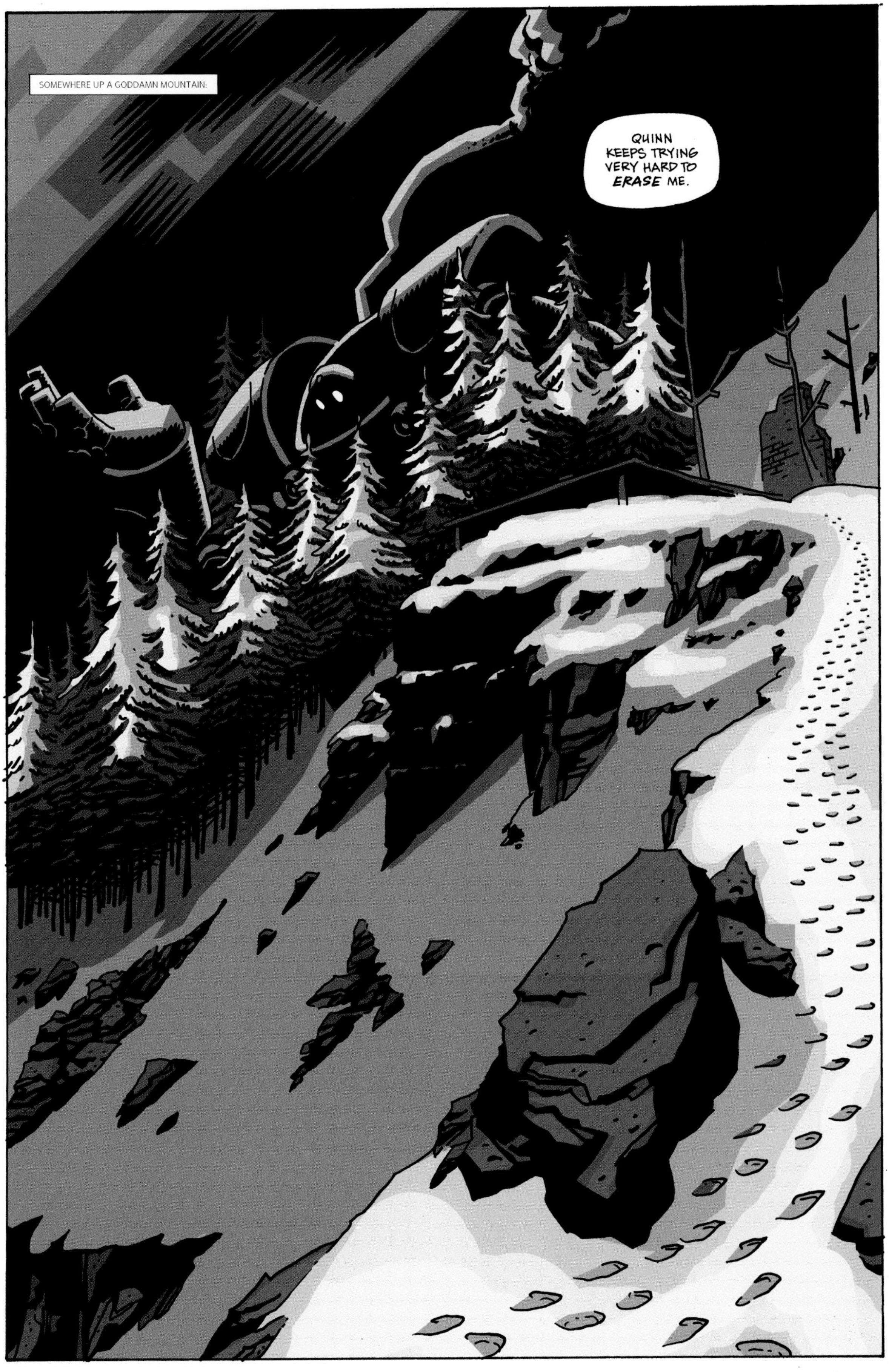
SOMEWHERE UP A GODDAMN MOUNTAIN:
QUINN KEEPS TRYING VERY HARD TO ERASE ME.

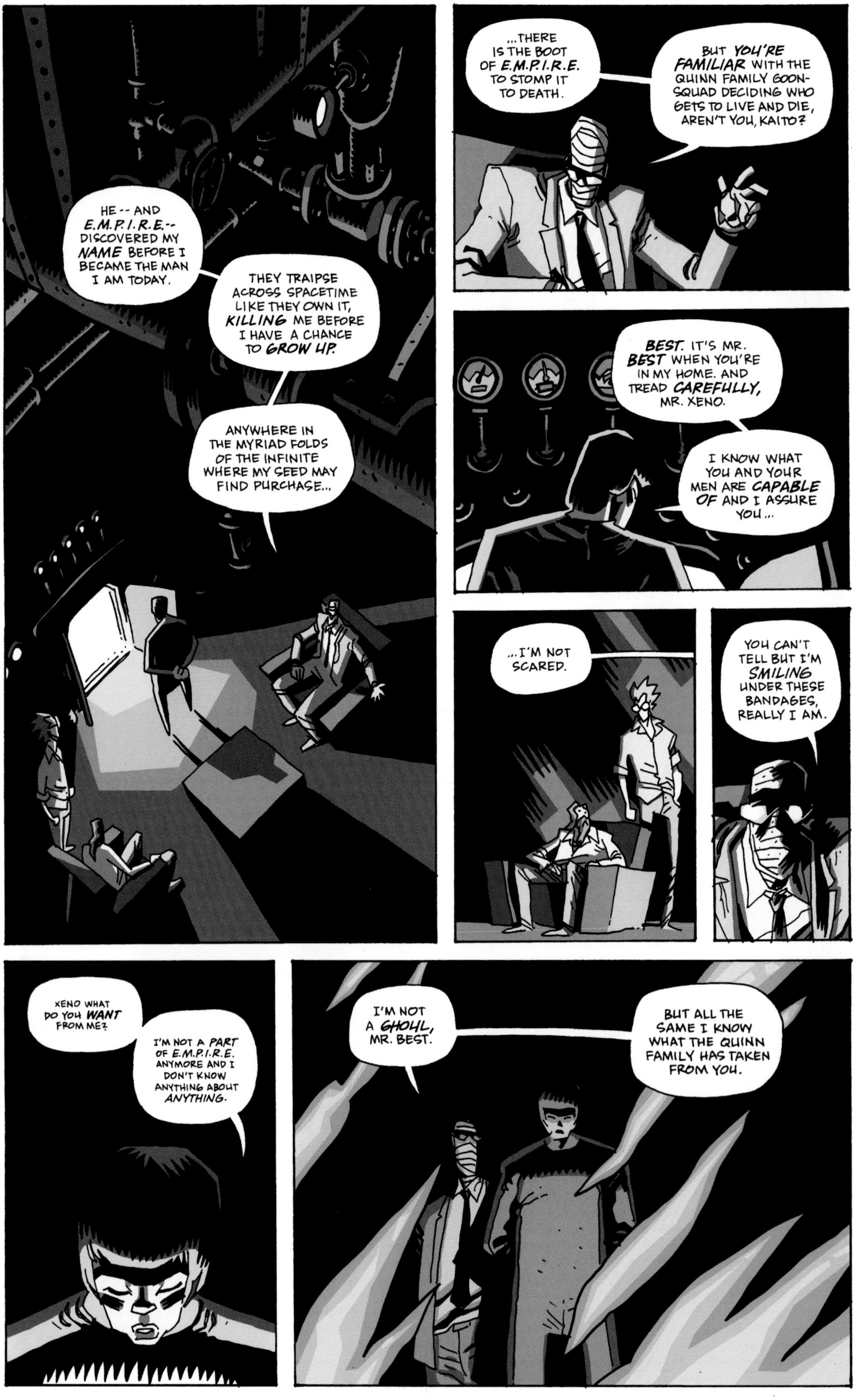
HE -- AND E.M.P.I.R.E.-- DISCOVERED MY NAME BEFORE I BECAME THE MAN I AM TODAY.
THEY TRAIPSE ACROSS SPACETIME LIKE THEY OWN IT, KILLING ME BEFORE I HAVE A CHANCE TO GROW UP.
ANYWHERE IN THE MYRIAD FOLDS OF THE INFINITE WHERE MY SEED MAY FIND PURCHASE...
...THERE IS THE BOOT OF E.M.P.I.R.E. TO STOMP IT TO DEATH.
BUT YOU'RE FAMILIAR WITH THE QUINN FAMILY GOON-SQUAD DECIDING WHO GETS TO LIVE AND DIE, AREN'T YOU, KAITO?
BEST. IT'S MR. BEST WHEN YOU'RE IN MY HOME. AND TREAD CAREFULLY, MR. XENO.
I KNOW WHAT YOU AND YOUR MEN ARE CAPABLE OF AND I ASSURE YOU...
...I'M NOT SCARED.
YOU CAN'T TELL BUT I'M SMILING UNDER THESE BANDAGES, REALLY I AM.
XENO WHAT DO YOU WANT FROM ME?
I'M NOT A PART OF E.M.P.I.R.E. ANYMORE AND I DON'T KNOW ANYTHING ABOUT ANYTHING.
I'M NOT A GHOUL, MR. BEST.
BUT ALL THE SAME I KNOW WHAT THE QUINN FAMILY HAS TAKEN FROM YOU.

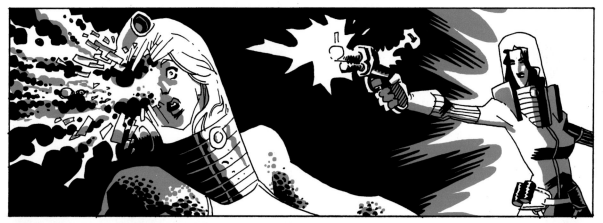

AND I KNOW YOU COULD KILL HIM AT ANY TIME, FOR *ANY* REASON.

LET ALONE THE VERY *SPECIFIC* REASON YOU HAVE...

WHAT ARE YOU WAITING FOR?

SKYLABS ARE FALLING, MR. BEST.

AREN'T YOU THE BEST KILLER IN THE WORLD?

HE IS.

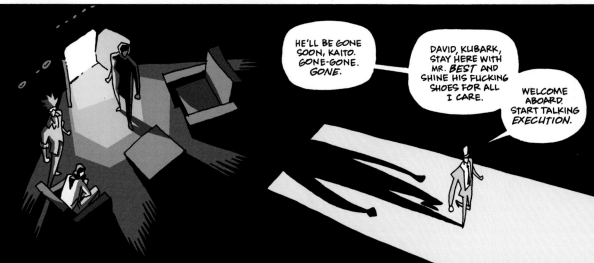

HE'LL BE GONE SOON, KAITO. GONE-GONE. GONE.

DAVID, KUBARK, STAY HERE WITH MR. *BEST* AND SHINE HIS FUCKING SHOES FOR ALL I CARE.

WELCOME ABOARD. START TALKING EXECUTION.

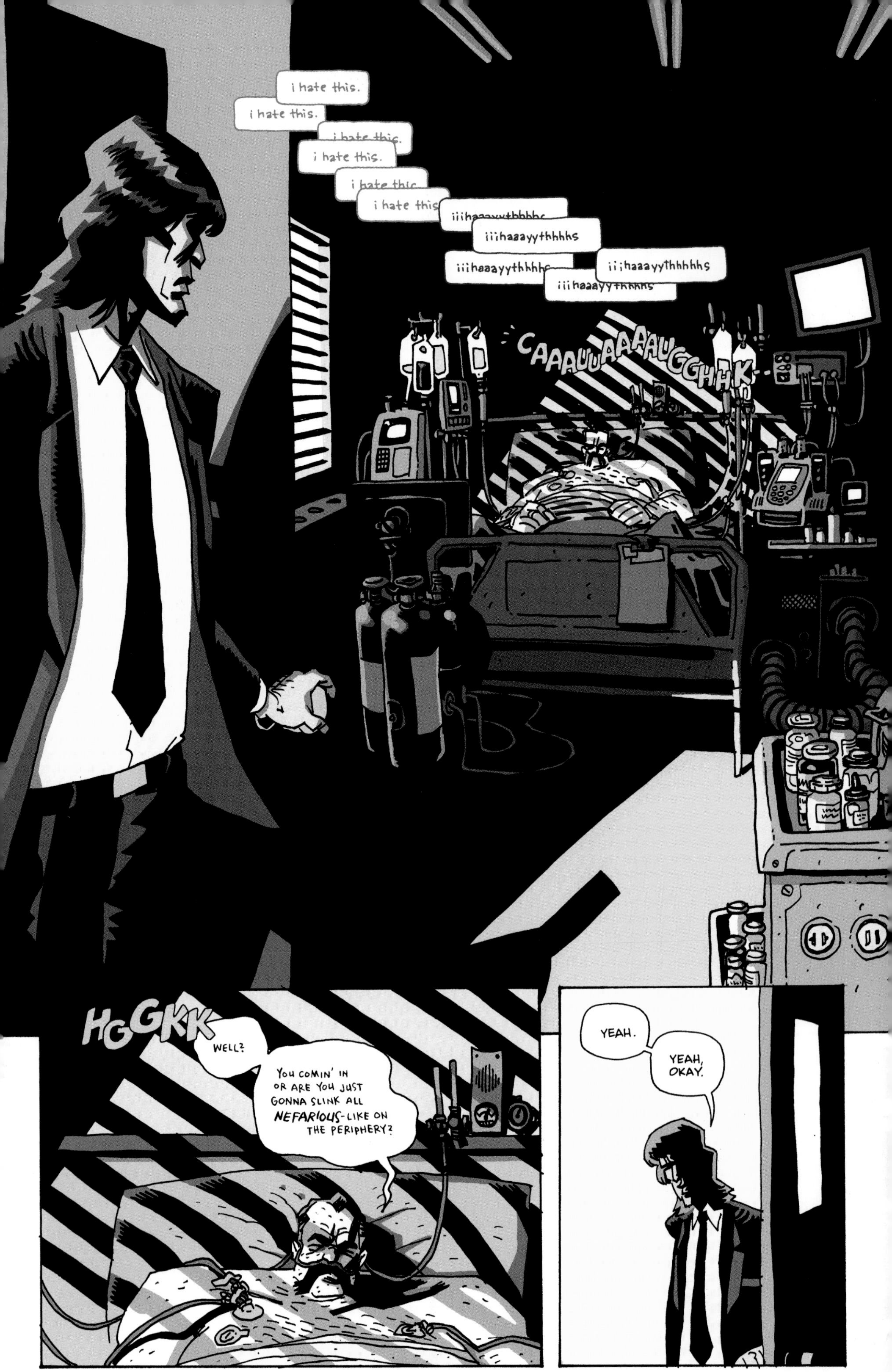

i hate this.
i hate this.
i hate this.
i hate this
iiihaaayythhhhs
iiihaaayythhhhs
ii;haaayythhhhhs
CAAAUUAAAAAUGGHHK
HGGKK
WELL?
YOU COMIN' IN OR ARE YOU JUST GONNA SLINK ALL *NEFARIOUS*-LIKE ON THE PERIPHERY?
YEAH.
YEAH, OKAY.

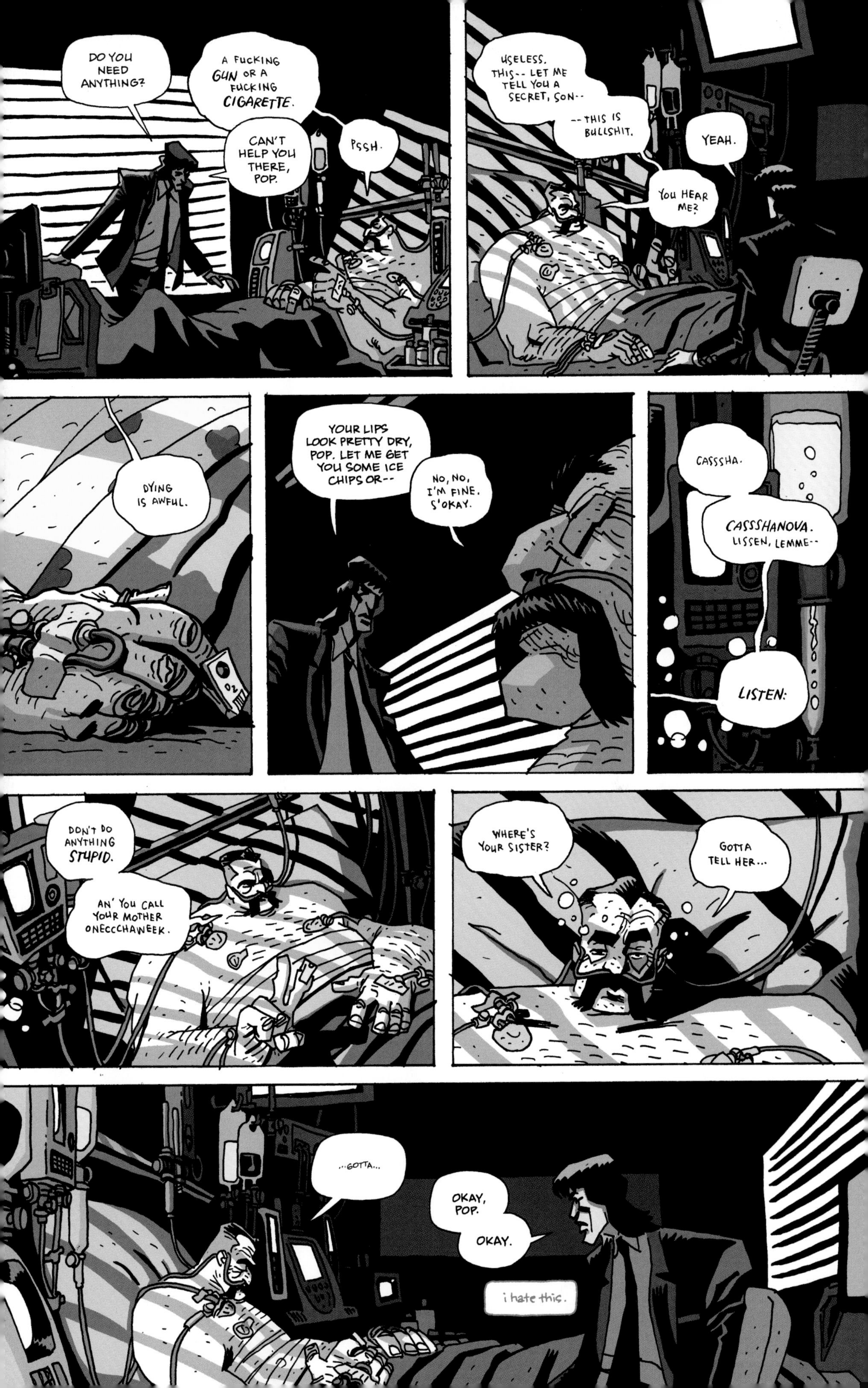
DO YOU NEED ANYTHING?
A FUCKING GUN OR A FUCKING CIGARETTE.
CAN'T HELP YOU THERE, POP.
PSSH.
USELESS. THIS-- LET ME TELL YOU A SECRET, SON--
--THIS IS BULLSHIT.
YEAH.
YOU HEAR ME?
DYING IS AWFUL.
YOUR LIPS LOOK PRETTY DRY, POP. LET ME GET YOU SOME ICE CHIPS OR--
NO, NO, I'M FINE. S'OKAY.
CASSSHA.
CASSSHANOVA. LISSEN, LEMME--
LISTEN:
DON'T DO ANYTHING STUPID.
AN' YOU CALL YOUR MOTHER ONECCCHAWEEK.
WHERE'S YOUR SISTER?
GOTTA TELL HER...
...GOTTA...
OKAY, POP.
OKAY.
i hate this.

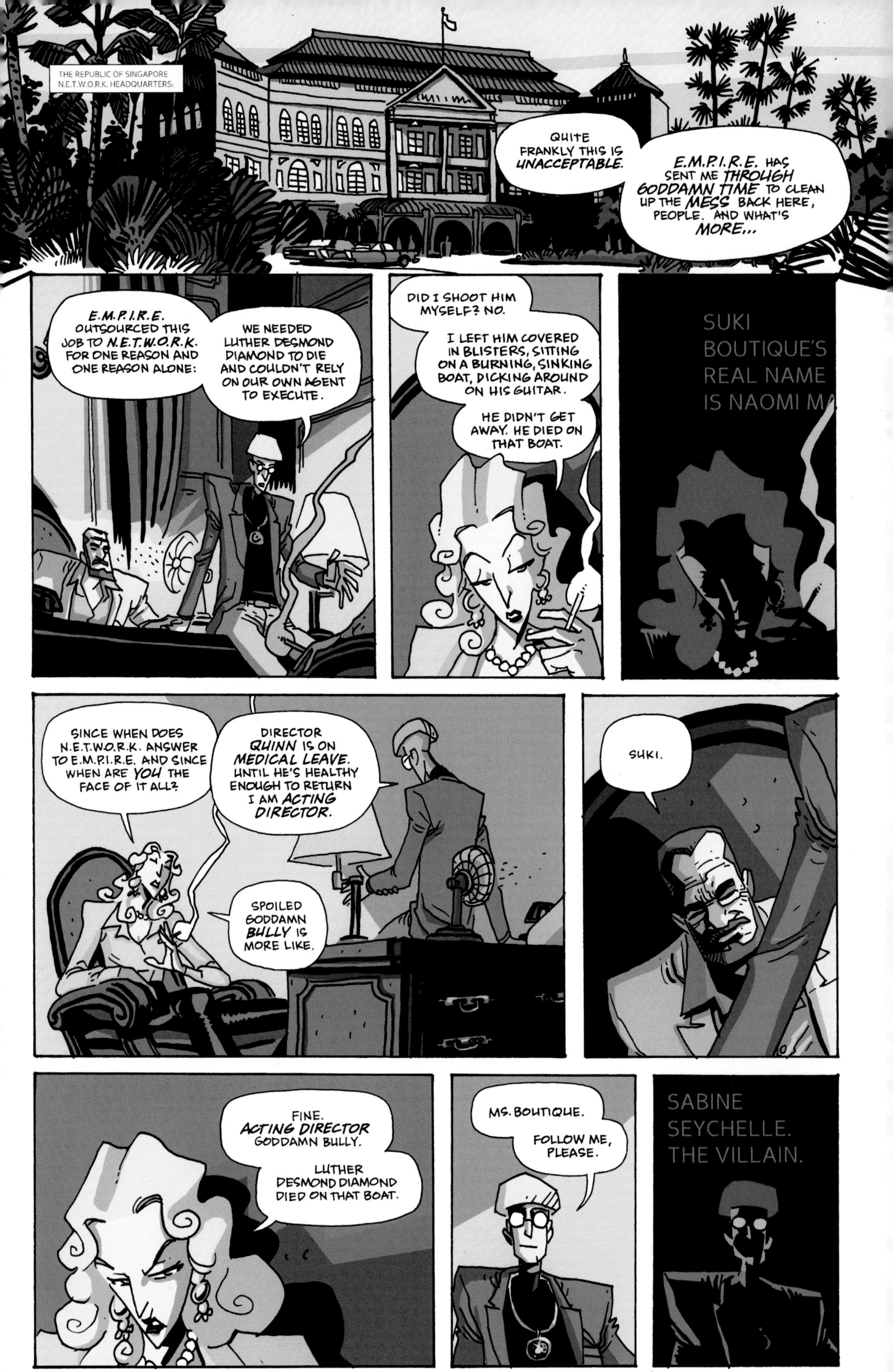
THE REPUBLIC OF SINGAPORE N.E.T.W.O.R.K. HEADQUARTERS:
QUITE FRANKLY THIS IS UNACCEPTABLE.
E.M.P.I.R.E. HAS SENT ME THROUGH GODDAMN TIME TO CLEAN UP THE MESS BACK HERE, PEOPLE. AND WHAT'S MORE...
E.M.P.I.R.E. OUTSOURCED THIS JOB TO N.E.T.W.O.R.K. FOR ONE REASON AND ONE REASON ALONE:
WE NEEDED LUTHER DESMOND DIAMOND TO DIE AND COULDN'T RELY ON OUR OWN AGENT TO EXECUTE.
DID I SHOOT HIM MYSELF? NO.
I LEFT HIM COVERED IN BLISTERS, SITTING ON A BURNING, SINKING BOAT, DICKING AROUND ON HIS GUITAR.
HE DIDN'T GET AWAY. HE DIED ON THAT BOAT.
SUKI BOUTIQUE'S REAL NAME IS NAOMI MA
SINCE WHEN DOES N.E.T.W.O.R.K. ANSWER TO E.M.P.I.R.E. AND SINCE WHEN ARE YOU THE FACE OF IT ALL?
DIRECTOR QUINN IS ON MEDICAL LEAVE. UNTIL HE'S HEALTHY ENOUGH TO RETURN I AM ACTING DIRECTOR.
SPOILED GODDAMN BULLY IS MORE LIKE.
SUKI.
FINE. ACTING DIRECTOR GODDAMN BULLY.
LUTHER DESMOND DIAMOND DIED ON THAT BOAT.
MS. BOUTIQUE.
FOLLOW ME, PLEASE.
SABINE SEYCHELLE. THE VILLAIN.

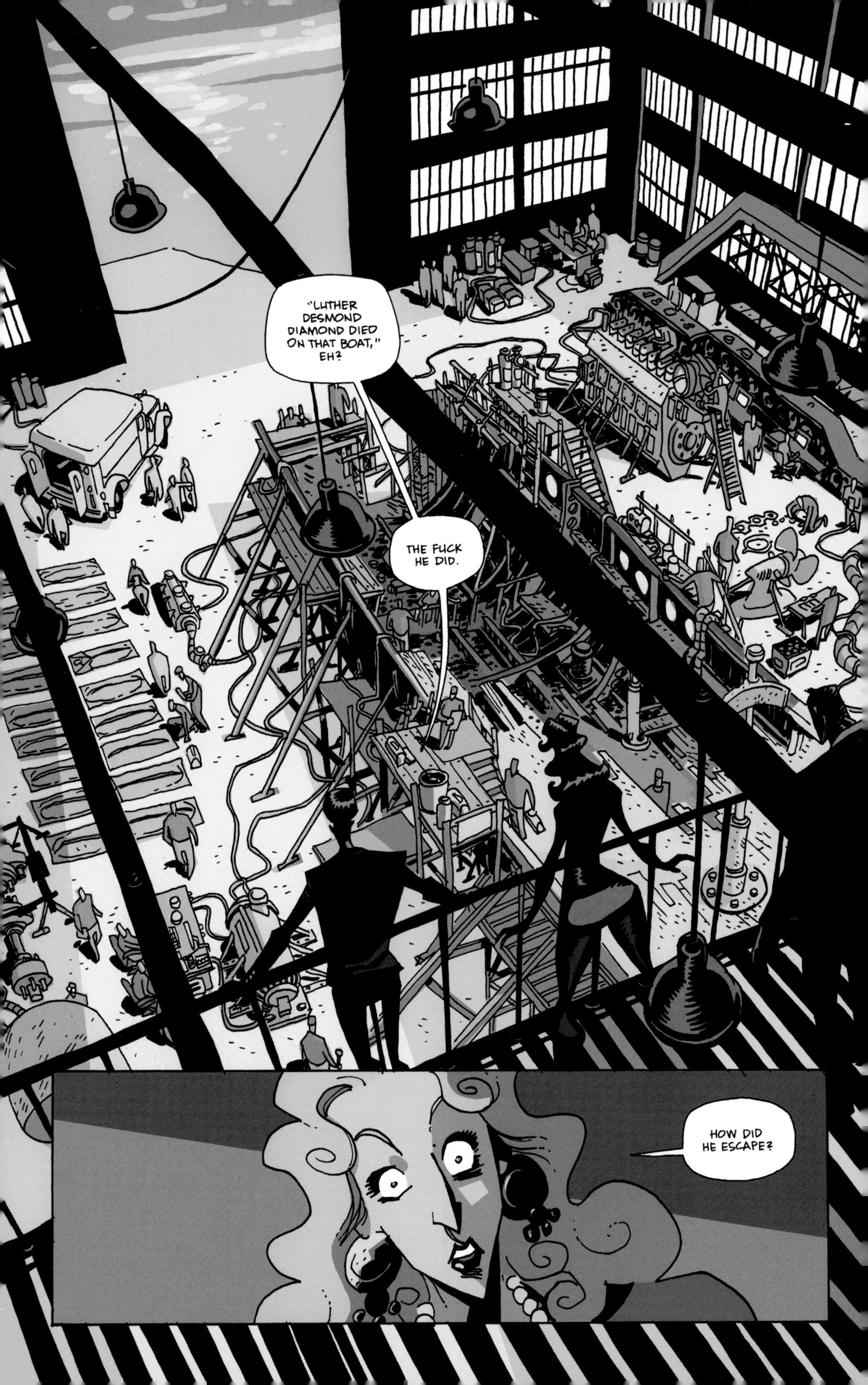
"LUTHER DESMOND DIAMOND DIED ON THAT BOAT," EH?
THE FUCK HE DID.
HOW DID HE ESCAPE?

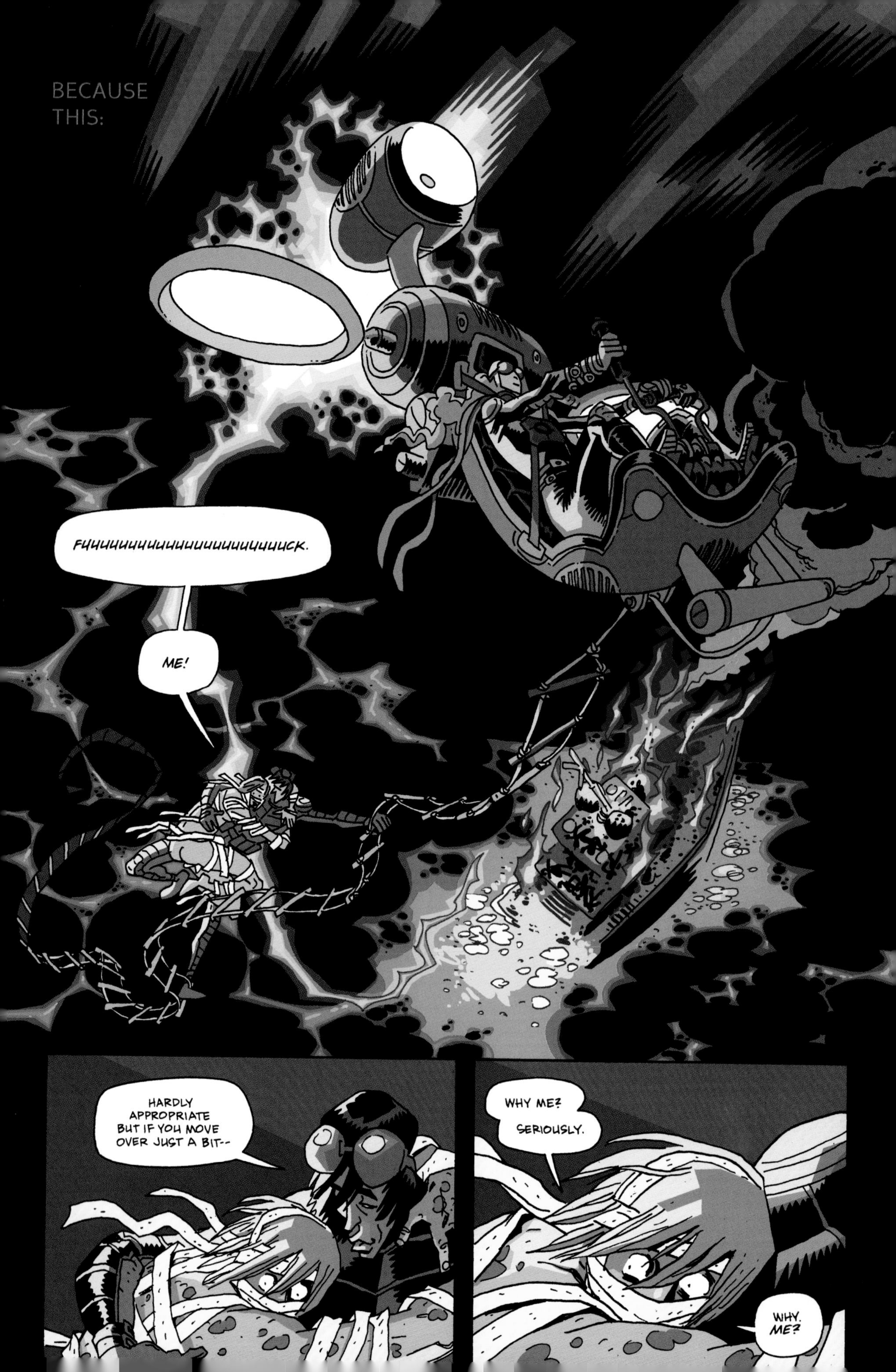
BECAUSE THIS:
FUUUUUUUUUUUUUUUUUUUUUUUCK.
ME!
HARDLY APPROPRIATE BUT IF YOU MOVE OVER JUST A BIT--
WHY ME?
SERIOUSLY.
WHY. ME?

BECAUSE LATER:

BUT THE THING IS:

YOU SHOULDN'T HAVE DONE THAT.

I DIDN'T DO THAT.

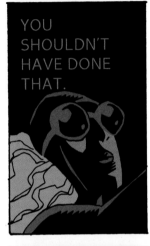

BUT YOU WILL.

AND I'LL HELP YOU DO IT.

WHY WOULD YOU DO THAT?

BECAUSE YOU NEEDED ME TO.

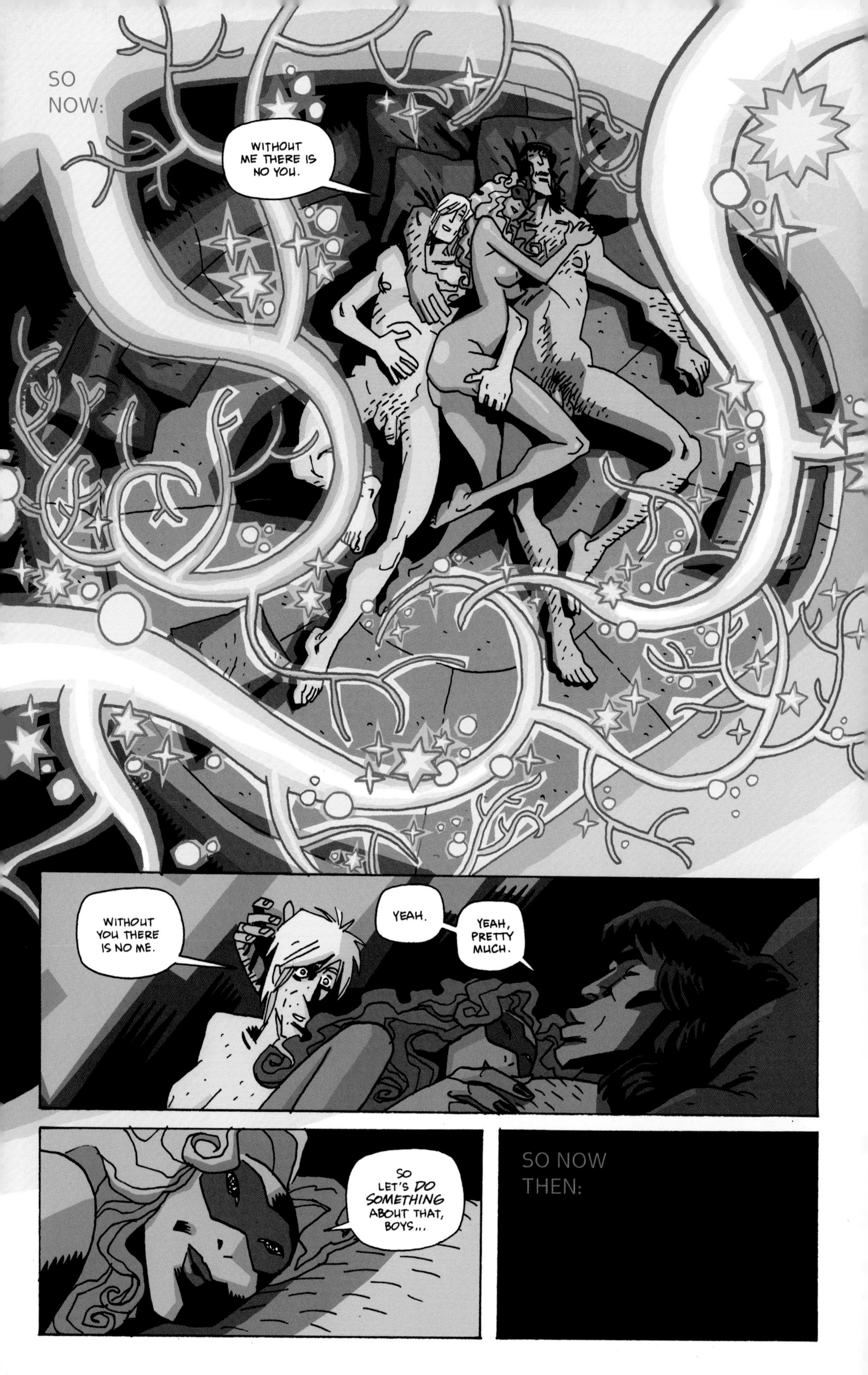
SO NOW:
WITHOUT ME THERE IS NO YOU.
WITHOUT YOU THERE IS NO ME.
YEAH.
YEAH, PRETTY MUCH.
SO LET'S *DO SOMETHING* ABOUT THAT, BOYS...
SO NOW THEN:

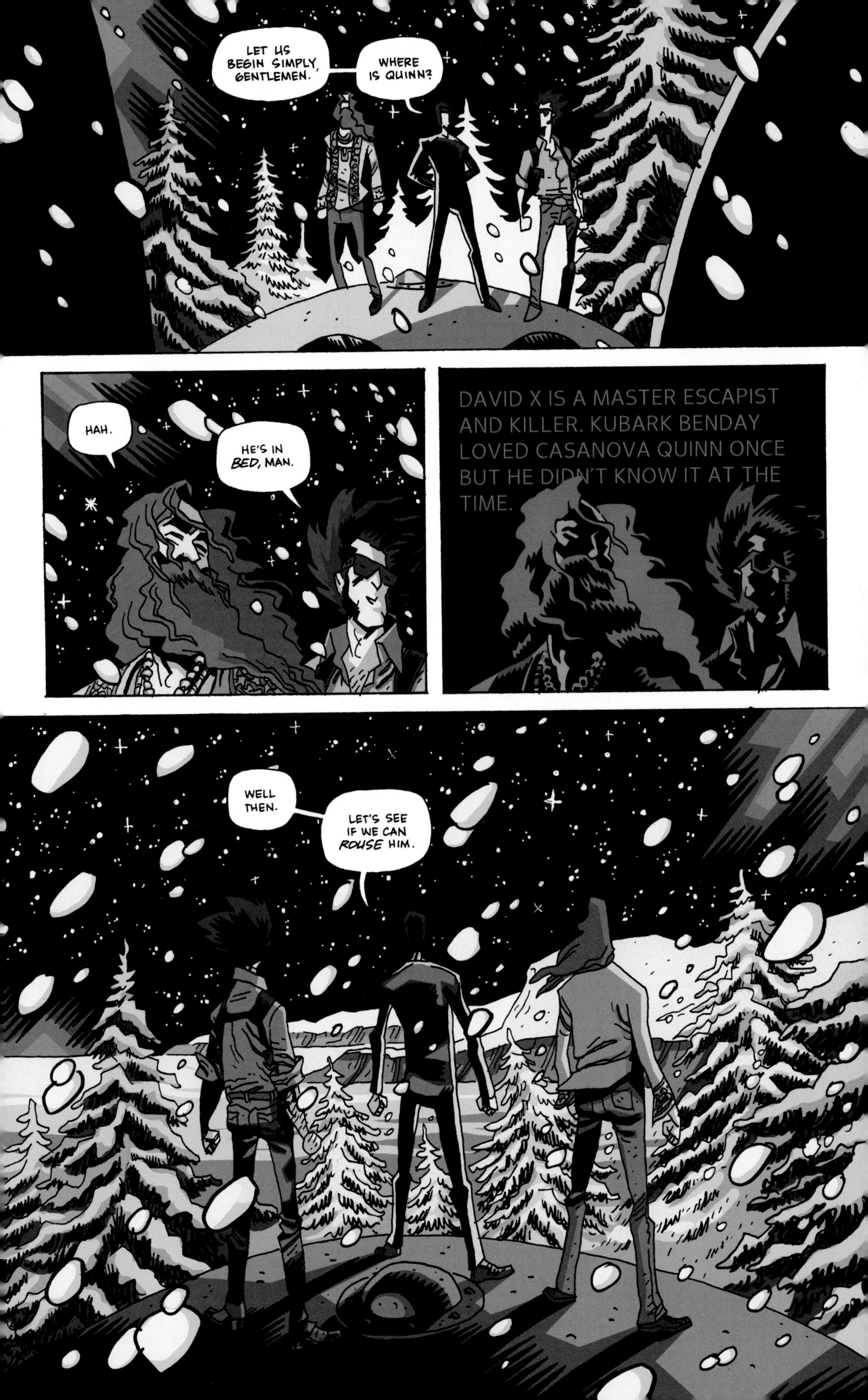
LET US BEGIN SIMPLY, GENTLEMEN.
WHERE IS QUINN?
HAH.
HE'S IN BED, MAN.
DAVID X IS A MASTER ESCAPIST AND KILLER. KUBARK BENDAY LOVED CASANOVA QUINN ONCE BUT HE DIDN'T KNOW IT AT THE TIME.
WELL THEN.
LET'S SEE IF WE CAN ROUSE HIM.

8. LA RITOURNELLE

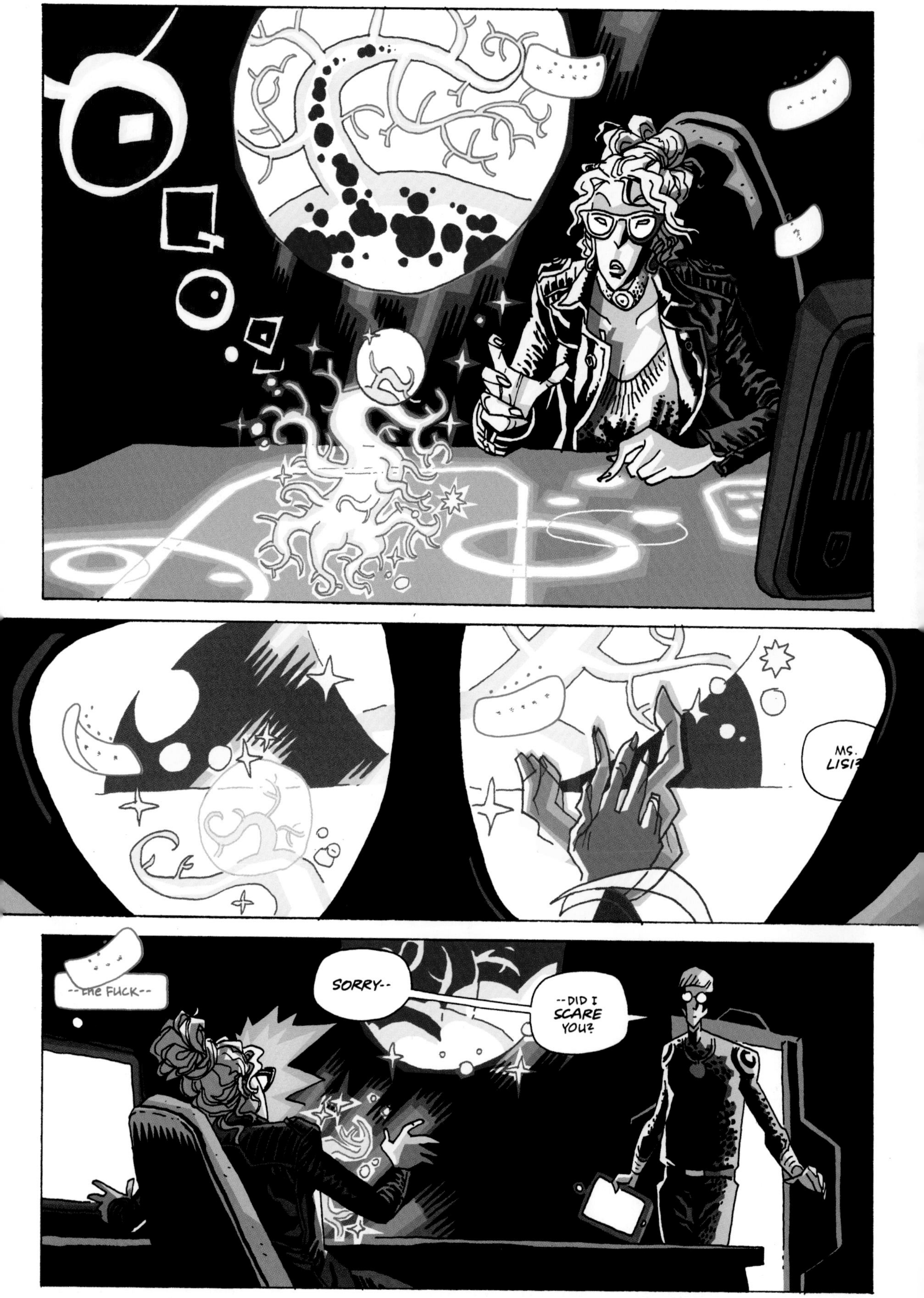

MS. LISI?
--the FUCK--
SORRY--
--DID I SCARE YOU?

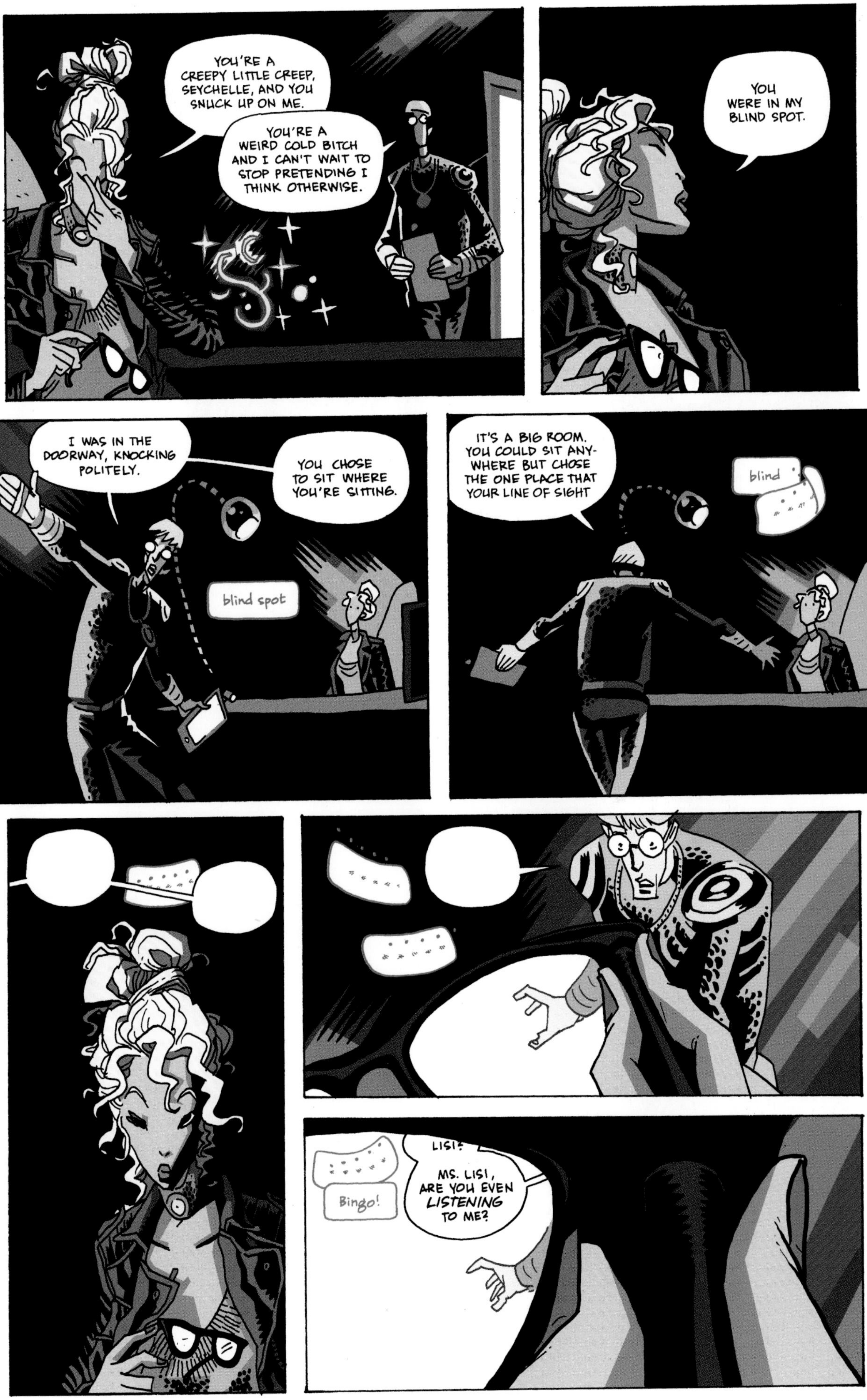
YOU'RE A CREEPY LITTLE CREEP, SEYCHELLE, AND YOU SNUCK UP ON ME.
YOU'RE A WEIRD COLD BITCH AND I CAN'T WAIT TO STOP PRETENDING I THINK OTHERWISE.
YOU WERE IN MY BLIND SPOT.
I WAS IN THE DOORWAY, KNOCKING POLITELY.
YOU CHOSE TO SIT WHERE YOU'RE SITTING.
blind spot
IT'S A BIG ROOM. YOU COULD SIT ANY-WHERE BUT CHOSE THE ONE PLACE THAT YOUR LINE OF SIGHT
blind
LISI?
MS. LISI, ARE YOU EVEN LISTENING TO ME?
Bingo!

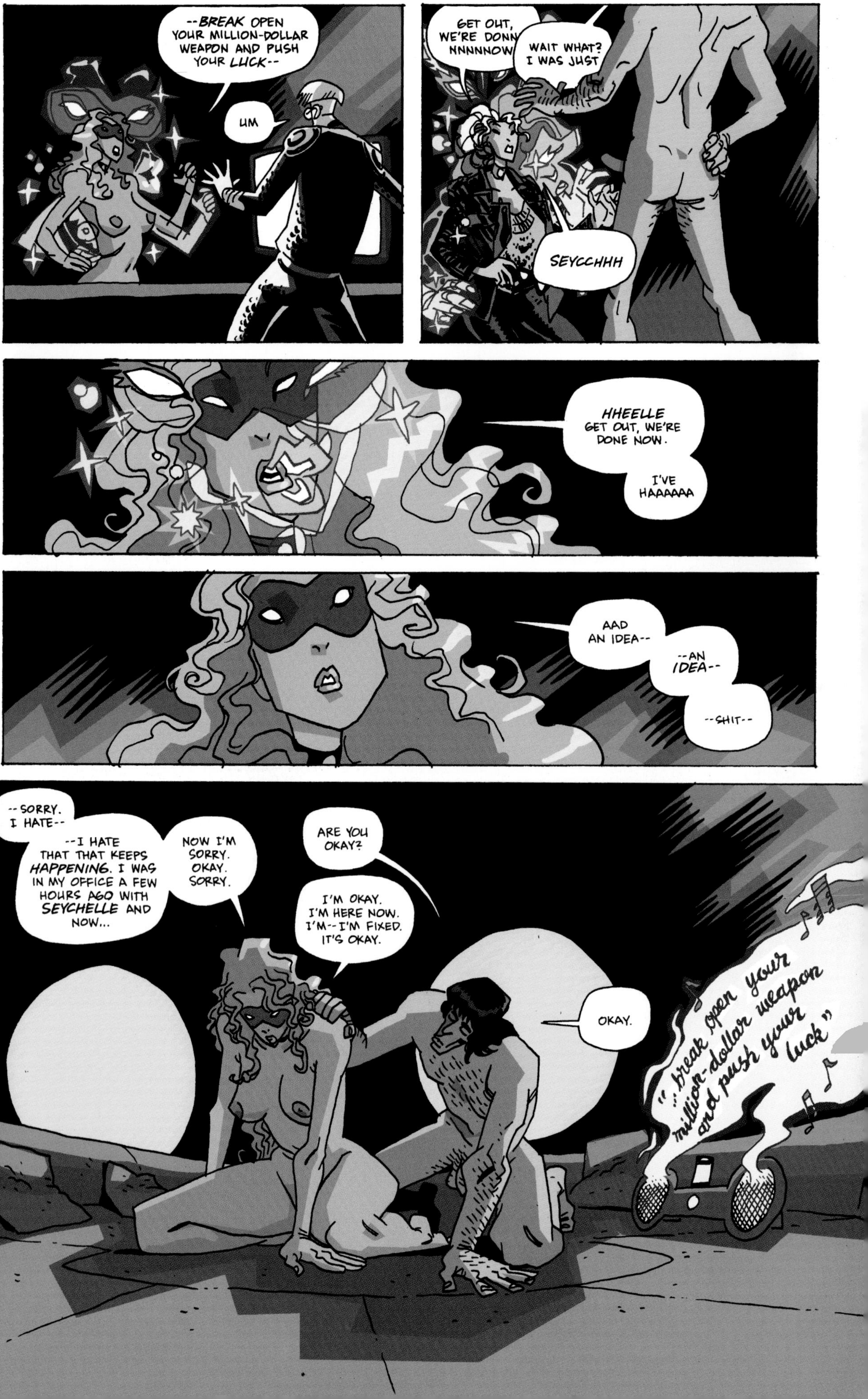
--BREAK OPEN YOUR MILLION-DOLLAR WEAPON AND PUSH YOUR LUCK--
UM
GET OUT, WE'RE DONN NNNNNOW
WAIT WHAT? I WAS JUST
SEYCCHHH
HHEELLE GET OUT, WE'RE DONE NOW.
I'VE HAAAAAA
AAD AN IDEA--
--AN IDEA--
--SHIT--
--SORRY. I HATE--
--I HATE THAT THAT KEEPS HAPPENING. I WAS IN MY OFFICE A FEW HOURS AGO WITH SEYCHELLE AND NOW...
NOW I'M SORRY. OKAY. SORRY.
ARE YOU OKAY?
I'M OKAY. I'M HERE NOW. I'M--I'M FIXED. IT'S OKAY.
OKAY.
"...break open your million-dollar weapon and push your luck"

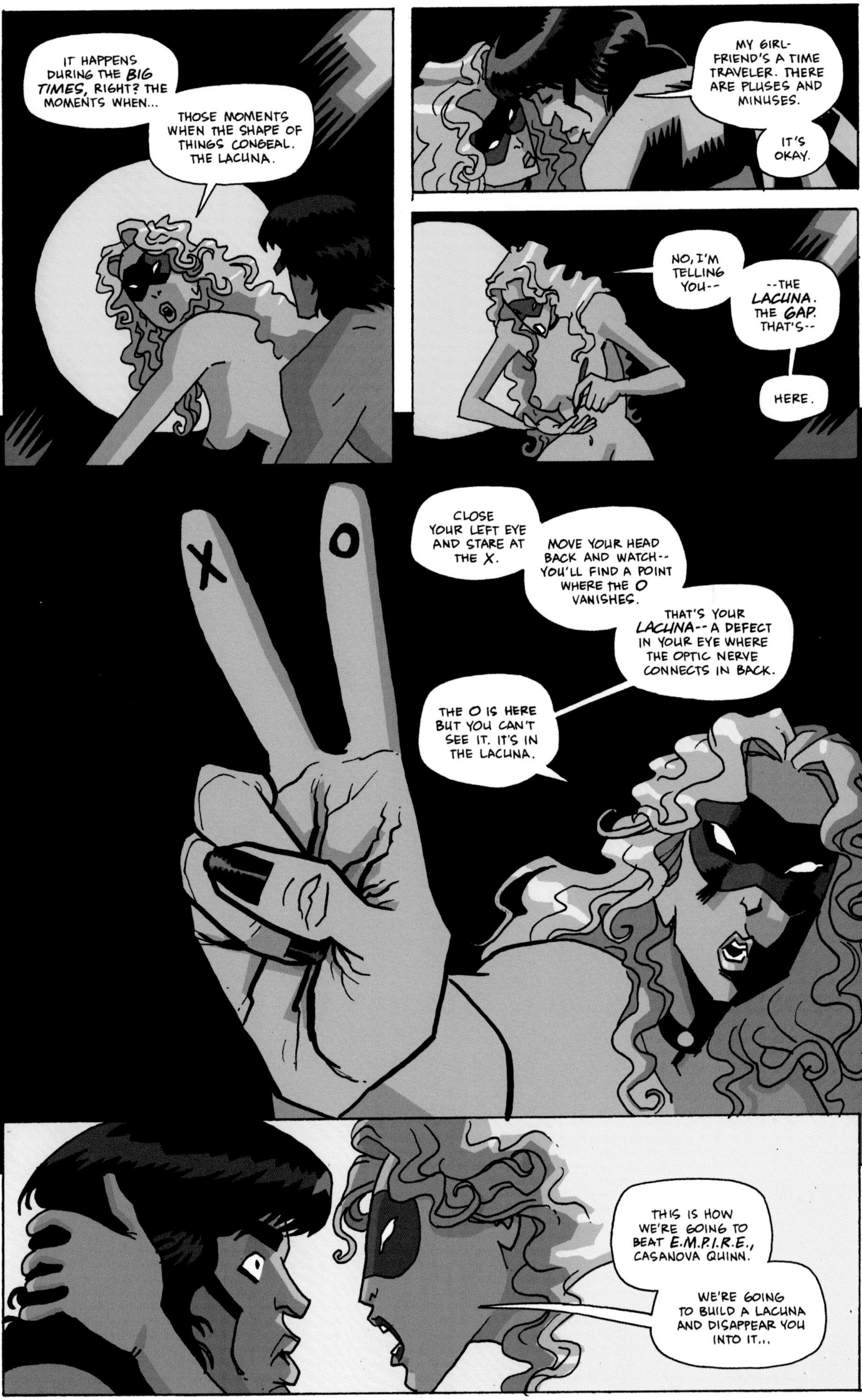
IT HAPPENS DURING THE BIG TIMES, RIGHT? THE MOMENTS WHEN...
THOSE MOMENTS WHEN THE SHAPE OF THINGS CONGEAL. THE LACUNA.
MY GIRL-FRIEND'S A TIME TRAVELER. THERE ARE PLUSES AND MINUSES.
IT'S OKAY.
NO, I'M TELLING YOU--
--THE LACUNA. THE GAP. THAT'S--
HERE.
CLOSE YOUR LEFT EYE AND STARE AT THE X.
MOVE YOUR HEAD BACK AND WATCH-- YOU'LL FIND A POINT WHERE THE O VANISHES.
THAT'S YOUR LACUNA-- A DEFECT IN YOUR EYE WHERE THE OPTIC NERVE CONNECTS IN BACK.
THE O IS HERE BUT YOU CAN'T SEE IT. IT'S IN THE LACUNA.
THIS IS HOW WE'RE GOING TO BEAT E.M.P.I.R.E., CASANOVA QUINN.
WE'RE GOING TO BUILD A LACUNA AND DISAPPEAR YOU INTO IT...

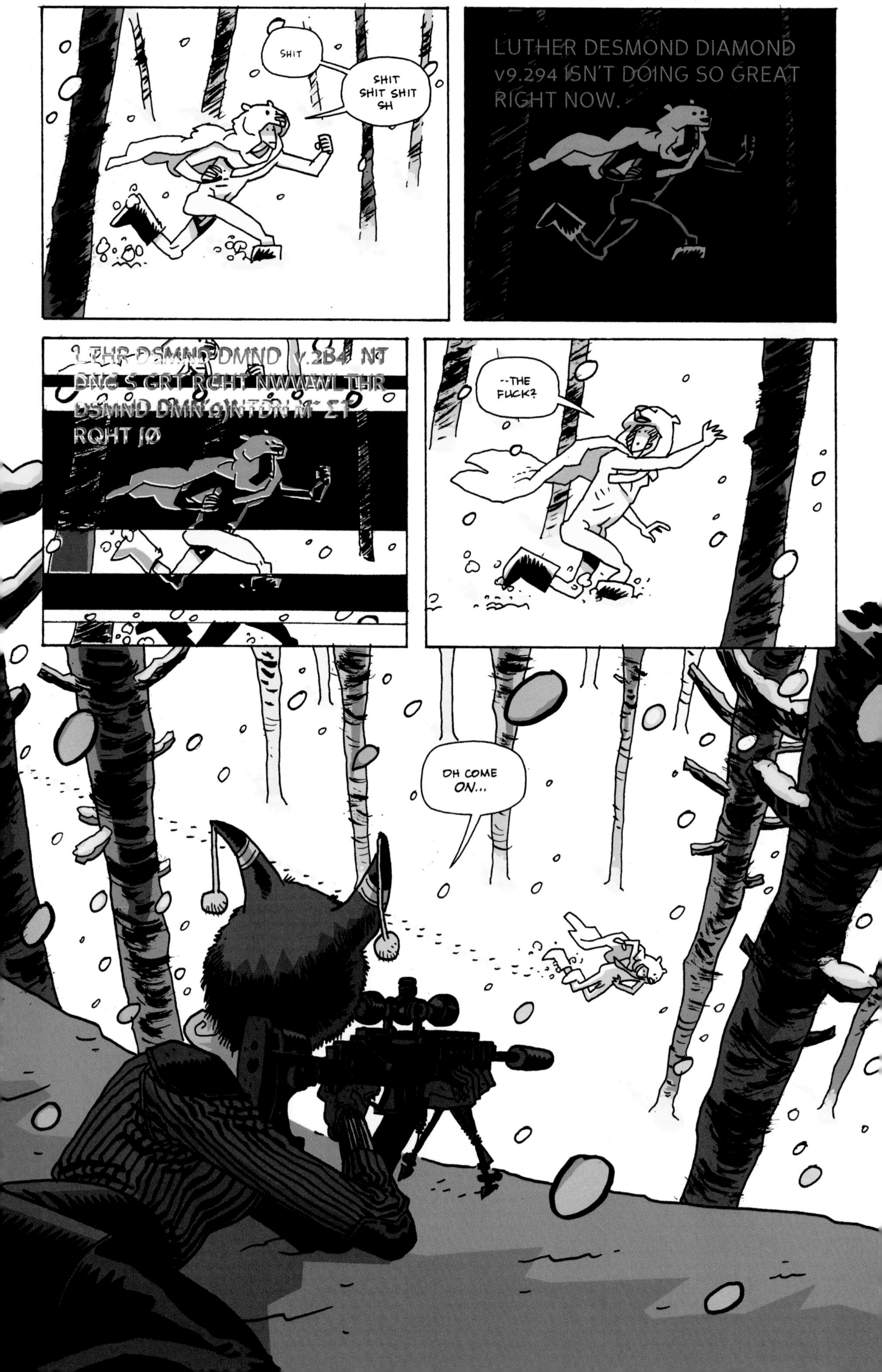
SHIT
SHIT SHIT SHIT SH
LUTHER DESMOND DIAMOND v9.294 ISN'T DOING SO GREAT RIGHT NOW.
L THR DSMND DMND v.2B4 NT DNG S GRT RGHT NWWWL THR DSMND DMN Ω)NTDN M ΣT RQHT JØ
--THE FUCK?
OH COME ON...

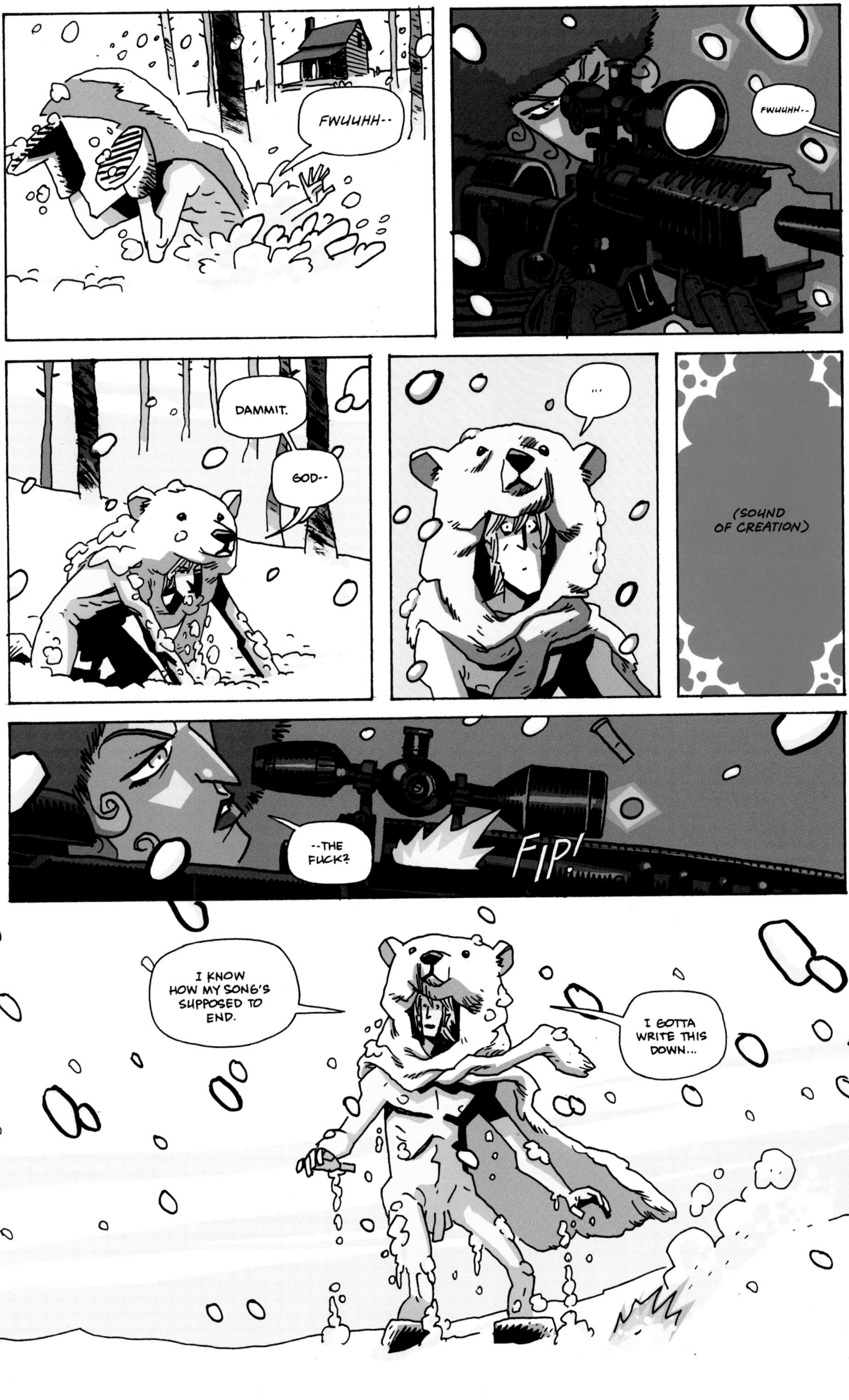
FWUUHH--
FWUUHH--
DAMMIT.
GOD--
...
(SOUND OF CREATION)
--THE FUCK?
FIP!
I KNOW HOW MY SONG'S SUPPOSED TO END.
I GOTTA WRITE THIS DOWN...

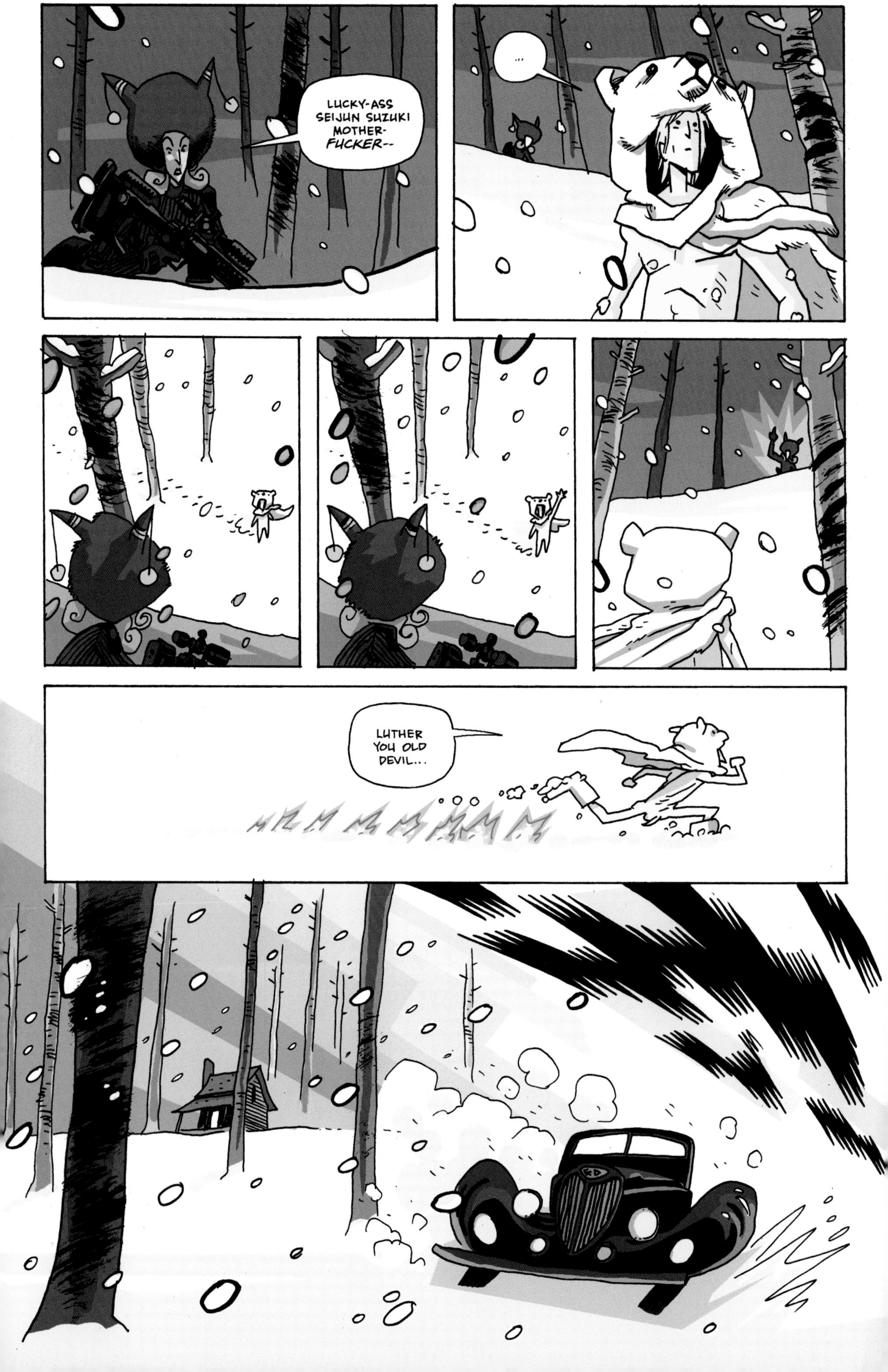
LUCKY-ASS SEIJUN SUZUKI MOTHER-FUCKER--
...
LUTHER YOU OLD DEVIL...

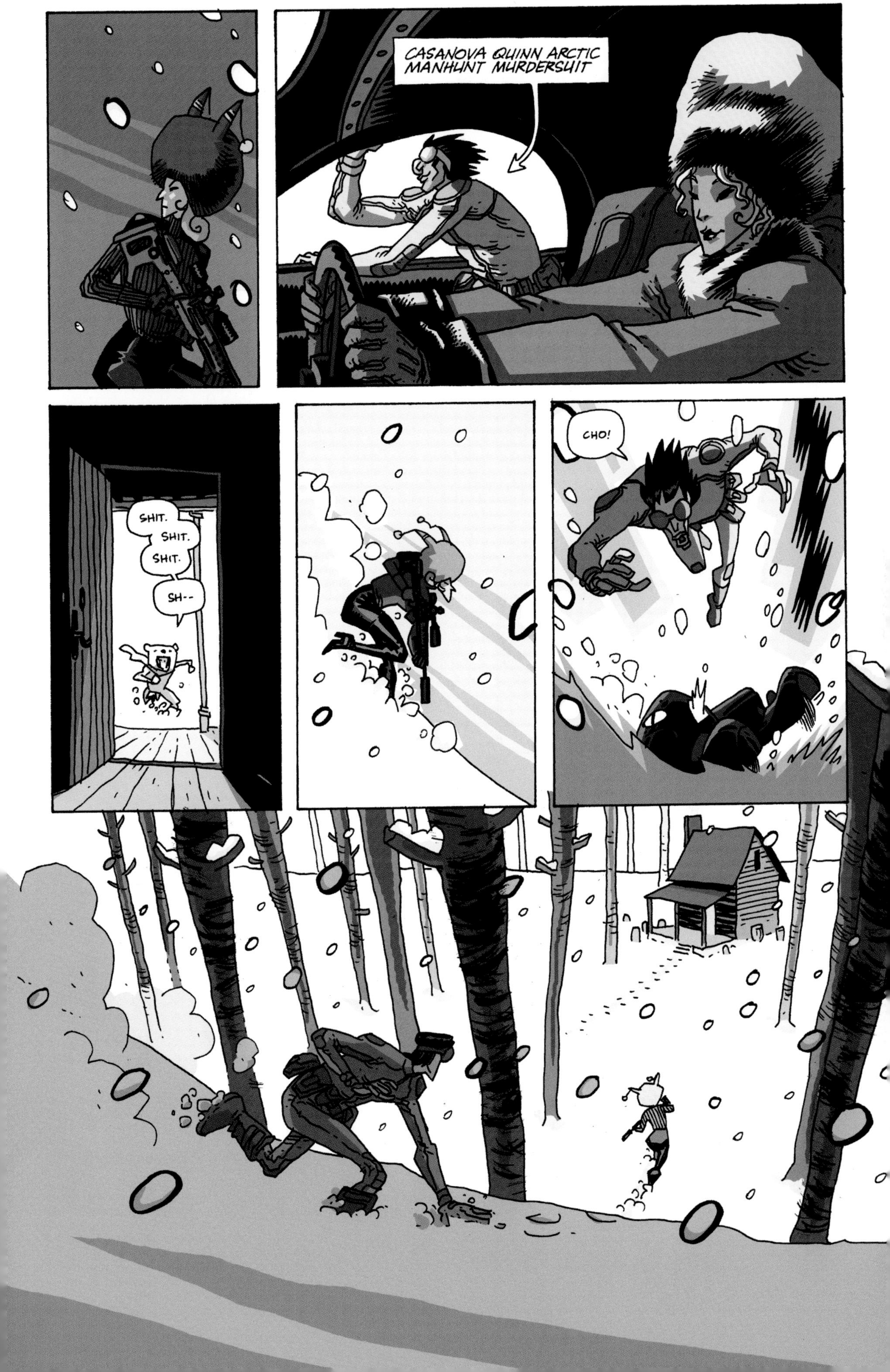
CASANOVA QUINN ARCTIC MANHUNT MURDERSUIT
SHIT.
SHIT.
SHIT.
SH--
CHO!

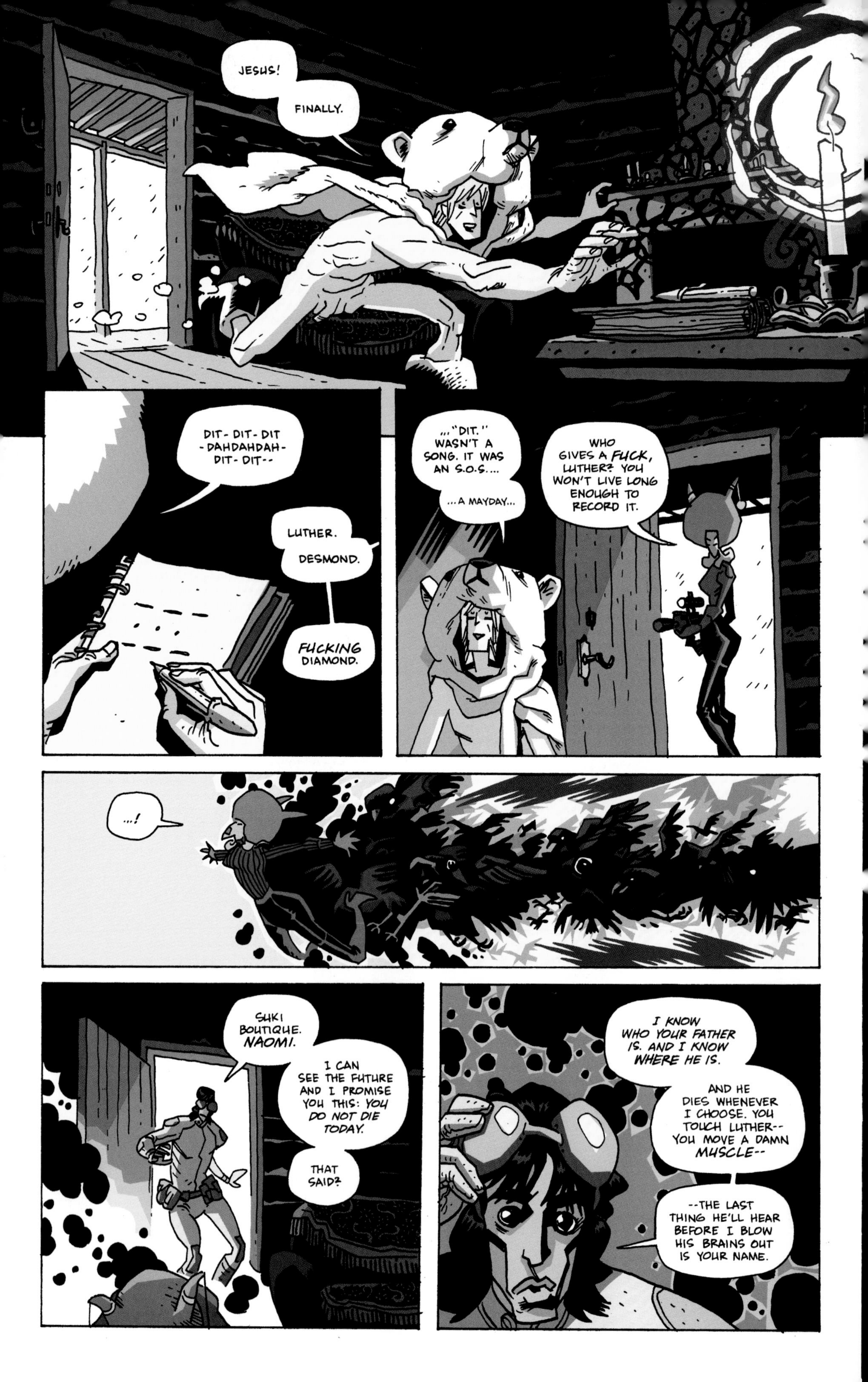
JESUS!
FINALLY.
DIT- DIT- DIT -DAHDAHDAH- DIT- DIT--
LUTHER.
DESMOND.
FUCKING DIAMOND.
..."DIT." WASN'T A SONG. IT WAS AN S.O.S....
...A MAYDAY...
WHO GIVES A FUCK, LUTHER? YOU WON'T LIVE LONG ENOUGH TO RECORD IT.
...!
SUKI BOUTIQUE. NAOMI.
I CAN SEE THE FUTURE AND I PROMISE YOU THIS: YOU DO NOT DIE TODAY.
THAT SAID?
I KNOW WHO YOUR FATHER IS. AND I KNOW WHERE HE IS.
AND HE DIES WHENEVER I CHOOSE. YOU TOUCH LUTHER-- YOU MOVE A DAMN MUSCLE--
--THE LAST THING HE'LL HEAR BEFORE I BLOW HIS BRAINS OUT IS YOUR NAME.

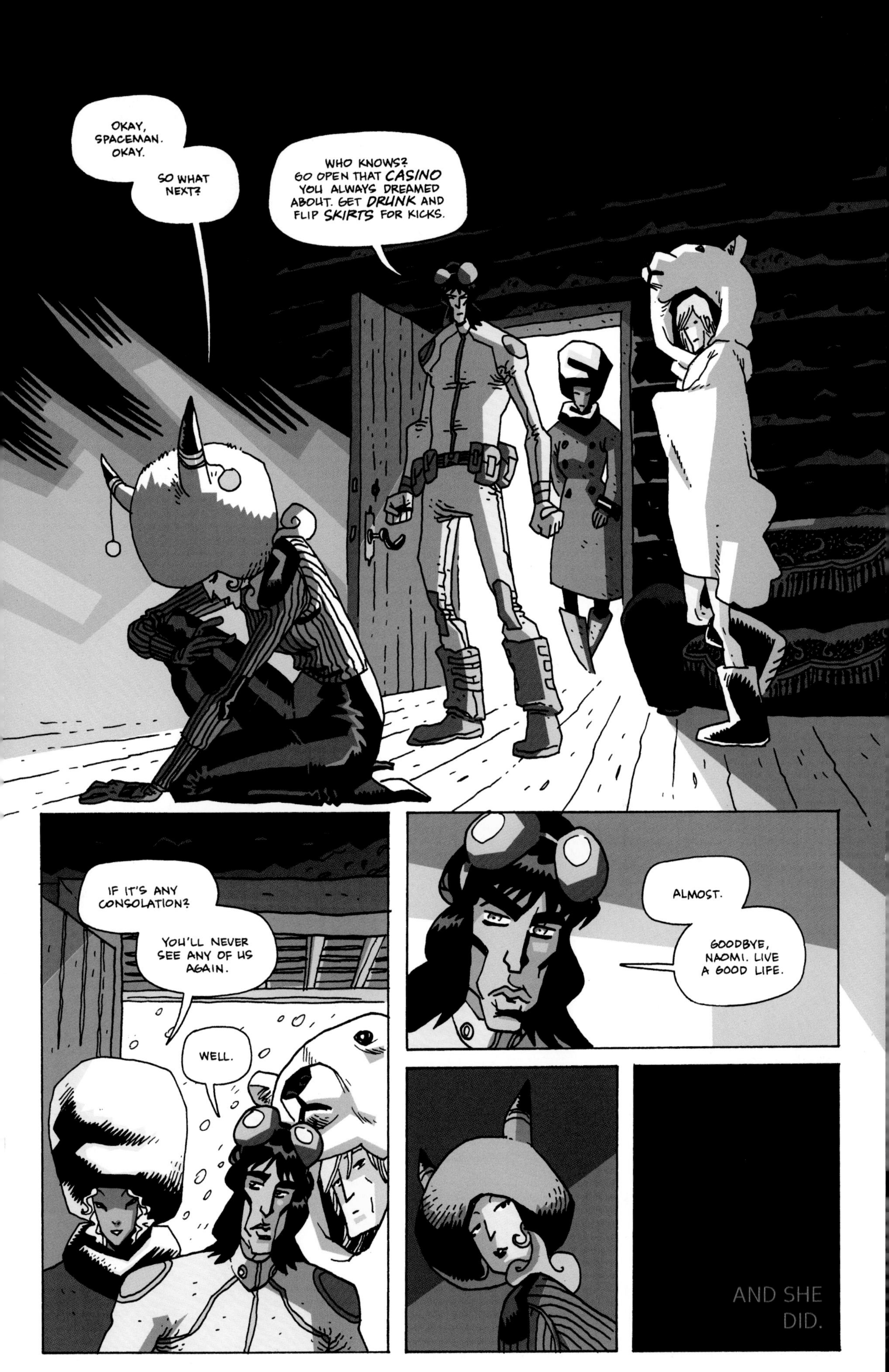
OKAY, SPACEMAN. OKAY.
SO WHAT NEXT?
WHO KNOWS? GO OPEN THAT CASINO YOU ALWAYS DREAMED ABOUT. GET DRUNK AND FLIP SKIRTS FOR KICKS.
IF IT'S ANY CONSOLATION?
YOU'LL NEVER SEE ANY OF US AGAIN.
WELL.
ALMOST.
GOODBYE, NAOMI. LIVE A GOOD LIFE.
AND SHE DID.

9. YOU'RE JUST A PRODUCT OF THE TIMES

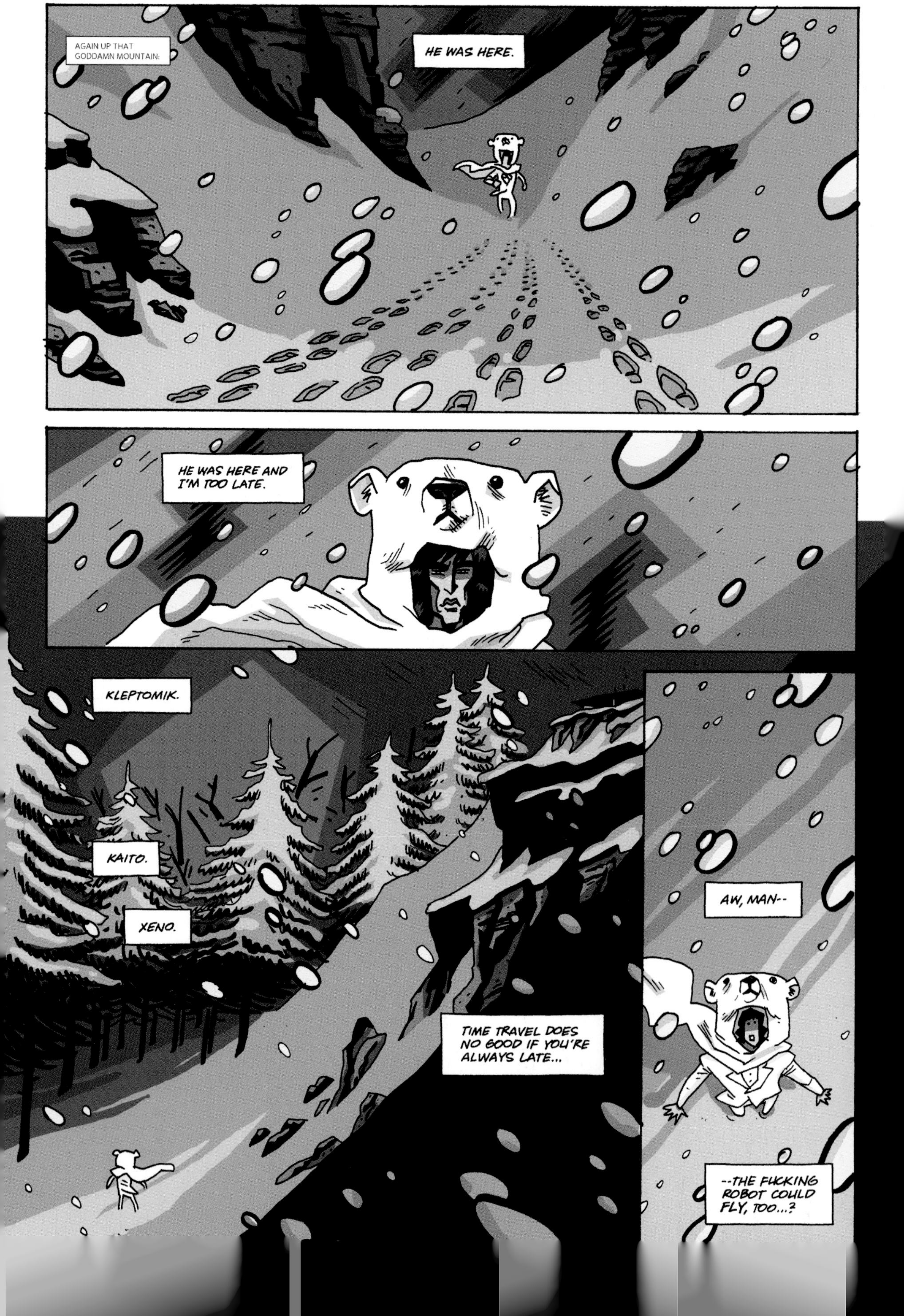
AGAIN UP THAT GODDAMN MOUNTAIN:
HE WAS HERE.
HE WAS HERE AND I'M TOO LATE.
KLEPTOMIK.
KAITO.
XENO.
AW, MAN--
TIME TRAVEL DOES NO GOOD IF YOU'RE ALWAYS LATE...
--THE FUCKING ROBOT COULD FLY, TOO...?

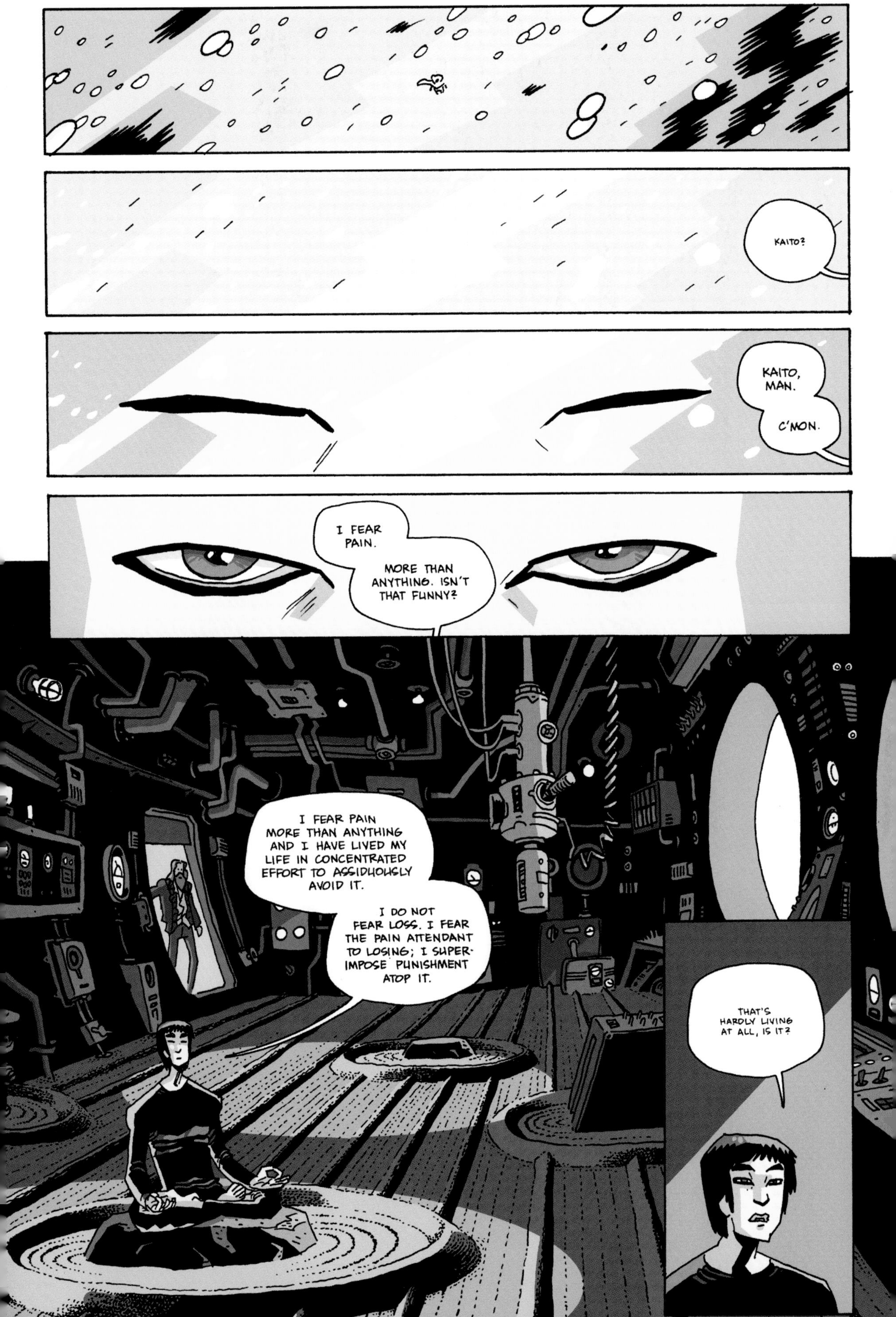
KAITO?
KAITO, MAN.
C'MON.
I FEAR PAIN.
MORE THAN ANYTHING. ISN'T THAT FUNNY?
I FEAR PAIN MORE THAN ANYTHING AND I HAVE LIVED MY LIFE IN CONCENTRATED EFFORT TO ASSIDUOUSLY AVOID IT.
I DO NOT FEAR LOSS. I FEAR THE PAIN ATTENDANT TO LOSING; I SUPER-IMPOSE PUNISHMENT ATOP IT.
THAT'S HARDLY LIVING AT ALL, IS IT?

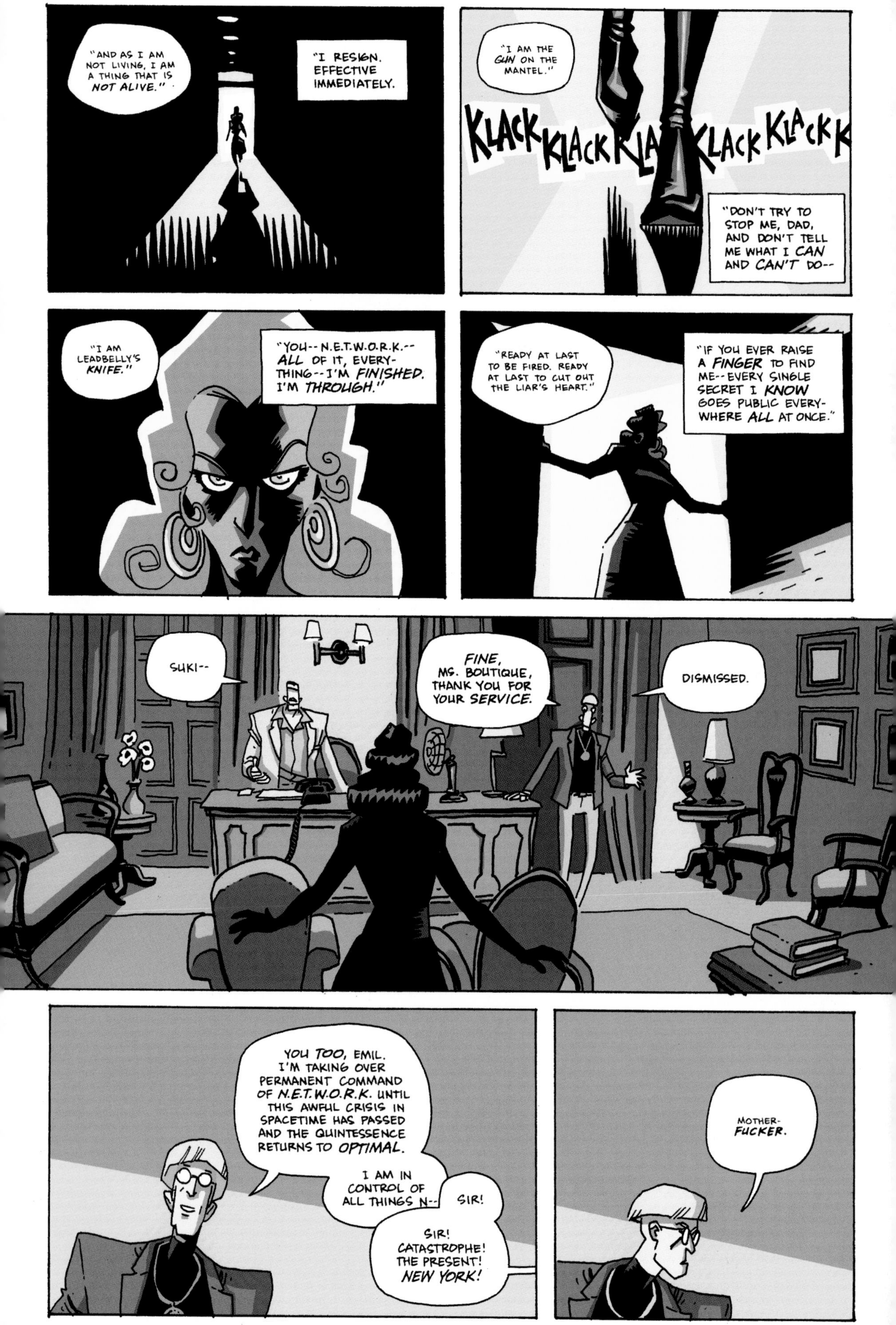
"AND AS I AM NOT LIVING, I AM A THING THAT IS NOT ALIVE."
"I RESIGN. EFFECTIVE IMMEDIATELY.
"I AM THE GUN ON THE MANTEL."
KLACK KLACK KLA KLACK KLACKK
"DON'T TRY TO STOP ME, DAD, AND DON'T TELL ME WHAT I CAN AND CAN'T DO--
"I AM LEADBELLY'S KNIFE."
"YOU--N.E.T.W.O.R.K.--ALL OF IT, EVERY-THING--I'M FINISHED. I'M THROUGH."
"READY AT LAST TO BE FIRED. READY AT LAST TO CUT OUT THE LIAR'S HEART."
"IF YOU EVER RAISE A FINGER TO FIND ME--EVERY SINGLE SECRET I KNOW GOES PUBLIC EVERY-WHERE ALL AT ONCE."
SUKI--
FINE, MS. BOUTIQUE, THANK YOU FOR YOUR SERVICE.
DISMISSED.
YOU TOO, EMIL. I'M TAKING OVER PERMANENT COMMAND OF N.E.T.W.O.R.K. UNTIL THIS AWFUL CRISIS IN SPACETIME HAS PASSED AND THE QUINTESSENCE RETURNS TO OPTIMAL.
I AM IN CONTROL OF ALL THINGS N--
SIR!
SIR! CATASTROPHE! THE PRESENT! NEW YORK!
MOTHER-FUCKER.

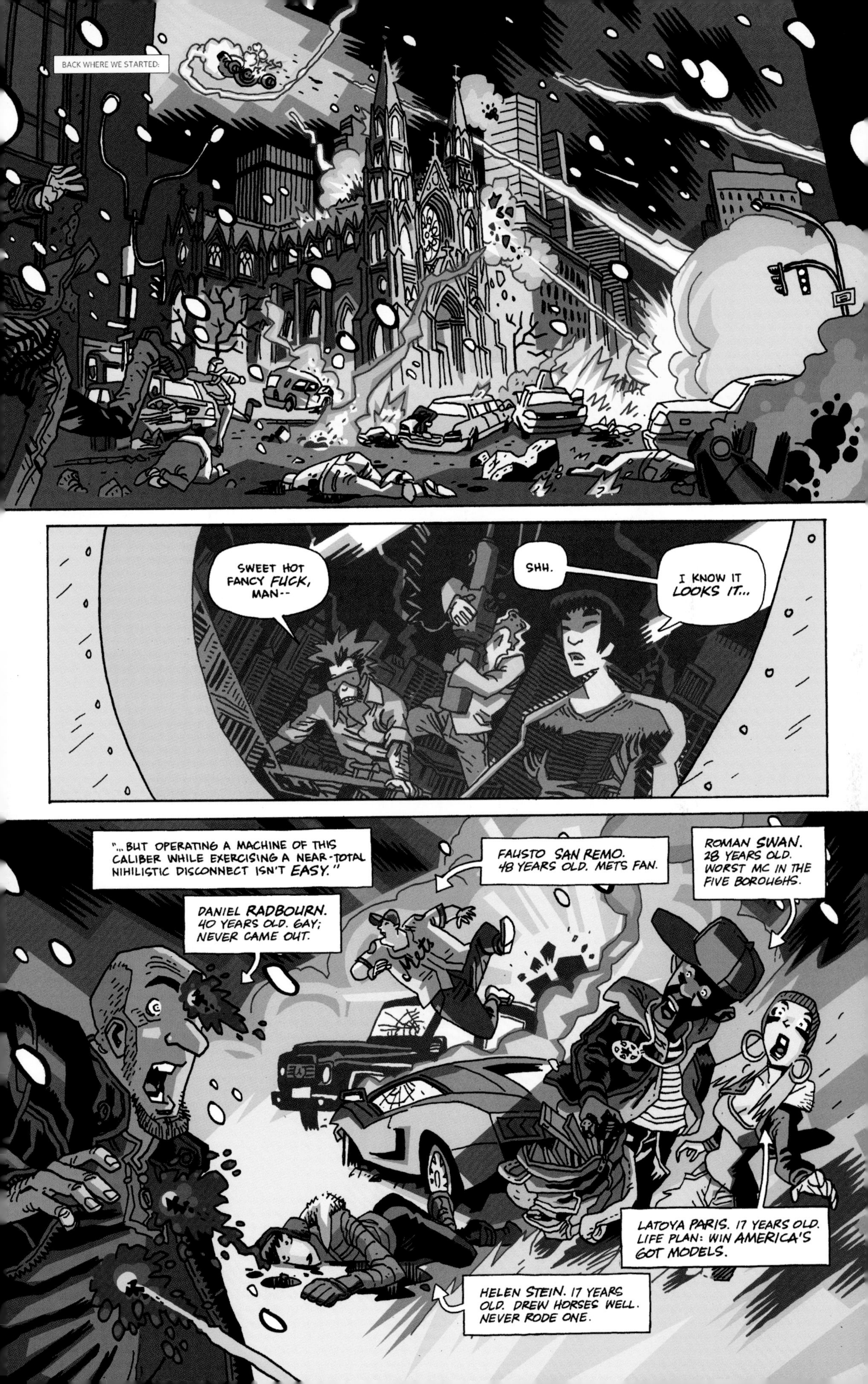
BACK WHERE WE STARTED:
SWEET HOT FANCY FUCK, MAN--
SHH.
I KNOW IT LOOKS IT...
"...BUT OPERATING A MACHINE OF THIS CALIBER WHILE EXERCISING A NEAR-TOTAL NIHILISTIC DISCONNECT ISN'T EASY."
FAUSTO SAN REMO. 48 YEARS OLD. METS FAN.
ROMAN SWAN. 28 YEARS OLD. WORST MC IN THE FIVE BOROUGHS.
DANIEL RADBOURN. 40 YEARS OLD. GAY; NEVER CAME OUT.
LATOYA PARIS. 17 YEARS OLD. LIFE PLAN: WIN AMERICA'S GOT MODELS.
HELEN STEIN. 17 YEARS OLD. DREW HORSES WELL. NEVER RODE ONE.

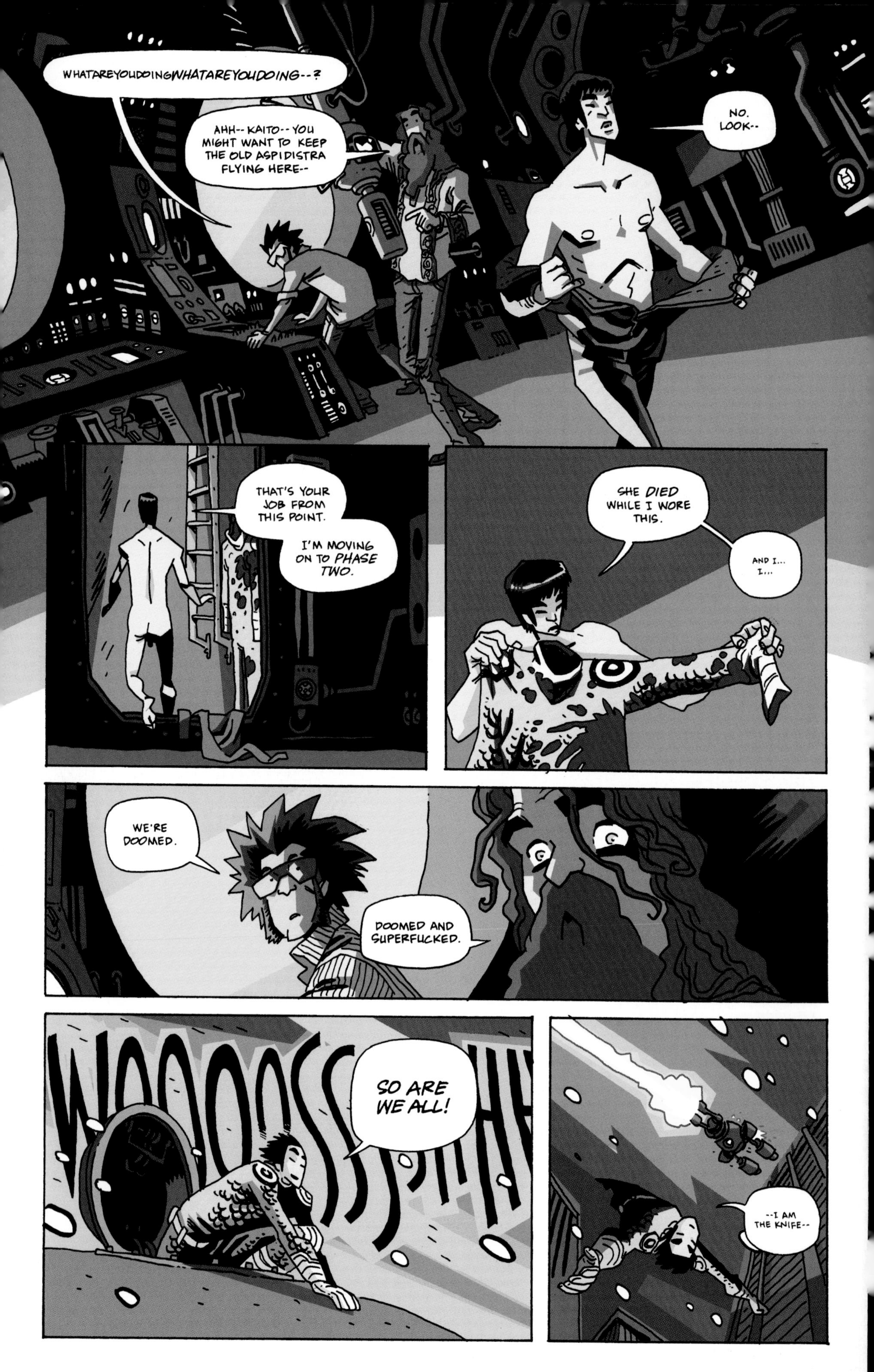
WHATAREYOUDOINGWHATAREYOUDOING--?
AHH-- KAITO-- YOU MIGHT WANT TO KEEP THE OLD ASPIDISTRA FLYING HERE--
NO. LOOK--
THAT'S YOUR JOB FROM THIS POINT.
I'M MOVING ON TO PHASE TWO.
SHE DIED WHILE I WORE THIS.
AND I... I...
WE'RE DOOMED.
DOOMED AND SUPERFUCKED.
WOOOOSSHH
SO ARE WE ALL!
--I AM THE KNIFE--

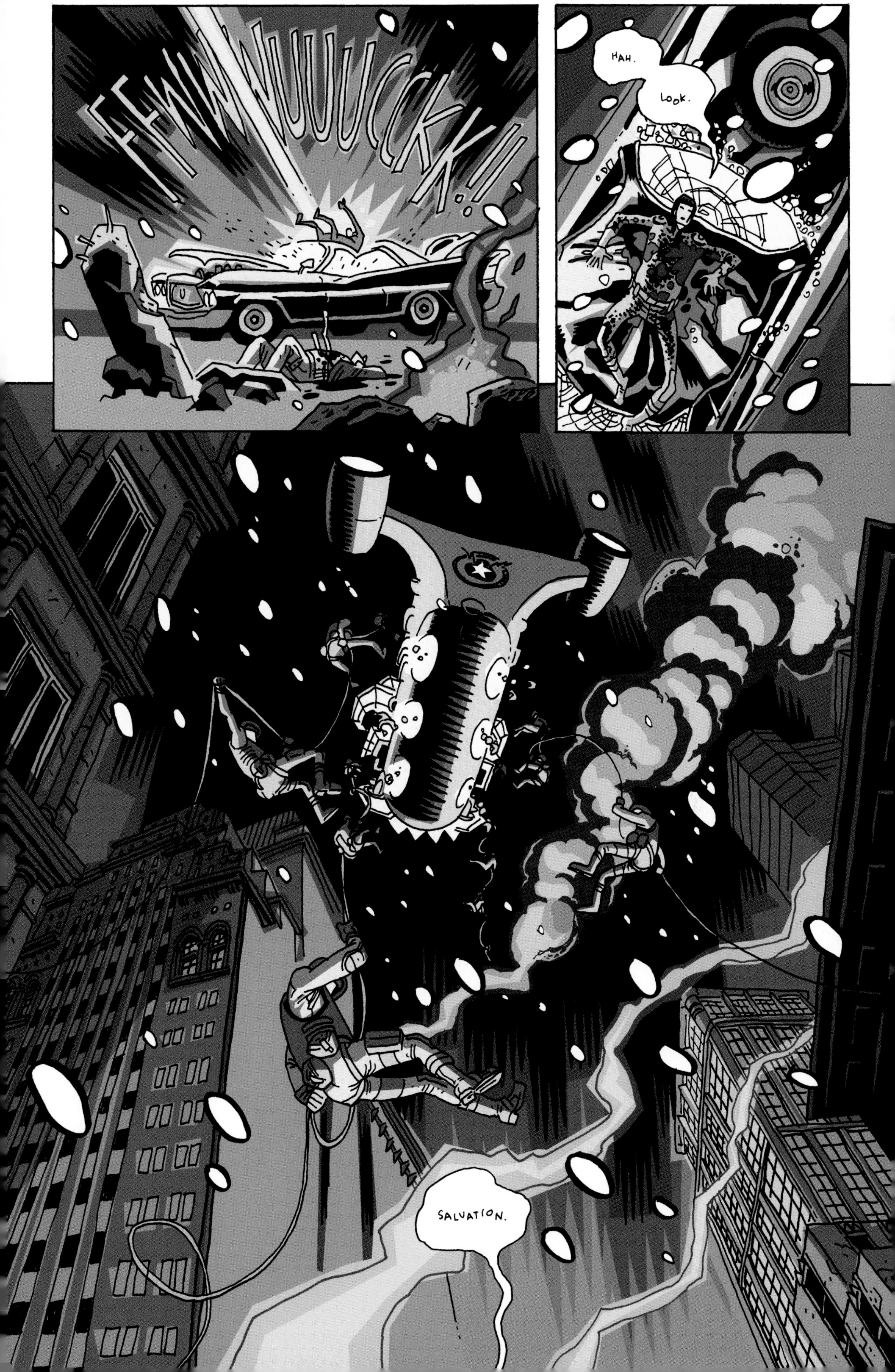
FFWWUUUCKK!!!
HAH.
LOOK.
SALVATION.

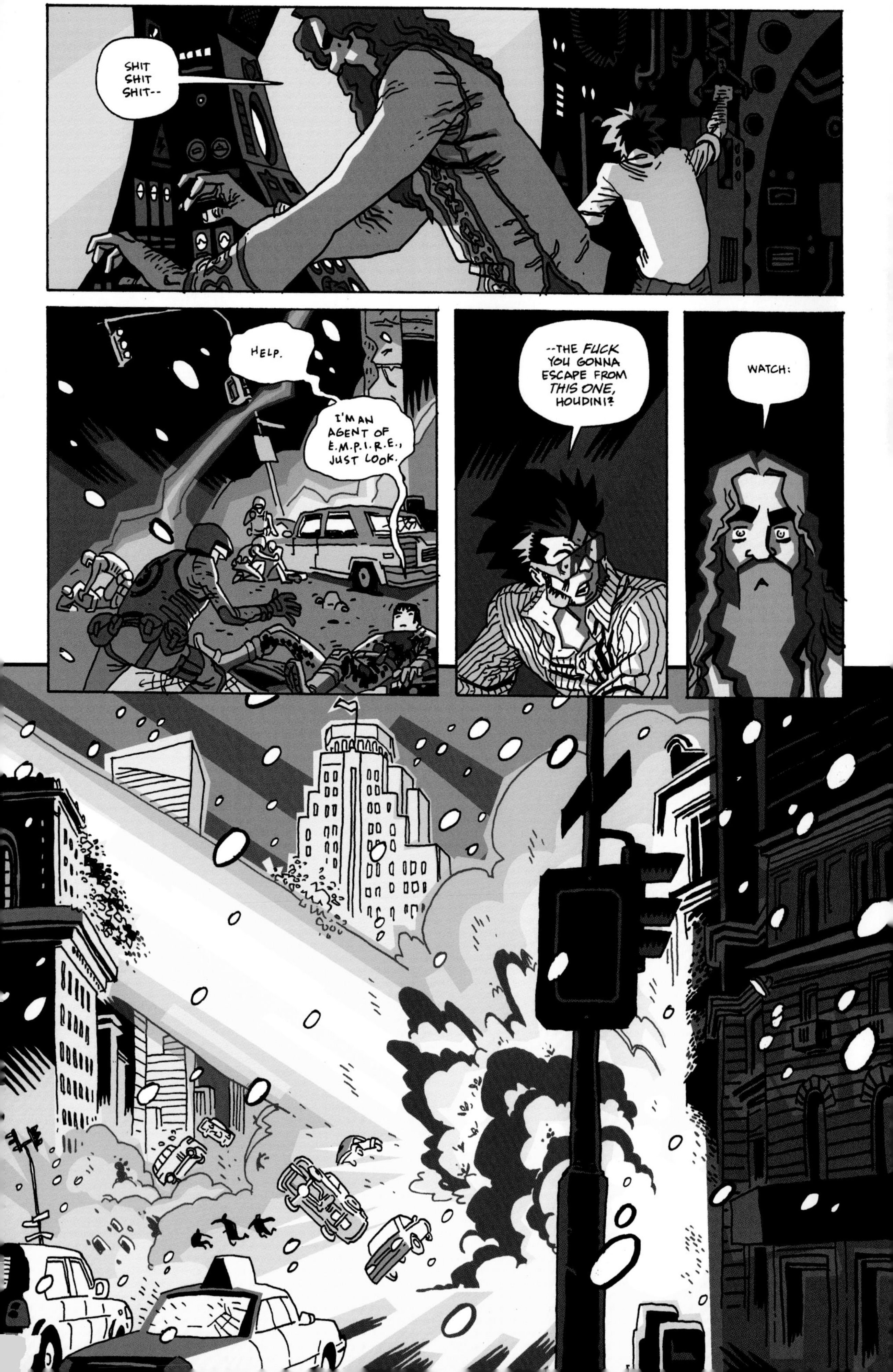
SHIT SHIT SHIT--
HELP.
I'M AN AGENT OF E.M.P.I.R.E., JUST LOOK.
--THE FUCK YOU GONNA ESCAPE FROM THIS ONE, HOUDINI?
WATCH:

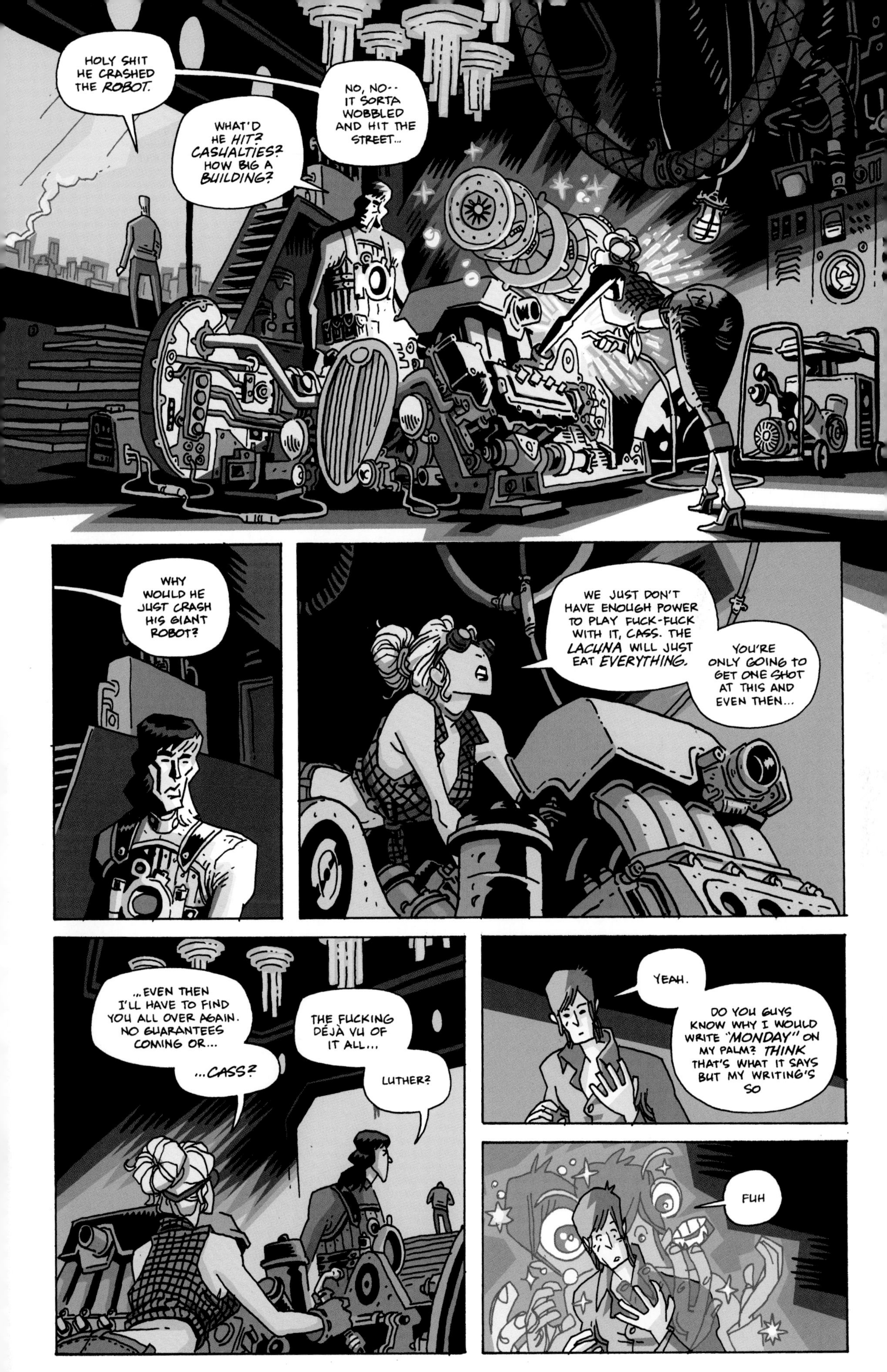

HOLY SHIT HE CRASHED THE ROBOT.
WHAT'D HE HIT? CASUALTIES? HOW BIG A BUILDING?
NO, NO-- IT SORTA WOBBLED AND HIT THE STREET...
WHY WOULD HE JUST CRASH HIS GIANT ROBOT?
WE JUST DON'T HAVE ENOUGH POWER TO PLAY FUCK-FUCK WITH IT, CASS. THE LACUNA WILL JUST EAT EVERYTHING.
YOU'RE ONLY GOING TO GET ONE SHOT AT THIS AND EVEN THEN...
...EVEN THEN I'LL HAVE TO FIND YOU ALL OVER AGAIN. NO GUARANTEES COMING OR...
...CASS?
THE FUCKING DÉJÀ VU OF IT ALL...
LUTHER?
YEAH.
DO YOU GUYS KNOW WHY I WOULD WRITE "MONDAY" ON MY PALM? THINK THAT'S WHAT IT SAYS BUT MY WRITING'S SO
FUH

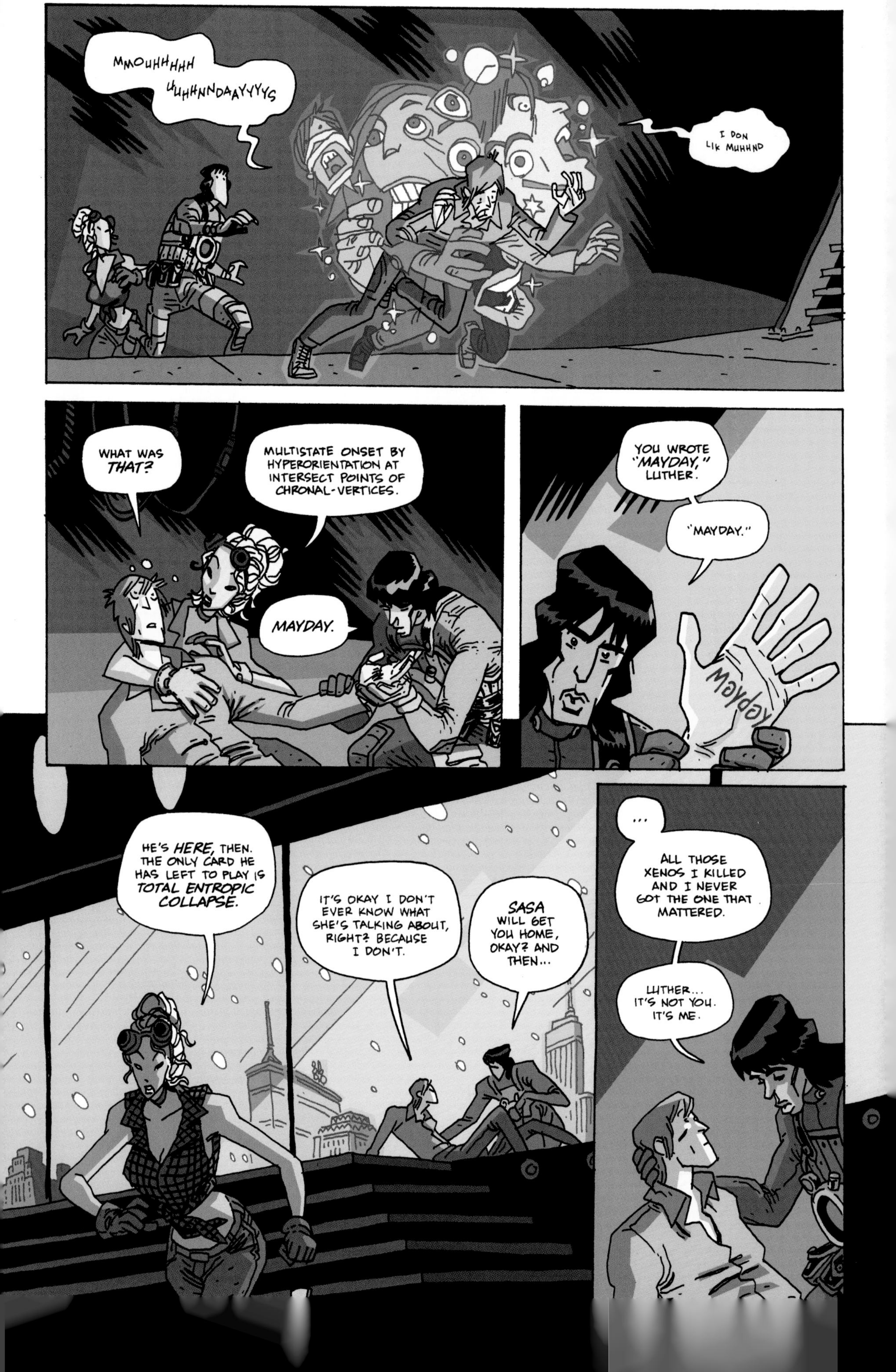
MMOUHHHHH UUHHNNDAAYYYYG
I DON LIK MUHHND
WHAT WAS THAT?
MULTISTATE ONSET BY HYPERORIENTATION AT INTERSECT POINTS OF CHRONAL-VERTICES.
MAYDAY.
YOU WROTE "MAYDAY," LUTHER.
"MAYDAY."
Mayday
HE'S HERE, THEN. THE ONLY CARD HE HAS LEFT TO PLAY IS TOTAL ENTROPIC COLLAPSE.
IT'S OKAY I DON'T EVER KNOW WHAT SHE'S TALKING ABOUT, RIGHT? BECAUSE I DON'T.
SASA WILL GET YOU HOME, OKAY? AND THEN...
...
ALL THOSE XENOS I KILLED AND I NEVER GOT THE ONE THAT MATTERED.
LUTHER... IT'S NOT YOU. IT'S ME.

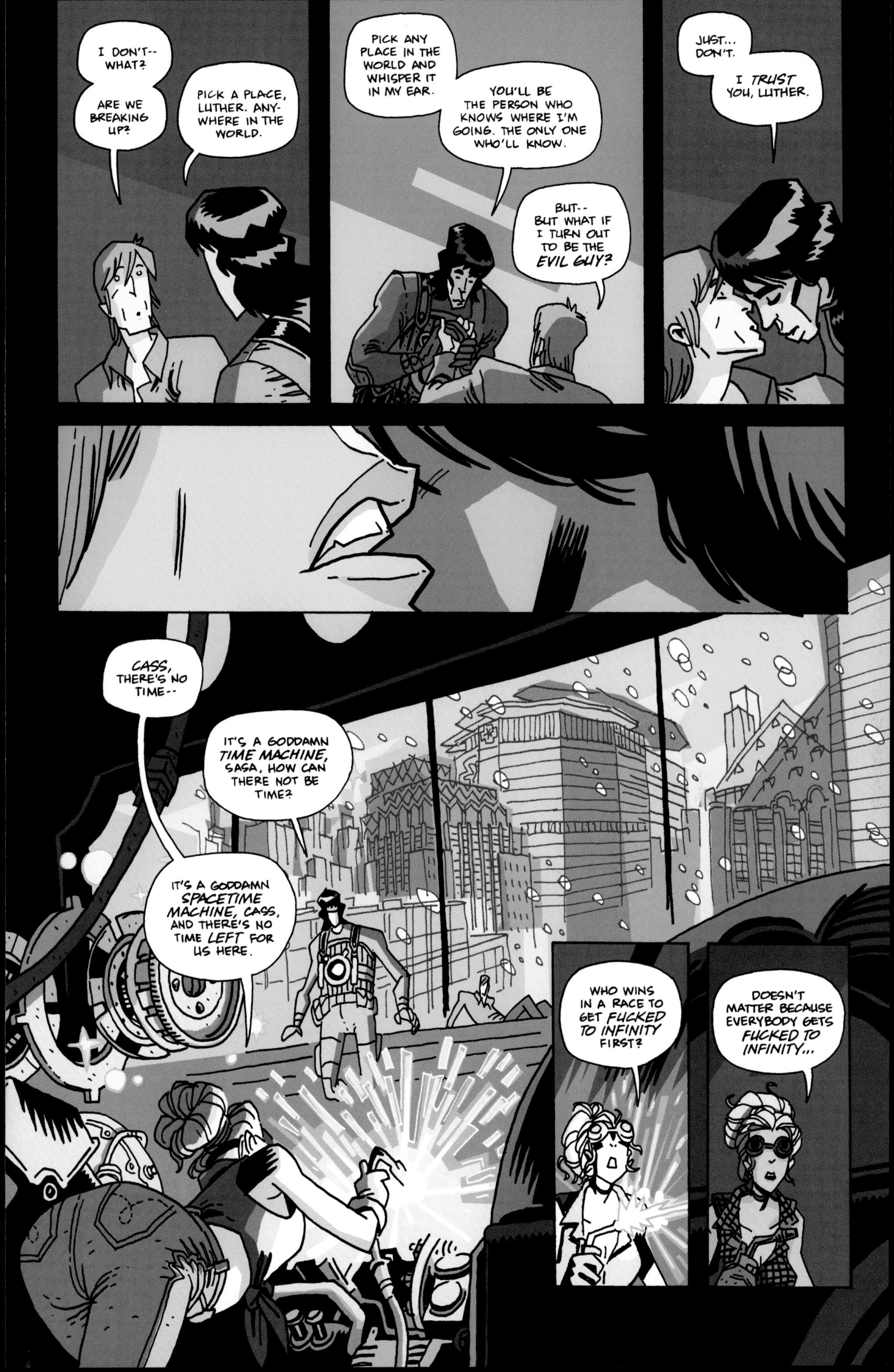
I DON'T-- WHAT?
ARE WE BREAKING UP?
PICK A PLACE, LUTHER. ANYWHERE IN THE WORLD.
PICK ANY PLACE IN THE WORLD AND WHISPER IT IN MY EAR.
YOU'LL BE THE PERSON WHO KNOWS WHERE I'M GOING. THE ONLY ONE WHO'LL KNOW.
BUT-- BUT WHAT IF I TURN OUT TO BE THE *EVIL GUY?*
JUST... DON'T.
I *TRUST* YOU, LUTHER.
CASS, THERE'S NO TIME--
IT'S A GODDAMN *TIME MACHINE,* SASA, HOW CAN THERE NOT BE TIME?
IT'S A GODDAMN *SPACETIME MACHINE, CASS,* AND THERE'S NO TIME *LEFT* FOR US HERE.
WHO WINS IN A RACE TO GET *FUCKED TO INFINITY* FIRST?
DOESN'T MATTER BECAUSE EVERYBODY GETS *FUCKED TO INFINITY...*

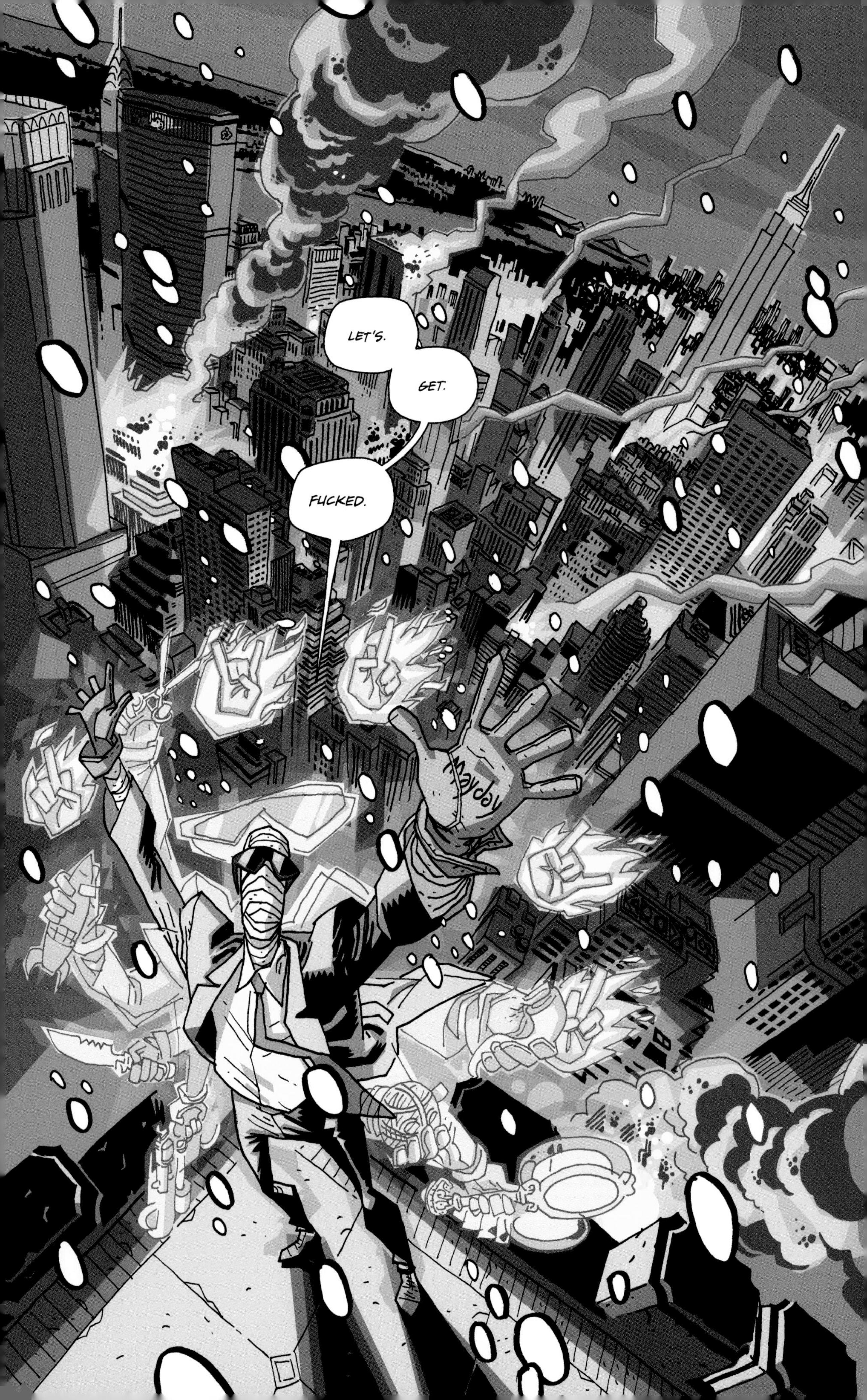
LET'S.
GET.
FUCKED.

W.A.S.T.E.-FREE WILDERNESS

WHAT IF IT'S NEVER ENOUGH

HARM REDUCTION

RELAXED IN PERSON

BACKMATTER

10. CAMERAS IN BROOKLYN

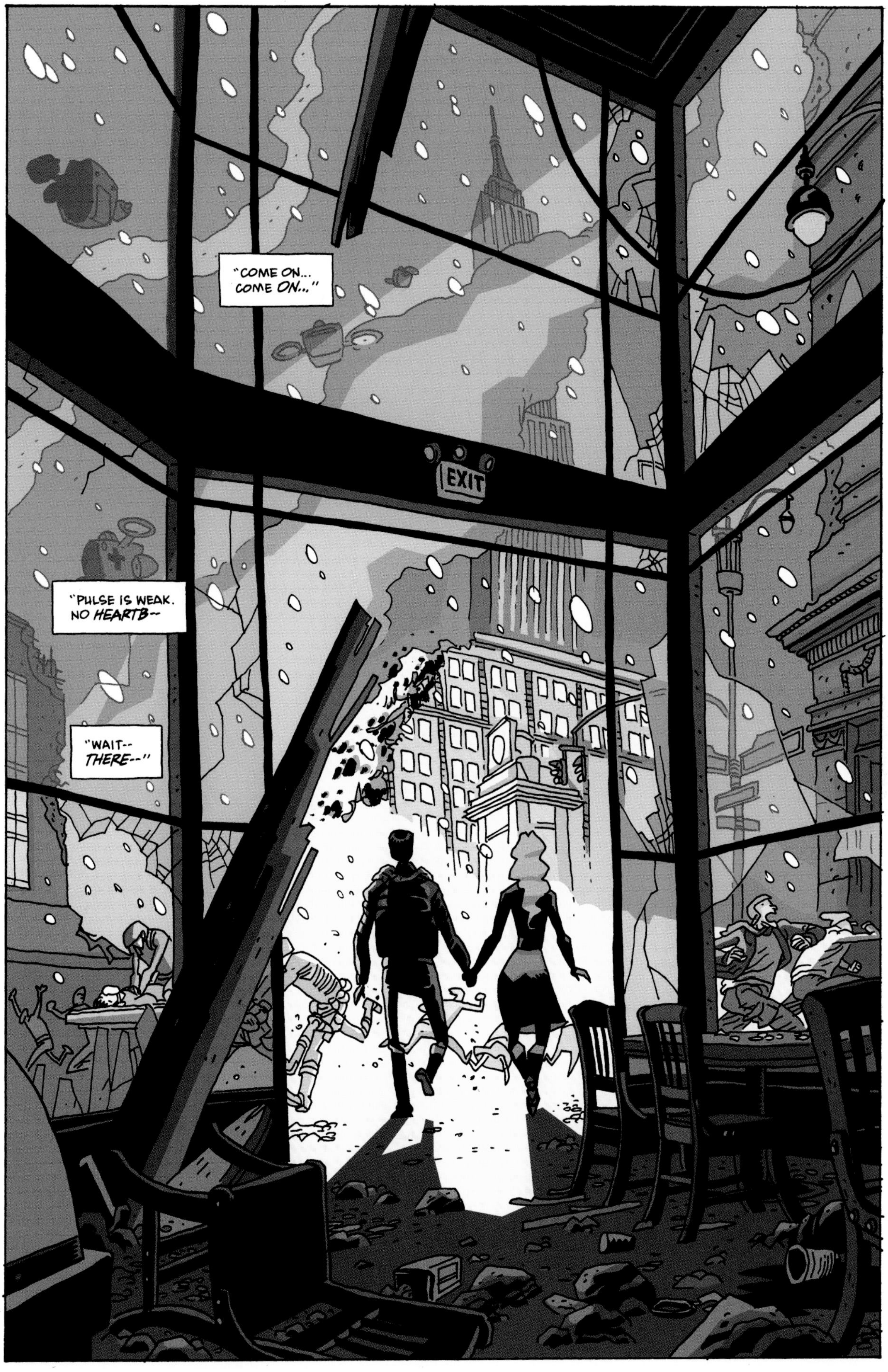
"COME ON... COME ON..."
EXIT
"PULSE IS WEAK. NO HEARTB--
"WAIT-- THERE--"

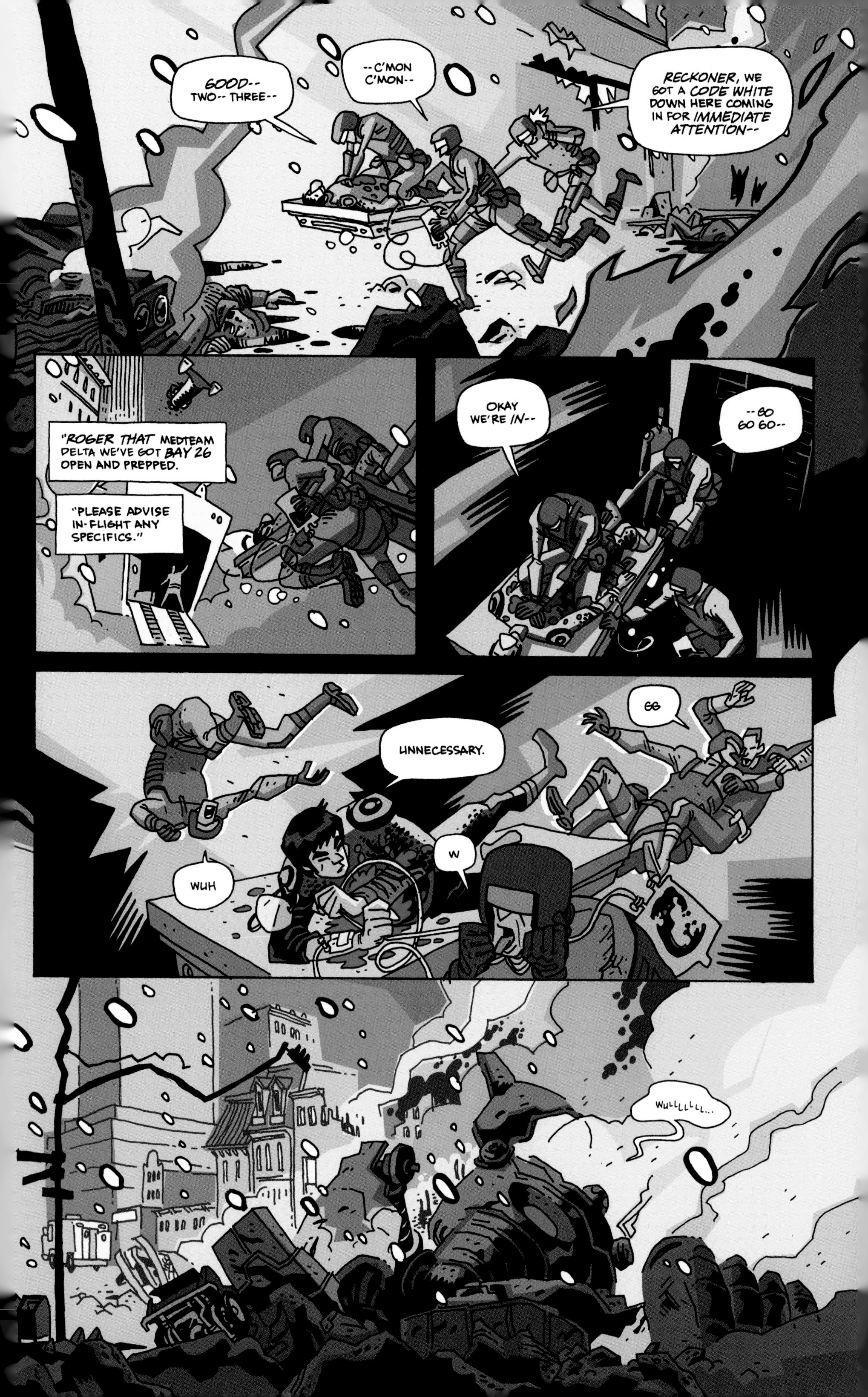
GOOD-- TWO-- THREE--
--C'MON C'MON--
RECKONER, WE GOT A CODE WHITE DOWN HERE COMING IN FOR IMMEDIATE ATTENTION--
"ROGER THAT MEDTEAM DELTA WE'VE GOT BAY 26 OPEN AND PREPPED.
"PLEASE ADVISE IN-FLIGHT ANY SPECIFICS."
OKAY WE'RE IN--
--GO GO GO--
UNNECESSARY.
GG
WUH
W
WULLLLLLL...

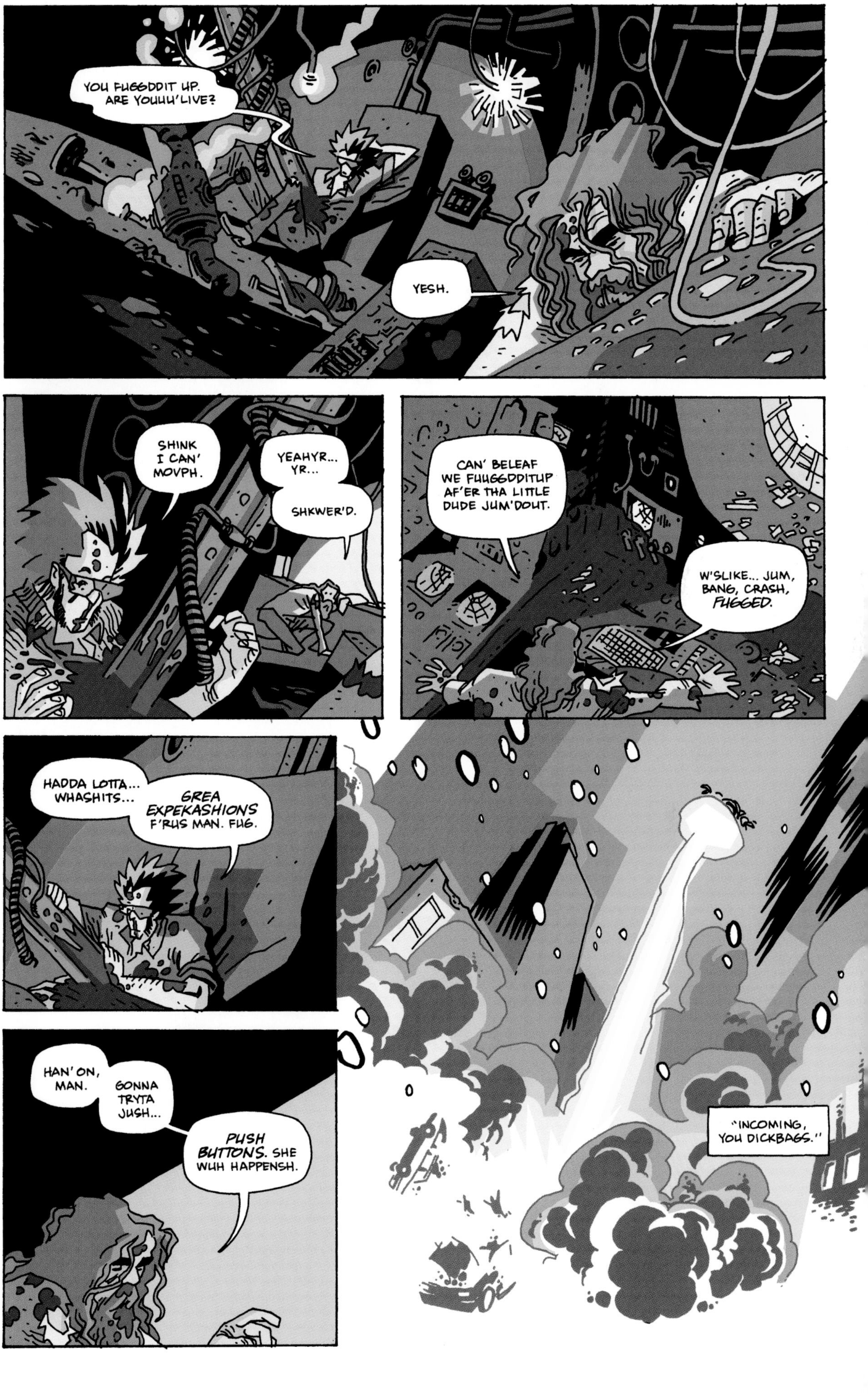
YOU FUGGDDIT UP. ARE YOUUU'LIVE?
YESH.
SHINK I CAN' MOVPH.
YEAHYR... YR...
SHKWER'D.
CAN' BELEAF WE FUUGGDDITUP AF'ER THA LITTLE DUDE JUM'DOUT.
W'SLIKE... JUM, BANG, CRASH, FUGGED.
HADDA LOTTA... WHASHITS...
GREA EXPEKASHIONS F'RUS MAN. FUG.
HAN' ON, MAN.
GONNA TRYTA JUSH...
PUSH BUTTONS. SHE WUH HAPPENSH.
"INCOMING, YOU DICKBAGS."

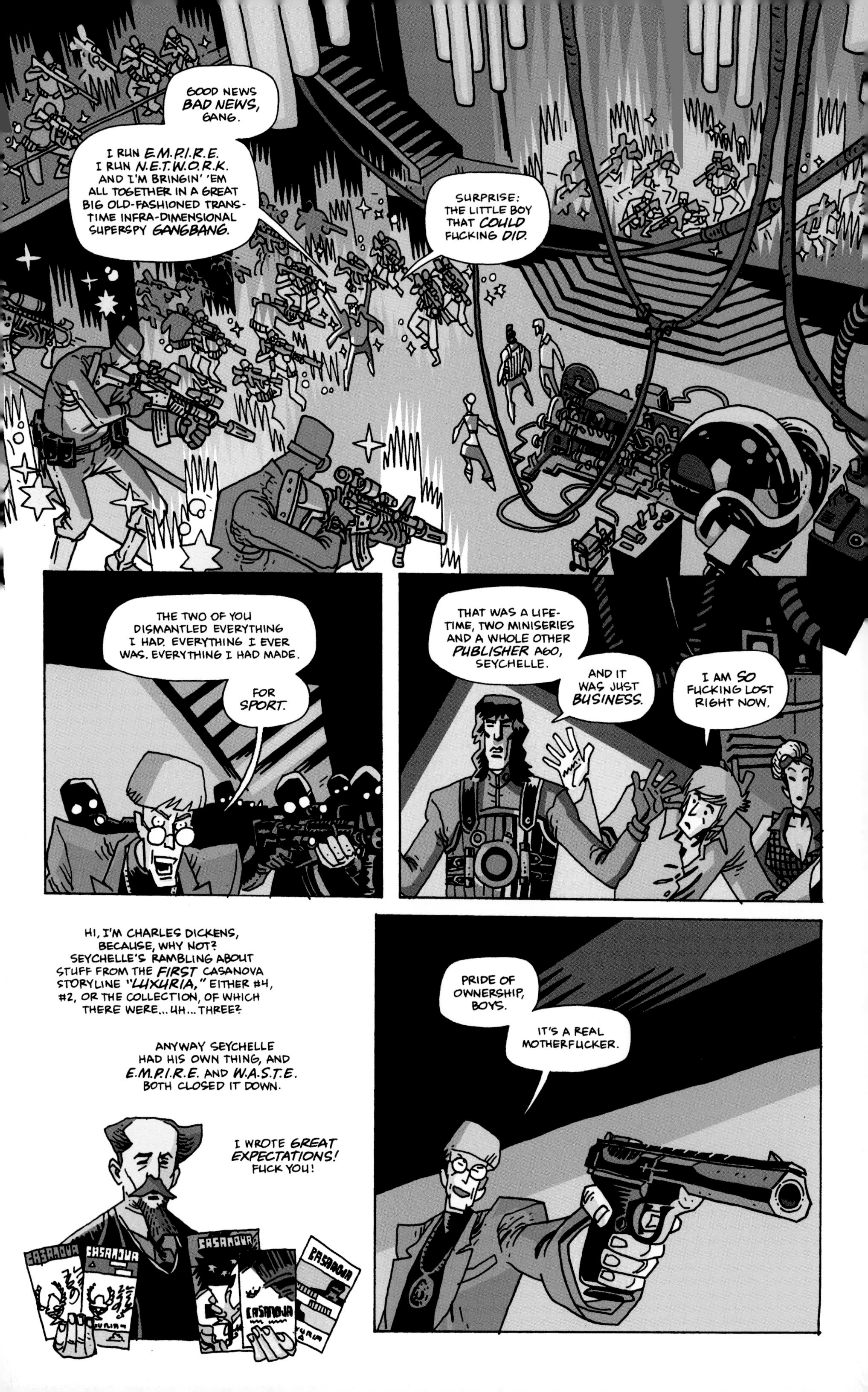
GOOD NEWS BAD NEWS, GANG.
I RUN E.M.P.I.R.E. I RUN N.E.T.W.O.R.K. AND I'M BRINGIN' 'EM ALL TOGETHER IN A GREAT BIG OLD-FASHIONED TRANS-TIME INFRA-DIMENSIONAL SUPERSPY GANGBANG.
SURPRISE: THE LITTLE BOY THAT COULD FUCKING DID.
THE TWO OF YOU DISMANTLED EVERYTHING I HAD. EVERYTHING I EVER WAS. EVERYTHING I HAD MADE.
FOR SPORT.
THAT WAS A LIFE-TIME, TWO MINISERIES AND A WHOLE OTHER PUBLISHER AGO, SEYCHELLE.
AND IT WAS JUST BUSINESS.
I AM SO FUCKING LOST RIGHT NOW.
HI, I'M CHARLES DICKENS, BECAUSE, WHY NOT? SEYCHELLE'S RAMBLING ABOUT STUFF FROM THE FIRST CASANOVA STORYLINE "LUXURIA," EITHER #4, #2, OR THE COLLECTION, OF WHICH THERE WERE... UH... THREE?
ANYWAY SEYCHELLE HAD HIS OWN THING, AND E.M.P.I.R.E. AND W.A.S.T.E. BOTH CLOSED IT DOWN.
I WROTE GREAT EXPECTATIONS! FUCK YOU!
PRIDE OF OWNERSHIP, BOYS.
IT'S A REAL MOTHERFUCKER.

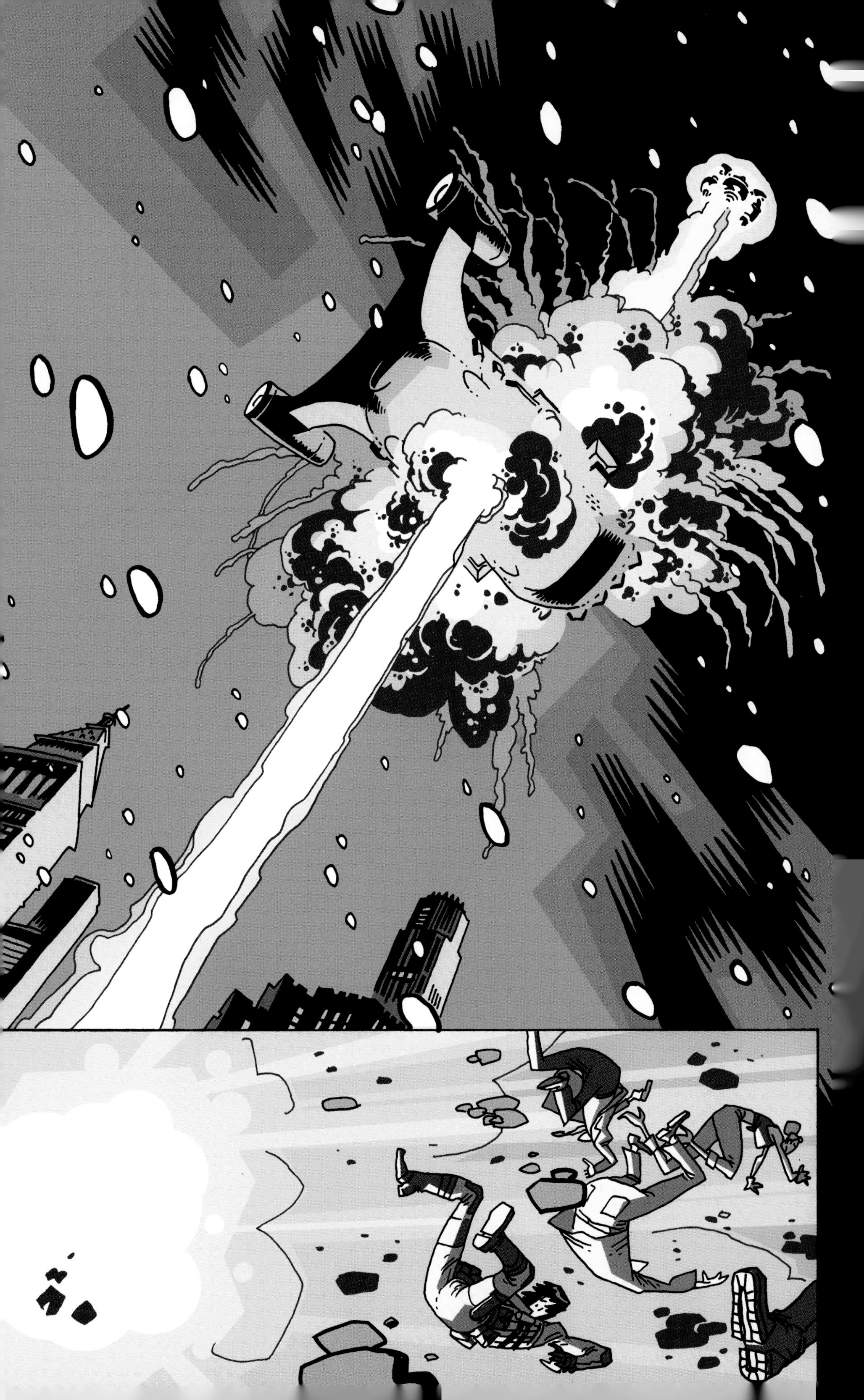

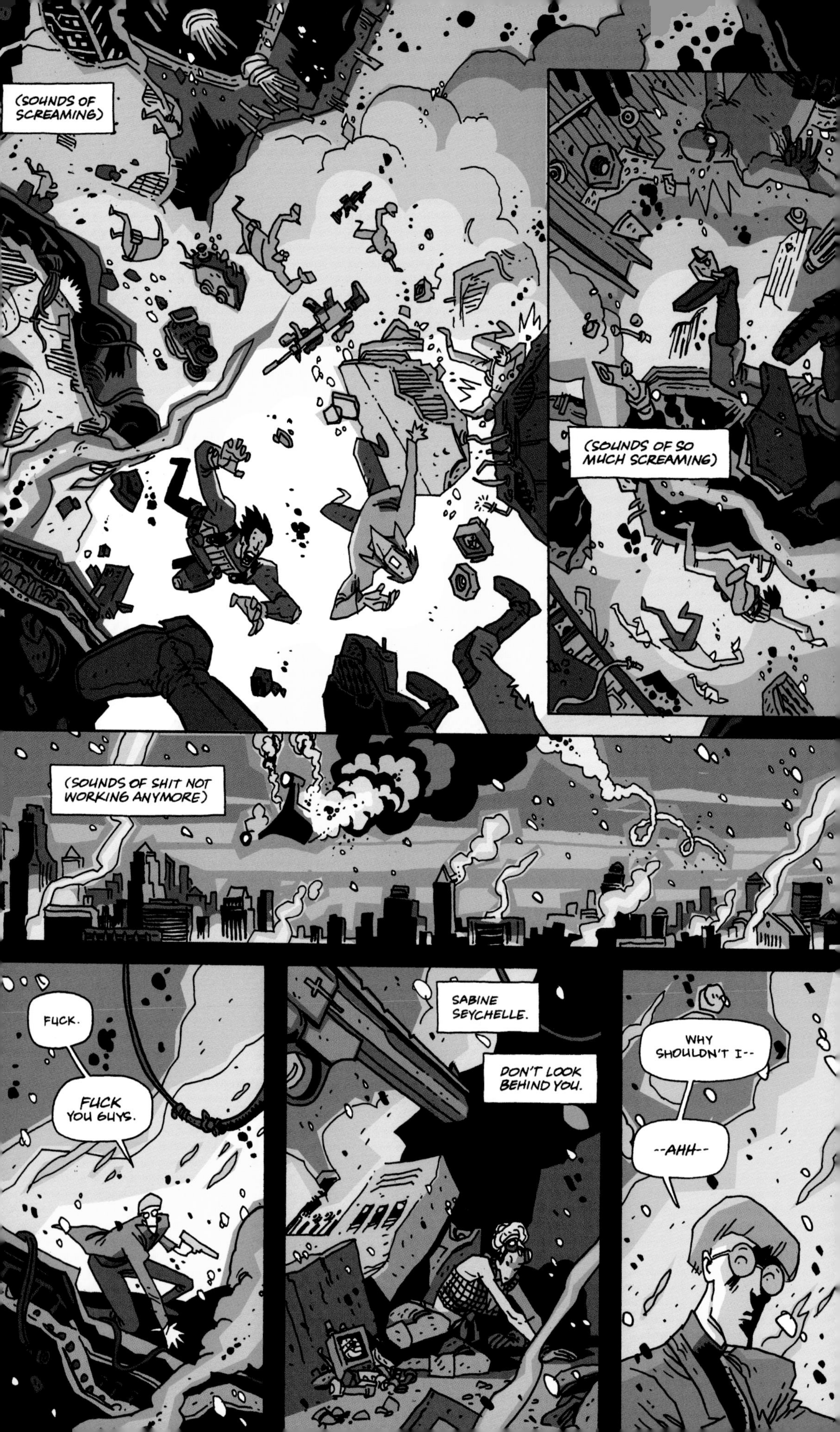
(SOUNDS OF SCREAMING)
(SOUNDS OF SO MUCH SCREAMING)
(SOUNDS OF SHIT NOT WORKING ANYMORE)
FUCK.
FUCK YOU GUYS.
SABINE SEYCHELLE.
DON'T LOOK BEHIND YOU.
WHY SHOULDN'T I--
--AHH--

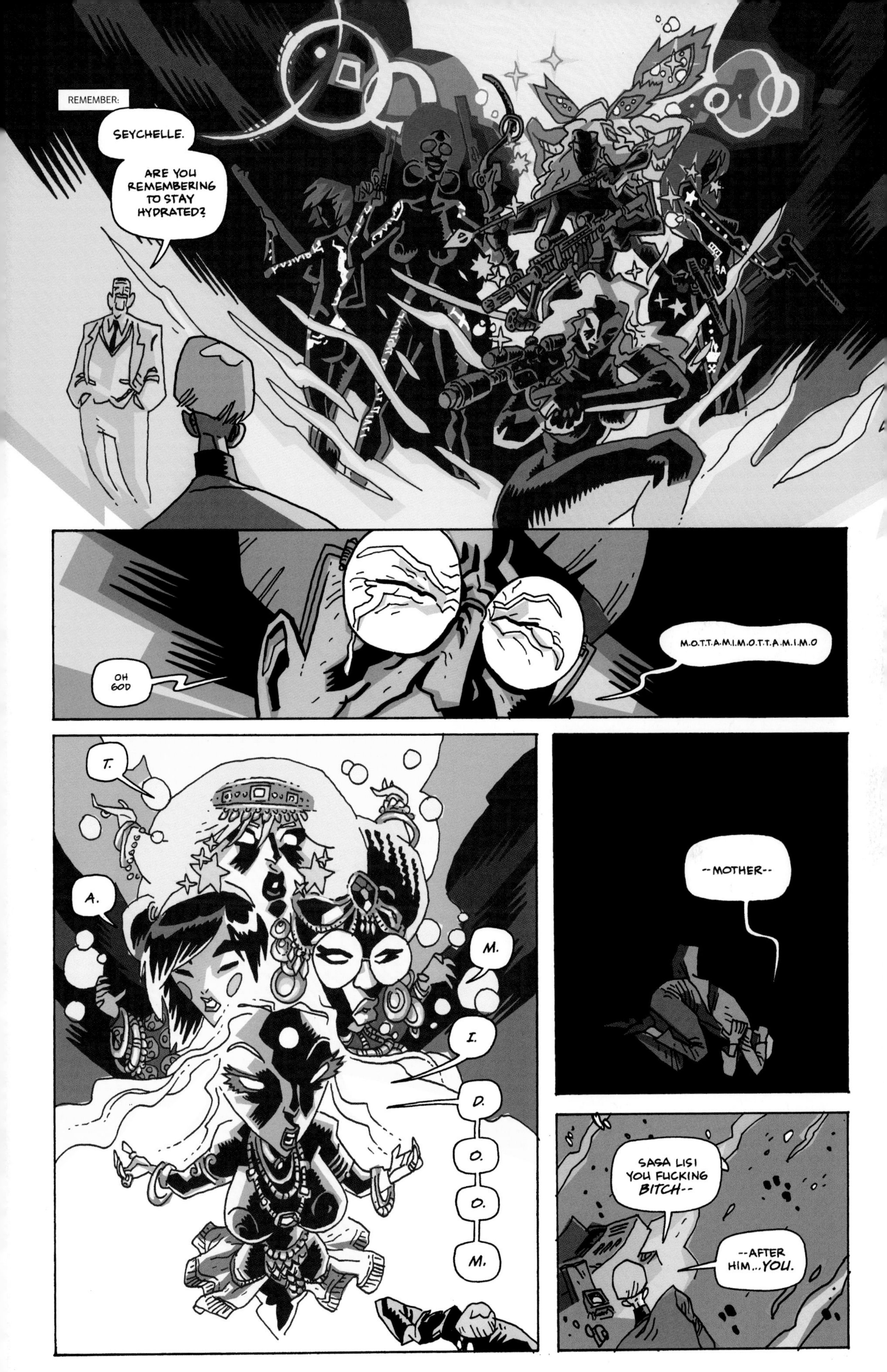
REMEMBER:
SEYCHELLE.
ARE YOU REMEMBERING TO STAY HYDRATED?
OH GOD
M.O.T.T.A.M.I.M.O.T.T.A.M.I.M.O
T.
A.
M.
I.
D.
O.
O.
M.
--MOTHER--
SASA LISI YOU FUCKING *BITCH*--
--AFTER HIM...*YOU*.

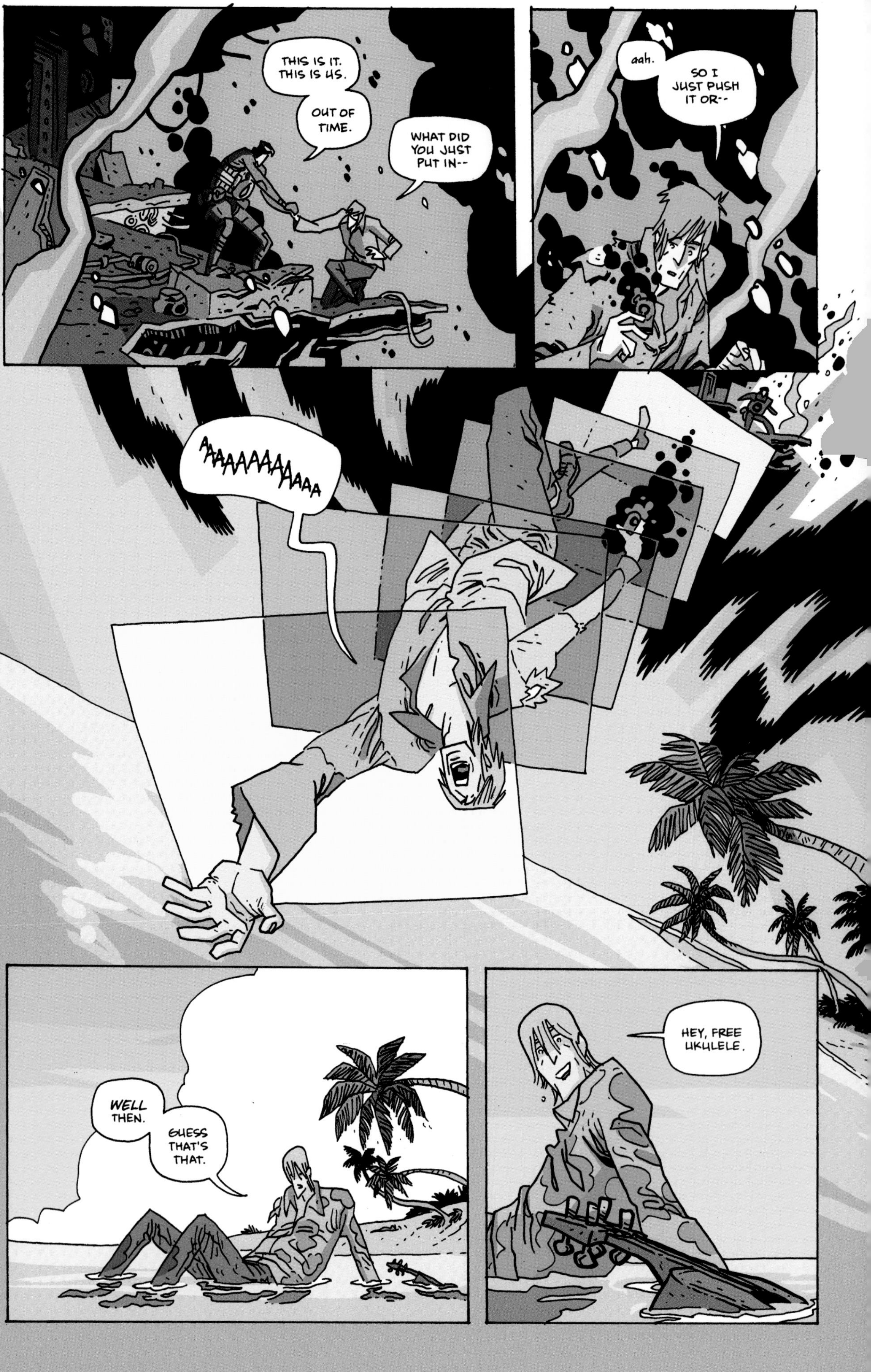
THIS IS IT. THIS IS US.
OUT OF TIME.
WHAT DID YOU JUST PUT IN--
aah.
SO I JUST PUSH IT OR--
AAAAAAAAAAAAA
WELL THEN.
GUESS THAT'S THAT.
HEY, FREE UKULELE.

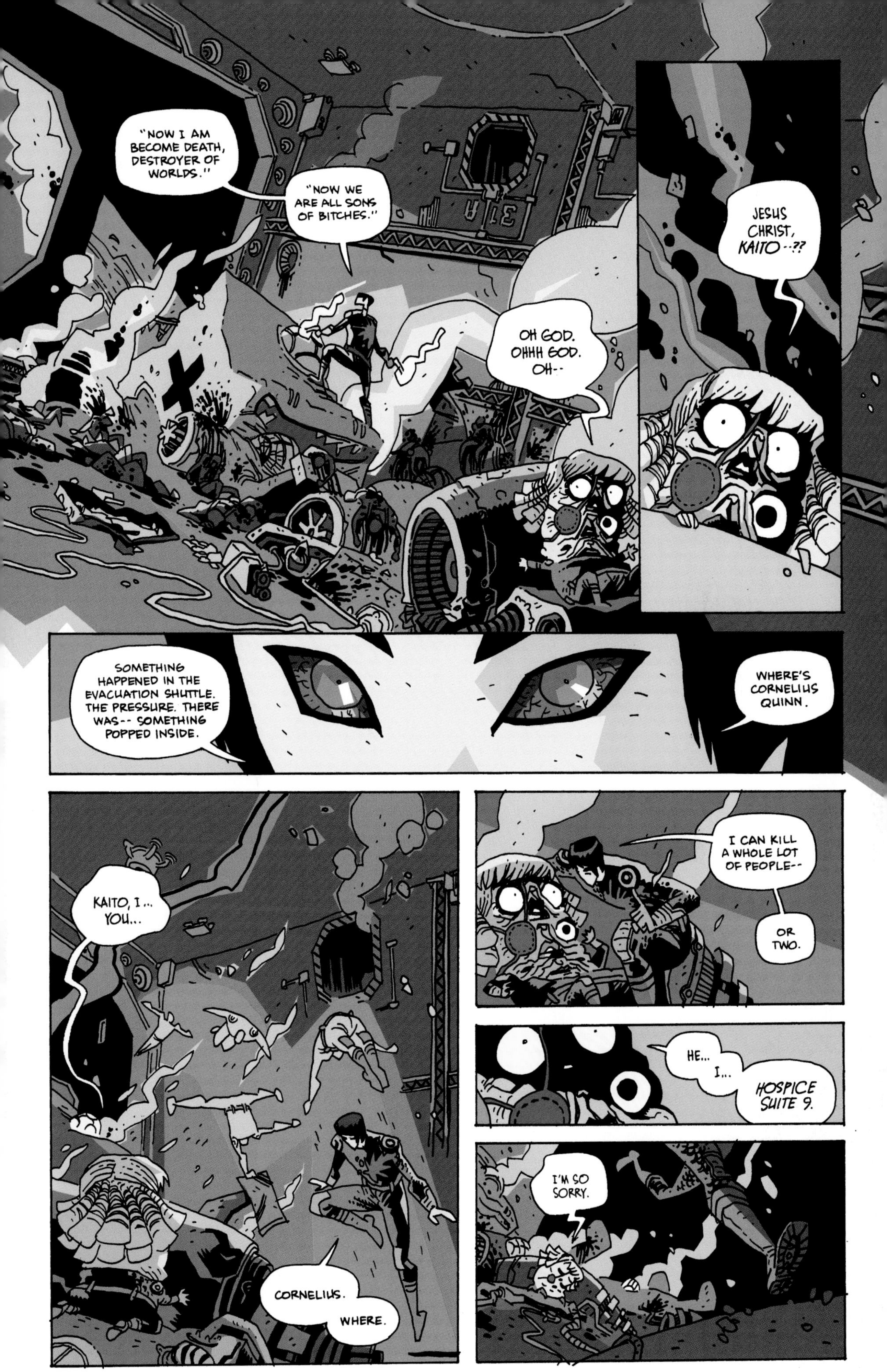
"NOW I AM BECOME DEATH, DESTROYER OF WORLDS."
"NOW WE ARE ALL SONS OF BITCHES."
OH GOD. OHHH GOD. OH--
JESUS CHRIST, KAITO--??
SOMETHING HAPPENED IN THE EVACUATION SHUTTLE. THE PRESSURE. THERE WAS-- SOMETHING POPPED INSIDE.
WHERE'S CORNELIUS QUINN.
KAITO, I... YOU...
CORNELIUS.
WHERE.
I CAN KILL A WHOLE LOT OF PEOPLE--
OR TWO.
HE...
I...
HOSPICE SUITE 9.
I'M SO SORRY.

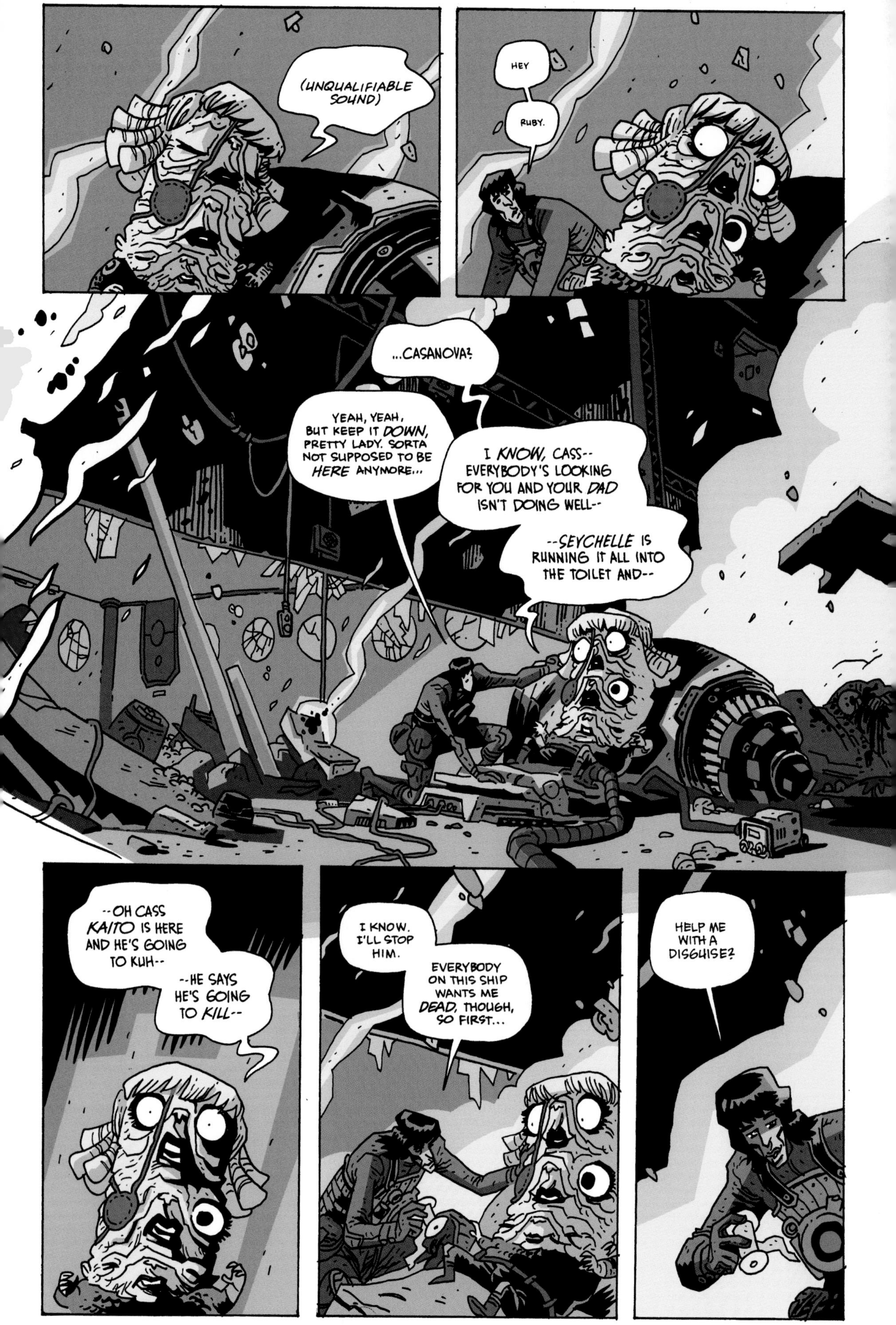
(UNQUALIFIABLE SOUND)
HEY
RUBY.
...CASANOVA?
YEAH, YEAH, BUT KEEP IT DOWN, PRETTY LADY. SORTA NOT SUPPOSED TO BE HERE ANYMORE...
I KNOW, CASS-- EVERYBODY'S LOOKING FOR YOU AND YOUR DAD ISN'T DOING WELL--
--SEYCHELLE IS RUNNING IT ALL INTO THE TOILET AND--
--OH CASS KAITO IS HERE AND HE'S GOING TO KUH--
--HE SAYS HE'S GOING TO KILL--
I KNOW. I'LL STOP HIM.
EVERYBODY ON THIS SHIP WANTS ME DEAD, THOUGH, SO FIRST...
HELP ME WITH A DISGUISE?

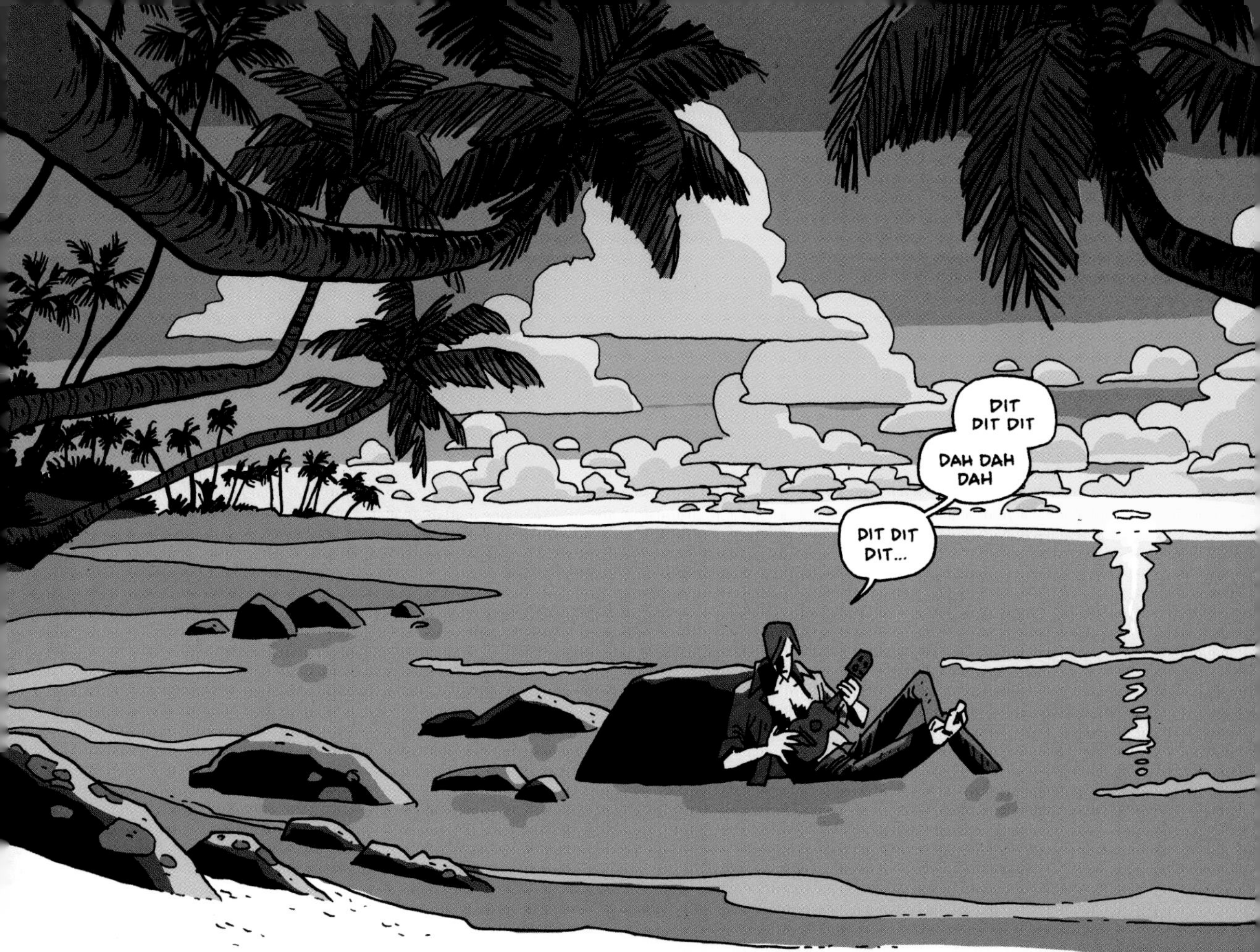
DIT
DIT DIT
DAH DAH
DAH
DIT DIT
DIT...

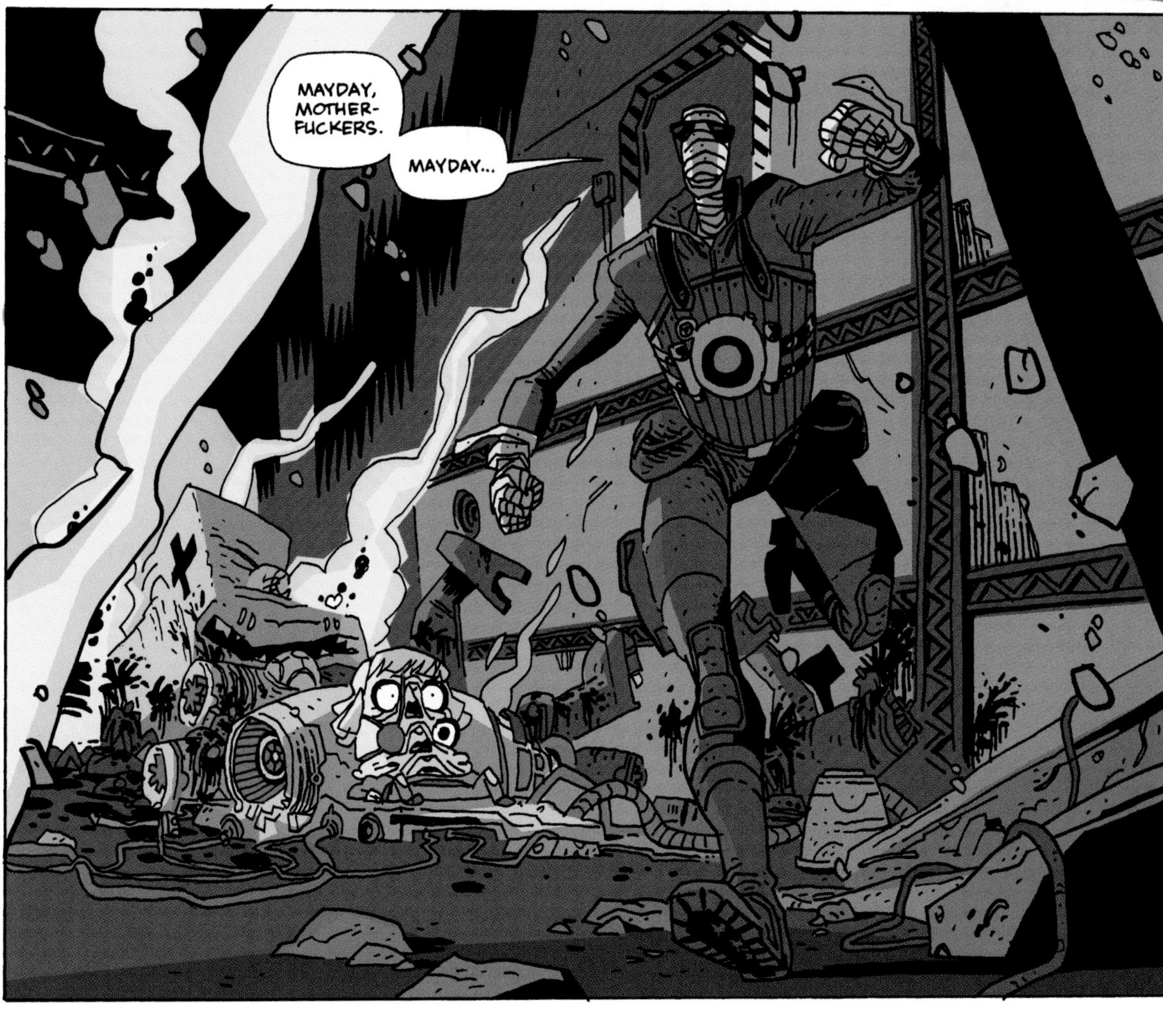
MAYDAY, MOTHER-FUCKERS.
MAYDAY...

11. PEOPLE ARE TURNING TO GOLD

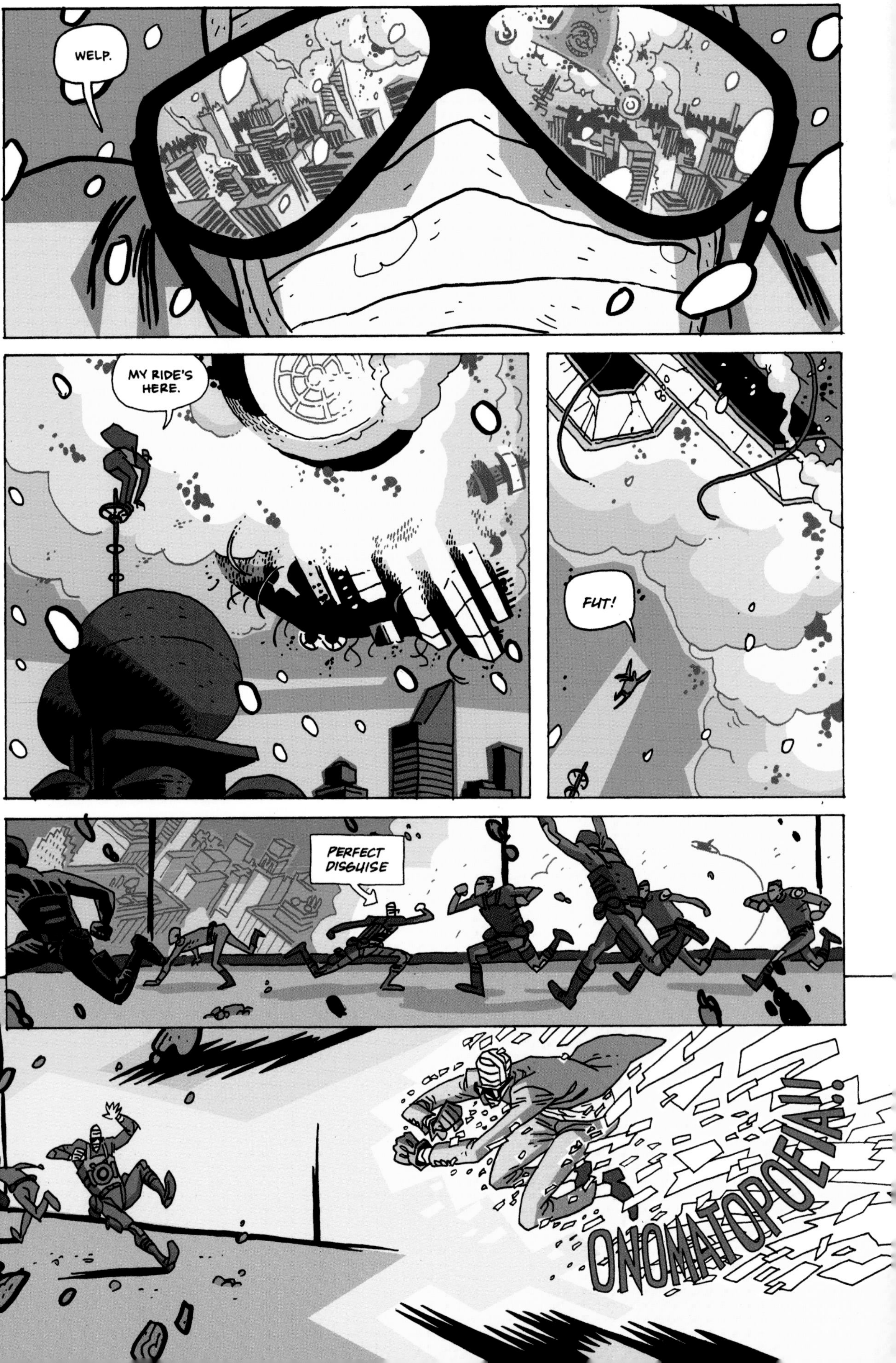
WELP.
MY RIDE'S HERE.
FUT!
PERFECT DISGUISE
ONOMATOPOEIA!!

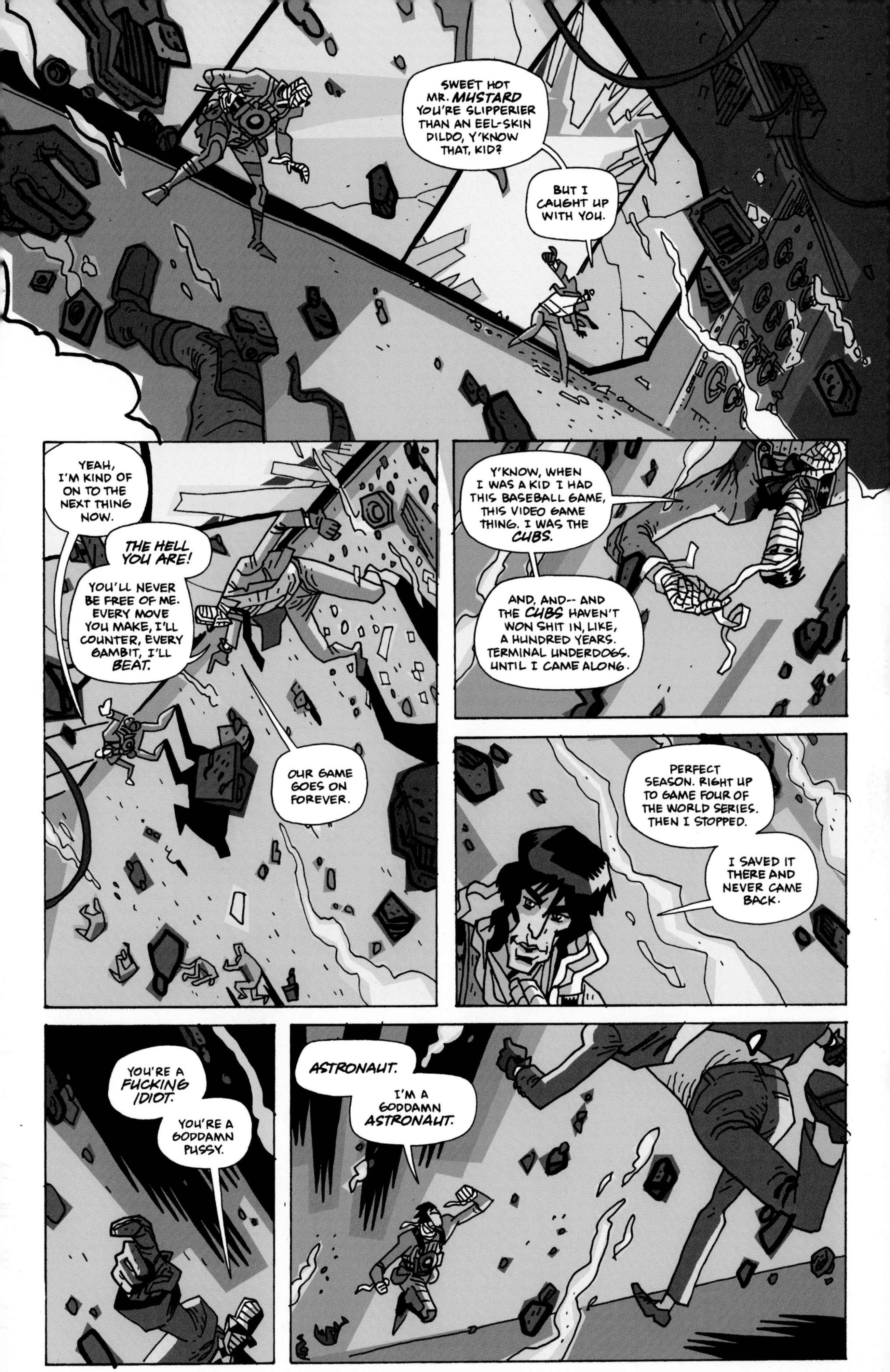
SWEET HOT MR. MUSTARD YOU'RE SLIPPERIER THAN AN EEL-SKIN DILDO, Y'KNOW THAT, KID?
BUT I CAUGHT UP WITH YOU.
YEAH, I'M KIND OF ON TO THE NEXT THING NOW.
THE HELL YOU ARE!
YOU'LL NEVER BE FREE OF ME. EVERY MOVE YOU MAKE, I'LL COUNTER, EVERY GAMBIT, I'LL BEAT.
OUR GAME GOES ON FOREVER.
Y'KNOW, WHEN I WAS A KID I HAD THIS BASEBALL GAME, THIS VIDEO GAME THING. I WAS THE CUBS.
AND, AND-- AND THE CUBS HAVEN'T WON SHIT IN, LIKE, A HUNDRED YEARS. TERMINAL UNDERDOGS. UNTIL I CAME ALONG.
PERFECT SEASON. RIGHT UP TO GAME FOUR OF THE WORLD SERIES. THEN I STOPPED.
I SAVED IT THERE AND NEVER CAME BACK.
YOU'RE A FUCKING IDIOT.
YOU'RE A GODDAMN PUSSY.
ASTRONAUT.
I'M A GODDAMN ASTRONAUT.

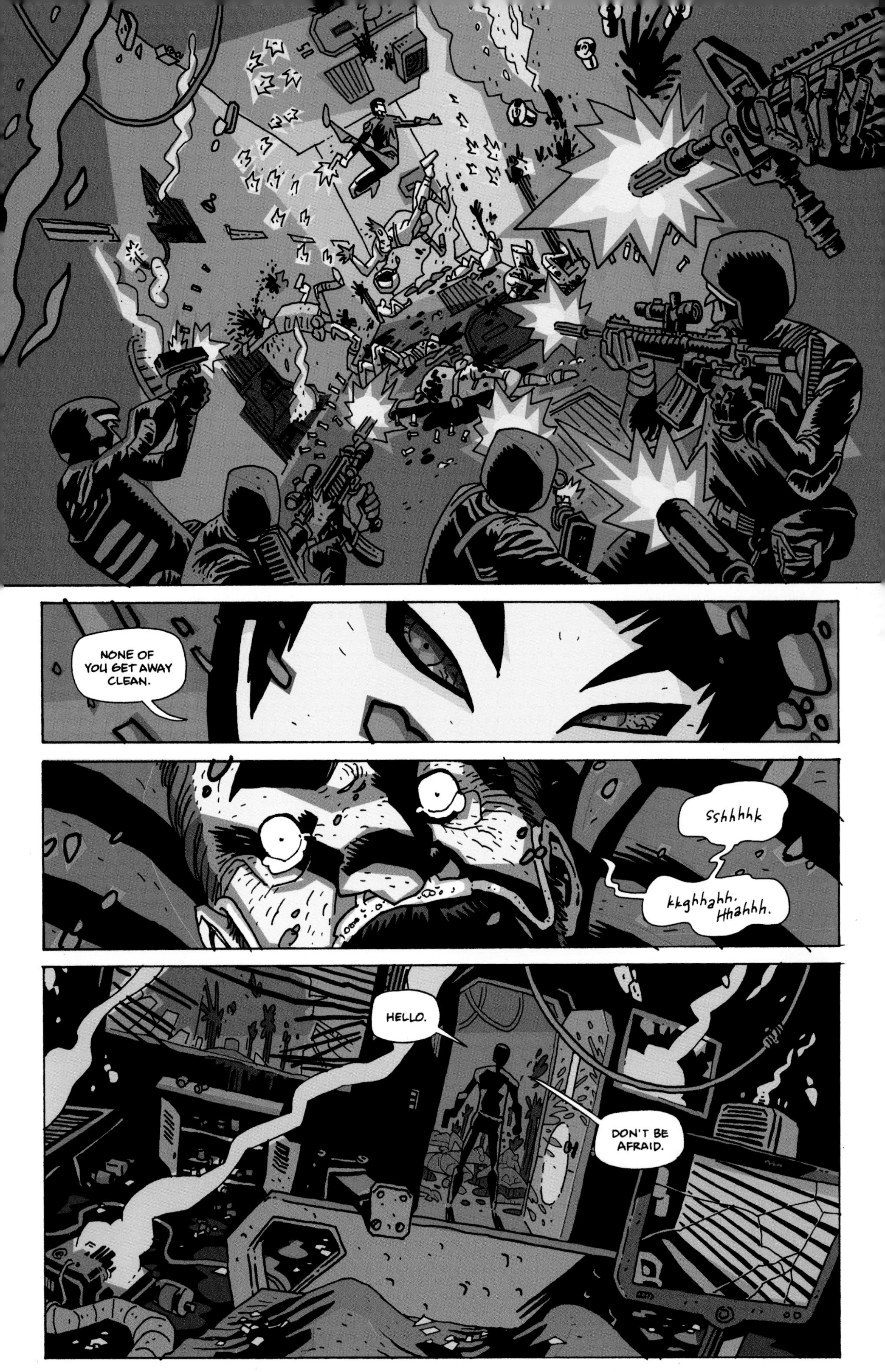
NONE OF YOU GET AWAY CLEAN.
sshhhhk
kkghhahh. Hhahhh.
HELLO.
DON'T BE AFRAID.

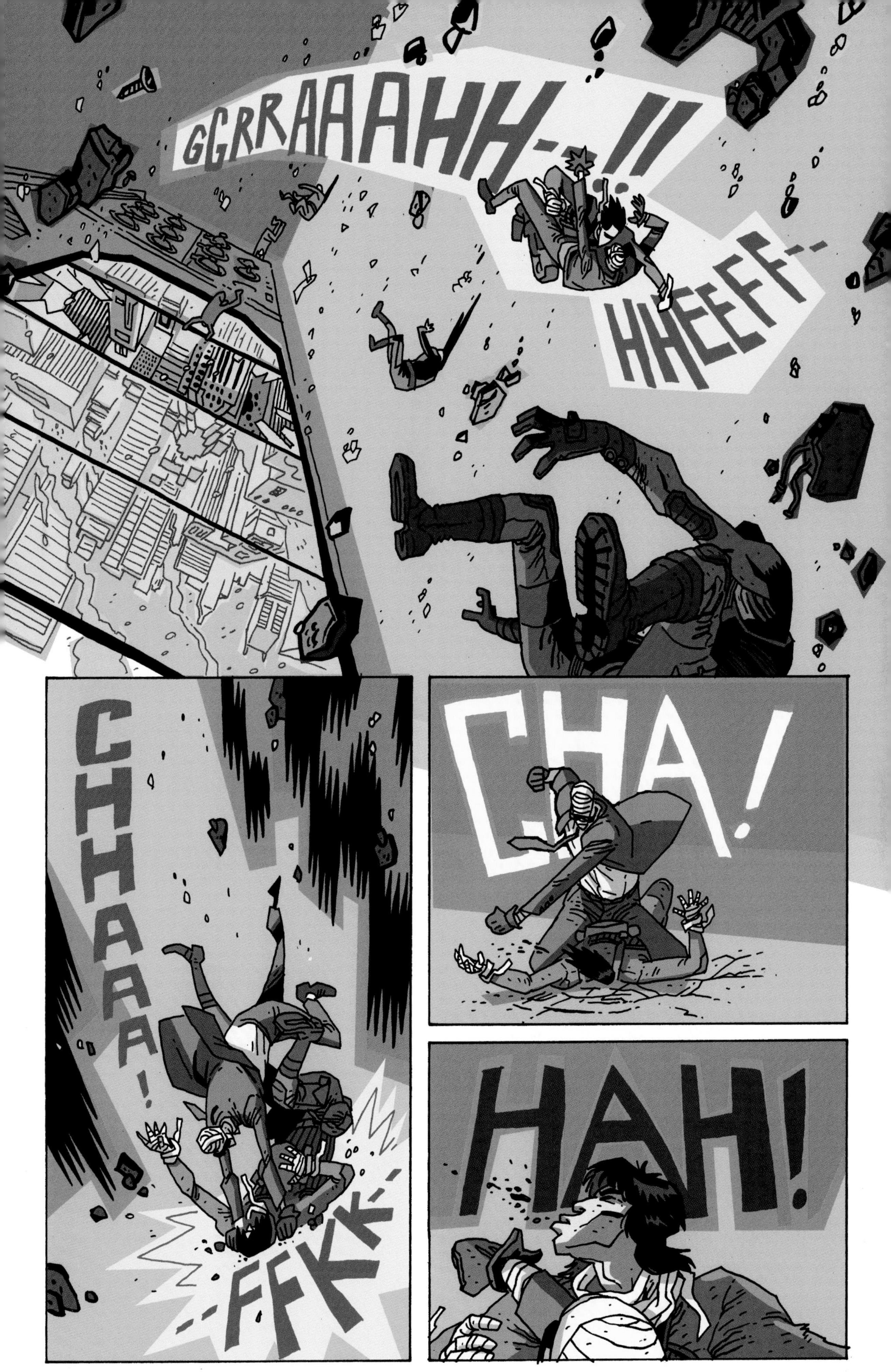
GGRRAAAHH--!!
HHEEFF--
CHHAAAA!
--FFKK
CHA!
HAH!

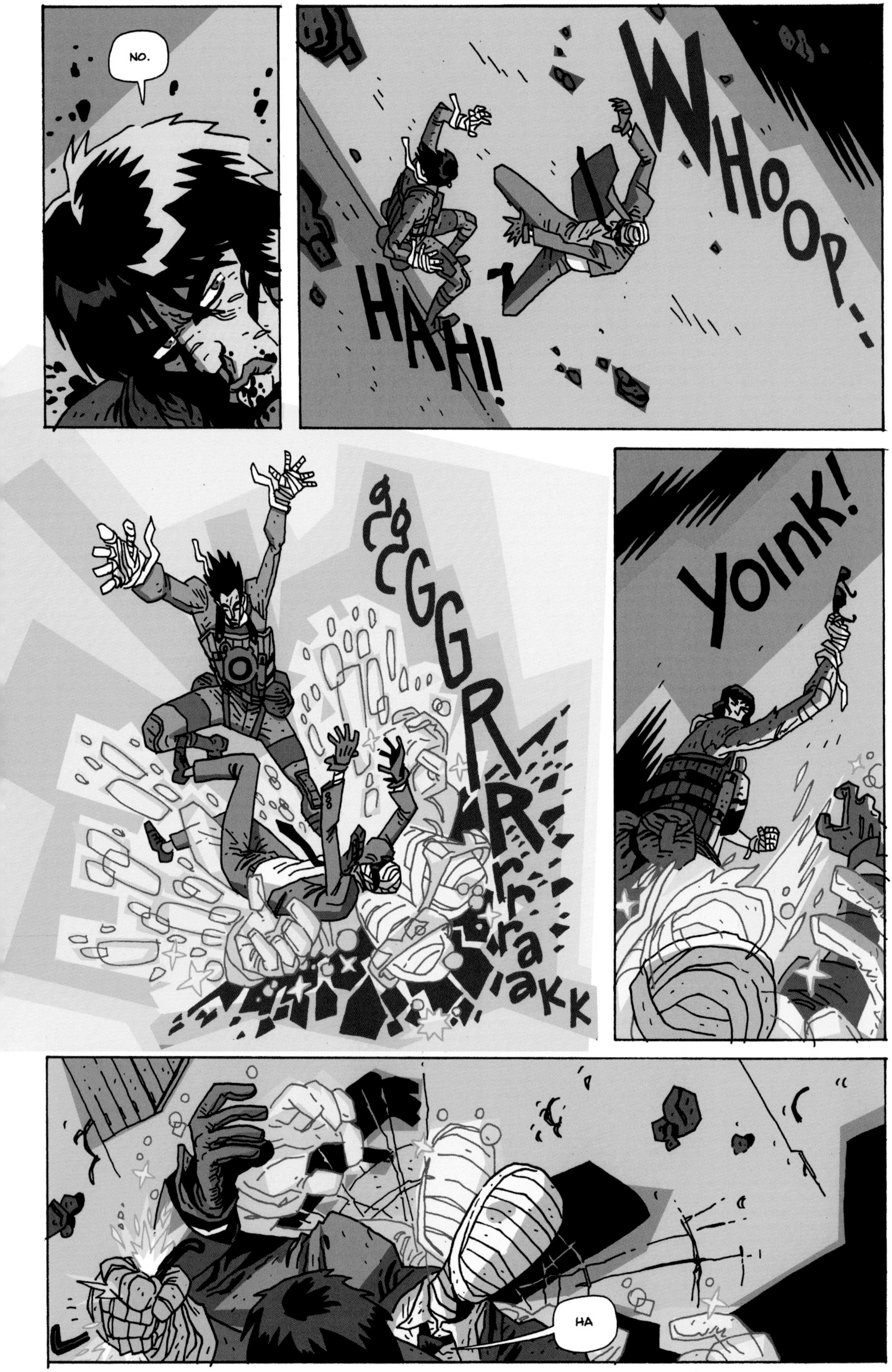
NO.
WHOOP..
HAHI!
ggCGGRRRrrrrraakk
YOINK!
HA

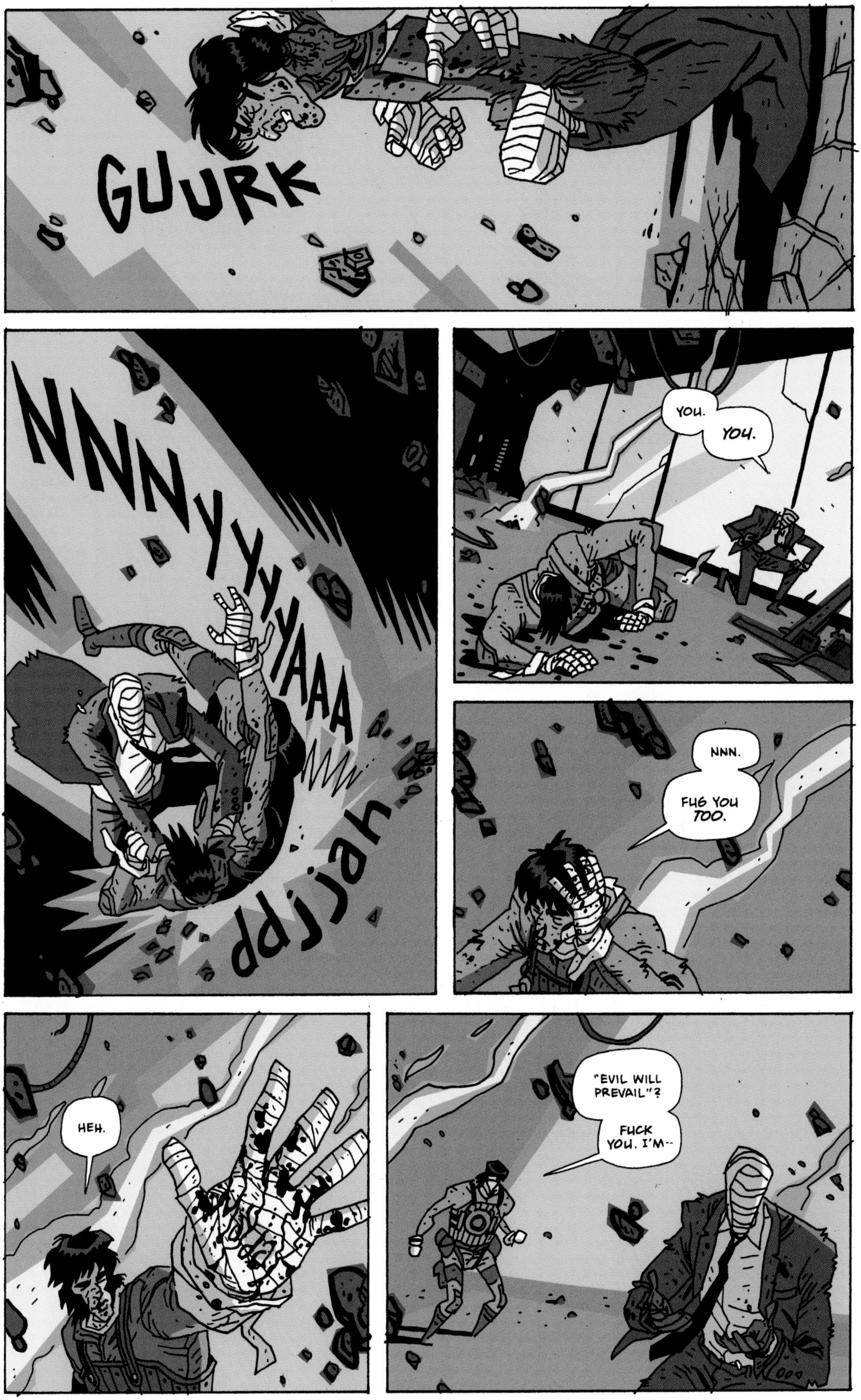
GUURK
NNNyyyyYAAA
ddjjah
YOU.
YOU.
NNN.
FUG YOU TOO.
HEH.
"EVIL WILL PREVAIL"?
FUCK YOU. I'M--

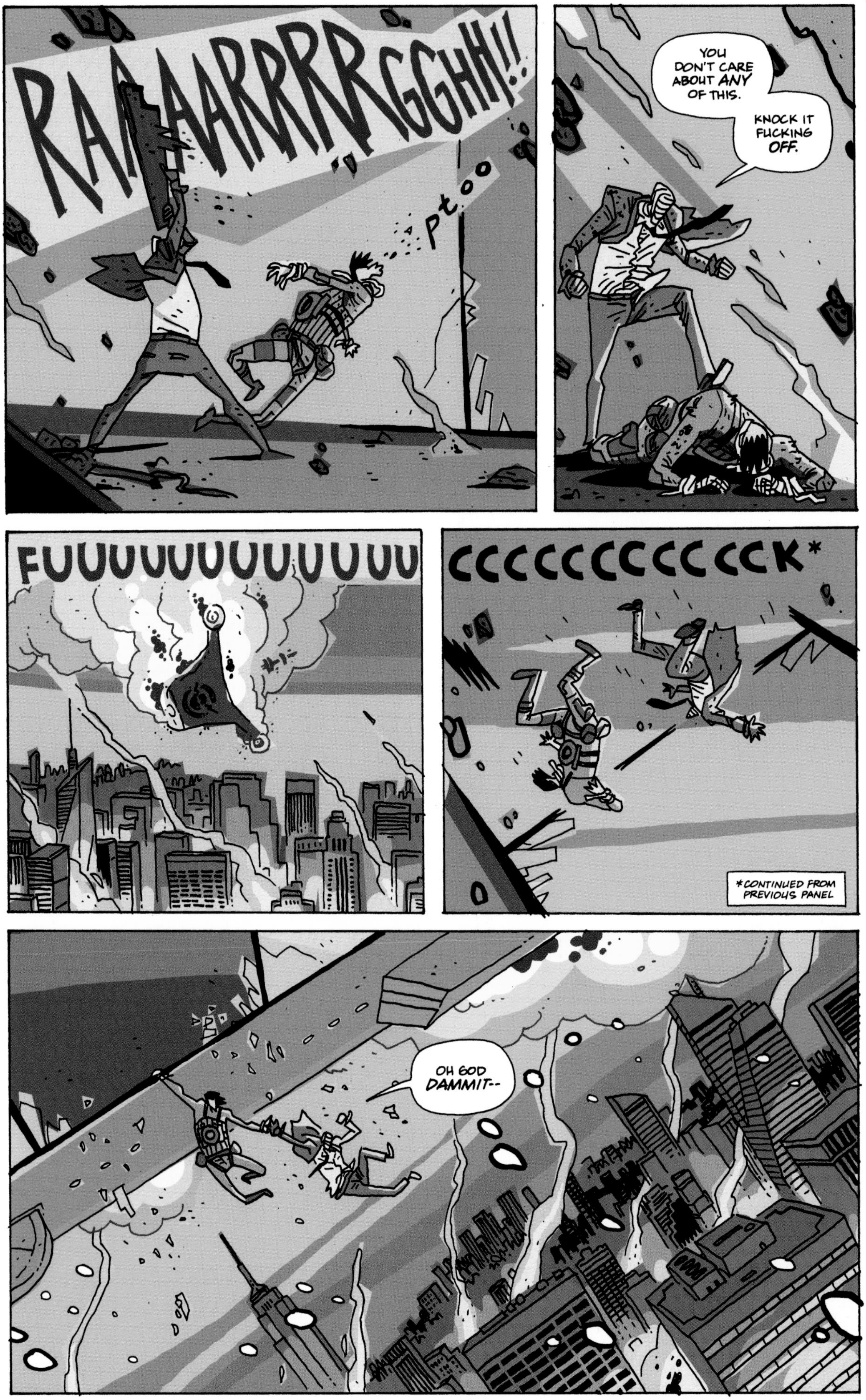
RAAAARRRRGGHH!!
ptoo
YOU DON'T CARE ABOUT ANY OF THIS.
KNOCK IT FUCKING OFF.
FUUUUUUUUUUUU
CCCCCCCCCCCK*
*CONTINUED FROM PREVIOUS PANEL
OH GOD DAMMIT--

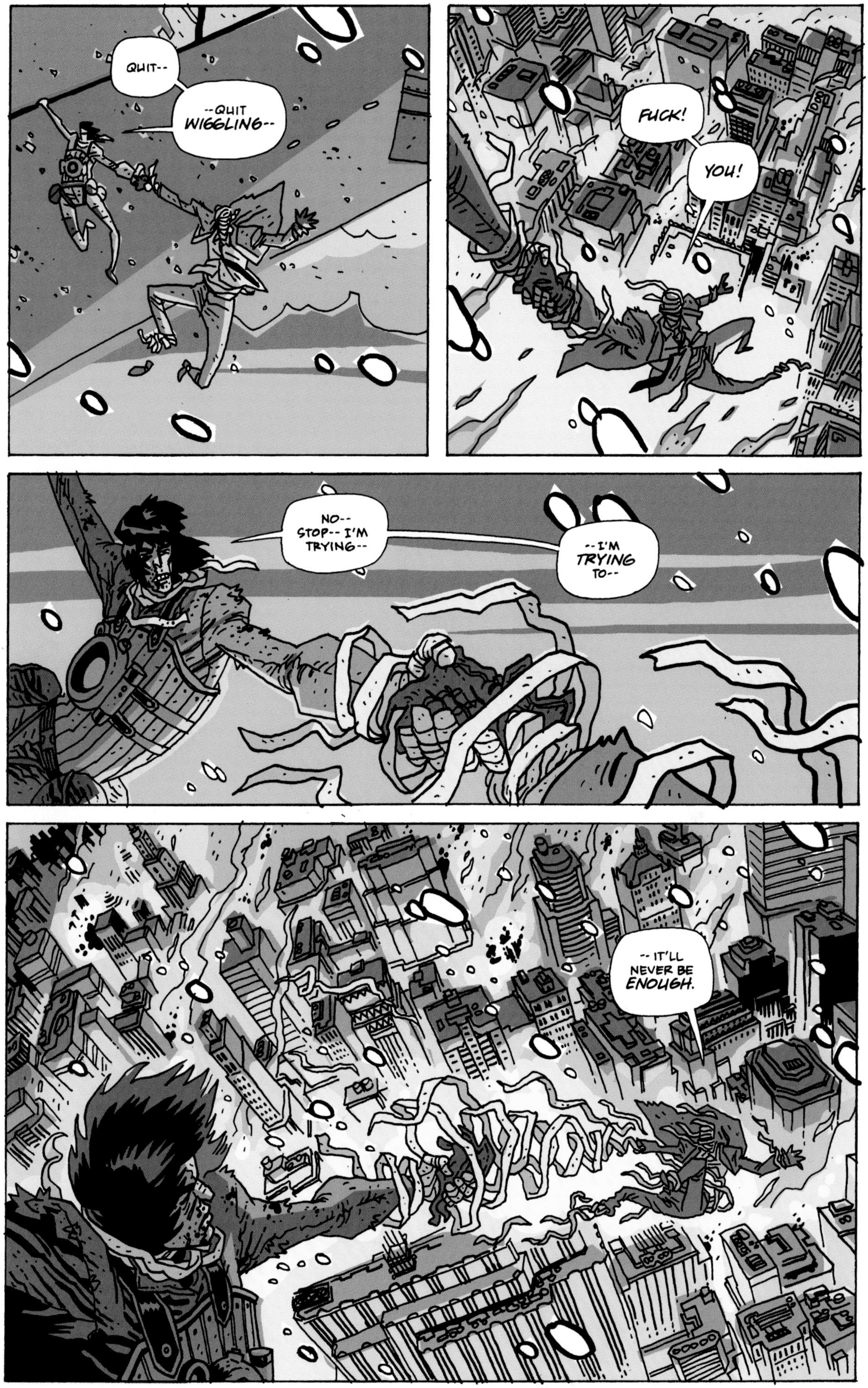
QUIT--
--QUIT WIGGLING--
FUCK!
YOU!
NO-- STOP-- I'M TRYING--
--I'M TRYING TO--
--IT'LL NEVER BE ENOUGH.

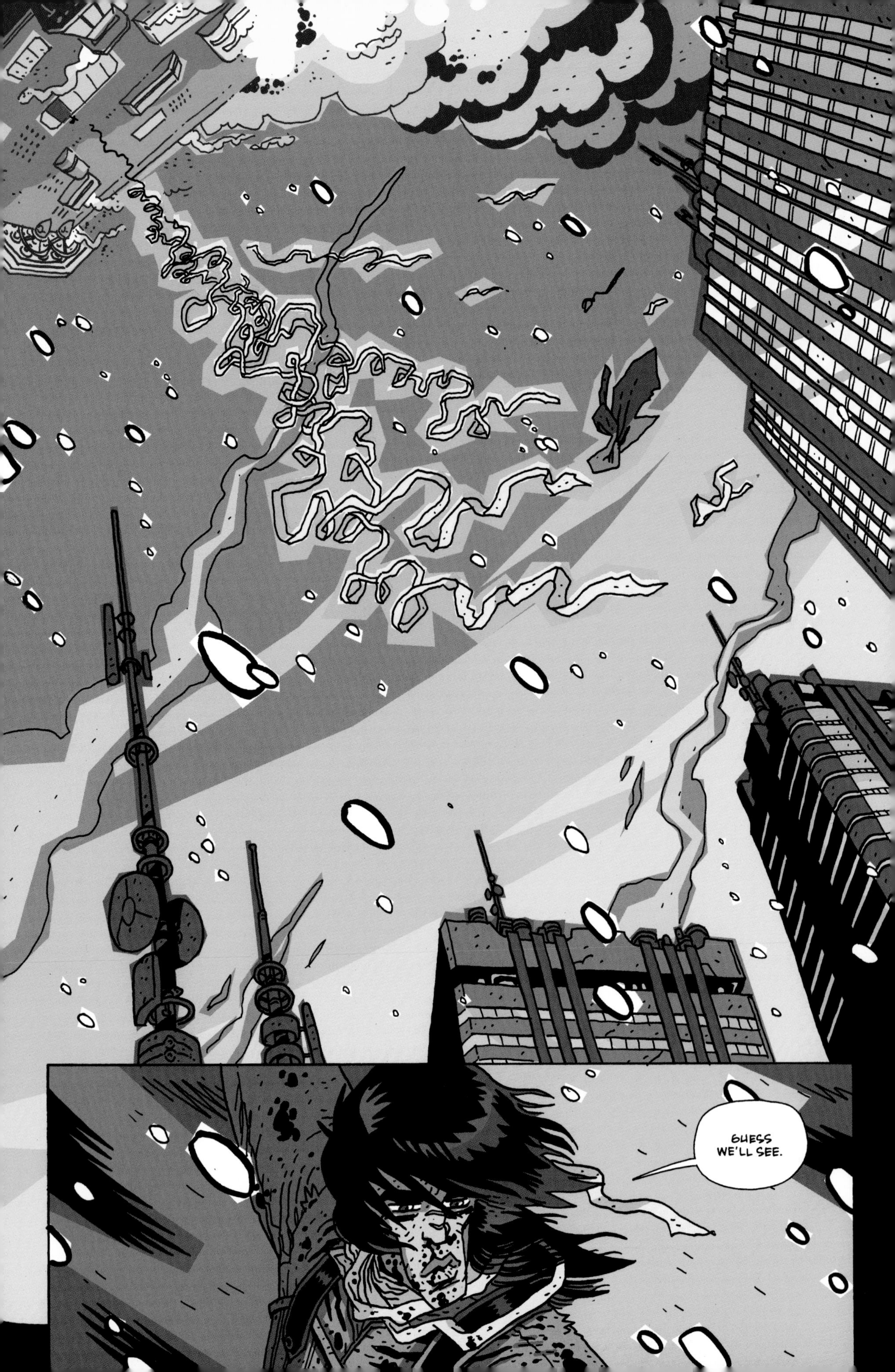
GUESS WE'LL SEE.

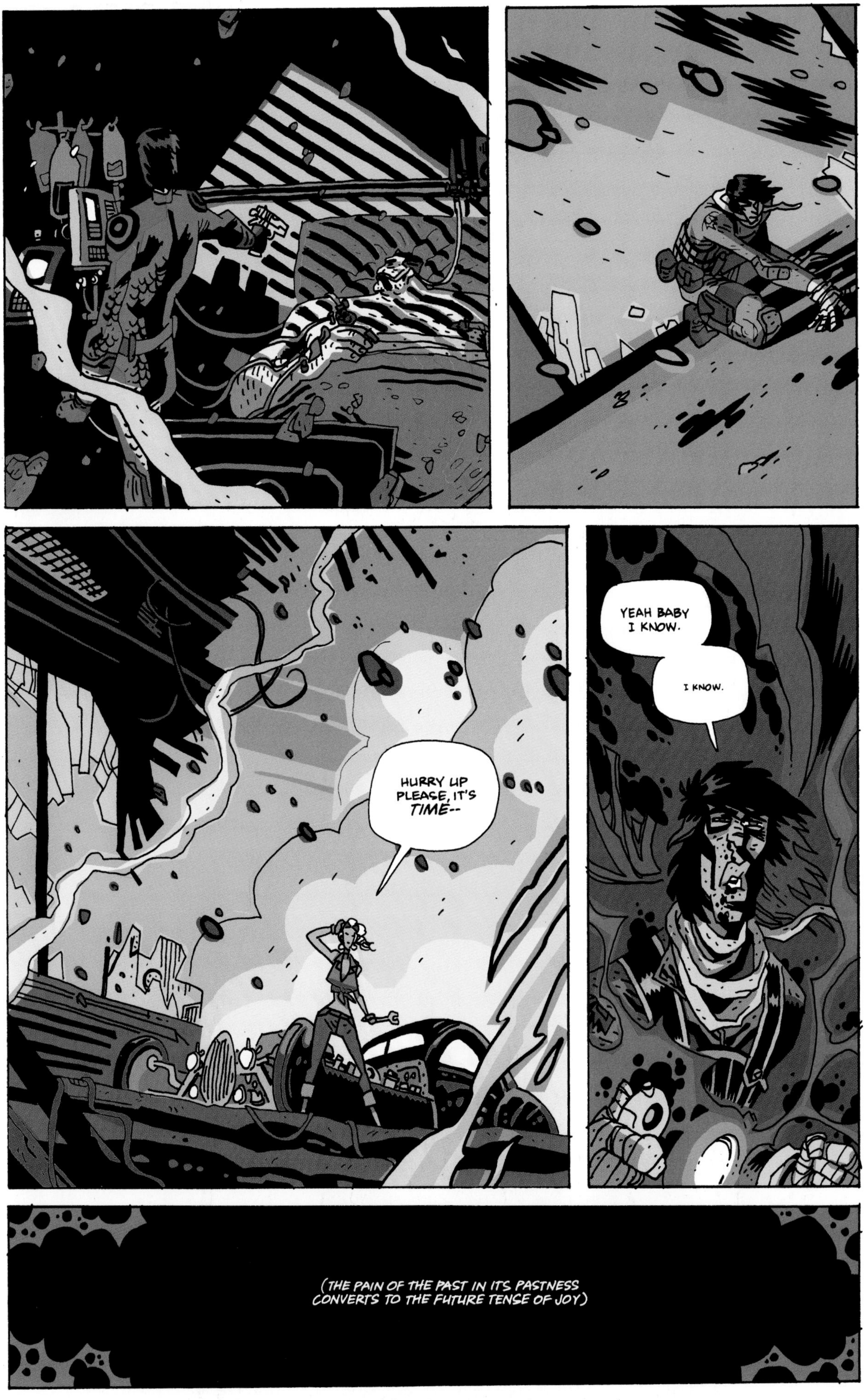
HURRY UP PLEASE, IT'S TIME--
YEAH BABY I KNOW.
I KNOW.
(THE PAIN OF THE PAST IN ITS PASTNESS CONVERTS TO THE FUTURE TENSE OF JOY)

12. WE ARE THE DEAD

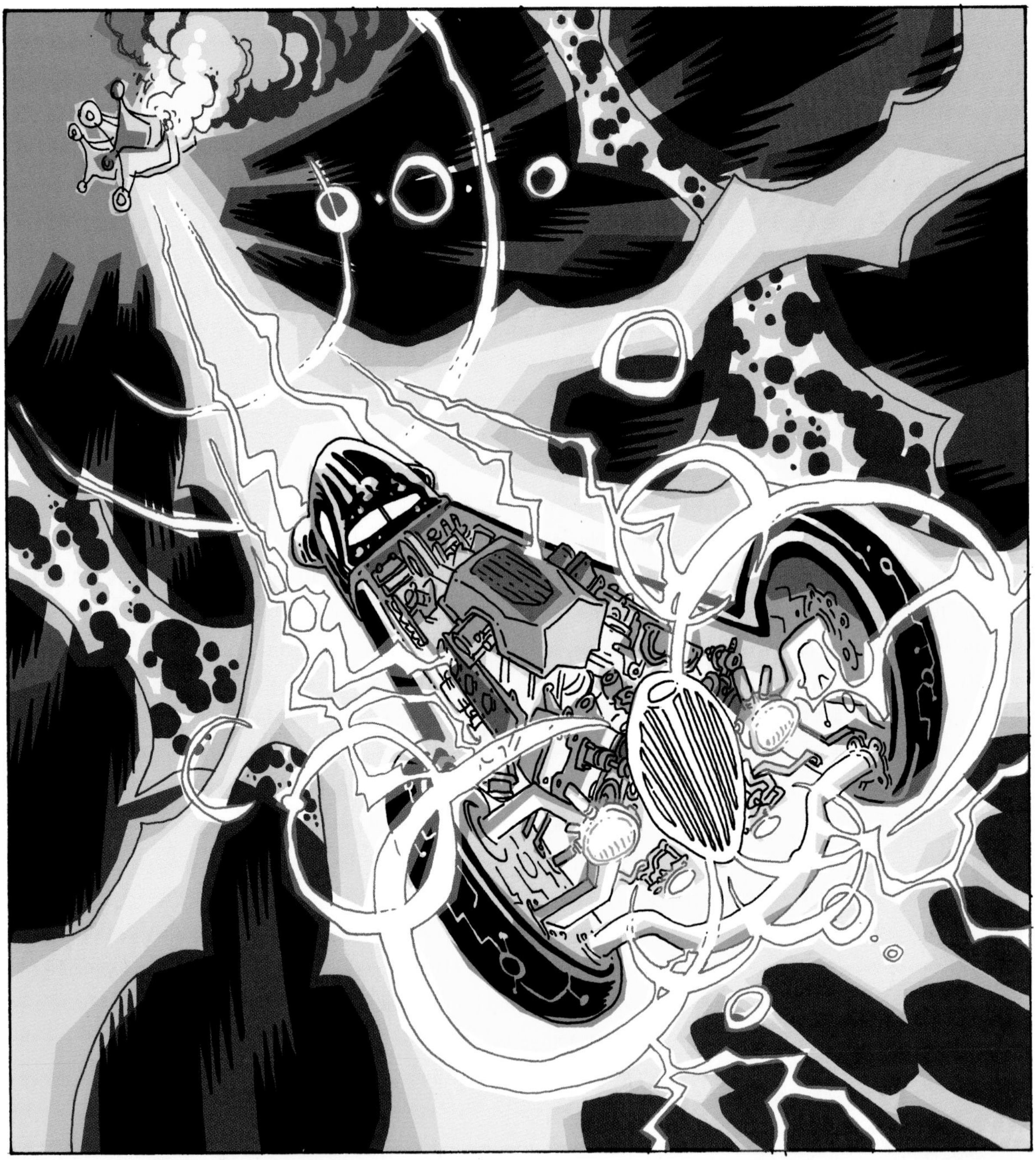

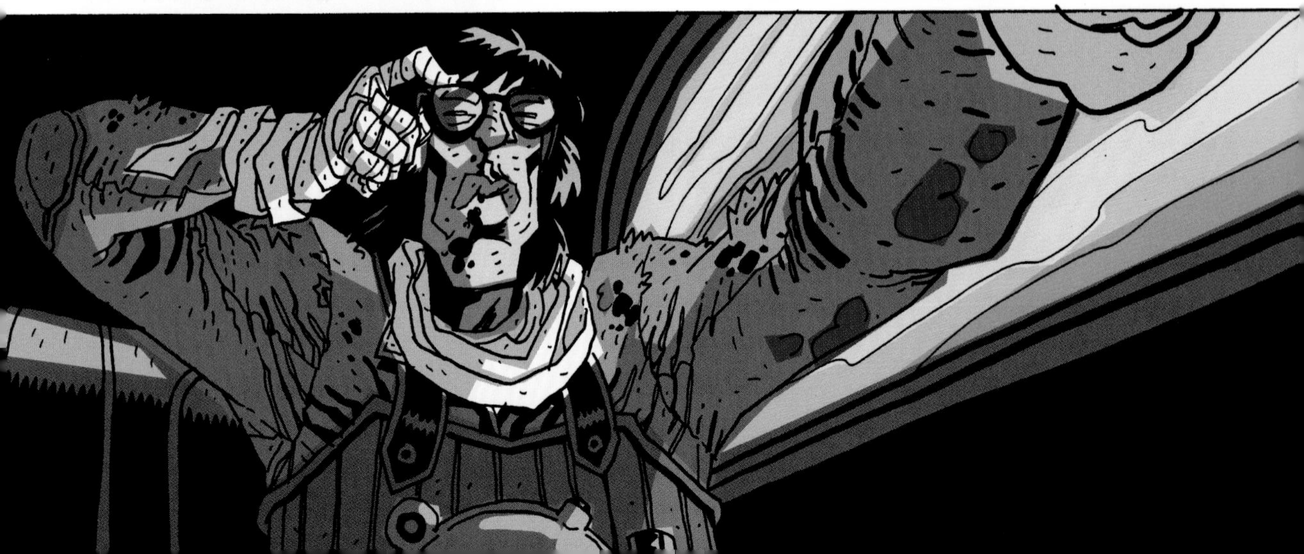

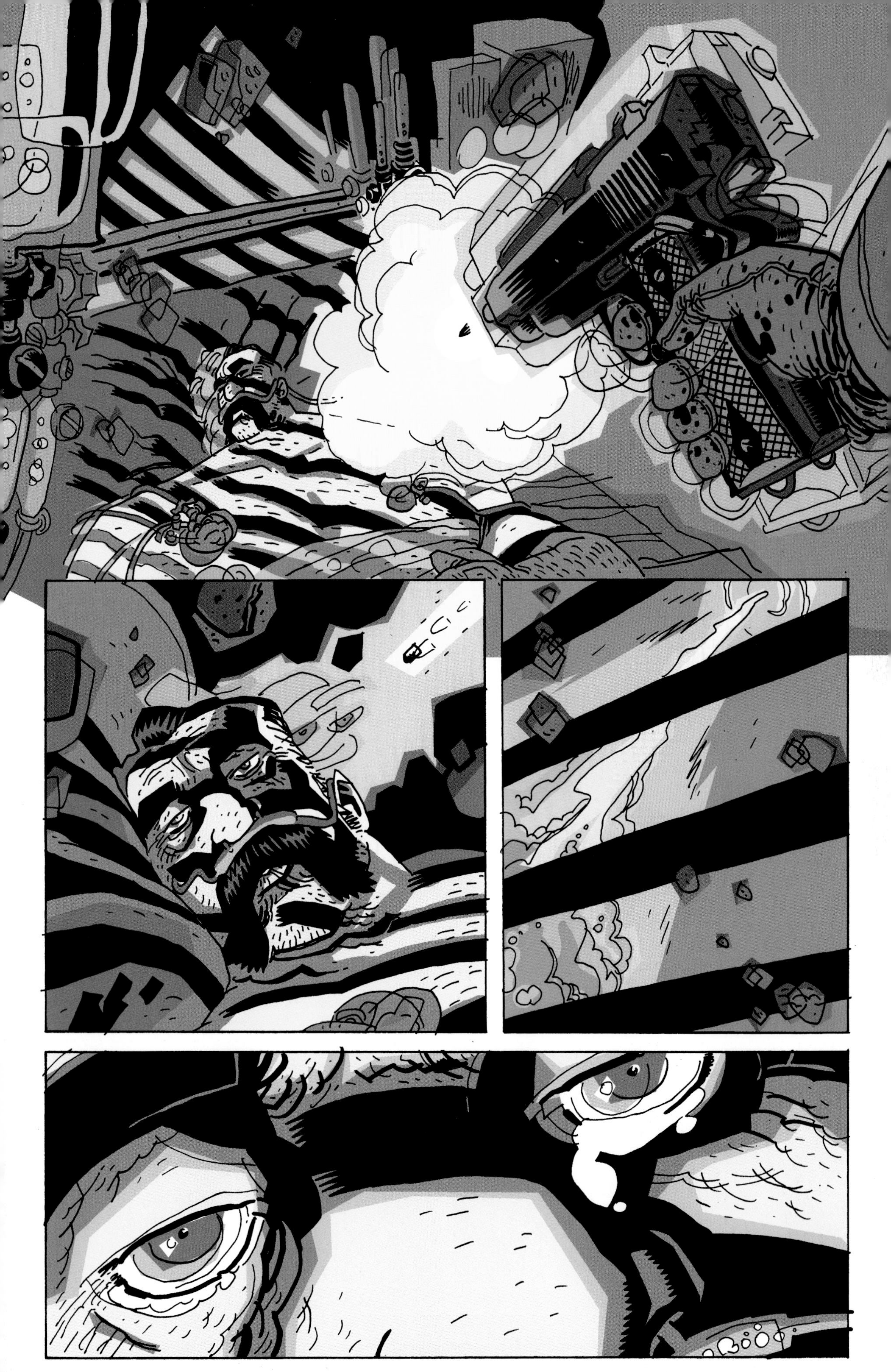

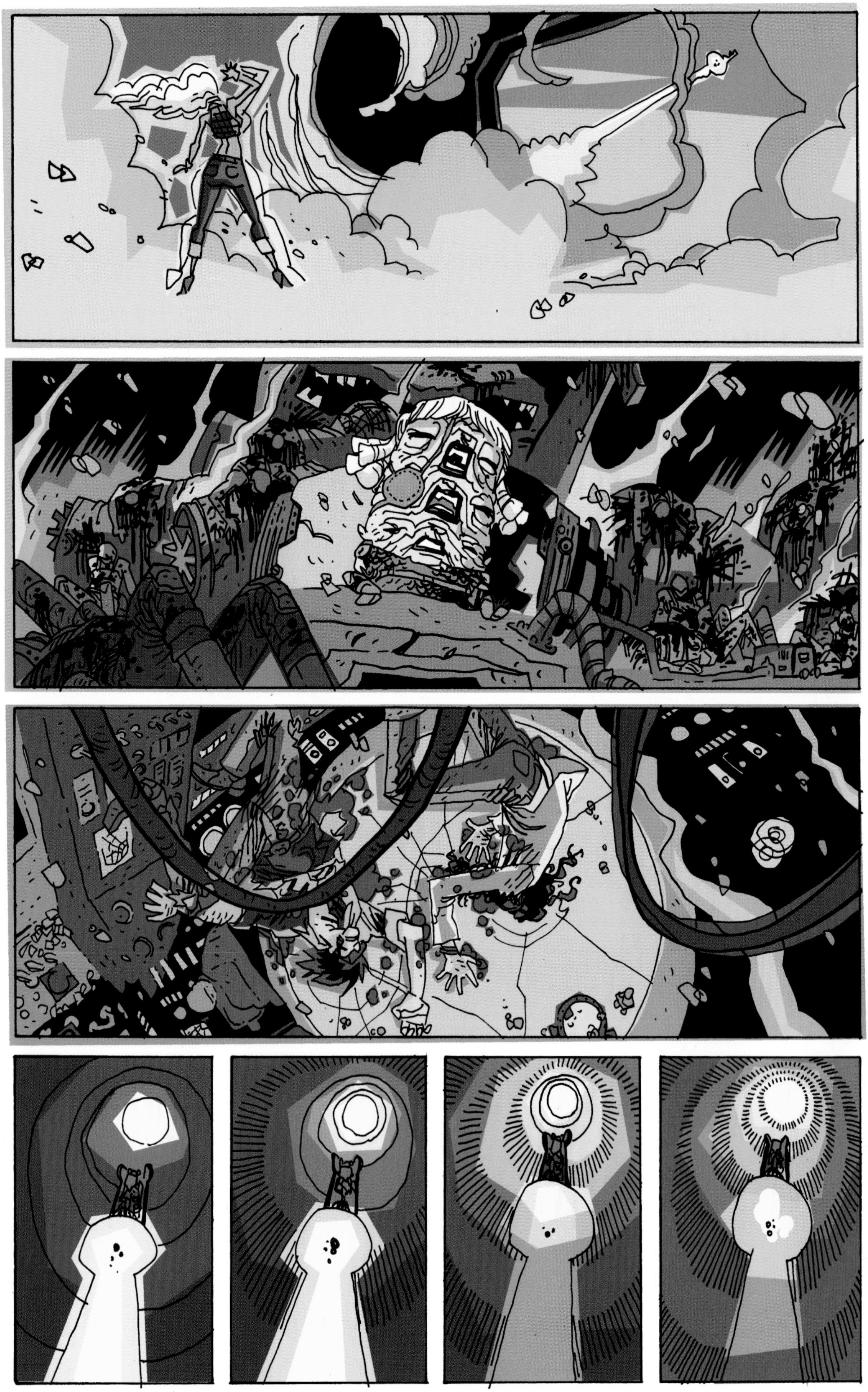

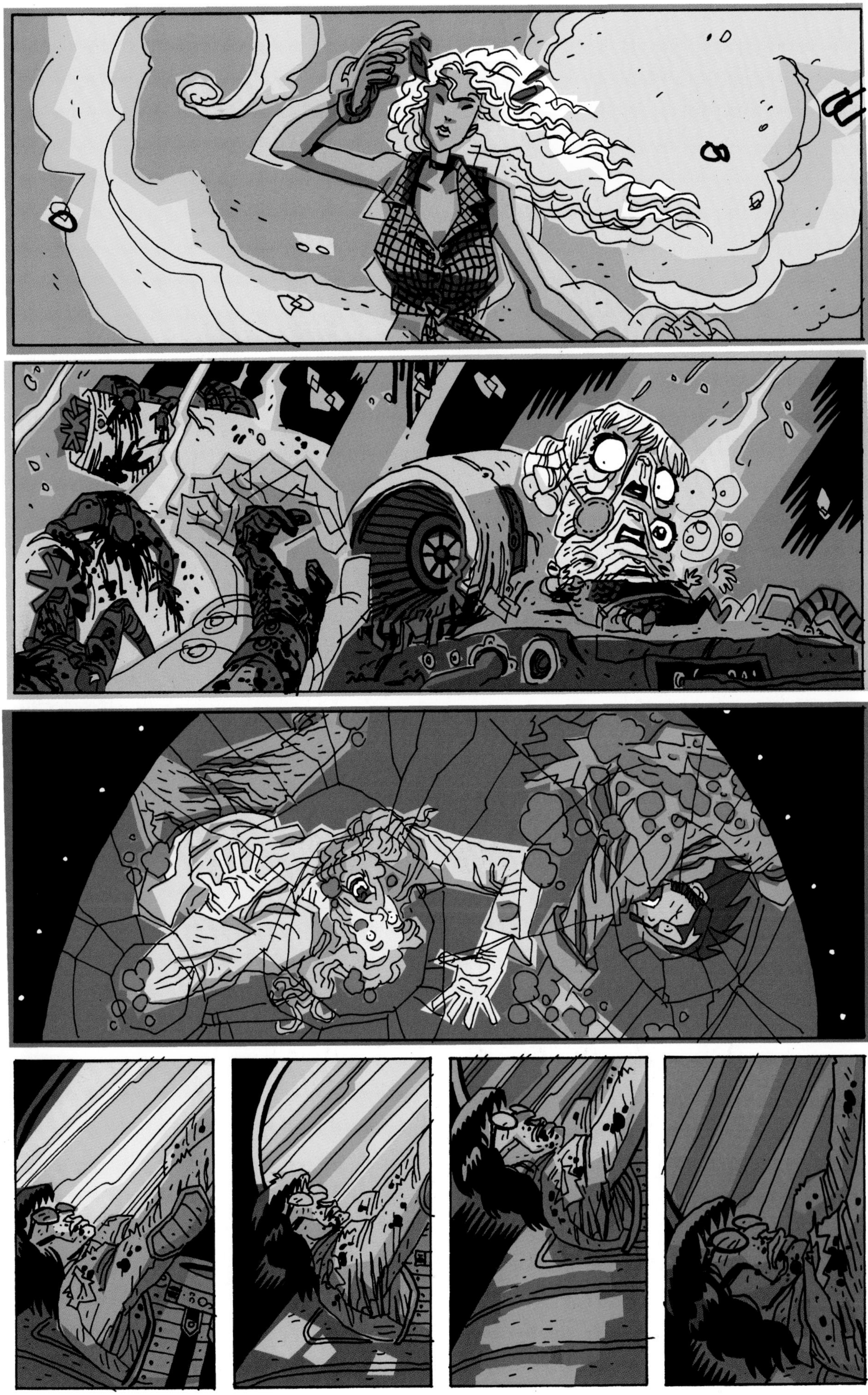

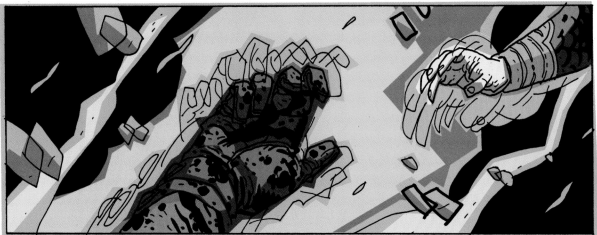

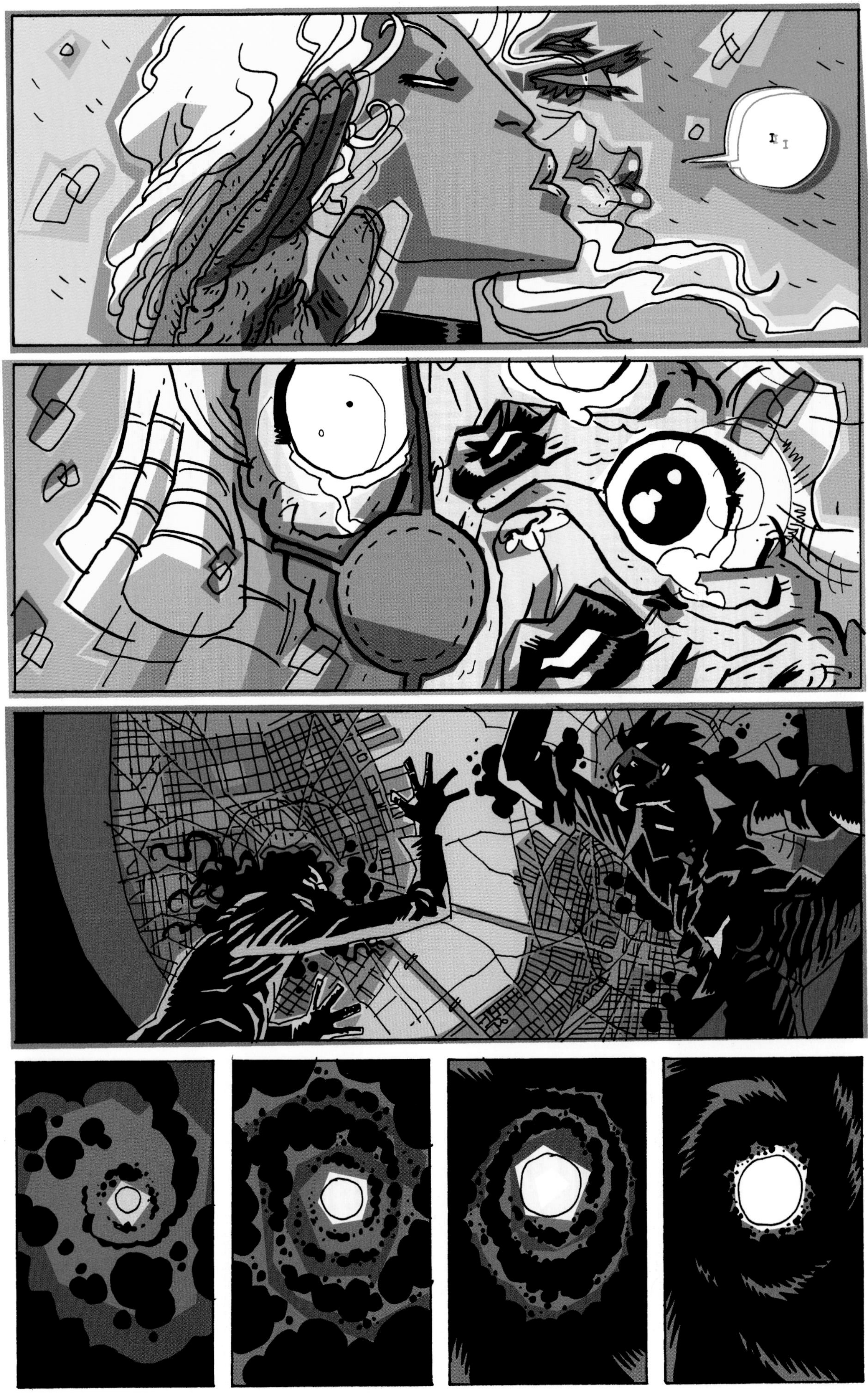
I I I

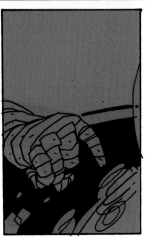

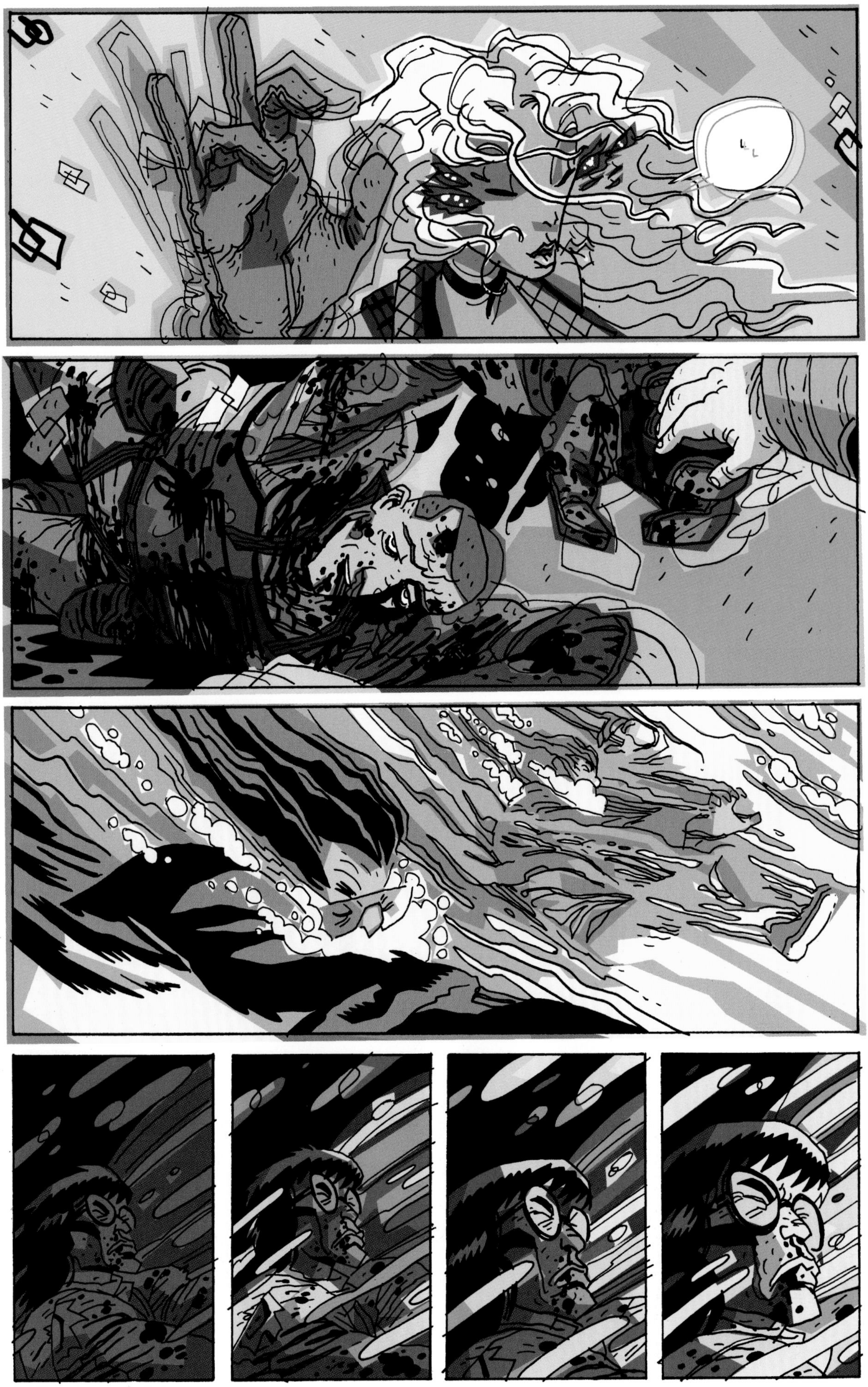

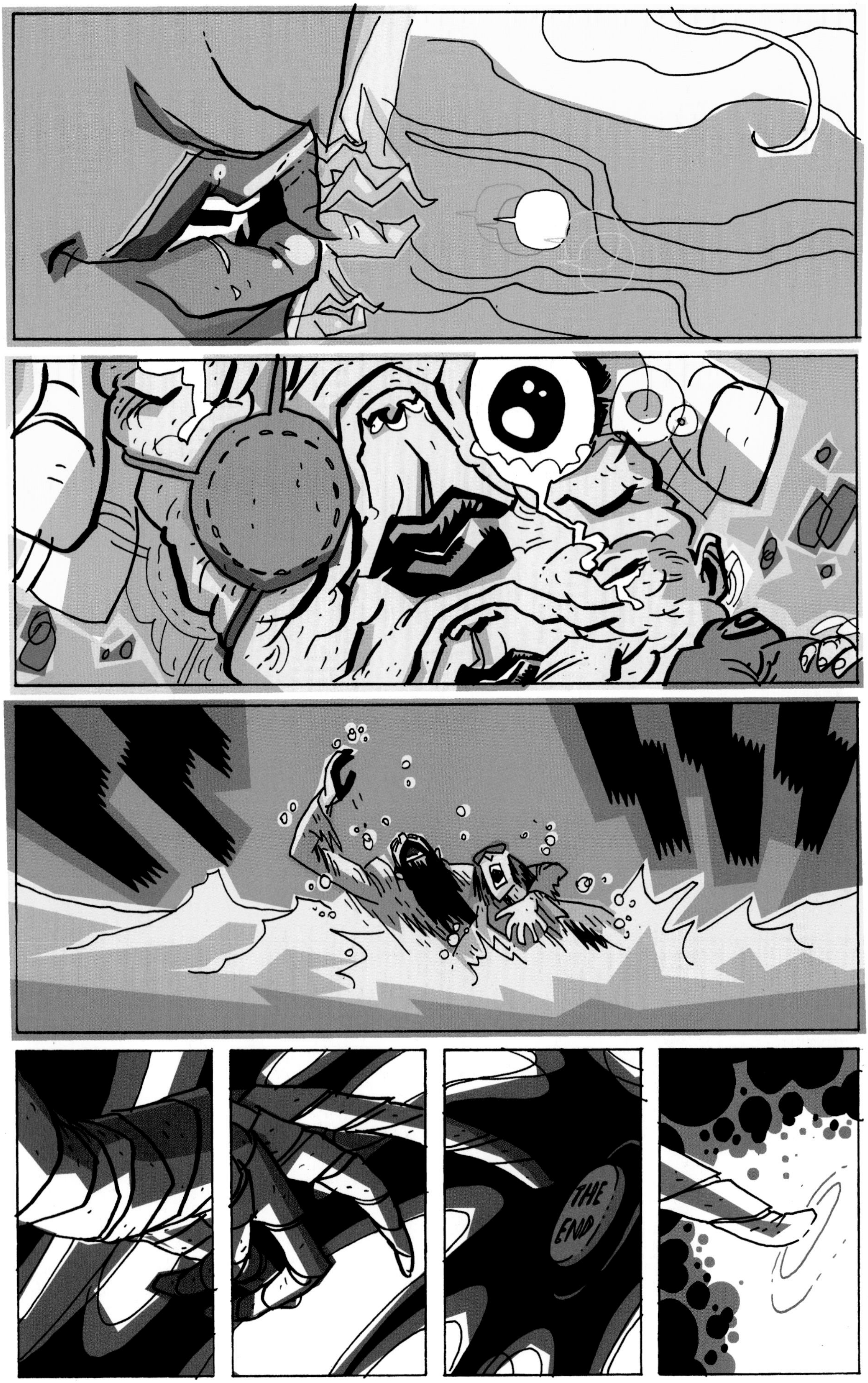
THE END

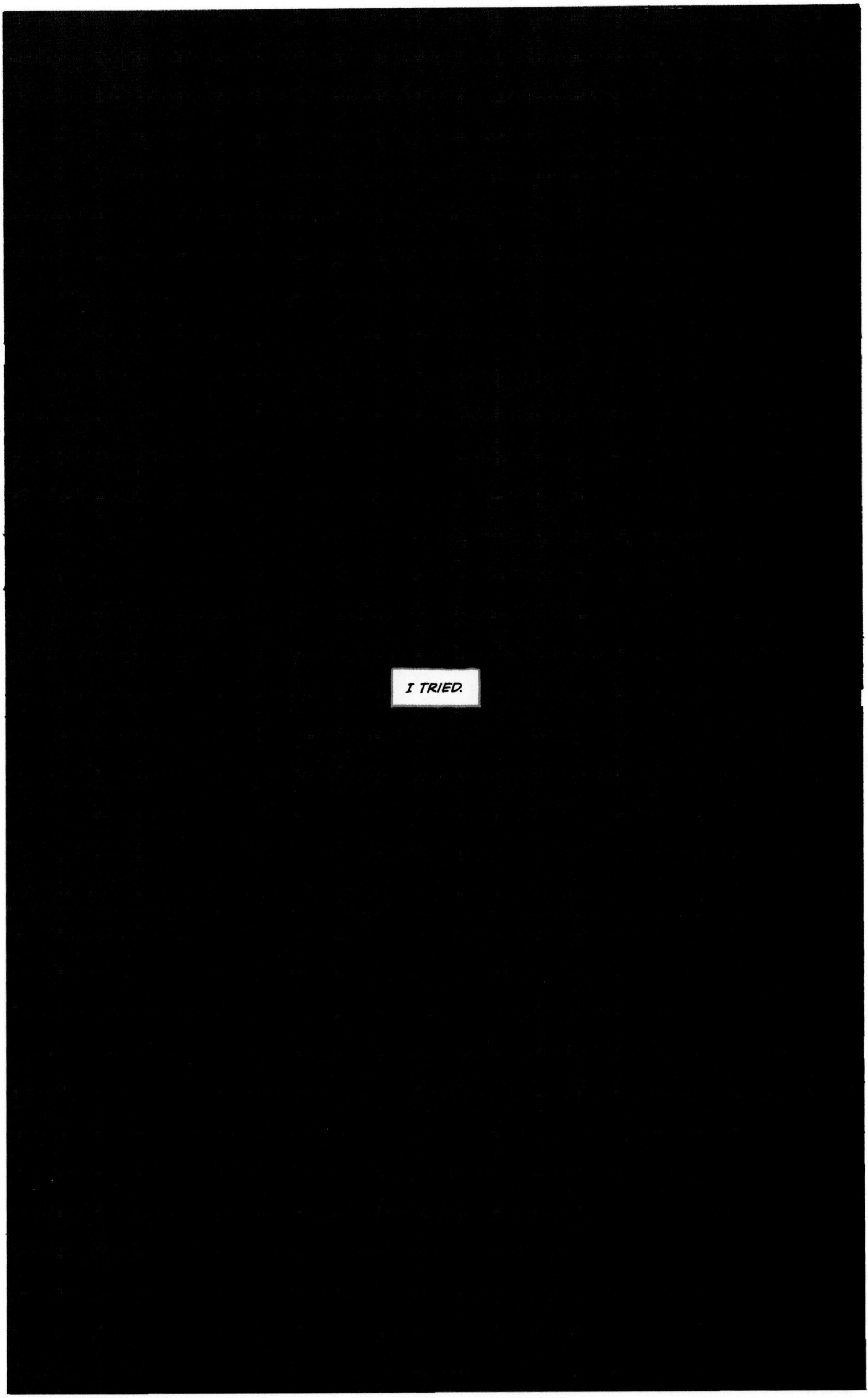
I TRIED.

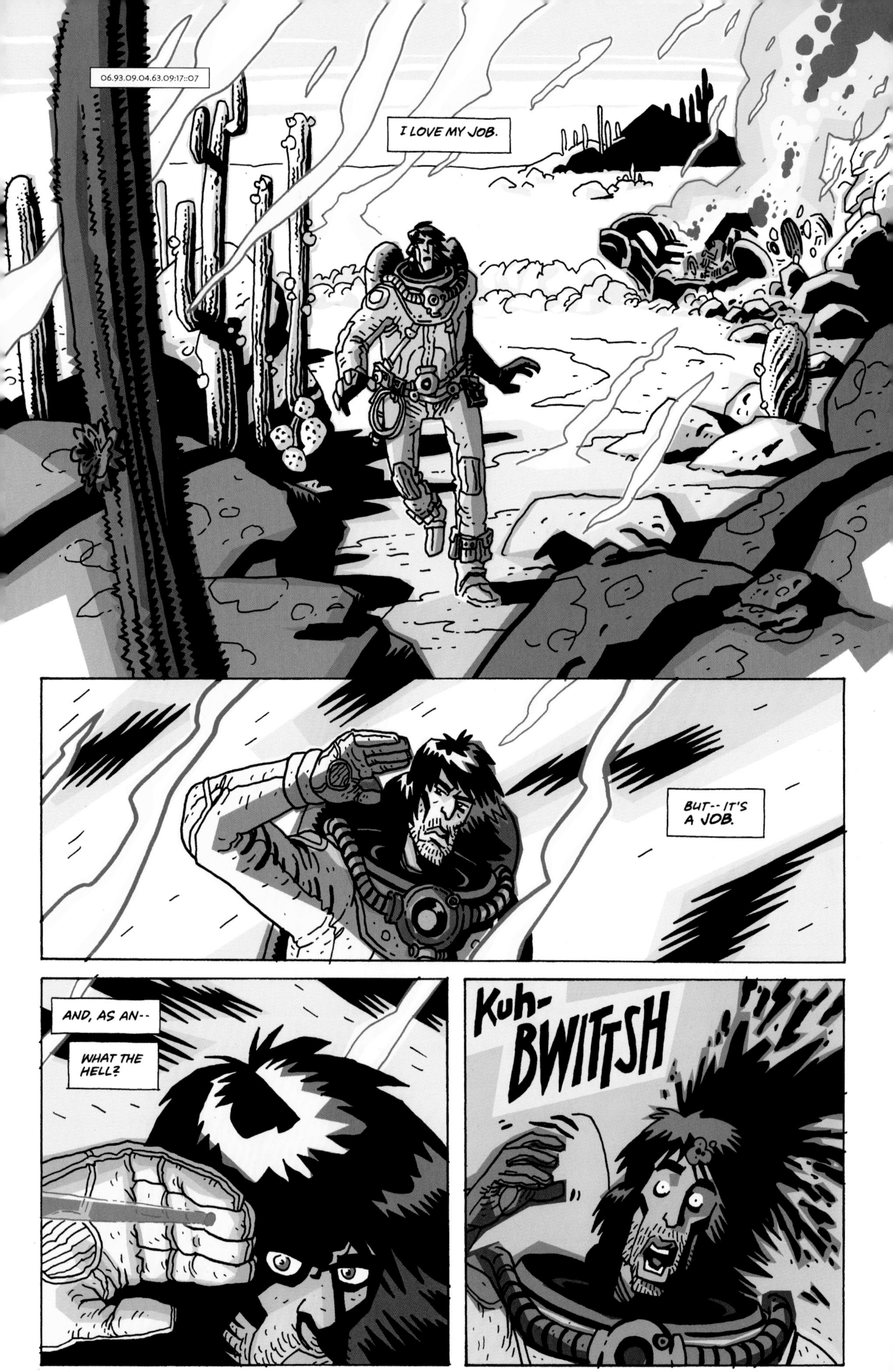
06.93.09.04.63.09:17::07
I LOVE MY JOB.
BUT-- IT'S A JOB.
AND, AS AN--
WHAT THE HELL?
Kuh-BWITTSH

CASANOVA
QUINN
V6.93

CASANOVA
QUINN
V3.z2

CASANOVA
QUINN
V2.a35

CASANOVA
QUINN
VA.A7o

CASANOVA
QUINN
V5.we

CASANOVA
QUINN
V8.d#t21

CASANOVA
QUINN
V3.o2h33

CASANOVA
QUINN
V6.1ddO4

CASANOVA
QUINN
VO.3t-2°°

CASANOVA
QUINN
V4.d0p8

CASANOVA
QUINN
V1.2zon

CASANOVA
QUINN
V5.oVa3t

CASANOVA
QUINN
Va.-

CASANOVA
QUINN
VK.30t-2

CASANOVA
QUINN
V1

GOD
DAMMIT.

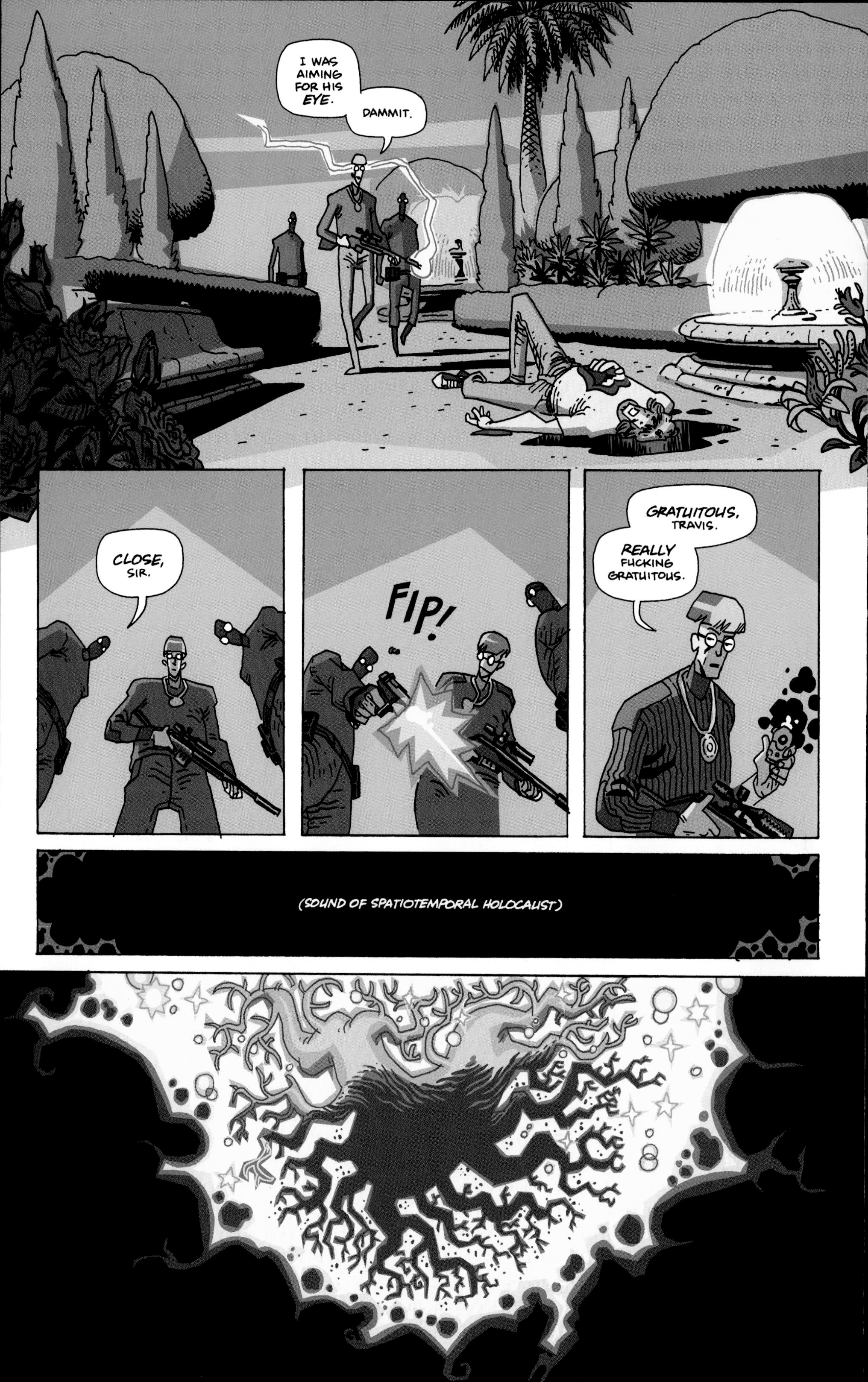
I WAS AIMING FOR HIS EYE.
DAMMIT.
CLOSE, SIR.
FIP!
GRATUITOUS, TRAVIS.
REALLY FUCKING GRATUITOUS.
(SOUND OF SPATIOTEMPORAL HOLOCAUST)

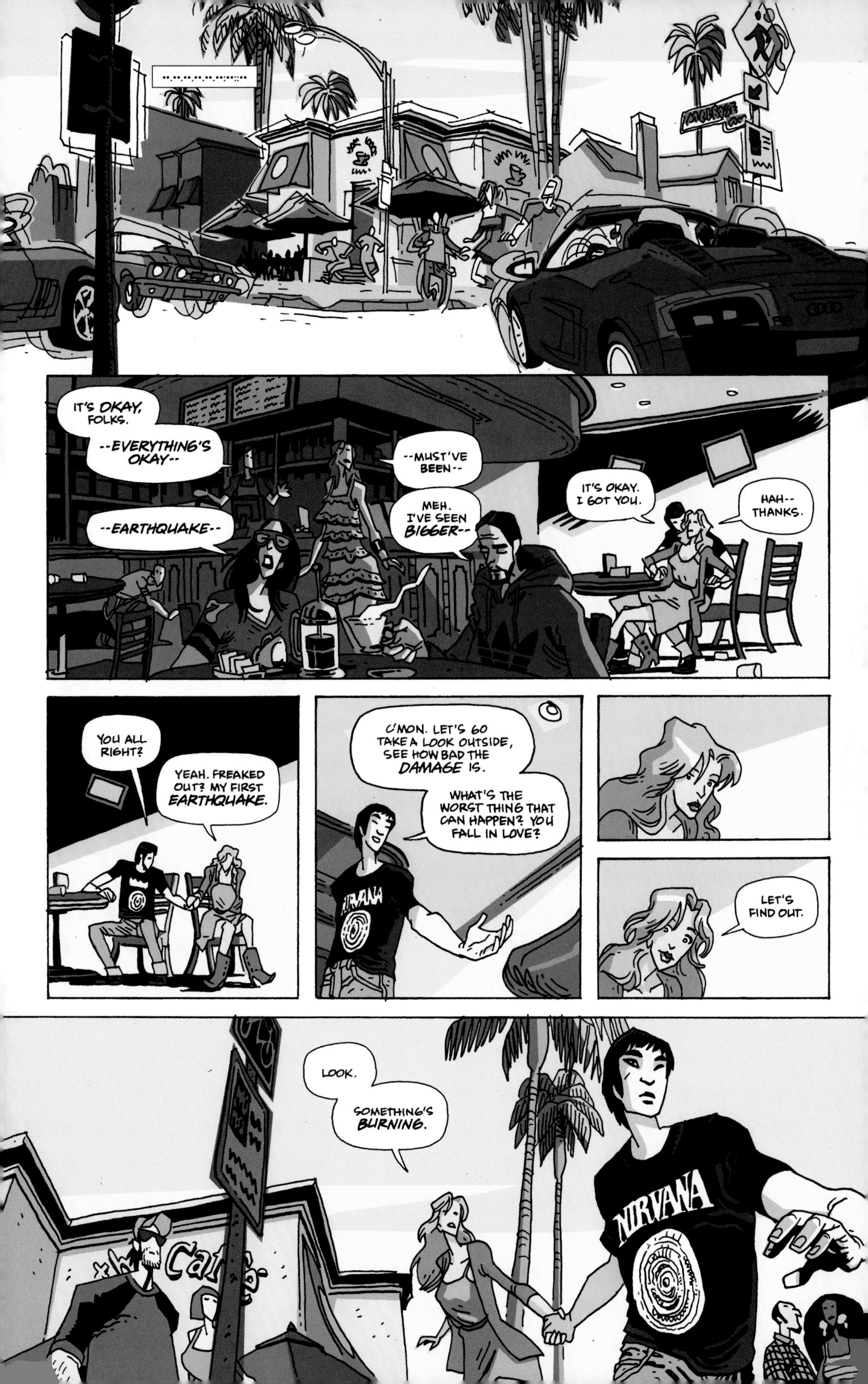
IT'S OKAY, FOLKS.
--EVERYTHING'S OKAY--
--EARTHQUAKE--
--MUST'VE BEEN--
MEH. I'VE SEEN BIGGER--
IT'S OKAY. I GOT YOU.
HAH-- THANKS.
YOU ALL RIGHT?
YEAH. FREAKED OUT? MY FIRST EARTHQUAKE.
C'MON. LET'S GO TAKE A LOOK OUTSIDE, SEE HOW BAD THE DAMAGE IS.
WHAT'S THE WORST THING THAT CAN HAPPEN? YOU FALL IN LOVE?
LET'S FIND OUT.
LOOK.
SOMETHING'S BURNING.
NIRVANA
NIRVANA
Cafe

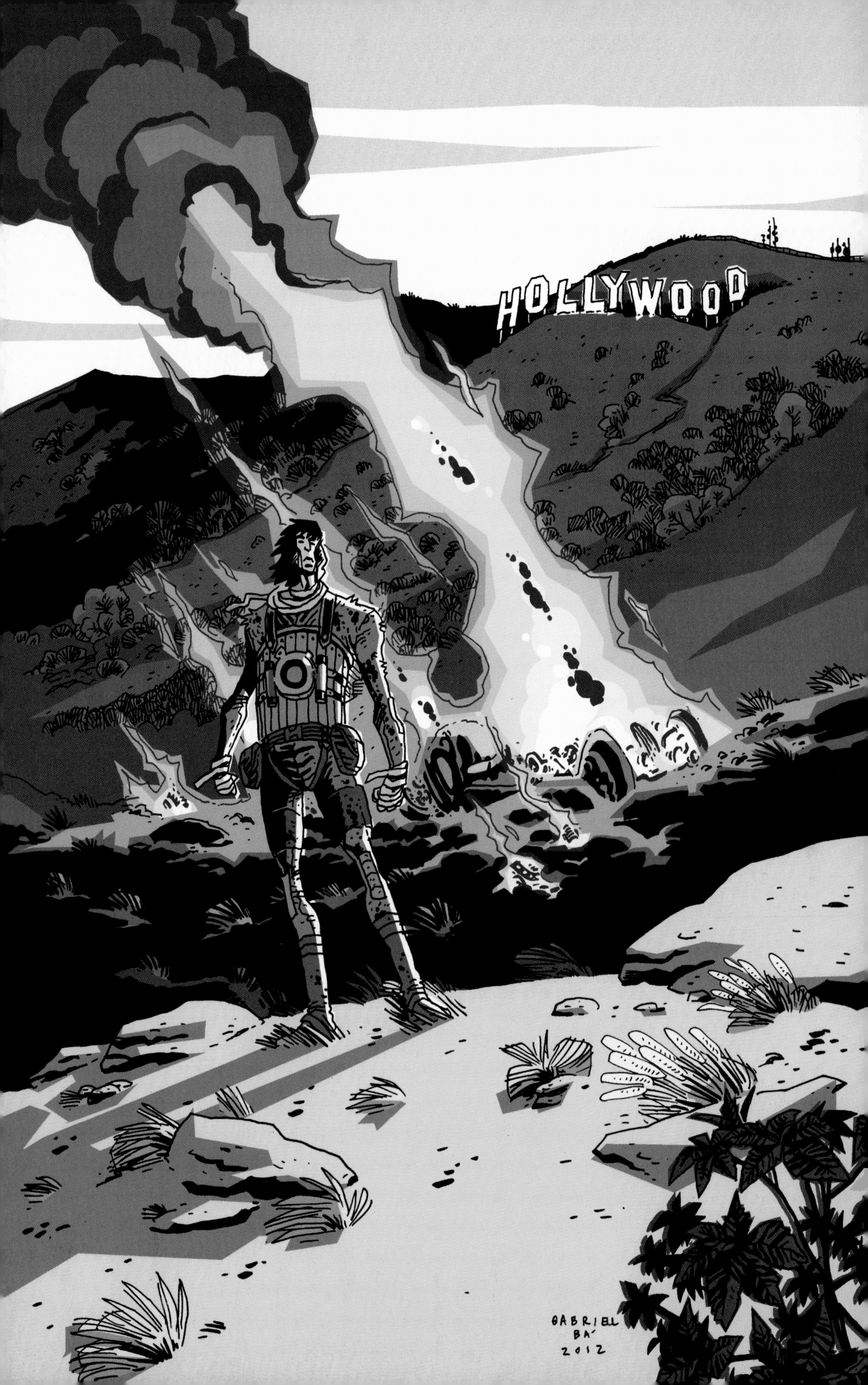
HOLLYWOOD
GABRIELL BÁ 2012

W.A.S.T.E.-FREE WILDERNESS

WHAT IF IT'S NEVER ENOUGH

HARM REDUCTION

RELAXED IN PERSON

BACKMATTER

AVARITIA[1] 1 (Icon Comics, 2011)

As I was saying.

Welcome back, cats and kittens (and crypto-cisgendered post-binary QYTTNS, I suppose), to CASANOVA. How you been? You're looking good.

I am looking old. I got grey hairs and started naming them after X-Men[2]. I got a daughter and it's completely blown up the way everything looks to me forever. The twins are looking famous. They have won more awards than the god of awards and have been perched atop the *New York Times* best-seller list[3]. Cris, goddess of all spectra, is seeing things beyond the veil of mortal man, and Dharbin is seeing many many things that are very very tiny. Including many tiny Robocops[4]. Did you know that a 'björk' is the proper collective noun for multiple Robocops? It is. A 'björk of Robocops.'

I wrote this issue all over the world over a very long year. Or rather, I rewrote this issue, literally, over a calendar year. Getting a little bit into it, blowing it up, starting again. Stalling, restarting, re-attacking, and reworking. Reading more and more brilliant things, finding new veins of inspiration and feeling like a giftless hack and doing it all over again[5]. There were easily twice as many pages thrown out as were actually delivered to the boys for their art-ening (that's a technical term fuck you I went to art school). *Missgeburt*, as the Germans[6] say. "Messy birth."

See, thing is this: when we wrapped GULA we didn't know when AVARITIA was going to happen and simply went into hibernation. Once we got the where and when of CASANOVA'S triumphant return (and, believe me, it WAS triumphant—the reprints doing as good or better than the originals ever did), I sat down and re-read all of LUXURIA and GULA and came away with one single thought that haunts every page of AVARITIA to date:

"This is not so good."[7]

So it took a while BECAUSE I AM CRAZY.

We're back now. Hi.

Rather than bloviate endlessly in these pages[8], I want to open them up and start having dialogues with you folks. It's a dead art, the comic book letter column, and I miss it. The argument was that social networks, or ur-social networks, nascent social networks, etc., made them obsolete and, in a sense, they did; why read what people were thinking three months ago about a book that came out six months ago? However now, to me, as social networks have become constant dopamine triggers maximized at 140 characters, speed and ubiquity have, as always, replaced depth[9].

I never gave a shit about what people thought about the comics I read, not in particular, anyway; I gave a shit about dialogues with the creative teams, the glimpses behind the scenes, the hint, however subtle, at meaningful conversation. The feeling that I and the other people that actually *read the letter columns too* were, in some way, connect to everything[10]. THE INVISIBLES had a great letter column. TRANSMETROPOLITAN. The backmatter of HATE[11]. I even loved STAN'S SOAPBOX. There are a dozen more I'm sure—and no, don't say CEREBUS as I've never read it and have no interest, quite frankly—but I'm on a plane as I type this part[12] and have no shelf of books to stare at to jog my memory.

---

1   Oh, oh god, oh god how I've resisted writing this. I literally made this book slip out of its schedule because I didn't want to revisit AVARITIA.

Well, let's start at the start, I guess. AVARITIA happened later and later in our creative lives ('our' meaning the twins and mine) for this reason or that, and because "I haven't lived enough life yet to write it" feels like the only important one here, now, in 2015, looking back. I think about the old sculptor's canard, about knowing the statue's form, hiding inside the block of marble, and the sculptor's job meant the removal of every bit of marble NOT the statue. I recall feeling a lack, an absence of experience; in my life things happened that had not resolved and I recall feeling that I couldn't write AVARITIA until some form of resolution came.

AVARITIA started about half-way through a really hard five year stretch, an annus horribilis that just kept growing and growing. I remember thinking, oh, god, I hope this isn't growing up. I hope life just doesn't turn into this because we reach half-way and everything goes downhill.

When my father was diagnosed with stage-three lung cancer, I knew I could start writing.

2   Absolutely true. The day my daughter was born, my wife handed her to me and, with love in her eyes, said "you've got grey hairs," referring, clearly, to this start of our journey into parents-of-two-dom; I, ruining the moment, said "I'm going to name them 'Scott' and 'Emma.'" She used to say she knew when I was working on X-MEN because I'd go stomping around the house in heavy boots. I do not miss it.

3   The dirty secret that, for a long time, only Gerard Way (Bá's collaborator on THE UMBRELLA ACADEMY and apparently a songster of some sort) and I knew: the twins didn't need to work with writers. Their brilliant, staggering, utterly human and lovely DAYTRIPPER pretty much told the whole world. Fuckers. Mother FUCKERS.

4   I have no idea.

5   Very true. Thirty, forty, fifty pages maybe never saw the light of day because... because more amazing comics kept happening and I felt I had to up my game.

6   So perfect. Missgeburt. Perfect.

7   Very true. I remember—my body remembers—the physical sensation of putting GULA down, on the night I started AVARITIA and realizing that this thing I thought had made my bones did not, in fact, cut the current mustard. It might have, for the writer I was in 2006 and 2008 but two years on from that... no. Humbling experience that.

8   Pfft.

9   I still think this! Way to go, past me!

10   While CASANOVA's publishing schedule remained too erratic to right this ship, I have experienced this phenomenon in my own comics now, namely with SEX CRIMINALS, whose letter columns *inspired a separate book* and have *gotten people laid* and *inspired readers to fuck one another's hair.* So clearly I wasn't the only one feeling that lack.

11   To this day, HATE #27 remains the high-water mark of great single issue of a comic. Of course, as per footnote 7, having not read the thing in a while, who knows. I still remember, though, the feel of it in my hands; of laughing so hard I started to cough; of reading then immediately rereading; of poring over the columns and backups (Alan Moore? Kool-Aid Man? What?), of feeling wholly *satiated.* Nothing, not even the relentless march of time, can change that.

12   America's airports and convention centers are one long smear of groggy memory and fluorescent-lit corridors with bad geometric carpets. I dream of endless labyrinthian conventions where we shuffle from one place to the next, never stopping, never arriving, simply traveling.

Because, here's the thing: I am 100% addicted to everything all the time. I try to limit my social network bullshit because it engulfs everything around me if left unchecked[13]. That means work doesn't get done, family doesn't get loved, life doesn't get lived—while there may be a few other issues that I push to the surface of things, the ultimate truth is that. I get engulfed, I don't write, I ignore everything and get super-direly unhealthy.

Anyhoo. Maybe we should aim for slower and deeper over faster and more furious, said the actress to the bishop's dick, which she held in her hand during a story that would later on be recounted to indicate possible a double entendre before being usurped by 'that's what she said.'

Oh! Oh, one more thing, in case you're returning to CASANOVA and didn't read the reprint stuff: I outed myself as an alcoholic and addict in recovery[14]. So if you've ever met me at a show and offered to smoke me out or toll or trip or buy me a drink—there have been many of you—and I demurred, I wasn't trying to come off like a dick. I was trying to not make you feel uncomfortable by saying, "No, thank you, I'm an alcoholic and an addict in recovery for years now, but thank you all the same."

OKAY shutting up. CASANOVA: AVARITIA letter column here we go:

Matt and Los Bros Bá-Moon, or is it Moon-Bá,

I can not even begin to state how excited I am that Vol 3 is ready to be birthed into the world and hopefully my iPad. Regardless the re-release of the first 2 volumes of CASANOVA gave me a good reason to further delve into why I love this book probably more than any other comic book.

The short and poignant way is the Secret Cinema. It showed with an economy of words and pictures what comics can do and why I still read them. I have given that issue to more friends than I can even count.

But I am equally excited because I have been desperate to know what happened to the real Zephyr since the release of 13 & 14 way back when, and it's finally about to happen.

So I will break out my W.A.S.T.E. sticker from Heroes Con '06, who knew that buying issue 1 from you and Kelly Sue would be the best 2 dollars spent on my entire trip down to NC.

We Are So Terribly Excited indeed!
-Neil Cameron

SECRET CINEMA[15] is a riff on the amazing short film by Paul Bartel from 1968. One of those things I saw in film school and haven't seen since. Bartel would go on to make DEATH RACE 2000 which, if for some reason you've never seen, SEE. It's dark and absurd and bleak and funny and fantastic for any number of reasons. I wear a Frankenstein 'F' shirt[16], I love this movie so much.

Also: No Zephr in AVARITIA. Sorry. But soon. We're not far away from her now. Our next arc, ACEDIA, which'll see Fábio back on board for art, will see the inevitable return of Zeph.

I think[17].

•

Dear Matt,

Aside from REALLY focusing on my "cobra kegels" nothing has improved my sex life as much as you and Fábio putting me in CASANOVA.

Love,
Shumphries

This is from Sam Humphries, the visual inspiration for Kubark Benday (Next month! Next month! Mmpph—) and the writer of the scifi cult sexplosion of a comic OUR LOVE IS REAL, drawn by my pal and comic-compatriot Steven Sanders. OLIR is so boutique[18] it makes Das Racist and Curenn$y tapes[19] look like fucking WATCH THE THRONE. Seek it out. Learn what love is. Shumphriesandersstyle.

•

---

13   As I type this I have numerous sites blocked on my browser, some forever, some until the evening, and have quit Twitter on ethical grounds (the righteous excuse I needed to break the habit). Everything is dangerous always.

14   Eight years and two weeks as I type this. This also might explain my natural aversion, frustration, and embarrassment when media—comics, music, movies, whatever—get saddled with the very lazy "___ on (drug)" comparison. First off, I've done a lot of drugs and at no point, not even on the most LSD or the most dusted, did I ever stop and think, "Gee, this is like if David Lynch directed PORKY'S" or "This must be what Phillip Glass hears on MDMA." Or maybe I feel self-righteous. I dunno. Write better, write smarter. "___ on (drug)" means you've run out of things to say and ways to say them.

15   OH HOLY SHIT IT'S ON YOUTUBE: http://youtu.be/lrtON7Sf3Mc

16   People thought it was F for "Fraction." Mike Allred even drew me wearing it in our cameo appearances in FF. Sorry. It's 'Frankenstein.'

17   Not so sure anymore. Maybe.

18   Since this writing Sam became one of Marvel's most prominent writers on the ascent.

19   Contemporary!

I found CASANOVA no. 9 in Nairobi!!

From the Image, two-tone color palette days. The day I found it I had to do math in my head to convert Kenyan shillings into US dollars. It was selling for the original cover price in a 24-hour supermarket in Nairobi, Kenya. I was there for other, more ridiculous reasons. I remember sitting that night, reading the issue for the first time in July 2010, in my shitty little hotel room at the Six-Eighty.

I went into Nakumart 24/7 to buy bottled water and look around. I found books. Off in one corner there's this stack of comics. A weird mix of stuff ranging from Marvel's last attempt at a Blade series (Chaykin!) and the sort of stuff you find in bargain bins at comic stores everywhere. And then CASANOVA 9.[20] I had a friend (Greg Nell, comic geek extraordinaire) who was searching every store in Jo'burg to find me all the back issues. I only had the hardcover (and now I have these Icon issues—you've Retail Superman'd me into getting the same title in 3 formats, Fraction![21]). This is a book that you've said yourself was not moving enough copies to make you any real money, and I found an original one in a 24/7 supermarket in a city in central Africa.

There weren't any Supermans, but there was a Casanova.

That night I wrote a letter to you about this that I never ended up sending.

I discovered this book when I used to sell comics in Cosmic Comics, Jo'burg. I picked it up because I liked THE ORDER[22] and because I liked Bá's work on UMBRELLA ACADEMY. I remember reading #1 in the store, putting the book down, certain that I wasn't getting something or that maybe it was shit. I don't know why I bought it after that, or why it sat on my shelf at home for a month before I cracked it open again and read it and fell in love with it. That's just how it had to happen, I guess. I've love it ever since. I've re-read that volume and shipped it out to people and sold the trades (and made my old boss order the trade even after I stopped working for him—popped it right next to Gillen's PHONOGRAM[23] on my list of things it would be impossible to sell without me in the store to sell them, and then occasionally popped by and sold them anyway).

Everything about this series reminds me why comics are awesome, why writing is awesome, why art is beautiful. It is music, but in pictures and amusing anecdotes. It is the comic that is like that quote about the Velvet Underground. Maybe it didn't sell any copies, but everyone who reads it will probably want to make comics[24]. I know I do. Thanks for making this comic and letting me know it's OK to enjoy the stuff that I do, and to be me. I can't wait for AVARITIA and whatever else you have up your sleeve.

P.S. Newman Xeno is not a subtle alias.

P.P.S. Sorry for the regrettable style and length of this one.

- Nas Who

Okay, that's fucking amazing. I'd give Dharbin's left dick for a picture of CASANOVA on a rack in a supermarket in Nairobi.

One time I found a copy of this graphic novel I wrote called LAST OF THE INDEPENDENTS in a Tower Records in Tokyo; it was the only time I ever saw a copy of the book somewhere not a comic book store in the United States. It remains one of my favorite moments about being a part of comics ever. I wrote my phone number and email inside of that copy of LOTI but never heard from anyone. Ahh, well. The ego is a monster.

Jesus, Nas, thanks for writing this. And thanks for triple-dipping, too. It wasn't ever my intention but I know Casanovanauts like you DID it and for that I'll never be able to thank you enough.

P.S.—I know!

•

Hey,

I guess that writing to you at the beginning and upon the completion of CASANOVA volumes has become somewhat of a habit for me.

I meant to write this email earlier (after reading you comments for the CASANOVA: GULA #4 backmatter), but I guess life got in the way. The reason I wanted to write this piece was because of the comments you've made regarding the retro backmatter and your tendency to ramble; I really loved the old backmatter and I always thought it was more than just 'backmatter' for the book. Hell, I was just as excited to read the backmatter as I was to read the issues themselves, and with me truly love this series, that means a lot.

I just want you to know that by no means did you talking about your work make it any less special. I don't care very much for reality TV and shows like BIG BROTHER make me sick, but there was something about that window to the soul of sorts that you gave us, the readers, with your former take on the backmatter. It made me feel as if I was right there with you when you were traveling from one place to another and trying to structure the issue and that weird connection between whatever happened to Cass on paper and

20   This remains one of my all-time favorite letters. How crazy is that to think of? A little two-dollar CASANOVA comic sitting in a pile in a convenient store in Nairobi.

21   Check out CASANOVA: ACEDIA #2 (on sale Feb or Mar 2015, depending on how the short month jacks up the print schedules) for information on joining the CASANOVA TRIPLE-DIPPERS CLUB. No shit.

22   A short-lived book I did at Marvel mostly with Barry Kitson in 2007.

23   I am unfamiliar with this.

24   See, why should *I* say nice things about myself and my work when people can write in and say it for me? LETTER COLUMNS!

what you experienced in real life[25]. It served as a companion piece to the issue, in my honest opinion. Your creative process was just intoxicating and I'm so very sad to bid it adieu. I wish you would reconsider it, but I fully respect your wishes.

And now on to actually discussing AVARITIA: while I do enjoy some of your 'work for hire' books, I think that CASANOVA brought out the best in you and challenged you the most (although it might have just been the Slimline format. Ha!). In previous emails I wrote to you about the effect CASANOVA had on my life. LUXURIA found me in a very dark place and helped me rediscover my identity and creativity, GULA found me in the midst of an experiment and trying to chart out the life I want to live, and now AVARITIA is coming out as I am bout to embark on yet another monumental step. I don't know why but I find a little comfort in growing up with this book and seeing it evolve and change as I am. I guess you could say that the previous two CASANOVA acts provided the soundtrack to two periods in my life, and it's only fitting to have the third volume drop as I begin yet another period. I love this book, man. It means a lot to me, and I'm just so very happy that you're back at it. I'm truly ecstatic to see Cass back, as well as the twins rocking every single page. And hell, maybe Cass' unreal estate agent will even make a comeback (although nowadays I don't really have a need for it as toll to attract hot comic book girls in Paris. And YES, they are quite hot and it makes absolutely no that you can find them browsing the new books right next to chubby, acne'd fanboys. Ha! A tangent within a tangent. Christopher Nolan should make a movie about me And back to the point: I guess there's no need for another 'I just got you laid' email from you :).

Before I wrap this up, I would like to thank you once again for creating this wonderful book that just always falls into that 'in the right time and in the right place' category for me.

This is going to be a great ride,
Shlomo Roman

SHLOMO ROMAN! The guy with the name so cool he became a character in CASANOVA.

Y'know what I've come to realize about the backmatter isn't that I mind talking, it's that I've come to mind very much talking so goddamn much about myself[26]. I felt like I'd drawn lines in the sand, I'd made these rules that I needed to follow, because otherwise, I was break the rules, cheating our of the deal, not following through or whatever, and I came to feel imprisoned by these wholly arbitrary things that only mattered to me, that is, *was I following the rules or not.*

I remember when someone asked Jack White about why he broke the rules of the White Stripes and made a record with bass and keyboard and such on it. And he said, 'Well, that was a stupid rule.'[27]

Not using these pages, as much of a hassle as assembling the content may be, felt like a rip-off, though.

So...so, like, I love going to shows and meeting the people and if nothing else, saying thank you for allowing me to have this completely ridiculous, completely amazing job. And, like, make no mistake: it is ridiculous and amazing, and thanking folks is literally no big deal[28]. Anyone in comics who behaves as though shows and talking to their readers is, like, some kind of Sisyphean ordeal

---

25   Writing the page of AVARITIA #1 (I'm not sure what the page number will be in the collection you've got in your hands) where 16 different Casanovas get assassinated and the page scans in either columns or rows took me most of an entire day to write. I planned it out in my .99-cent notebook ten ways to Tuesday before typing any of it.

I wrote it in a hotel a few miles away from Walt Disney World in Orlando, Florida. We went for my son's third birthday. My daughter, about six months old, sprouted a fever. Teething, probably. I remember driving down endless swamp highway looking for a drug store so I could buy her ibuprofen.

It was early September. My folks and Kel's family, all at the time living in Florida, came too. My father would have some of his lung removed and then start a combination of chemo and radiation at the end of the month. It hung over the whole trip for me, it hung over my whole life for a long time.

As, y'know, I suppose it should. I had to get Bá pages, though, and I stayed home from the park one day—I think maybe they did SEA WORLD?—so I could write. And while most times writing for me feels like using a teaspoon to dig a tunnel, that day all of the nervous energy and fear and anxiety came out through my pencil all day long as I planned and replanned and replanned that page. Eight hours? Nine? Maybe more—I don't remember now—but when it was all said and done I felt *is that all there is?*

And that night I kept feeling Tallulah's forehead, waiting for the fever to break, watching her sweat and sigh and moan inside that little baby tiger cage hotels give you to put 'em in. Is that all there is? Is this it?

26   I'm lying here in both cases. I want nothing more than to talk about myself. *It's why I'm a writer.*

27   I think I actually used this line in an earlier CASANOVA hardcover.

28   This remains true, if not, somehow, *more true*, were such a thing possible. I was sure, come 2012, that my career was over in comics. I mean, look, comics—at least work-for-hire comics but I suspect as the timeline on viable and healthy original comics extends and expands it'll hold there, too—and any pop medium obey certain rules of fashion. They have seasons, they have trends, they have supernovas and slow-burning stars and black holes and blue-shifting stellar collapses. And in 2012 I thought my season ended. Nobody gets a guaranteed career; nobody gets a 401K in comics. We don't retire; we quit, die, or stop working because the work goes away or the phone stops ringing or our health falls apart. So spring 2012 I felt, well, okay, shit, I guess I don't quite get the Hall-of-Fame career I hoped for; time to, I dunno, go back to advertising or get other stuff going somehow. I had a show so bad—not in terms of what I sold (although that was lousy too) but in terms of response and...and *vibe*—that I knew my worm had turned. In the world of work-for-hire comics anyway.

I'd deprioritized work I'd created in favor of work that'd pay on delivery of script regardless of sales (for books you create and publish somewhere like Image, the deal is the book comes out, makes its cost back, Image gets their take, and then what's left goes to the creative team according to whatever split they've agreed to beforehand... ninety days after publication.) and set about making the opposite true. We moved to Portland, see, in 2009, very suddenly. A carjacking terminated in our front yard back in ol' Kansas City—literally a car almost crashed into my house but its axel got tangled up in a small tree it ran over first and they weren't going fast enough to uproot the thing—and we moved, figuring that if you went across the street or across the country packing your shit meant the same pain in the ass either way so we might as well move somewhere we wanted to live. So Portland.

We got out here. The house we were set to buy fell apart on inspection. We lived in Brian and Alisa Bendis' spare bedroom as we tried to figure out what came next when we discovered Kelly Sue had gotten pregnant. Not an unwelcome development at all but an unanticipated one—with our son we needed a stellar abacus and half a chemistry set to get and stay pregnant, so a Luke Skywalker-in-the-trench-esque insemination never occurred to us as possible—and one that meant getting out of Chez Bendis and into a place as quick as we could. So we rented a big ol' house halfway up a goddamn mountain on the outskirts of Portland and cooked the baby.

And then discovered we owed the IRS forty-some thousand dollars from the sale of the house in KC we thought our accountant had paid? Or... or something? Suddenly I had two kids and five figures of debt and a dad with cancer and...

And so I felt I didn't have the wiggle room to risk independent, original, work.

I'm writing this, I realize, to somehow appease the Past Matt of Art School, who'd sneer (while cashing checks mom and dad sent him to live on) at the guy I became and demand to know when why and how he sold out, and how can you do that to us. That's how it happens, Past Matt. It's just that easy. Sneer and skulk and snark all you can from the confines and safety of youth, all of you; one day you'll have a Scott and an Emma of your very own and realize there are oh so many more important and interesting things than *keeping it real.* And from that your humanity and compassion will grow and if you are very lucky you'll stop being such a judgmental little fuck.

from which they will never be free should be ridden out of town on a fucking rail.

And, god, there are dudes that are like that and it infuriates me. Guys who go to shows, who do press, who do whatever and make sure everyone knows they're doing it through gritted teeth and a nose pinched tightly shut...y'know, doing shows, doing podcasts, doing interviews, or whatever...it's not mandatory, you ass[29]. That pained artiste bullshit drives me crazy.

Anyway, so I'd much rather use this as the world's slowest moving convention table than a journal, and hopefully whatever small exchanges we have will be, y'know, fun, or...something. Not work, anyway. That might be what life is all about: avoiding work as long as possible.

I'd agree with you that CASANOVA has brought out the best in me, but I think that's because I'm not just writing the book, I'm writing the rules at the same time. Does that make sense? Like, it's not appropriate to write, say, UNCANNY X-MEN with the CASANOVA pen. Because you've been hired to write UNCANNY X-MEN and that comes with its own guidelines and such so you rise or fall or suck or win based on how one performs within those guidelines. Why force apples to be bananas? Or something? It's a disingenuous state of criteria. Maybe my apples suck; maybe you love my bananas. One cannot and will never be the other, though.

Shlomo, I hope AVARITIA find you well, strong, healthy, happy, superhuman, invincible, kind, wise, and limber of mind, body, and tongue.

Wait, ew.

•

Dear Matt, Gabriel, Fábio, Cris and Dustin,

Thank you for making CASANOVA.

Honestly, it's been way too long since GULA originally ended, and while seeing the original stories in full color is great, nothing beats a new, full-length Cass story.

I expect you guys to mess with my head, fill it with ideas and gorgeous visuals, just like you did when you first started the book.

Welcome back, guys. You were missed.

- Pat Lokia

Pat Loika is a dude whose hobby, beyond comics, seems to be going to comics shows. I knew him from the internet, or rather, knew him as an internet presence, and so the first time I ever saw him, I knew who he was and what he was about before we'd actually met—the effect was to greet a stranger as though he were an old pal. I honestly think he's maybe done more conventions than I have in the five years that I've been working full-time in comics.

Pat is like the Comics Superfan #1 and it's always a good time to see him. Dude loves comics like the lunatics that make comics love comics.

Thanks, Pat[30].

•

Dear Casanova,

I just wanted to write and let you know that I love you. I love you more than I have ever truly loved a woman. Which is slightly sad and pathetic, but most of the women I know don't treat me as nicely as you do. When women abandon me and move to the nearest college town, you are there for me. When women kick me in the emotional balls, you are there for me. You and your proud papas in this wall of sound pop trash glory rag: Matt Fraction, Gabriel Bá, and Fábio fucking Moon. You and your giant robots, you and your multiple timelines, you and your incorporation of my favorite Strokes[31] tune. You are awesome.

I love you Casanova.
-Curt Pires

───────────────

29   See, because, here's the kicker: *the worm turned again.* I didn't stop giving a shit about what I was writing, regardless of whether or not I owned it or someone else did and did my level best to write like a motherfucker. And the work-for-hire stuff I did became the most critically-received (kind of important) and the most commercially-received (VERY important when your paychecks get cut by a publicly-held company) work of my for-hire career, with next to no support, from those that hired me. That's not a criticism or a hurt accusation or recrimination; it's the weather report; it was the way it was. I mean, I literally paid to make promo postcards and buttons for one of my Marvel books out of my own pocket, and gave 'em away all summer long. I worked on projects no one expected to last beyond six issues all while setting up original stuff the best I could (including what you're reading now, SATELLITE SAM, SEX CRIMINALS, and ODY-C) in anticipation of the day that there was no seventh issue and no more paychecks coming in. I went to any show that'd have me and said thank you and shook every hand I could on the way down as I did on the way up and then what I thought was an exit was really just a revolving door and suddenly I had a bigger career than I knew what to do with. And it's still an honor and privilege to say thank you and shake your hand and sign my dumb fake name a few times. I can think of ten thousand other ways I'd like to express my gratitude.

I feel like I had seven points I tried to make between these last two footnotes but fuck if I think I actually made 'em. I dunno what the moral of the story is. *Everything will be okay in the end and if it's not okay then it's not the end,* as my sponsor likes to say.

Also comics dudes who go to cons and act like it's community fucking service some judge somewhere forced them to do are fucking assholes. If you don't want to go don't fucking go and hold your nose, prick.

30   This remains true. Pat now has a podcast called LOIKAMANIA that you should check out. You can hear who Pat is and how great a guy he is and how crazy-deep he loves this crazy-ass medium.

31   Hey remember the Strokes?

CASANOVANAUTS: I think we might need to get Curt quality-laid. Or a quality car so he can go to the nearest college town. How can we do that? Is that something we Kickstarter or what?

•

New CASANOVA is a beautiful thing, mostly for the ways it's going to infect my life. So much of CASANOVA seems to come directly from Matt's life/experience based on the copious and moving backmatter from the first two volumes, but I always found the series and backmatter to oddly end up directly relating to what was going on in my life. Whether it was blowing up my headspace or talking about movies like KILLER OF SHEEP that just happened to be playing at my school that very night, CASANOVA burrowed its way in and then left that space empty for far too long. Now that it's back, I'm looking forward to more story and more co-opting of my brain space, because my brain's been solely my own for too long.

-Logan Ludwig

Logan, I sincerely hope your year has been better than mine[32].

•

ODE TO CASANOVA QUINN

Lovechild of the mongoose
and a chromatic blender, you fuck nurses
and nurses' nurses
in technicolor bachelor pads

and triangulated stairwell closets. O, yeah,
leather in the summer, silk in the winter,
you are big, quiet.
You laugh at calendars and clocks,
ruby lenses to match the socks. Razzmatazz
on a cracker, you bunch panties
and get chubs like Olympus Mons
as you jeet-kune-do in a field of retired batteries.

No 'Theory of Everything' can outlaw you
as you emaciate the skin of space-time's mango.
Hobo of love, no one lined up for your birth
unless you fell for them first.

-Dave Landsberger

A POEM! A POEM! WE GOT OUR FIRST POEM!

We've had tattoos before but a POEM! My word.

Next issue will be all brown and purple and printed on a grocery bag and we will have totally brought '90s Vertigo BACK[33]!

•

Dear Matt, Gabriel, Fábio, Cris and Dustin,

As I write this letter (my first letter to any publication), I have received word that Rebecca Black has moved schools due to bullying. I think, should this be printed in the back of CASANOVA: AVARITIA, it will really date it. Like DAREDEVIL, the Ben Affleck masterwork, is dated by its awful, awful soundtrack (Evanescence up in this piece). My kids are going to have a lot of questions for me some day, like who Rebecca Black[34] is, and why anyone cares about her education (because, future children, education is the most important. SO IMPORTANT). I plan on giving them CASANOVA as soon as they're old enough to not make me feel back about giving them a comic that has boobies in it.

CASANOVA came to me originally in a time of great transition for me in my personal life, it was the first comic book that I loved (I think the second was NEXTWAVE by Ellis and Immonen), I used it to replace the love of a woman. CASANOVA never made me feel guilty for eating whole box of cookies, CASANOVA never told me that CASANOVA is a dumb name for a firstborn, and though CASANOVA left me, it came back, because it truly loves me. I am incredibly excited to finally read some new CASANOVA, I sincerely hope it doesn't suck, but you'll have my money anyways.

Love,
Joe Menjivar

Joe, you and Curt up there should maybe meet and be, like, co-wingmen or something. Not in a Dylan-and-Eric way, either.

---

32   There should be a font that universally means "cry for help."

33   I keep thinking this is the meanest thing I ever wrote. I didn't mean it to be.

34   I had to google it.

Eating a whole box of cookies: one time, when I was a kid, I ate two entire containers of vanilla cake frosting, because I felt sad.

Later, I drank!

Also I hope this doesn't suck either. I've absolutely no perspective on these things anymore.

•

Hey Cosmic Love Spies,

I'm quite excited for AVARITIA but when do we get the hardbacks of everything else??[35]

Rock on.

-Pete Buser

Y'know, I should have some better optics on that (that's a thing that people say now, that they have 'optics' on stuff) a month or so after this sees print. We'll know how the GULA trade did (if it's anything like the LUXURIA trade, it'll be fairly awesome-doing) and I can start talking to Icon about that[36].

We're going to be releasing a new version of my very first graphic novel LAST OF THE INDEPENDENTS, with stunningly good art by Kieron Dwyer, through Icon. So...there's that? Look, news! I just broke news[37].

I also daydream of doing a one-color GULA collection to match the old one-color AVARITIA collection somewhere someday because I have mild OCD and it makes me insane[38].

•

Well, that's AVARITIA #1 at long last. I hope you enjoyed it. Thanks to everyone that wrote in—sorry we didn't have the room to run it all.

Let me know what you're thinking, what you're doing, what you're seeing. Tell me about amazing things or sad things or funny things. It's nice to hear that you like CASANOVA but you don't even have to talk about it. Please: help me grow my understanding of the world and the people in it.

Drop a line to CasanovaQuinn@gmail.com. I'm assuming all received mail is OK to print so tell me otherwise.

Fraction
PDX
33,000 Feet Above the Dog Day of Summer[39]

AVARITIA II (Icon Comics, 2011)

BAM! BUM BAAHHH BUMMMMM!!!

Look not for anything but look at the goddamn bottom of those sneakers on David's feet. Look! Look. GABRIEL BÁ LADIES AND GENTS. Nobody would draw like that.

I am writing this in New York City. It's about 1:45 in the morning and everybody at my house back in Oregon is sick, feverish, throwing up, having a first day of school, or having a birthday[40], and I'm here, doing this, and arguing with grown men about comic books all day long. Ahh, Christ.

So the first issue of CASANOVA: AVARITIA #1 has been released for real for really real and for real and for true and I kind of totally can't believe it. Hey, so, if you bought it, and now you bought this, thank you. I hope you dug it. I hope you dug this last one, too.

The next one'll probably be a week or two late, because I'm way late getting it written. It got tricky and I had to figure it out. You know how it goes, right? Right. Anyway: #3 is coming, just maybe not 28 days from now.

I cannot speak more highly of Marc Maron's WTF podcast. I know I'm late on the bandwagon but if you're a fan of comedy, of the creative process, of laughter, of human beings baring their souls, of humans, of souls, of podcasts—go for it. Comedy nerds and

---

35 2014 and 2015, it turns out.

36 I did and they didn't care. Their model of trade success and the original-market's ideas are wildly different.

37 This didn't happen at Icon and hasn't happened yet at Image.

38 This will literally never happen.

39 I think I was flying home to be with my parents during my father's surgery and to help my mom for the first few weeks that came after.

40 I let myself be talked into going to a Marvel editorial retreat that meant I missed both my son's birthday and first day of pre-kindergarten. Now, granted, he was four and wasn't quite acutely aware what was happening, but I still haven't forgiven myself. The whole reason I left the straight world was so I'd never do stuff like that and yet, boom, I did. That's how easy it is to sell out, it seems.

human beings alike, WTF is a treasure.

This past season of LOUIE has been remarkable—so real and hilarious and so painfully honest and true that I can't even express what it is I love about it so. I love it so much, and I love what Louis C.K. does as a writer and performer that it, along with discovering WTF, is really what's inspired me to do this goofy-ass letter column. Anyway, if you're looking for stuff... go look at that.

Nothing sounds good to me these days[41].

I read a comic that made me cry—Jaime Hernandez's Maggie stuff in LOVE AND ROCKETS: NEW STORIES #4. I am certain anyone can read the story and enjoy it, but unless you've maybe read the whole of LOCAS maybe it won't ding for you like it did for me. So, look, go read MAGGIE THE MECHANIC, THE GIRL FROM H.O.P.P.E.R.S., PERLA LA LOCA, PENNY CENTURY, ESPERANZA, then get LOVE AND ROCKETS: NEW STORIES 1-4. If you don't week on the last page too I'll buy 'em all back from your soul-dead ass.

Drop us a line. Join the conversations. Casanovaquinn@gmail.com is the magic address. Anything going on in your mind.

Anything at all.

•

I'm in a place where I feel like my destiny was to do something great and I missed my shot.

Oh, shit, that's *rough*. I get that. I know that. I remember that. And dude it's fucking *rough*.

So, hey, then, at least there's this—you're still around, and today ain't your day to run the company, and, so, who the fuck knows.

I was in a car crash this one time. Or rather—this one particular car crash I was in this one particular time—and this one car crash was kind of a doozy. My window was down; it was August in North Carolina and we just got through a crazy, like, monsoon-blast of rain so everything was just starting to get over being wet. I was delivering pizzas at the time and we were running late because of the rain. I had to drive way the fuck out to this one asshole's place and because it took longer than thirty minutes from when he called—didn't matter that we weren't Domino's—he was angry and not only yelled at me for being late he stiffed me on the tip.

ANYWAY SO I am, for the first time that day, driving back slowly, ears sorta stinging and generally surly from getting stiffed—I got paid five bucks cash an hour under the table plus tips, so I was pretty much living on tips—when I thought I need to hurry up. I didn't DO anything about it; I just remember having the thought as the rear end of the car started to slide out from under me. It hooked backwards and left, swerving into the oncoming lane.

I saw a pick up truck coming at me. Time turns into a 32-panel Gabriel Bá page of wholly discrete, wholly independent imagery now—time might not be relative but *our ability to experience it is* and I swear to god you can train yourself to think faster[42]—I see a Dad driving, a Kid in the middle, a Mom on the end. All three cover their faces defensively as we're about to crash. Seriously—like a cartoon. EEEK! And Dinosaur Jr. is playing. WHERE YOU BEEN? "I Ain't Sayin'" is the track. *And I'm rolling home to you.* The terrified family ready for impact. *Fuck it*, I think, and mash the brake as hard as I can and whip the wheel hard in the other direction. The car leaves the earth. I whip around hard 180 degrees and start to violently roll. Remember the window is down—my head smashes out every time I'm driver-side-down and I think—*this is when you die, Matt. Something's going to stab you through your skull. The car is going to crush your head*—and then as the car rights itself and keeps rolling, I think—I swear to god every work of this is true—*that didn't kill me*—and I keep going and going. The car comes to a stop facing the opposite direction it started. I had missed the truck. I severed three telephone poles at the ground and ran into a fourth. Snapped both axles. The front right wheel was folded under the car. The whole of the passenger side caved in. I look at the tape deck—out pops Dinosaur Jr. I take the tape and the money bag. The door is crushed. I have to kick it open. I do. I get out. I go into shock.

The next morning, you'd only be able to tell I was in a wreck from the seat-belt-shaped welt across my neck and chest. I was completely fine. Not even concussed.

I tried to go back to work—again, I was in shock—and eventually the dad from the truck convinces me to sit down. I plop down flat on my ass like it was a cartoon and wait for the cops and the ambulance to come.

So, okay, the whole thing—scary enough, I suppose. Like, as an event, it's not really the kind of thing you just shake off. I was supposed to be on the front page of the paper but there was a wreck like mine that killed a kid later that day and so that made it instead. What really fucked me up though was…like…I remembered thinking *that didn't kill me* again and again. Every time my head slammed out of it, every time I felt dirt *go into my ear*—I had dirt in my goddamn ear!—like, in my mind, I was readying, on some channel, for the end while, on another, realizing the end hadn't come.

So…so why was I still alive? I remember writing it in giant letters in my sketchbook. WHY ARE YOU STILL ALIVE?

(I also may have written a piece of sage-like advice gleaned from Old Ben Kenobi: *in my experience, there's no such thing as luck.*

There is nothing on this sweet earth quite like a STAR WARS nerd at art school.)

It was my first encounter with my utter abject and absolute powerlessness in the face of an unmanageable problem disguised as an

---

41   Am I crazy or has it been some lean-ass years for music?

42   In my good music drought I've gone backwards and rediscovered Eno's HERE COME THE WARM JETS. Reading up on him and on it, I came across this article: http://music. hyperreal.org/artists/brian_eno/interviews/Peopl83a.html

In which he recounts a similar experience. Also, go read TIME WARPED by Claudia Hammond if horology and the way our minds process time is your bag.

ultimately unanswerable question[43]. That was the damage that came from the car crash; it wasn't physical, it was, like, psychic. I was seventeen and I was alive for no reason I could discern. That's maybe a child's luxury, in a way, having that kind of existential angst to climb to as you're trying to define what shape of an adult you're going to take...I feel embarrassed to even admit it now. What I see now is that, as a nascent alcoholic and drug addict, it was an encounter with the powerlessness I have in life, ultimately, and the unmanageability the things in that life are, in spite of desires to the contrary. In the same way that I was unable to control my desire to get high, to get drunk, to get fucking cross-eyed wasted as early and often as possible no matter what, I was unable to control why I'd live or die in a fucking car crash from which it was, quite frankly, counter-intuitive to survive, let along come away sans injury.

I don't know if I'm making sense but: once upon a time I thought I could control everything and, surviving this catastrophic thing, was a kind of monumental reminder that, no, shithead, you don't get to control anything. *And I didn't know what to do with that.*

I had no answers then and remain, still, to this day, unconvincing and unconvinced in or by my arguments one way or the other. *Faters gonna fate.* I don't believe in destiny and fate and that kind of magical thinking like I used to; if you do, though, then...then hey, if it's your destiny, and you're still alive, then it'll make its damn date with you in its own sweet time. Otherwise it's not destiny; it's an *errand.*

And either way—it ain't your day to run the company. You know what I mean? Jesus I wrote like ten thousand words in response to your one line WHAT IS WRONG WITH ME.

•

Dear Gentlemen Fraction, Bá, Moon, Harbin, Arbona, and Ms. Peter:

Forgive me, I was kind of scrambling to get something in so I apologize if this comes off half baked and not fully thought out. Today, I was re-reading AVARITIA 1 on the train back to Astoria from my job as a college assistant at Brooklyn College and I started thinking about all the little references that I've come to love reading in all of these iterations of CASANOVA. I was trying to gain a higher understanding of What It All Means in an attempt at trying to wrap my brain around this truly spectacular series that has affected pretty much everything I do from a writing standpoint.

The understanding I come to is how all the ingredients, from the color scheme, to the music song title chapters, the names, and the references to movies and other comics clarified in the backmatter, are a way of showing us where creativity comes from. The often sneered and jeered question, "Where do you get your ideas from?" gets something of an answer, well maybe not so much an answer but a clarification, in the backmatter. The interviews, the personal stories, and the appendixes of stuff that fueled that issue are an attempt at showing that you creativity comes from the stuff you love and mashed together helps to make CASANOVA.

I just want to say thanks for those enlightenments because it expanded my world. I may not have seen (Oh the shame) Danger: Diabolik or read American Flagg! if you didn't always advocate it. I probably would have seen and read those works at some point, but probably not if I didn't read this book. Just like those works helped to fuel CASANOVA, this work helps to fuel what I want to do and I think that's why you do it; you want us to pose over it, examine it, dissect it, and finally be fired up enough by it to up our game and create something. So, thank you.

Question: you all going to NY Comic Con? I think it's been about a year and half since I last saw you, Matt, in the halls of Marvel after a retreat (I was working for Agent M at the time).

Sincerely,
Dave Press

Hey, Dave, thanks for the kind words.

I sort of hope this book is sort of less about *what it all means* the more it goes on. I hope it just kind of means CASANOVA. As just as surely everything in my life is slowly becoming CASANOVA. Like...like that stuff, it's all nods and winks and color but I hope it's about more than what DVD I bought yesterday or whatever.

I had this—I've told this story before but I dunno if I've ever told it here in CASANOVA—but when Image Comics came to me and offered the chance to do a book in the slimline format, I was convinced I'd never get another chance to do another comic anywhere. So rather than, like, create another comic that was another rip-off of BATMAN or whatever, I wanted to make the book I wanted to read. And so here we are.

I'm glad that I was able to shine a little light on some of the amazing stuff that fueled—and fuels—me. Somehow it seems the least I can do?

And yeah, I'll be at NYCC. I think the boys will be there too. CASANOVA party!

•

Dear Mr. Fraction and company,

Before I start I obviously have to let you know that I am a big fan of all your work. I got into your writing when you started writing Invincible Iron Man and have been picking up almost all of your work since. When I saw that they were reprinting an old comic you did for Image about time-traveling spies, I was instantly intrigued. Luckily, it was pretty awesome.

This letter is not so much about that though. I am writing to ask your opinion on something that I know a lot of comic book creators kind of joke about, but none of them ever seem to talk about openly: downloading comic books illegally.

---

43 It is also, my therapist assures me, a TRAUMATIC EXPERIENCE that I'm really only just now starting to unpack and figure out. I read the glibness with which I responded to this and shudder.

Although I know very little about downloading comic books (I really prefer to hold the actual comic in my hand), I know a great deal about downloading music. I have been playing in bands since I was about 16; going on tours around the country, putting out records (actual records, not compact discs), printing t-shirts in our living room, etc. etc. and all these things were done generally DIY. It was never my day job, but I definitely invested countless hours, dollars, and sweat into all of it. Everything we did, we did because we loved doing it, as I'm sure you did when you first started writing (and hopefully still do).

When I would see my band's music on some forum, or on a torrent site or what have you, I was legitimately excited. I was always thrilled that someone appreciated something I had created enough to take time to upload it on to the Internet and share it with other people. The thought of being upset that someone "stole" music from myself or my band never even crossed my mind.

I am curious how you feel about this. Are you ever okay with people downloading your work for free? Was it acceptable when you were a hungry young writer just trying to get you name out there? Is it more acceptable now that you are well established, and I'm sure have set salary in your contract? I know most comic book writers are probably not making Kanye West money (I have no qualms with downloading Watch the Throne for free), but I assume you make a comfortable living. When you see a mediafire link for every issue of Casanova for download, are you flattered or hurt? Thanks for your time, and keep up the great work.

-Matt Vicars

P.S. One of the things I really love about DIY punk bands is the general passion that comes along with it. A hand-screened seven inch with a hand-painted cover is much more a labor of love, rather than just a commodity with a price tag on it. The people who created it leave a piece of themselves with every copy. I get a similar feeling with this backmatter, and I really think it adds a lot to the comic.

Hey Matt—it's tricky, the piracy thing. I am both flattered and hurt[44].

I want to make it clear I am only speaking about my experiences with CASANOVA and other creator-owned books here; not because I'm not allowed to voice my opinions on all things Marvel but my opinions on all things Marvel with regards to piracy and such is wildly different and not wholly applicable or relatable to CASANOVA. So as you read this, I am speaking about THIS and not THAT.

It was, literally, June of 2011 that I first made money in independent comics. Money came in, yes, but my deals to date with my collaborators have always been to pay them out first. Only then was I comfortable enough to get paid. And we JUST got to that point. So...so from 2006 until now, all my independent work was done pro bono. I even *still* don't get paid for CASANOVA, but the backlist moves so the money comes from there. It's all back-end for me. There are guys in comics who can make that work for them and do GREAT. I am not them and CASANOVA isn't that book. We're a little book and we live on a narrow margin. AND we happened to launch new material in a month when retailers were locked into a fucking stare-down with a mega-massive re-launch of an entire line of comic books[45] so their money was spoken for on more-sure bets than this. It's tough out there, cats and kittens, without having to stare down Greg Lantern[46], y'know?

(We're doing OK, don't worry. Just saying.)

So, okay, let's say this: if every single download represents one lost sale, then, based on a few sites I've seen the book up on, that is a life-changing, game-changing amount of money lost from the literally thousands of people who have downloaded CASANOVA illegally.

IF none of them bought the book. Which I don't believe to be the case at all though; or, at least, I cannot allow myself to believe that. Because I read comics. I love comics. I need 'em around.

I tell myself and believe very much on some level that digital piracy, especially on weird-ass books like ours, serves as the best advertising we could ever do for the book. I tend to think of it as promotional, in a way, because I know shops under-order the book, don't push the book, don't shelve it. I know people can't find it because they tell me all the time. And look, I get it, the market's murder right now. So maybe people download the book and order it or buy the trades or whatever. Some of 'em gotta be, anyway.

Due to the nature of my deal with Icon I don't have control over CASANOVA as a digital product; if I did, it would be 99 cents an issue. That'll come, but we're not there yet. I mean, shit, we're supposed to be day/date digital with AVARITIA and as of this instant, we're not. It's a weird machine that doesn't work perfectly yet[47].

I'm rambling. Look: it's theft. It's also great promotion for books like CASANOVA. I believe comics fans do in fact have a need and desire for physical artifacts and I believe downloaders that discover comics like CASANOVA through piracy will seek out and buy physical copies.

In other words: it hurts. And it's thrilling.

I wish those scan-y pirate douchebags would've fucking color-corrected the green in the first run of LUXURIA though. Seriously it looked like a fucking bottle of Mountain Dew. Weirdly enough that's what hurt more than the ostensible "theft." It was so BADLY scanned and color-corrected. UNACCEPTABLE, SCANNERS[48].

---

44 I have friends that fall on all sides of this issue, just as much now as then, and I still don't have any better grasp on it. I guess it's maybe like a toothache you can't stop poking because it *feels so good?*

45 I can't wait for the history of the New 52 to be written. It was an incredibly weird time to be working in the comics mainstream and those books—OOPH those BOOKS.

46 Still makes me laugh, fuck you.

47 It's better now. Image is pretty close to perfect now. DRM-free in multiple formats day and date as the comics themselves. Soon we'll crack the price point and then it's game on.

48 This remains infuriating. Especially when review or commentary or critical pieces get written about CASANOVA and use ganked images from these shitty pirated versions. Like, it makes me want to punch a pirate in the face. It's one thing to rip me off. It's another thing *to destroy my shit.*

Tell you what—straw poll. Did you discover CASANOVA from download sites? Did you download CASANOVA "illegally" to encounter it for the first time? Did you download CASANOVA because you couldn't find a copy of it in your local store? Any pirates out there that dig the book—reach out, let me know what you're thinking: casanovaquinn@gmail.com[49].

Okay. It's now 3:30 in the morning and I gotta get up and fight with grown men about comics books in like five and a half hours. See you next time, earthmen. Thanks to everyone that wrote in. This is fun.

And it should be, right? It's fun. It's all fun. I write comics so I don't have to have a real job. I might have been born yesterday but I stayed up all night, son[50].

Matt Fraction
NYC
09 Sept 11

AVARITIA III (Icon Comics, 2012[51])

HIYAH EARTHMEN:

The CASANOVA inbox remains amazing, life-affirming[52] and work-invigorating and I've not replied to NEARLY as many emails as I should've. I read every single one, though, and can never thank you enough for taking the time out of your life to reach out to use with whatever's on your mind, like along if that's something complimentary, so this meager thank you will have to suffice.

Last time—remember last time? Does anyone remember laughter?[53]—I asked about digital, well, let's use the value-neutral term "acquisition" here…the digital acquisition of CASANOVA, and if it led readers to acquiring physical copies. What follows is a cross-section of the huge volume of mail we've received.

I've reduced the letter-writers' names to initials; while I appreciate their honesty (or creativity, if they signed off with a pseudonym) I don't wish anyone to be shamed for being honest here.

This is a straw poll, anecdotal at best, but I have to say that, time and time again, my suspicion about digital acquisitions were proven to be correct: digital files are value-less unless publishers and creators assign them value. They are at best spoiler-laden promotional tools that drive physical sales and at worst the e-version of guys standing in a shop, reading a book, and putting it back on the shelf.

I believe digital comics should cost nothing, or next to nothing, and be value-added incentives that come with the acquisition of physical copies of our books. Nearly everyone who wrote in reinforced that in my mind. Was there some degree of privileged justification and doth-protesting-too-much? Sure. And, look, maybe don't plead poverty via high-speed internet connection from your Apple-branded whatnot, as more than a few did. That said: those folks later bought, too. The WHY does not matter. It's the WHAT COMES NEXT that matters.

(Weirdly enough, if I had to boil CASANOVA down to a dozen words…)

Because I'm in a minority, and a hostilely treated one at that, what follows are your own words, your own thoughts, your own justifications for making the decisions that you made, and it makes my case far more persuasively than I could.

I've said this before but I think that, while not everybody that reads comics reads CASANOVA, by the time we're done, I'll have met or heard from everyone that DOES. And, again, thanks.

(Also of note: LOTS of non-American readers writing in. Lots more than usual, anyway.) Next time: more actual letters, more responses, I swear, I promise. CASANOVAQUINN@GMAIL.COM. No delays for next issue. Or very minor ones at best. We're on it. We'll see you soon for the finale of AVARITIA.

LET'S. GET. FUCKED.

•

DR:

I would like to say I have purchased every issue of CASANOVA since the Image days. I would also like to say I have purchased every trade since then too. I have also downloaded every issue illegally to read on my Galaxy Tab.

I'm sure that there are many more like me, who want digital copies, but after buying the physical, do not want to shell out additional money. I mean after buying a CD, I don't have to buy a digital comic for my iPod. So after buying a comic, I do not want to buy a

---

49   This remains the single most valuable thing to come out of this letter column—as you'll see going forward.

50   This is so thickly encoded and bitter I flinch to read it. I missed my kid's birthday and I was mad. Never again, never again.

51   Wow! Late! That's…I recognize the dangers of lateness with periodical publication, but, at the same time, one of the best things about independent comics remains the power the creators have to refuse to be a part of the weekly comics content machine that, post-New 52, power the big publishers. It hurts me, it hurts the retailer…but it doesn't hurt the work, because the work is *right* and goddamn if it isn't hard, if not impractical, to not want to prioritize the product above all else. Well, romantic if not impractical.

52   Eh.

53   ALWAYS makes me laugh.

digital copy for my Galaxy Tab[54] (...)

•

LV:

(...) I wanted just to tell you me experience regarding pirated comics and the like, especially after reading fellow Casanovanaut Mitt Vicar's letter, especially as I read my copy of AVARITIA #2 quite comfortably on my iPad after downloading the scan from some site hosted somewhere in Southeast Asia or an equivalently remote location.

I am, of course, in an equally remote location as well. I currently work in Capiapó, Chile[55] (also known as the desert town where those trapped miners hailed from) and there's not a single [local comic shop] here. Even in Santiago things are hard to find and you get charged pretty much double the price per issue. So I naturally download most of my comics and I order the trades of the ones that truly satisfy me from amazon. The rest I delete promptly from my hard drive and that's about it. Last year I was in the States, getting my Master's in English and living the life on loans as these things are wont to be, and head the praise for this book, so I promptly downloaded the pirate copy the day it came out and then bought the issue on Comixology. I hope to do the same thing next week, and I have also bought the other Cassignles that way. Because, ultimately, the one thing I'm really scared of here is that sales won't be enough and someone pulls the plug on this awesome, awesome comic.

I am a cheap bastard and play the "living in the third world card" when it comes to most corporate comics, though. But in these days when people debate the whole 3.99 or 2.99 or something-something .99 price tags on comic books, I can only say that as long as the quality is there and we readers feel directly involved in the survival of the books we love, things would be all right. (...)

•

MP:

(...) In print, bought, simultaneously reading forward while going backwards to score the rest of the series. So I ended up reading LUXURIA something like this: 6, 7, 2, 3, 1, 4, 5 or close to it...I didn't get to read the series straight until 11 I think and once you finished the second album, I read the whole series straight through, backmatter and all.

However, I also, upon discovering download sites, downloaded CASANOVA even tho' I had it already (and yeah, the green is quite a bit stronger than it is in print so I get the Mountain Dew comment...thankfully, the newer scans just adjust the contrast slightly, leaving the colors as they should be) between the end of the Image run and the beginning of the Icon run. Why? Because I like reading digital books on my laptop or e-reader (prefer a laptop tho'). One a laptop, you can look at the comic at the same size the artist drew it as, 10 by 15/11 by 17 and it really brings out the artwork. Not to mention, I like having the ability to have a sizable chunk of my comics with me should I feel like reading them.

But there are a ton of people out there that have either gotten back into comics (and yes, buying them) because of scans or gave something a try that they normally wouldn't. And you are right, most people would prefer to have the book in their hands, which is why people still buy the book if it's something they liked. That's why I have a real issue with companies that state illegal downloading is what's causing sales to drop. I honestly don't believe that. I think it has to do with people having less money these days for thrills with more content fighting for that dollar. The cover price isn't helping either. I never quite understand why no one looks at the correlation of dropping sales going hand in hand with rising prices. When I was a kid just starting out in the '80s, two bucks and some change could net me five comic books (six on those days mom would give me bus money, only to walk home to get that last book or two). Now, I can't even get a book for two bucks. Image started out at 1.95 and then jumped to 2.50, where it stayed for quite some time. I believe both Marvel and DC were 1.99 around that time and I was still buying books like I was when I was younger and twenty bucks (my monthly allotment for comics) went far. Now, married, but still with the twenty bucks, you can barely get five books for that at 3.99 price points. So lately, I've taken to reading trades/[original graphic novels] more and more and leaving the floppies alone (except for the books that aren't automatic sellers to that I can try to make sure it keeps going) (...)

•

SA:

(...) I just read the letters page from the last issue of CASANOVA: AVARITIA, and I would lie if I say I don't download comics illegally every week. Fuck, I downloaded C:A #2 illegally.

I'm trying my best not to sound like an arsehole, or giving dumb excuses, but I suppose I can't help it right now[56]. I frequent a few comic forums, and the current pricing seems to be a concern shared among American readers. You can imagine that goes double when comics cost three or four times more in asstard third-world countries like the one I live in. I download comics and music illegally, yes, but I also love having the actual physical thing in my hands (a good book is the second best partner you can get into your bed, I always say). (...)

(...) Sometimes the availability of the material in reprint form is the issue. Other times, the issue is the availability of money to purchase all the good stuff I enjoy.

The same goes with music: if an album of a band I like gets leaked a couple of weeks before the official release sale, I'll download it, listen to is, and buy it if I enjoyed it. If I don't, it wont' be taking any space in my hard drive.

Some people say uploading/downloading comics is like borrowing a book from a friend. I can buy my own copy and keep buying

---

54   I think that's been a particularly brilliant thing Marvel's done, the free download code-with-purchase thing. I should look into that for my stuff now.

55   This no longer holds sway as an argument as we've been published around the world in a half-dozen languages.

56   Sure you can, you could just, y'know, not steal comics from the internet. "But I Want It" doesn't actually serve as moral justification for theft.

the series if I like it, or just give it back and forget all about it if I don't. I understand that not everybody does that, and then the illegal downloads don't work as a kind of advertisement, as Matt said. Most people download their shit and the company/artists/whatever never sees a cent from the fuckers. Even if they did enjoy the work they so eagerly downloaded. Cheap fuckers. (...)

•

DF:

(...) I downloaded it because it was easy, and I supported it because I loved it. That's not to say that I don't recognize the damage pirating can do for a creator-owned series[57], and there are more than a few I've read and enjoyed and not bought. On the other hand, there are so very many that I downloaded first and bought later, stuff that I'd have never looked at had they not been freely, readily available, and CASANOVA is among them. (...)

•

RF:

Yes, I purchased CASANOVA (and your other stuff) after discovering your writing/it in torrents (I won't say piracy[58], as I didn't get it at sea at the business end of a cutlass). In fact, I bought it directly from you at a con. I tend to prefer monthlies/single issues, though, over trades, [quarterly publications], what have you, as trades don't open flat; most of the art gets locked into the gutter. (...)

(...) it continues to be foolish of the major comics publishers to not offer digital comics in formats for CDisplay. They should've done that long ago, getting the jump on DCP and Minutemen. The music industry made the same mistake until iTunes. Not excusing it, just being honest.

•

KdB:

(...) I buy comics because I kike them filling up my personal space but the cost makes me choosy. CASANOVA: I first came across you because one of the local retailers sometimes drops the price on all recent back issues to $2 per mag to clear them out and at times like those I buy stacks of things that look interesting. It's how I tuned in to the Image run of CASANOVA, and other stuff by other people. I didn't write just to tell you that. Something about piracy...?

That's right, I lived in Indonesia the past couple years. Piracy is everywhere. There are huge stores all over the place where you can spend say 40 US cents to rent a pirated copy of software that would otherwise cost hundreds of dollars. Pirated movies and music for sale in the big malls, photocopied book markets etc etc. The Hollywood boycott of Indonesia (2) has bolstered movie piracy, but piracy seems to have always thrived because the majority of people simply cannot afford the genuine article. I guess in the US and Australia, the big problem is piracy on the internet, but in Indonesia it's on the sidewalk (...)

(...) So Indonesia is the place where I first learned of comic piracy. It all started when a friend gave me a disc full of downloads. Then I worked out how to download stuff that I actually wanted to read/keep up with; mostly creator-owned/co-owned stuff, which I justified to myself easily since I had no other way to acquire them while in the country. The cost to have them shipped was incredibly prohibitive since I was subsisting on $600 a month; things have a way of getting lost in the Indonesian postal system; books like CASANOVA would never make it through postal screening anyway due to the nudity on the page; and the humidity would absolutely destroy them pretty quickly. So there's all that. Besides which, the internet there is so slow that I only ever downloaded a few titles each month (...)

(...) Paid digital downloads. Yes, yes, it'll be great when digital comics ARE cheaper than buying a printed copy. My copy of AVARITIA #2 cost me $7.50 so for Australians they already are. (...)

•

NO:

(...) in answer to your question, yes, I discovered CASANOVA by stealing it off the interwebs. I did so because I was between cities and comic book stores when it first came out and it completely passed under my radar. By the time I caught wind of it, it was too late. That ship had sailed, it was nowhere to be had. So I nicked it. Having scanned comics in no way makes up for the real thing (although you can read them on your laptop at work when you're pretending to do something else) but sometimes needs must. The thing is, had it not bee for those illicit downloads I would not have fallen big time for the mighty pen of Fraction and subsequently bought all those issues of UNCANNY X-MEN and INVINCIBLE IRON MAN and IMMORTAL IRON FIST and MIGHTY THOR etc etc. And I also wouldn't have gotten a raging hard-on for the brothers Moon/Bá and bought all those issues of THE UMBRELLA ACADEMY and (the amazing) DAYTRIPPER, or the DE:TALES and PIXU books (which in turn led me to pick up DEMO cos I fell in love with the fabulous Becky Cloonan). And then ultimately I did end up buying CASANOVA anyway, cos you reprinted it, in lovely full colour. So everyone's happy! So yes, while illegal downloads are evil and destroying the world and bla-bla-bla they are handy for filling in gaps, and they do act as a perfect gateway drug. Anyone who claims one illegal download represents one lost sale is a twat. But it is very annoying when the pages have been numbered wrong and it's not until you reach the end and find all those double-page spreads, which would have made far more sense had you read them in the correct order! Bastards. (...)

•

---

57   I wonder what the legal ramifications of writing "only illegally download comics whose underlying intellectual properties are owned by massive megacorporations" could be? I better not write it I guess.

58   This still cracks me up. I mean, a lot of this stuff cracks me up to reread, the equivocating and excuse-making, but that line especially. Jesus. "I'm not a thief as I have not acquired physical goods via illegal and thus resent being called a thief." Fucking classic.

MP:

(...) I didn't get into CASANOVA by my piracy but by OTHER people pirating it, and posting short sections of scans of it. I know that sometimes there are official preview pages put out there, but it's not the same as reading a blog post about how amazing a comic is and then seeing a few pages of it. It's caused me to buy comics before. I've also pirated CASANOVA, after I bought an issue, simple so I could post a single page here or there, and to have it in my computer so I can read it without stumbling into my closet. I also lent my friend the first 2 volumes, she had a house fire, so those are gone, these things happen. I also use comic piracy to help keep up as a fan, as if an issue is sold out of a series that I've been buying, I will tend to pirate the missing issues. But I've also had major income problems; as I was out of work for a while, I pirated what series I wanted and made up for it by spending what money I could on the comics I liked, maybe at a lower ration of what I actually read. (...)

(...) I think the biggest boom that piracy gives the comic industry is enthusiasm, as there are people talking about comics, sharing scans of a panel or page all over (...)

(...) But when it comes down to it, I can't think of a single comic/creator that I've pirated, enjoyed and didn't end up spending money on getting some of the comic that I enjoyed. (...)

•

NS:

I just read AVARITIA 1 and 2 for the second time today. The first time I read them was last night after torrenting them. I was going through the letter column and I saw you trying to reach out to the pirate community. And I'll keep this part short because there's some more I want to say (...) My copies of CASANOVA: AVARITIA 1 and 2 are sitting in my room at home right now but I can't go home. (...) I couldn't wait for CASANOVA, so I downloaded them too, and I'm glad.

•

KB:

(...) Yes, I pirate comics. Yes, I know it's wrong...but I do it anyway. I download comics I'm either not going to purchase anyway, or ones I want to try out before purchasing. Anyone that says every download is a missed sale is flat-out wrong and there's plenty of studies to prove it. I know there's a distinct difference, but I view illegal downloading as being roughly equivalent to flipping through a book at a local shop. I've been at this a long time, before previews of almost every major book were online, or places like Comixology and Graphicly existed. Old habits are hard to break. (...)

(...) What will get me to stop pirating comics is selling digital comics in a vendor-neutral, portable format. Oh, and at a decent price. Selling a digital comic wrapped in [digital rights management] for the same price as the paper version isn't even a contest. Your comment about selling CASANOVA for $0.99 would probably get me to buy it three times (floppy, digital, and trade) so long as the digital format allowed me to stick it onto a tablet, iPod, or anywhere else I wanted (...)

•

ED:

(...) I never would have heard about CASANOVA if not for another pirate on the internet. I never would have read it if I couldn't instantly find a download. I never would have spent money on it if I hadn't read it and re-read it and re-re-read it on an ill-suited monitor and decided, fuck it, I love this book.

I'm buying AVARITIA as it comes out, but I'll still buy a trade when that exists too. Hell, I wouldn't mind dropping $30 on a GULA hardcover in the original color, if you can make that happen. Gotta match my LUXURIA, even though I already have trades of both. All I know is, one download eventually translated into sales (...)

•

NR:

I did discover CASANOVA from download sites. I did download CASANOVA illegally. Did I like it? So freaking much!!! Did I buy it? Hell yeah!!! (...)

(...) I'm a Mexican guy who loves comics books but as most Mexican reader find myself "forced" to look for the independent comics at illegal sites because the very few comic book stores left because of the economic crisis basically focus on the "mainstream." We have "Marvel México" who translates them and distributes them at affordable prices in Mexican pesos. But if you want to read something outside those...you have to pay a whole bunch more, for example, AVARITIA I and II went from 4.99 to 8.00 USD since I had to buy then at an American store and pay shipping and handling. And we Mexicans are the lucky ones. Last year I went to Peru and man... those guys have it even worse, comic book prices are incredibly high and you have to buy the [trade paperback] version. And the same goes for all South American. (...)

•

FL:

I'm French and I live in France. I've loved comics since I was a child (learned to read with ASTÉRIX). I love alternative US comics. They are impossible to find here.

So I downloaded each and every issue of CASANOVA I could find.

I would buy high-quality electronic issues, though (for cheaper than paper issues) or mail order paper copies for a reasonable price.

And for the record I do think that in this age and time it should be possible to email original files to printers around the world and print locally instead of burning oil to move dead trees halfway around the globe. Yes I am dreaming up nonsense. I read comic books. And I love, just love your CASANOVA.

•

Oh hey—one more thing…

In 2012-2013, CASANOVA will be published in France, Argentina, Brazil, Chile, Italy, Portugal, San Marino, Spain, Spanish-speaking Central and Latin America, Switzerland and…

Wait for it…

Vatican City.

Daugard in France, Panini all the rest.

OK. See you in June, goddammit, JUNE.

MF
PDX
7MAR12[59]

AVARITIA IV (Icon Comics, 2012)

Dear CASANOVA Crew,

I'm sure you get tons of emails saying how amazing each issue has been, how each issue lives off every word that has come before it to create this psychedelic world(s) that Cass and company can't help but learn to live/destroy in it. I'm sure you get plenty of correspondence describing how every page holds a new discovery for your senses, not just when you reread them, but when you blink, or shift your eyes, or right before you're about to turn the page—but pause. So allow me instead to say a little something about our humble storytellers.

Over the last two years, I was lucky enough to meet the Twins and Mr. Fraction at the 2010 and 2011 New York Comic-Cons respectively. I have an identical twin brother and we are both Casanova fans from Day 1, so we were very excited to meet The Twins. We had a wonderful conversation with Gabriel and Fábio as we talked about Cass and Zeph's relationship and how the four of us connected to it. The passion in their eyes as we talked was piercing to say the least. My brother and I were being transported to this world that The Twins had been living in with Matt, just by seeing these stories from their perspective. During our journey, they also took turns drawing a sketch of Cass and Zeph back to back for us, each drawing one of the twins. The Twins drawing The Twins for the twins. Class Acts all the way.

Anyone that was at last year's NYCC knows how big/crowded/overwhelming the show gets year after year. After waiting in a long queue for Mr. Fraction, who was all smiles as he signed stack, and stacks and stacks of books for his fans, it was my turn. I had one book with me—a custom-bound hardcover of the Image releases of CASANOVA 1-14, with all the backmatter from the issues in an appendix at the back. The queue was just as long behind me, but Mr. Fraction took more than a moment to look through the book and compliment the design and passion behind it. Just like with The Twins, you could literally feel the creative forces that go into this series at that small table. We chatted a little bit more about Cass and he signed my book and it was back to the madness. Mr. Fraction wrote inside it, "For Mike—Creator of this wholly unique collection of CASANOVA. With thanks, Fraction!" Class Act all the way.

So we all know the joke is that, "you have to be a little crazy to be behind the typewriter and behind the artboard for this series,"" but in case any new readers are trying CASANOVA for the first time, please know that these guys have the right amount of world-building creativity AND the right amount of crazy to never give up on Cass. They will see Cass through to the end because when that first page was written, and then drawn, there was no stopping the journey.

Thanks for the best series of the last decade,
Mike H.

I remember this thing—this incredible, crafted, planned, thing—when I saw it. Aside from being flattering—and all of Mike's email up there is excruciatingly flattering—the thing I remember most about the book was feeling an odd sense of relief that there was someone else out there in the world that was AS obsessive about this stuff as I was. I dream of making my own collections of these things—I've come close more than once of custom-designing my own FINAL CRISIS edition that'd fold in a ton of the concurrent BATMAN stuff and side stuff in the proper reading order (in as much as you can do something like that), or collecting all of Paul Pope's short stories that I've gathered over the years from god knows how many places, or all the Al Columbia bits…

Anyway. To have had something to do with something someone felt that same kind of crazy about was pretty amazing. Thanks for sharing, Mike.

---

59   And I still feel the same way. I still think digital theft in the short term leads to physical sales in the long term and refuse to get worked up, pissed off, or anything about it beyond shrugging and trying to make it easier to get paid. Price point is next. I swear to you price point is next.

Also of note: my digital sales, and my wife's, are abnormally large. Like—like we are wreckers of the bell curve. Because of content, because of online outreach, because of… well, who knows? It's true though. So that might be skewing my perspective some.

The conversation continues…

-

What does Cass sound like, in you head? I always wonder that, especially because the art definitely dictates how I "hear" his voice when reading the books.

Thanks/I love comic books.
Jon

Sort of like Opus the Penguin mixed with Stark's Parker[60].

-

(...) I want to take a second and point out that I have no problem paying $4.99 for this book. I feel that it is completely worth it and, honestly, if it were necessary to charge more I'd pay more.

I've read in interviews that you're interested in exploring the [original graphic novel] format for Cass Vol. 4. I would miss the single issues but I'd love to see how Cass would evolve to envelop that format[61].

Have you thought about pursuing other formats? I know you just had a whole discussion of how digital comics are just advertisements for the finished print book but if any book could shatter that preconception it'd be Cass.

I really enjoyed how you GQ Bin Laden comic had commentary from you and I'd love something like that with Casanova.

Do you have any plans for more creator owned books in the near future? (...)

—Dave

I'm glad you stuck with us. I hated to jack the price up, but we've got more to pay for now, and eventually justified it to myself by realizing we're putting out sixty percent more book for just twenty-five percent more cost...

I was excited to explore OGNs but at least when the direct comics market is your primary retail audience and you're doing a non-established superhero, non-mainstream book, you die on the vine. The numbers just aren't there right now.

I'd also love to try and do digital-first work. Something is slowly cooking there, but who knows? It's virgin territory, it's wide open, nobody knows anything and somebody who's first to a particular digital comics market is gonna explode.

The backmatter in the old Image versions of CASANOVA were kind of like the GQ thing—for those of y'all wondering what he's talking about, me and Nate Fox did a piece about the killing of Osama bin Laden for GQ's MAN OF THE YEAR issue this past December, and they put it online with some making-of commentary from us.

Anyway, think I'm kind of done with that kind of thing, at least about CASANOVA. The OBL piece was nice, though, because I researched those pages as hard and as deep as any term paper I ever wrote in school.

Documentary comics is fun. It was as close to getting to do my Abraham Lincoln comic as I think I'll ever get.

-

Thanks for the CASANOVA series. Hell, thanks for your entire comic output.

And special thanks for the Suki Boutique winter scene where she has the most gorgeous outfit know to man.

Keep up the wonderful, insane work. I am buying.

—Pixie Solanas

This is very kind, but I'm only running this letter because your name is "Pixie Solanas."

-

Will you be releasing a volume for all seven deadly sins[62]? Sorry if you've clarified this elsewhere...

—Alee Karim

Assuming we get to publishing all of them, yes. In fact, AVARITIA will be collected in, like, twenty minutes. It'll be out in JULY and, as per the other Icon editions, will have all new exclusive making-of material that focuses on the artwork...

-

---

60   Which I guess means somewhere between Michael Bell and Jason Statham?

61   Oh, I'd forgotten about that. It'd still be fun to do something like that some day (I think about similar things for ODY-C) but I suspect would be more hassle than it's worth.

62   Well, it's a loose organizational principal rather than a straight-up, like, road map. The story I wanted to tell in CASANOVA, the story that got the ball rolling, will end up being the story we tell in Volume FIVE. Which is just the kind of rookie nonsense you'd expect someone to make their first time at the plate.

Dear Mr. Fraction and Co.,

Just to let you know, I love your love letter to life basically, so I got this one little question for you: as your life changes does it make you write CASANOVA differently?

Keep up the good work.

—Jack Higgins

Oh, yes. God yes. Absolutely.

And this one was no different. I think part of the problem with getting the right AVARITIA version rolling—it took forever and lots of false starts on my part—was because maybe some of those changes just hadn't stopped changing, maybe there was more of life that needed to be lived, lived through, survived, endured, I dunno[63].

I started this book wanting to not-write the Nth knockoff of BATMAN or WOLVERINE. I wanted to write a knockoff of DIABOLIK or BOND[64] and...and then it just became this entire other thing. And once I'd committed to what CASANOVA became...well, you had to stick with it.

When I first started, the notebook I had for LUXURIA was one of those five-subject sorts of deals, and the notes and stuff for LUXURIA ate up nearly the entire thing. Then GULA ate up a standard marble-cover notebook, almost to the page.

AVARITIA lives on just nine pages of new notebook, and that's including the two shorts that preceded it in the AVARITIA and GULA collections. It was almost entirely internal. It had to be lived.

Oh! There's a piece of scrap paper I wrote in a line about guilt on one night so I wouldn't lose it but ended up not putting it in the book. The line kind of summed the whole thing up but literally the morning it went to press, Dharbin talked me out of it. So there's that. And that was the end; that was what I needed to wrap AVARITIA #4.

Does that make sense? It barely does to me. I commit to things and stick with them far past the point of good sense sometimes[65].

Eh, fuck it. Beats not caring, right?

Next time: California and everything after.
Be seeing you.

Fraction
PDX
17 May 12

CASANOVA AVARITIA COLLECTION[66] (Icon Comics, 2012)

MATT FRACTION: So I think by the time Fábio and I finished GULA I felt like he'd taken CASANOVA away from you. In my head when I thought of the book I thought of his brush instead of your pen, almost. Then getting to write the short for him that came after the LUXURIA trade, where he got to not just revisit your characters but you "scenes" even more...I'd forgotten, in a way, what "your" CASANOVA looked like. Then starting with the DIT DIT DIT...short at the end of GULA you came roaring back and thoroughly seized it back. I'm wondering if you had a hard time finding your way back to CASANOVA after the break, and after Fábio's masterful turn behind the wheel.

GABRIEL BÁ: It really was a good choice to put Fábio in charge of the artwork of GULA and he surprised everyone and took over the series. Most of the characters became "his" characters after his interpretation. But Casanova himself was portrayed only on the first and last issues, so I still felt he was my character, the guy I created. I knew his tricks, his moves, his charm. And GULA was a lot more

---

63   So by the time I was writing this, my father had started and finished treatment for cancer and was in remission. The day he finished his chemo/radiation diet, my mother was diagnosed with breast cancer. Cancer had, at that point, spread though our family on either sides of the tree. I started wearing little bracelets with tiny skulls on my wrists, one side being people who were SICK the other side people who were WELL. I'm not religious, they weren't exactly prayer beads, but rather a kind of abacus that helped me chart my lucky stars and reminded me to think of my family and speak to them as much as I could. If anyone asked I told them Henry said I could never take them off (which he did, once, but he was three, and said all kinds of crazy shit) to hide from having to talk about it.

I wrote half the first issue of FEAR ITSELF in a hospital where my father was relieved the burden of a quarter of his lung. I wrote the second half at my parent's home, helping them find what the new normal looked like. And CASANOVA was happening the whole time in the background, a magpie perched atop everything I saw, everything I felt, pillaging it all for fuel.

Now, on the other side of 2014, there was good news and bad news. My wife says it's as if the top branches of our family tree have been lopped off. And it is. Not everybody died, but not everybody lived, and it kept adding *one more thing* when the last thing we needed was *one more thing*.

I was writing this book as a kind of real-time therapy, I think. Trying to process my own thoughts and feelings to the events transpiring all through my extended family and friends. All of CASANOVA has been autobiographical in some form or fashion, no matter how veiled the metaphor, and AVARITIA was no different.

64   Being Not Right but Wrong In Another Direction remains *my shit*.

65   And if you're reading this, so have you.

66   This back and forth was specially created for the AVARITIA collection.

straightforward story-wise than LUXURIA, I think, and when I got the first script for AVARITIA I realized we were back in psycho-crazy land again. What really worried me was the energy I had on the first series and if I could match or surpass that on the new one. The story was clearly more challenging, so I needed to up my game once more, which I didn't expect I would have to do this time. I thought I had CASANOVA all figured out—or that I had YOU figured out—and it would be a walk in the park to go back to the series. I was so wrong.

What about you? It obviously took you more brain-cracking to get back into the series. You really though it would be easier this time?

MF: No, no, god no. I don't know what I was thinking. I guess…I mean, I knew the gist, I knew the sweep of the story, but that's almost secondary to something like CASANOVA. I knew, though, that, whatever it was I came up with—by the time it saw publication—it would be a product of "we," of TEAM CASANOVA, that me, and you, and Cris, and Dharb would all have hands on it and whatever I was blowing, you guys, with your varied genius talents, would transform it into something Greater Than. So I guess…I guess what I'm saying is I had faith I could type "escape pod" and you guys would summon it from the grand unknown cosmic æther and we'd all fly away together. In a way, I think AVARITIA was more underwritten than the other CASANOVA issues—more trust, more faith. All of that somehow became paramount to being able to execute at all.

Did you feel something similar, having Cris and Dharb with us from the start, this time? Do you draw differently for "color," did you know where Dustin would come in? What was it like being more than just you, me, Fábio over your shoulder, and Mário cracking the whip?

GB: First of all, I have to say I got really overwhelmed by the amount of stuff that can be told in 32 pages. Every issue looking like a never-ending battle, full of blood, sweat and tears and all that jazz. And I really felt the scripts were beefier—as in a whole lot more stuff written in them—than the first two series. There's a lot in there to digest and end up on the page and that was more work than I expected. I guess you trusted me to understand all you meant, so you said everything you wanted on the scripts. As usual, I was really exhausted by the end of every issue, but completely satisfied by the result. These are my best pages.

About Cris and Dustin, I couldn't really imagine the look of this book without them.

On previous works like UMBRELLA ACADEMY and B.P.R.D., I got used to having my art colored and got a little lazy on the intensive use of black and white and I really wanted to get heavy on the inks on CASANOVA. I have to be honest and say I would still have the story in B&W or monotone because I love that look, so I would never have the guts to color these pages. Cris has no fear of doing that, she's having fun (not easy fun, but hard-working fun) and she totally owns it. We have gone a long way together over all the issues, and she really delivered what I expected and a little more. We still have a very unique-looking book.

And Dustin is the invisible man, in the best sense of the term. The handmade quality of his work is unbelievable and hard to describe and it fits the art so well it'll be hard to go back to digital lettering on my other projects. It seems almost unfair having him lettering our book instead of just having his stellar career as a cartoonist. We'll be lucky as long as we can hold him with us.

And now there's a hard question: Would you like the CASANOVA team to work on all your books? How different is the work dynamic with your other collaborators? What experiences do you want to transport to the super heroes and what you've learned from writing them that you used on CASANOVA? Or do you think they're two very different types of books that have nothing in common?

MF: The entire THING was overwhelming. Every issue. This book—this volume especially—was the hardest thing I've ever written, the more work-intensive. I spent a day's worth of work writing just one page, at one point, in the first issue, ten, twelve hours, something like that. It felt like reinventing itself every page-flip. And yes: I would work with you, Moon, Cris, and Dharb, on anything, everything, everywhere, whenever. It's not just that I'm such a fan, but that…I feel a strange and silent simpatico with all of you. A psychic… whatever goes unsaid I know you'll hear anyway, and understand. I mean, think about it—it wasn't until the VERY END of AVARITIA #4 that you had, I think, EVER written me for clarification and, let's be honest, things were pretty abstract at that point…

The best way I can explain this dynamic is this: when Kelly Sue first saw Cris' colors, she asked me, "Did you know it was going to look that good?" and I said "Yes, but I didn't know how to tell anyone." And I know you knew, too. I knew we were seeing that same thing in our heads when we thought of CASANOVA in color. And then comes Cris and not only delivers that but owns it and makes it her own.

This is the first ongoing series I've done that originated with the creative team—every other comic book I've done have been work-for-hire segments of a creative relay race. Which I can quite enjoy, both as a reader and a writer, but nothing replaces, as our dear Seychelle says, the "pride of ownership." For all the similarities in collaboration—and I've worked with, for my money, some of the very best—it's not the same as creating universe from scratch with your friends and then figuring out how it works as you play in it.

What about you? What's it like going form a phenomenon like UMBRELLA ACADEMY or a world-famous universe like HELLBOY'S for B.P.R.D. back to…um…planet weirdo?

GB: I consider CASANOVA: LUXURIA as my debut on the North American way of producing comics, to tell a story on a monthly series, and I'd day I had to learn it the hard way. After that, all other projects in that same universe were different and unique in their own way, but I had been well prepared by the fist run on CASANOVA, because of its dense storytelling and weirdness of the story.

Being the story on UMBRELLA ACADEMY as bizarre as it was, it was easier to understand and portray in the art than CASANOVA has ever been. And working on B.P.R.D. was the delight of a fan that loves not only Mignola's work, but has grown to love, admire and respect the world he has created. It is the closest I got to a work-for-hire kind of comic and pretty much the only one I would make this exception for.

So I thought that five years of experience with all these other projects, genres and creators would have built a stronger artist and that I would wheel the new CASANOVA pages with a hand on my back. That was very naïve of me and I have learned my lesson now. The depths this story can go, the dimensions—literally—it can reach, are really beyond the average comic book production and I'm glad I'm part of that. It's a comic that's hard to describe, hard to compare to just one thing instead of a mesh of different realms and forms of cultural production. It's a language-bender and that's what's most difficult about it, it will always be, and why I feel so good with the final result. I love my pages because I have to work so hard on them to do what I think is right for the story. Not a lot of comics are like that.

And the exciting moment of reaching the climax of the story you have told us six years ago, the one we've been waiting so long to reach. I have no idea what comes next and I know we can expect everything to change dramatically. But how much of the original story could you keep this far into the series and how much you adapted once it started getting a life of its own on the pages, with the characters getting faces and voices and all that. It's not just notes on a big bible notebook anymore. How does that help the rest of the story and now does it make it harder and more complex for you to move on?

MF: My metaphor has always been that...well, I have a couple metaphors. In terms of, I dunno how to put it, the Grand Design has pretty much remained fixed. In my head, there were these first three books formed a loose kind of trilogy; volume 4 is larely stand-alone; then there's another loose trilogy. With that in mind, the writing has been like taking a road trip without a map but a...y'know, vaguely functional sense of geography. I could leave my house and drive to New York in a few days' time but I have almost no notion of what roads I'd take. But I know it's east, and if I don't pass, like, the Great Lakes or the Mississippi, I've done something wrong. So you knew, six years ago, that Cass was going to end up holding that bandage with nothing underneath and so did I but I wasn't 100% on how he, or we, would get there. He ever says way back in LUXURIA he knows what's under the bandages...

So what I knew-knew about the book was very little but very important. Right? Like—there's 206 bones in the body, right? Pick the top ten. That sort of thing. I never really go lost when I wrote AVARITIA but there were times when I didn't know HOW to get there precisely. The good news was there was enough room so that...well, things like Luther, Luther became more than just a MacGuffin to me and to the story, so we had room to spend time with Luther. And still, Casanova had that date with Xeno's bandages.

Whatever comes next must be more simple and more kind, if for nothing else than I don't have anything else like this IN me right now. Whatever the next new sound is, is out there somewhere. Whatever ghosts and fuel I needed to burn out of me to get to Now are gone and done and burned. Life just needs to be lived.

Here's a question: I've said, for years now, that the dirty secret only me and Gerard Way knew was that you two had no use for the likes of us. The great thing we've NOT spoken of is DAYTRIPPER (which, for folks reading that might not, somehow, know, is your DC/Vertigo series done with Fábio). To say the response to DAYTRIPPER was positive is understating things—where do YOU go now, how do you two follow that up? Do you feel Sophomore Slump pressure? Are you gearing up for your Difficult Second Album?

GB: Shit, you're so right. We're really in a tight corner here. Well, what saves Fábio and me is that we have this balance between the types of books we work on that has really helped us to go through the years without struggling to have fresh ideas all the time. For as much as we understand its importance, we were not built for the monthly endless routine, not artistically and even less on the writing side of the deal. We are definitely not "idea machines," and in the end I think it's a good thing because when we have new idea, it's one we really thought it through and believe in. In the meantime, we have our "more commercial" comics like UMBRELLA and CASANOVA (and the fact that we only draw these comics makes it a lot easier on us too). These are comics that will never be "more of the same," so they help feed us with excitement for the job while exercising our artistic muscle.

In that same "commercial" zone, we are working with Mike Mignola on a new story, one we're both writing and drawing, which has been proving to be challenging and fulfilling at the same time. So that will keep us busy and we won't be away of the public eye for too long. That said, what will keep us away from the spotlight for some time is this massive novel from Brazilian literature we are currently adapting into a graphic novel. There has been a lot of book adaptations into comics here in Brazil over the last years, usually the classic ones that fall under public domain—even we did one back in 2007, "The Alienist," by Machado de Assis—but this one we're working on now is a modern classic written by a living author, maybe the most important living Brazilian writer, so the stakes are higher and the game is literally different. I can honestly say it will be our next biggest release, in similar way that the Parker books have been to Darwyn Cooke. We've been working on it for more than a year now and it'll still take us another year to see it all the way to completion.

We have the "second book" shadow all over us all the time, but we understood we don't have to hurry. The world we live in today—with the internet and its instantaneous pacing—really puts a lot of pressure on delivering new stuff right away, all the time, and we don't really work like that. I don't want to make something that is really good NOW. I want something that will endure.

What about you? I know we still have 4 entire series of CASANOVA to cover, but do you have something else you'd like to work on? Do you have one of those great ideas that come up in the middle of this very long project and made you almost wanna stop the presses and start this new project right away? Do you want CASANOVA to be over so you can jump on the next thing?

MF: Millions. All the time. Constantly. The burners atop my stove feel infinite, all covered with pot after pot of slowly bubbling ideas as CASANOVA does its all-encompassing, all-engulfing, all-consuming thing. The water boils and waits its turn.

GB: Being the über-writer of super heroes you have become, you completely master the North American mainstream market of comics, the craft, the way it works, the conventions, the characters, the readers, the format, as well as the wheels that make the machine keep pumping. Because you are part of this big industry of pop culture, your work reaches people all over the world. And now we have contract closed to publish CASANOVA in Italian, Spanish, French and Portuguese, so this book will break these borders as well. How often do you think about the differences your work can have on different readers, from different countries or cultures? And on the same not, CASANOVA drinks from a much bigger well than the regular comic and doing so can appeal to a different, more diverse kind of reader. With the great buzz that the super-hero movies have generated, comic creators are really in a big spotlight for a much wider audience. So what I want to know is: Do you think of comics as a bigger thing or are you happy with your role on this picture? Do you want to break this super-hero comics bubble and reach for the stars?

MF: That is...charming, to say the least. And I don't know that I think too terribly much about my books after they're done and set adrift on the currents of the world—but in terms of capital-C Comics, in terms of North American original works produced in English—yes, god, yes. My dream for those kinds of Comics is that they engulf the world like the virus in "Outbreak," that they spread internationally through airports, passed from world traveller to world traveller, devouring every inch of open air they can. And the only way that's possible is for as many kind of stories as there are stars to o the work; I like super-hero comics, I have fun writing them, I enjoy reading them, but this isn't the early day of the printed word, We don't need only the ILIAD and the Holy Bible to serve as the cornerstones of empire anymore. We need variety. That was always the dirty trick of CASANOVA to me: it looked like a "spy comic" (whatever that looks like) but I could tell whatever story I wanted. Ended up that I wanted to tell a story about every story that, y'know, took some time and bandwidth. In theory, though, it was a great plan.

But yes. Moving forward, the stuff that comes from me post-CASANOVA will be as different from CASANOVA as CASANOVA is from any super-hero stuff out there in the world.

I know you guys don't think about this stuff, but to me, that's the most insidiously ingenious thing about DAYTRIPPER—were it a novel there would be no wonder as to its success. Of COURSE it's an international best seller. Its idiom is human experience rather than, you know, one framed by American super heroes or whatever.

I get to do my first European shows this year; I did Brazil and the biggest show in the world last year with you two (and that was before CASANOVA had come out in Brazil)...and it's CASANOVA that's making that all possible, not the super-hero stuff. So, tell me—what's it like, making comics and going around the world, meeting comics readers, reading comics made thousands of miles away from where you come from? You've been everywhere now. What's the world like, through your eyes, for comics?

GB: I love comics and the more I travel and see it all over the world, more passionate I become.

What I've learned on my trips is that there is no ONE way to make comics, nor the BETTER way. Super heroes are mainstream in the U.S. and reach the whole world, but Bonelli's empire and characters like TEX, ZAGOR and MARTIN MYSTÉRE are the maintstream in Italy, as well as ASTERIX and TINTIN are still the big sellers on the French market, and every weekly massive MANGA sells more then the best-seller comics in Brazil or anywhere else, for that matter. And that's wonderful! And I believe there's space for everyone, everywhere. Readers and authors alike have plenty to learn it they look out to different comics—or any form of cultural and artistic production—then they're used to. I wouldn't be working on this book if I had not.

•

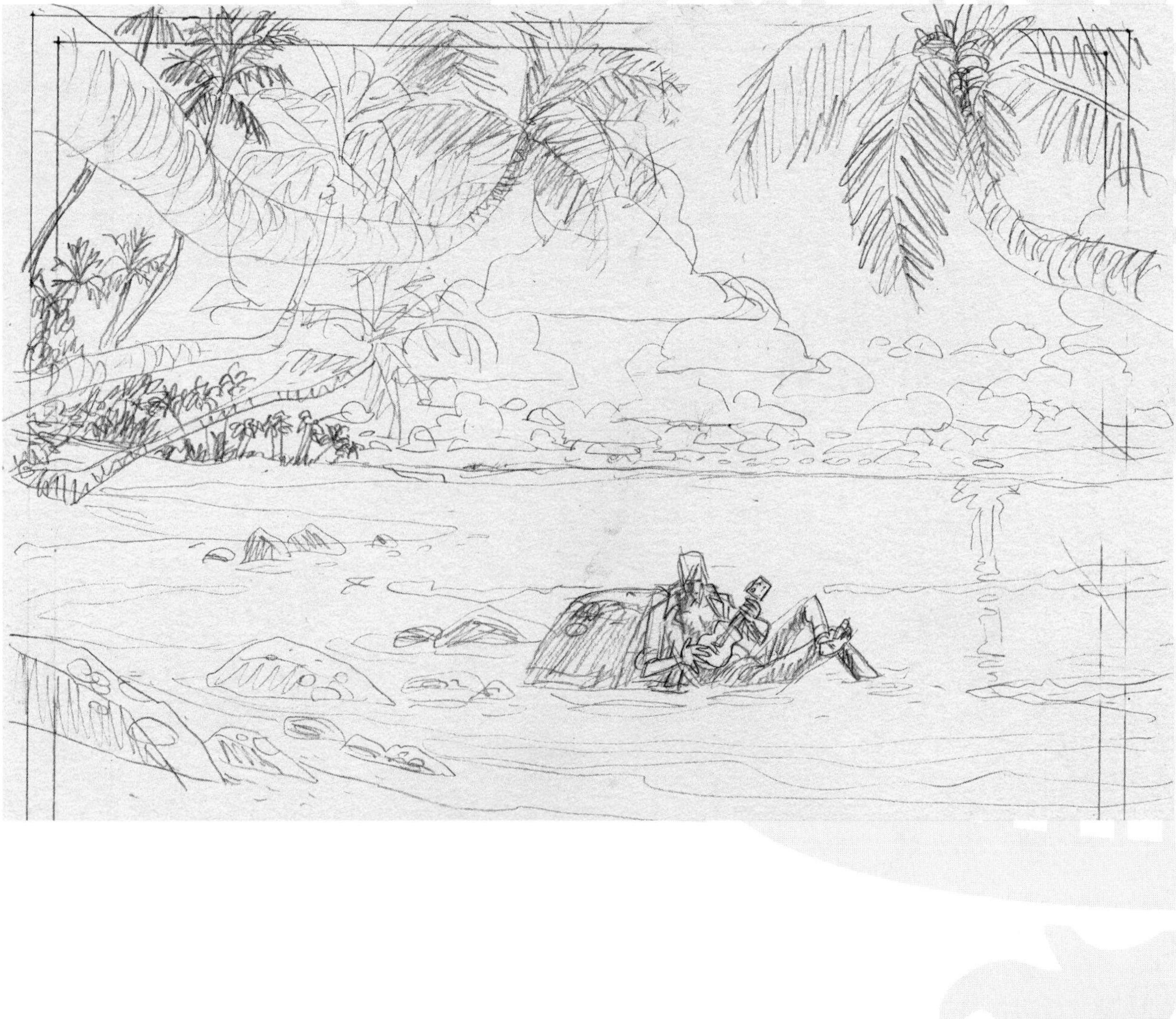

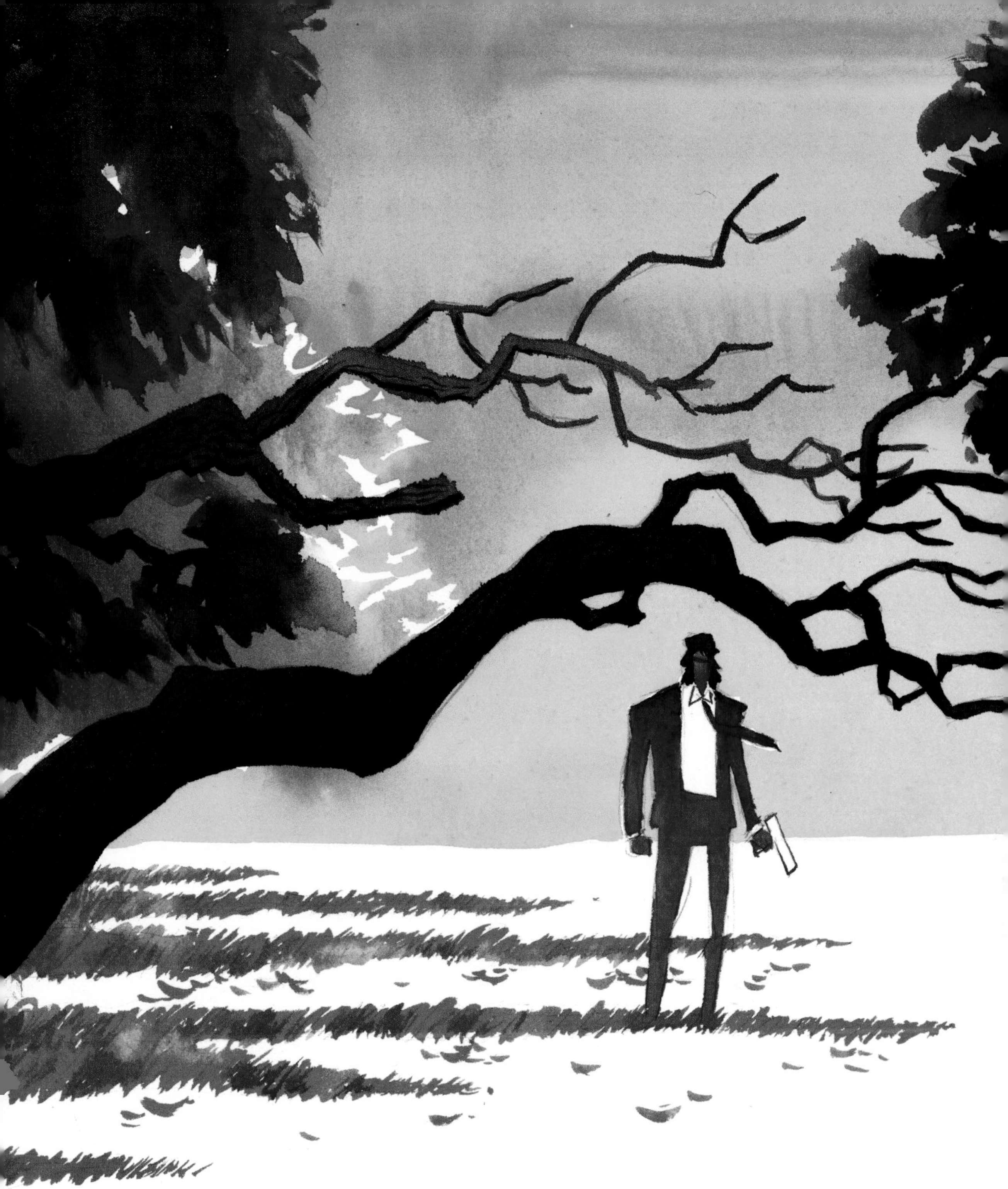
GABRIEL
BA
11

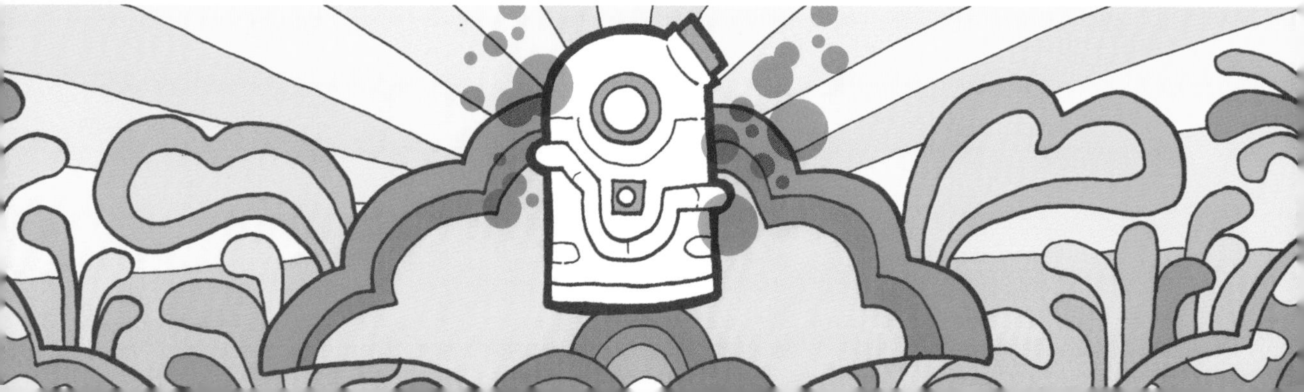

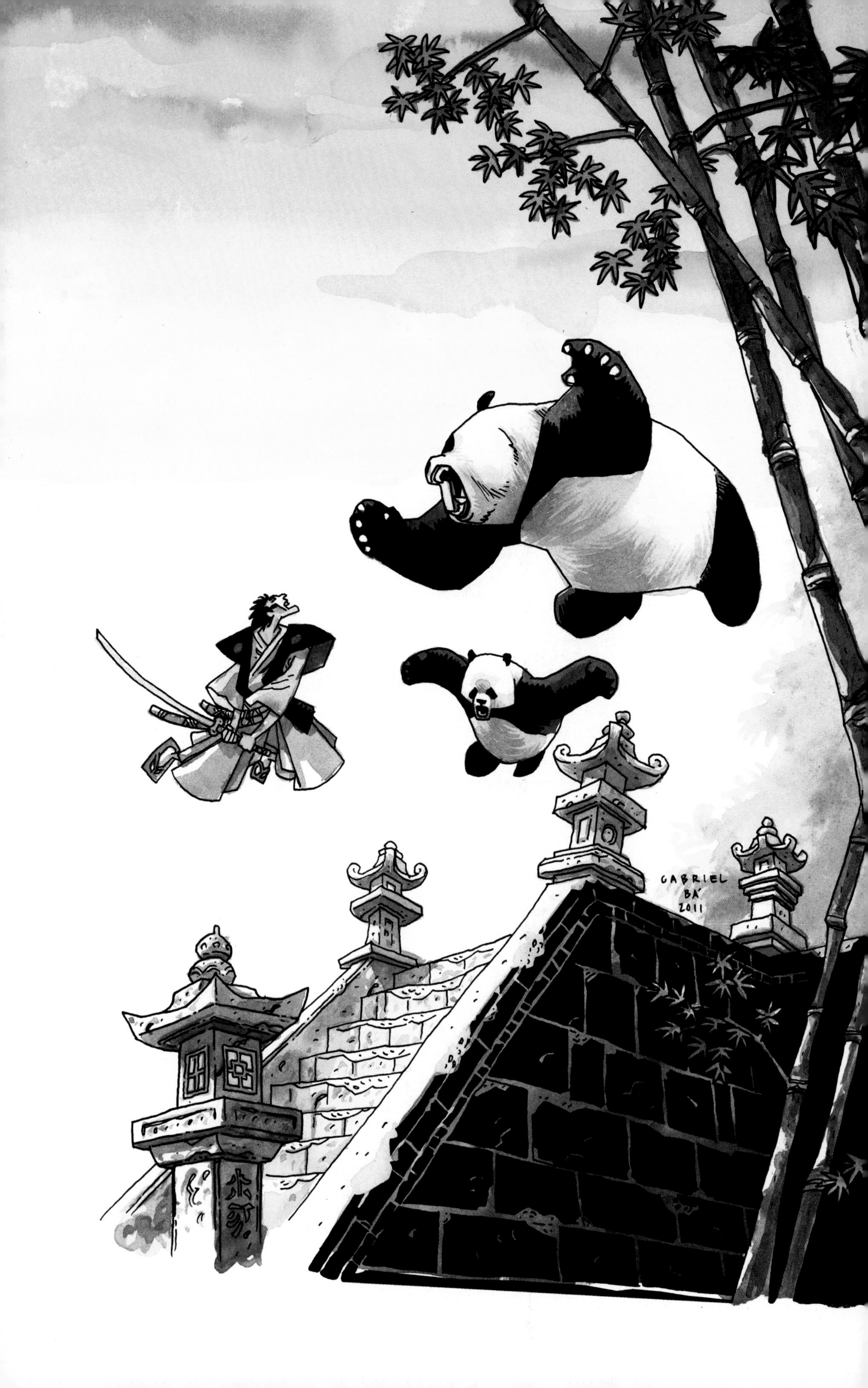
GABRIEL
BÁ
2011

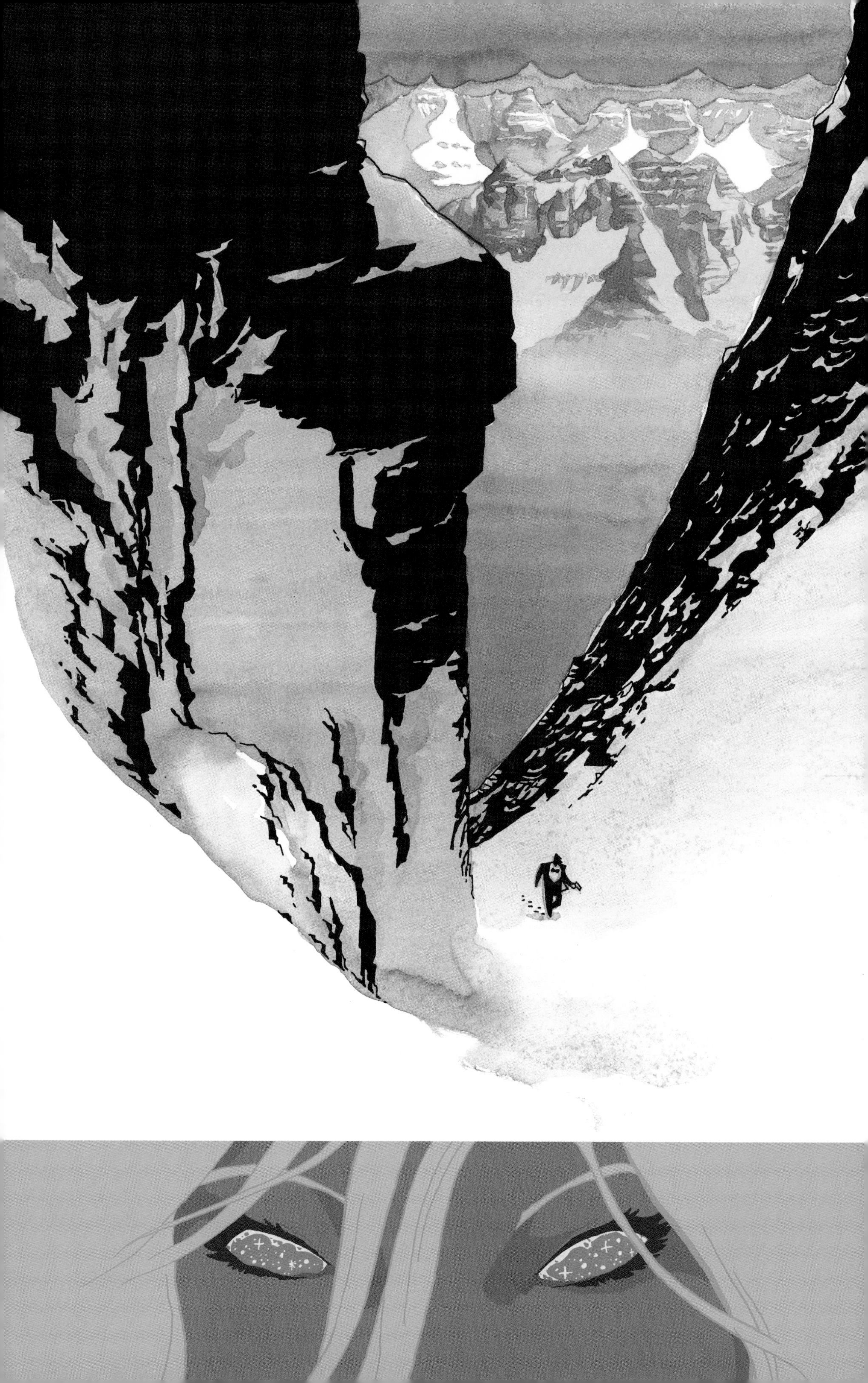

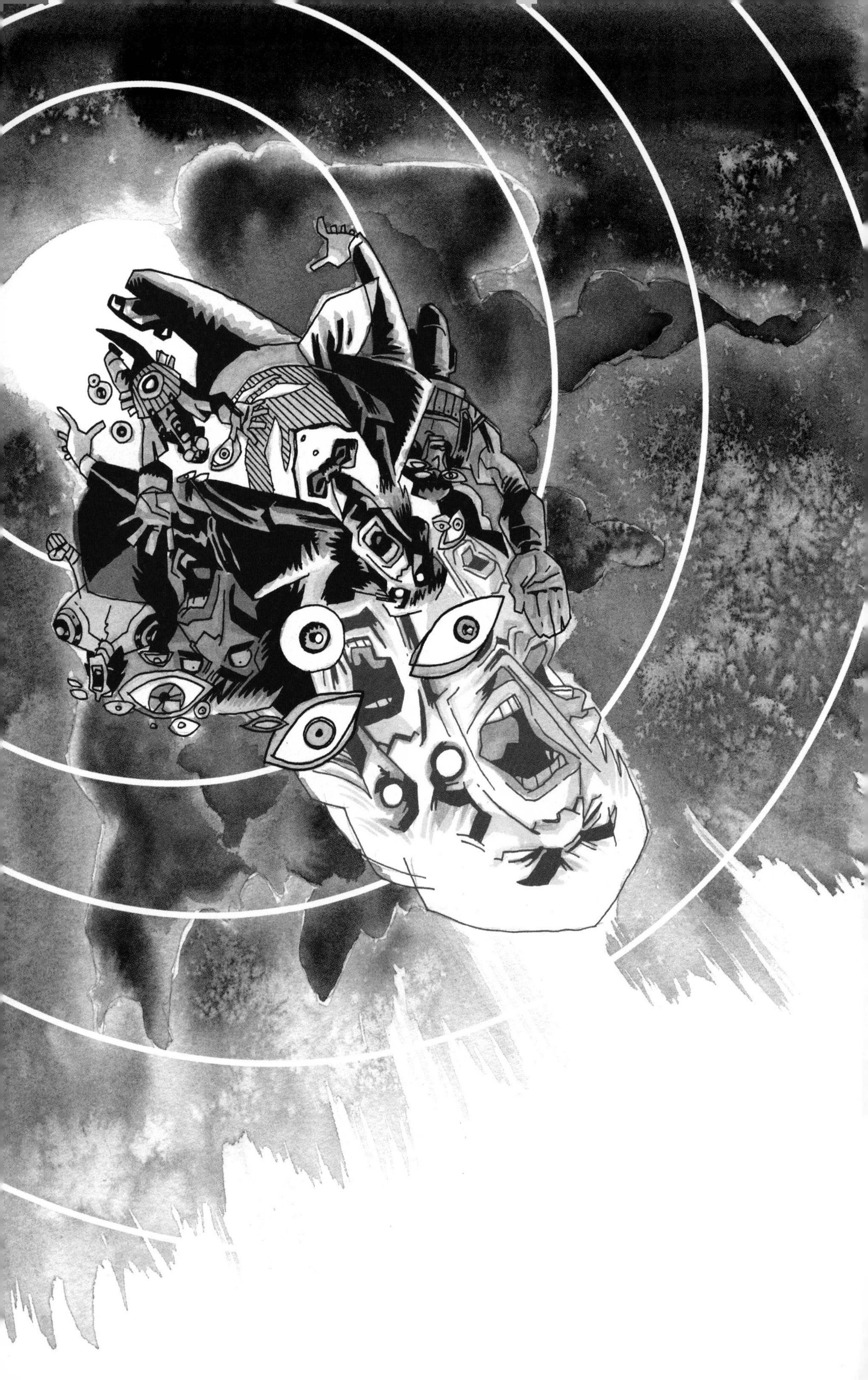

CASANOVA

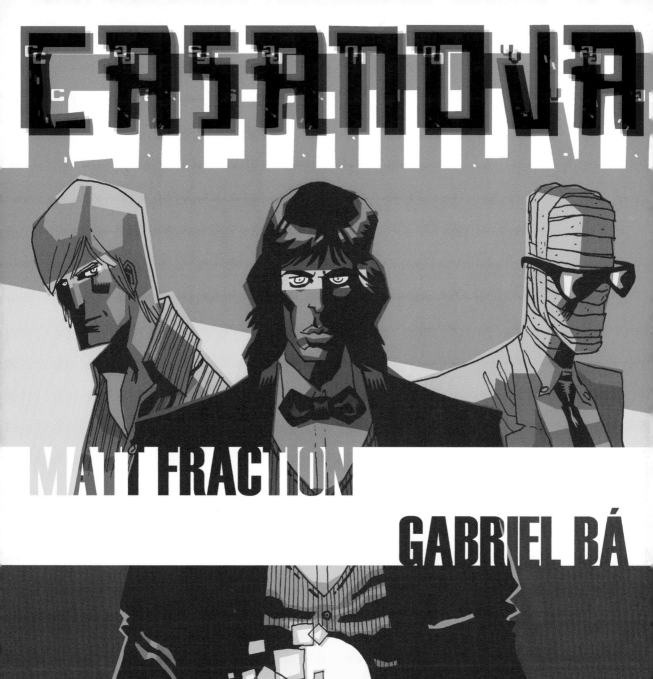

MATT FRACTION

GABRIEL BÁ

AVARITIA

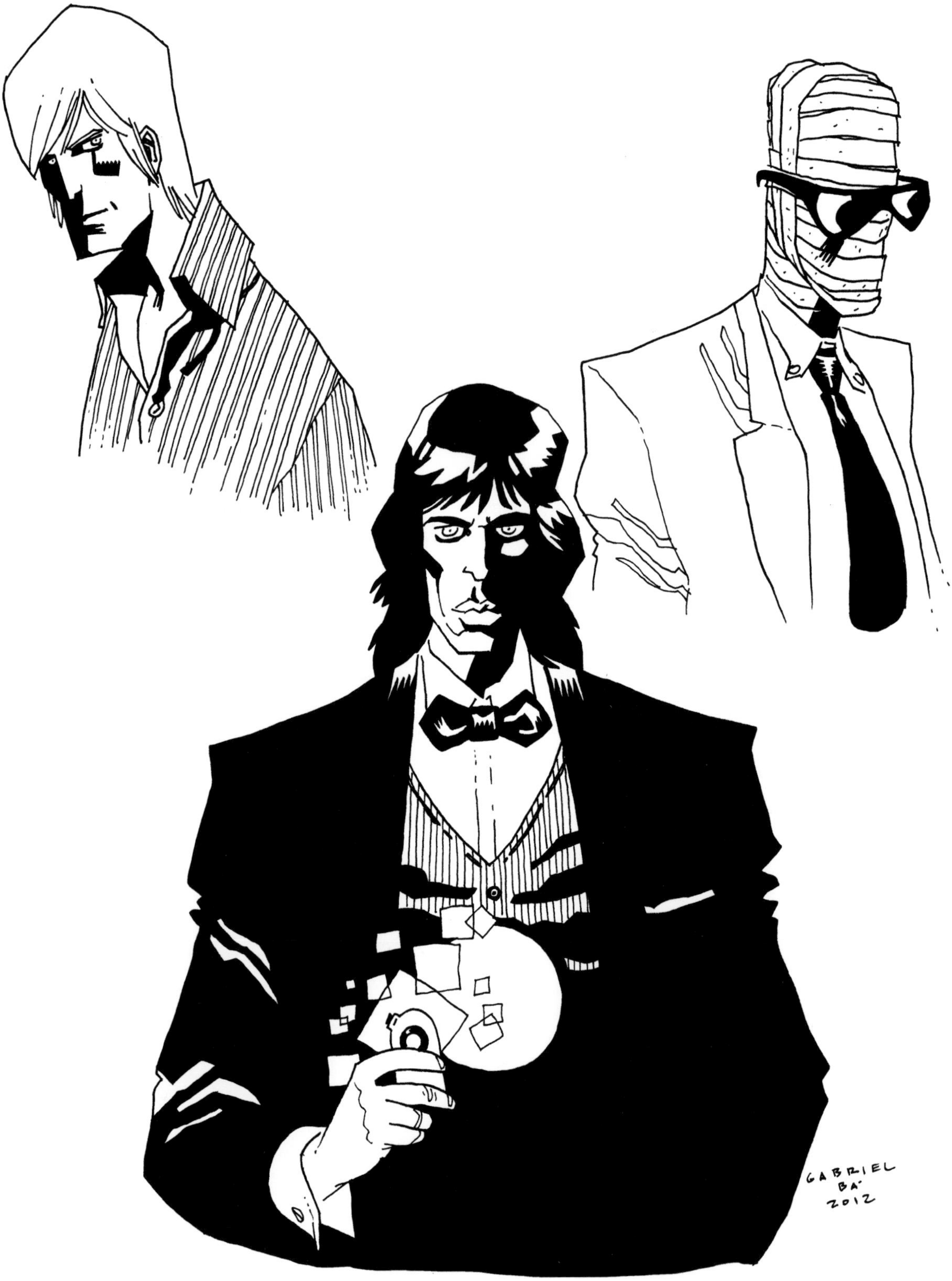
GABRIEL
BA
2012

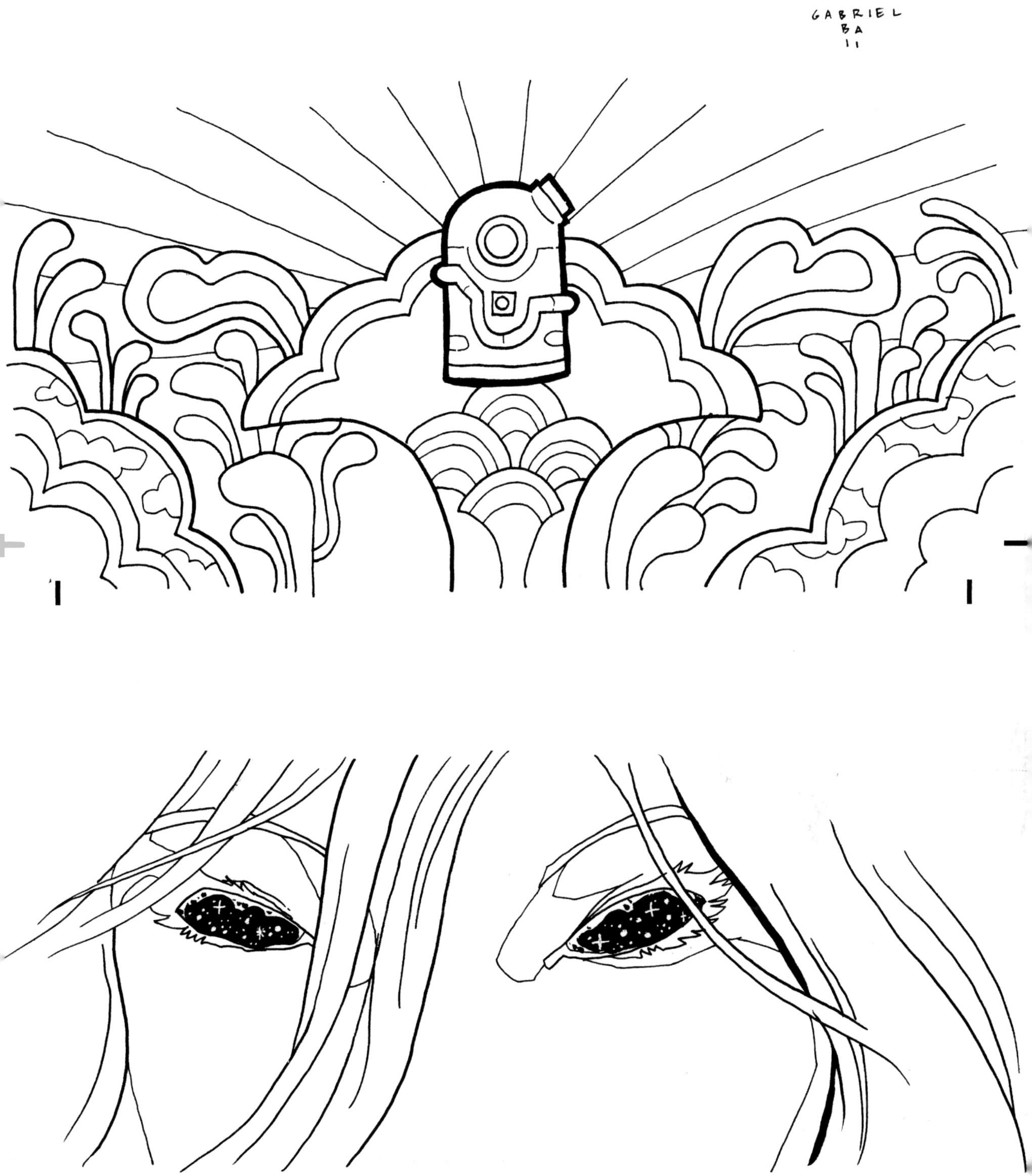
GABRIEL
BA
11

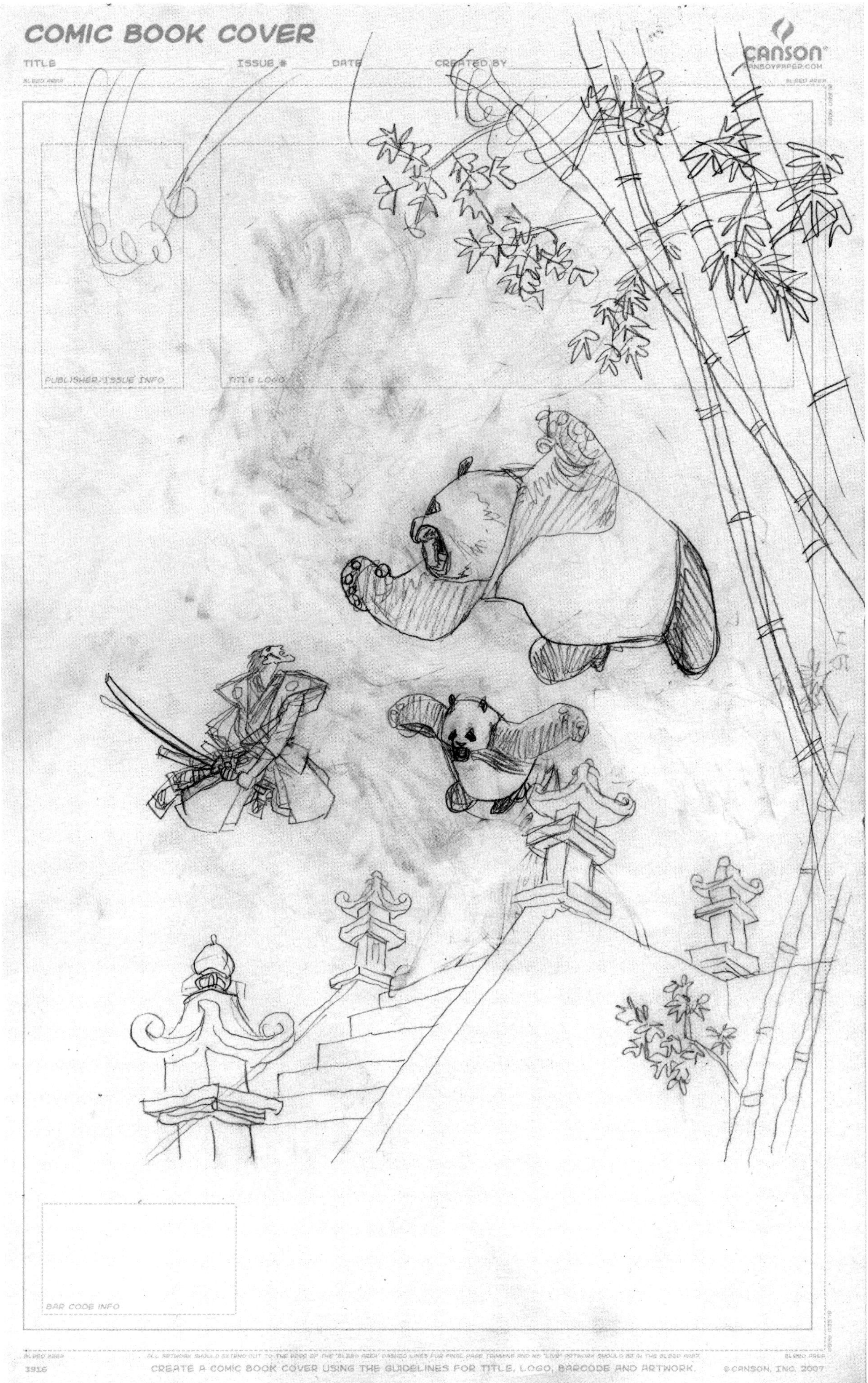
COMIC BOOK COVER
TITLE
ISSUE #
DATE
CREATED BY
CANSON®
FANBOYPAPER.COM
BLEED AREA
PUBLISHER/ISSUE INFO
TITLE LOGO
BAR CODE INFO
ALL ARTWORK SHOULD EXTEND OUT TO THE EDGE OF THE "BLEED AREA" DASHED LINES FOR FINAL PAGE TRIMMING AND NO "LIVE" ARTWORK SHOULD BE IN THE BLEED AREA
3916
CREATE A COMIC BOOK COVER USING THE GUIDELINES FOR TITLE, LOGO, BARCODE AND ARTWORK.
©CANSON, INC. 2007

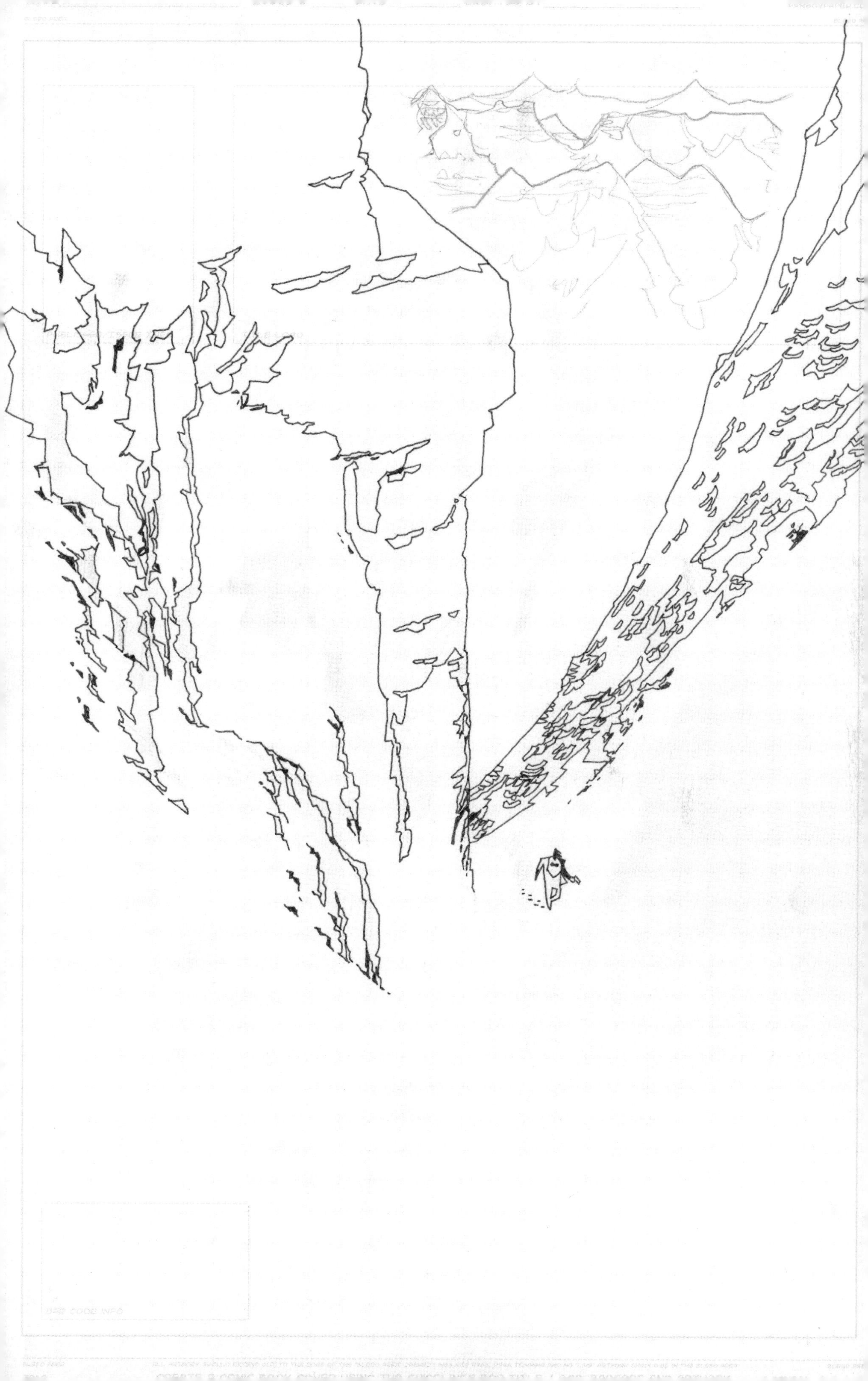
BAR CODE INFO

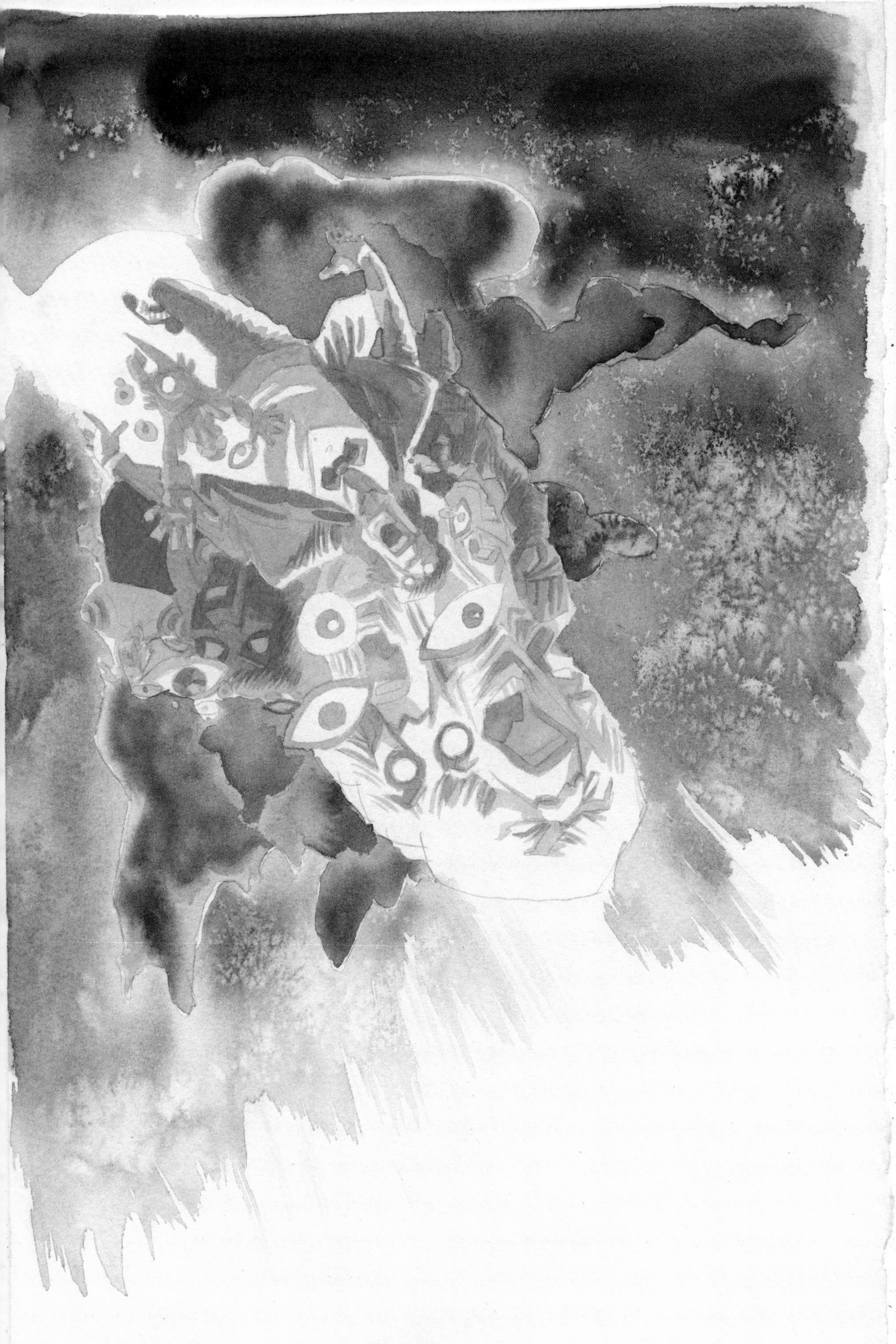

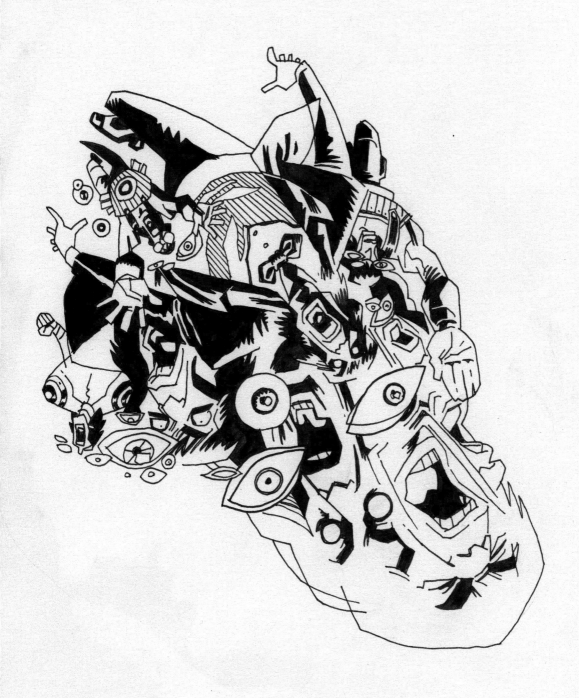

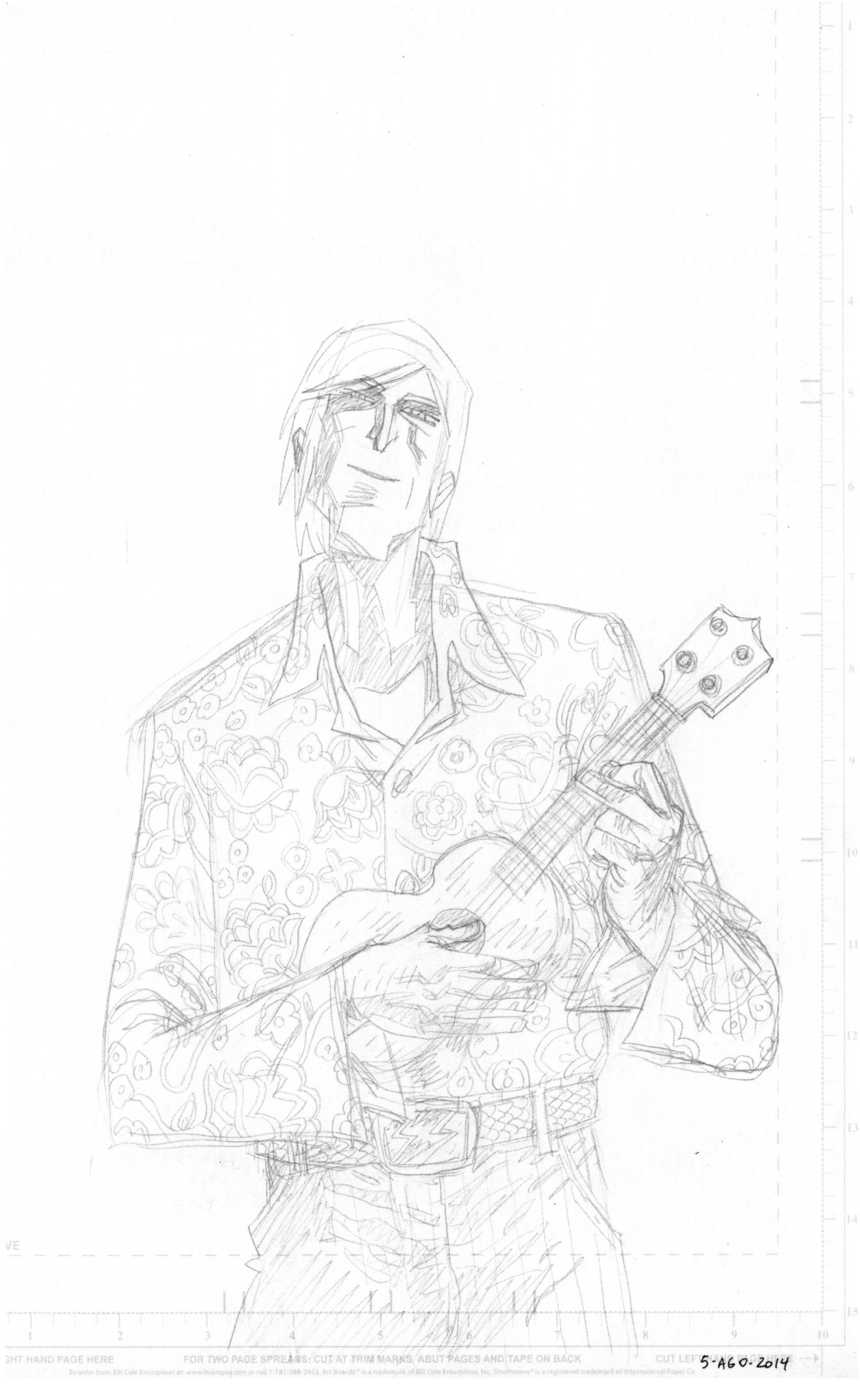
FOR TWO PAGE SPREADS- CUT AT TRIM MARKS, ABUT PAGES AND TAPE ON BACK
5-AGO-2014

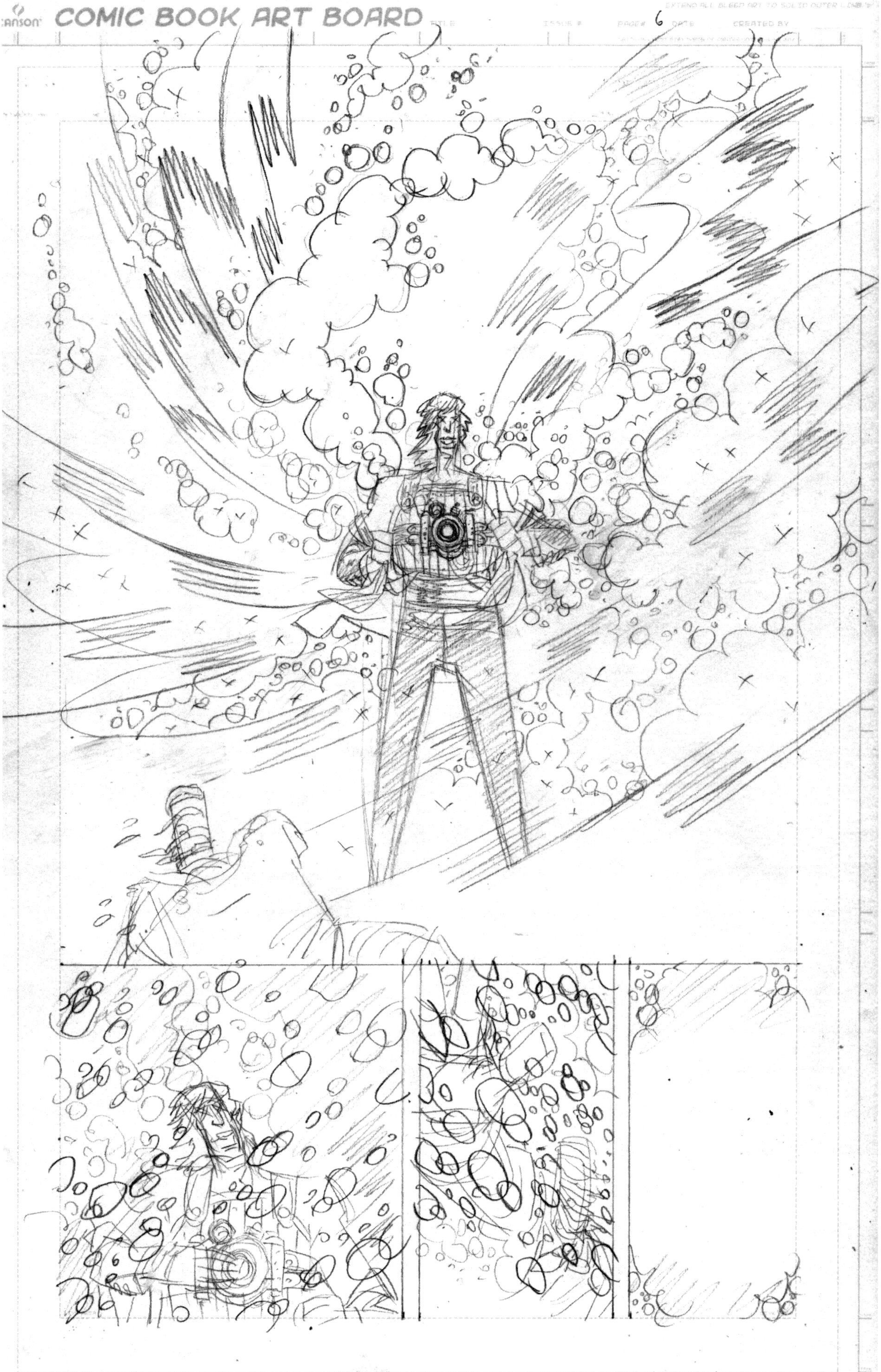
canson
COMIC BOOK ART BOARD
6
8-FEV-2011
FANBOYPAPER.COM ©CANSON, INC. 2007

Canson COMIC BOOK ART BOARD TITLE ISSUE # PAGE# 11 DATE CREATED BY

EXTEND ALL BLEED ART TO SOLID OUTER LINE

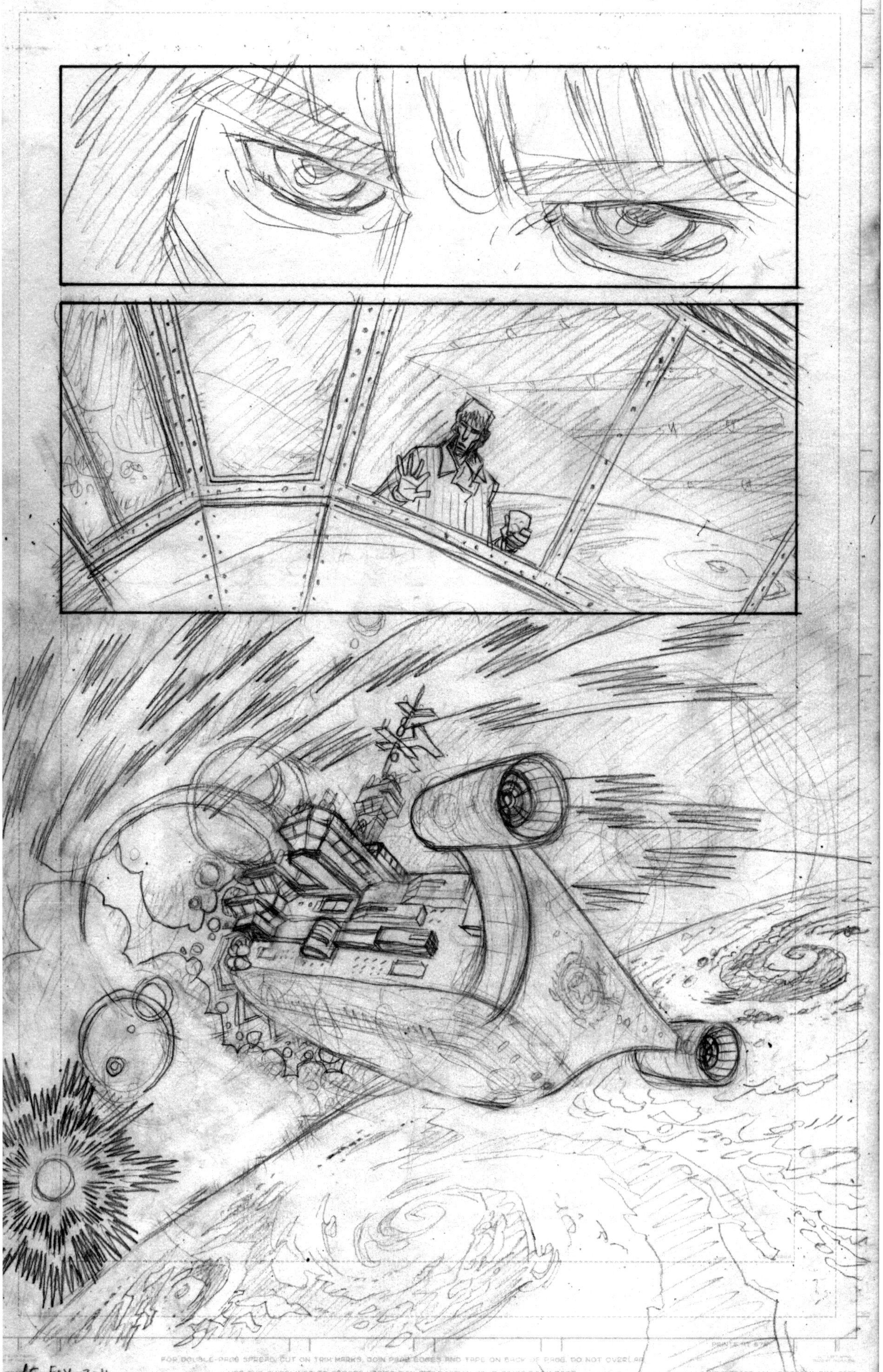

FOR DOUBLE-PAGE SPREAD, CUT ON TRIM MARKS, JOIN PAGE EDGES AND TAPE ON BACK OF PAGE. DO NOT OVERLAP

USE THE GUIDELINES TO CREATE VARIED BOX SIZES WITHIN YOUR COMIC BOOK PAGE

15-FEV-2011

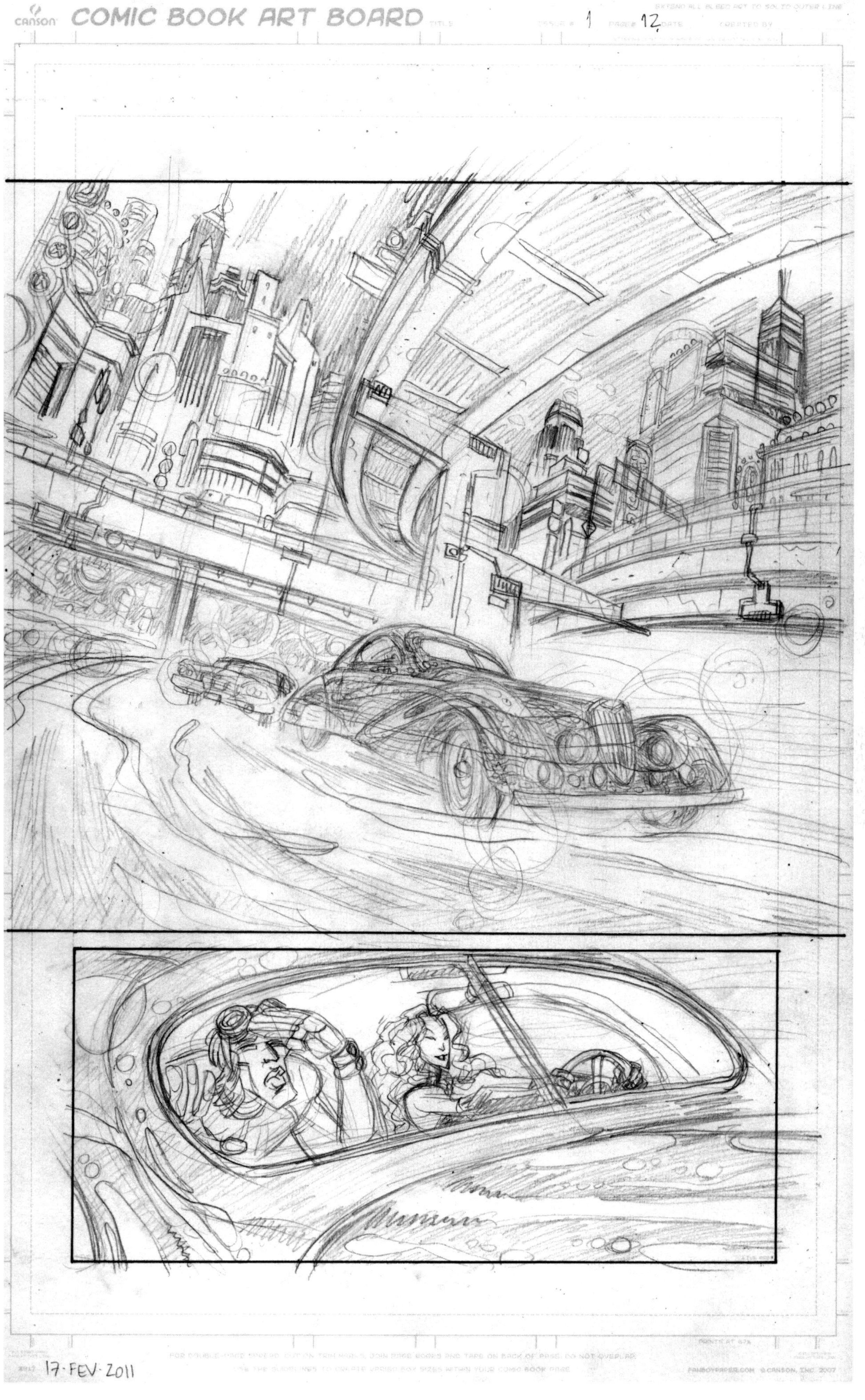

canson
COMIC BOOK ART BOARD
TITLE
ISSUE # 1
PAGE# 12
DATE
CREATED BY
EXTEND ALL BLEED ART TO SOLID OUTER LINE
17·FEV·2011
FANBOYPAPER.COM ©CANSON, INC. 2007

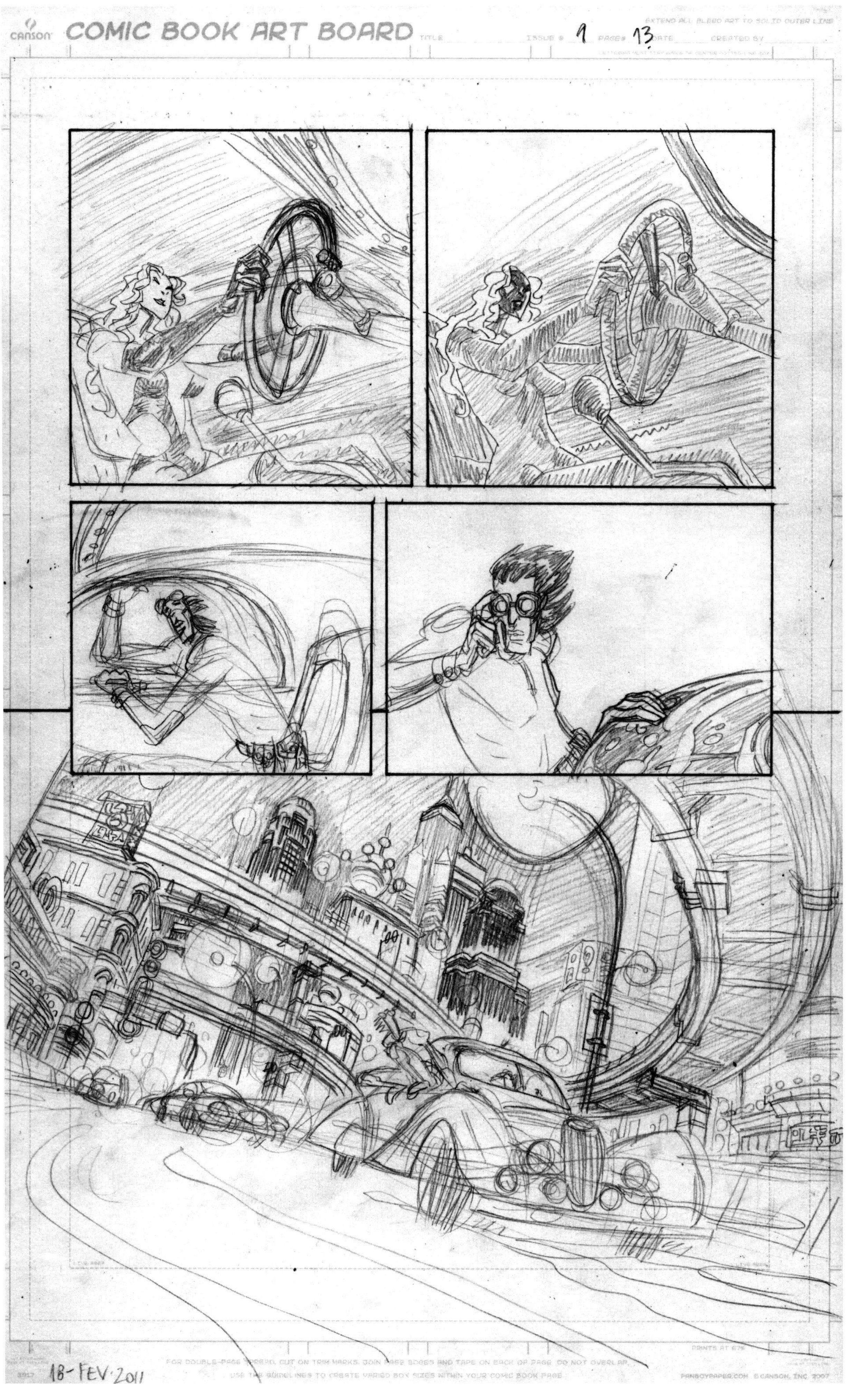

18-FEV-2011

CASANOVA: AVARITIA #2 P1

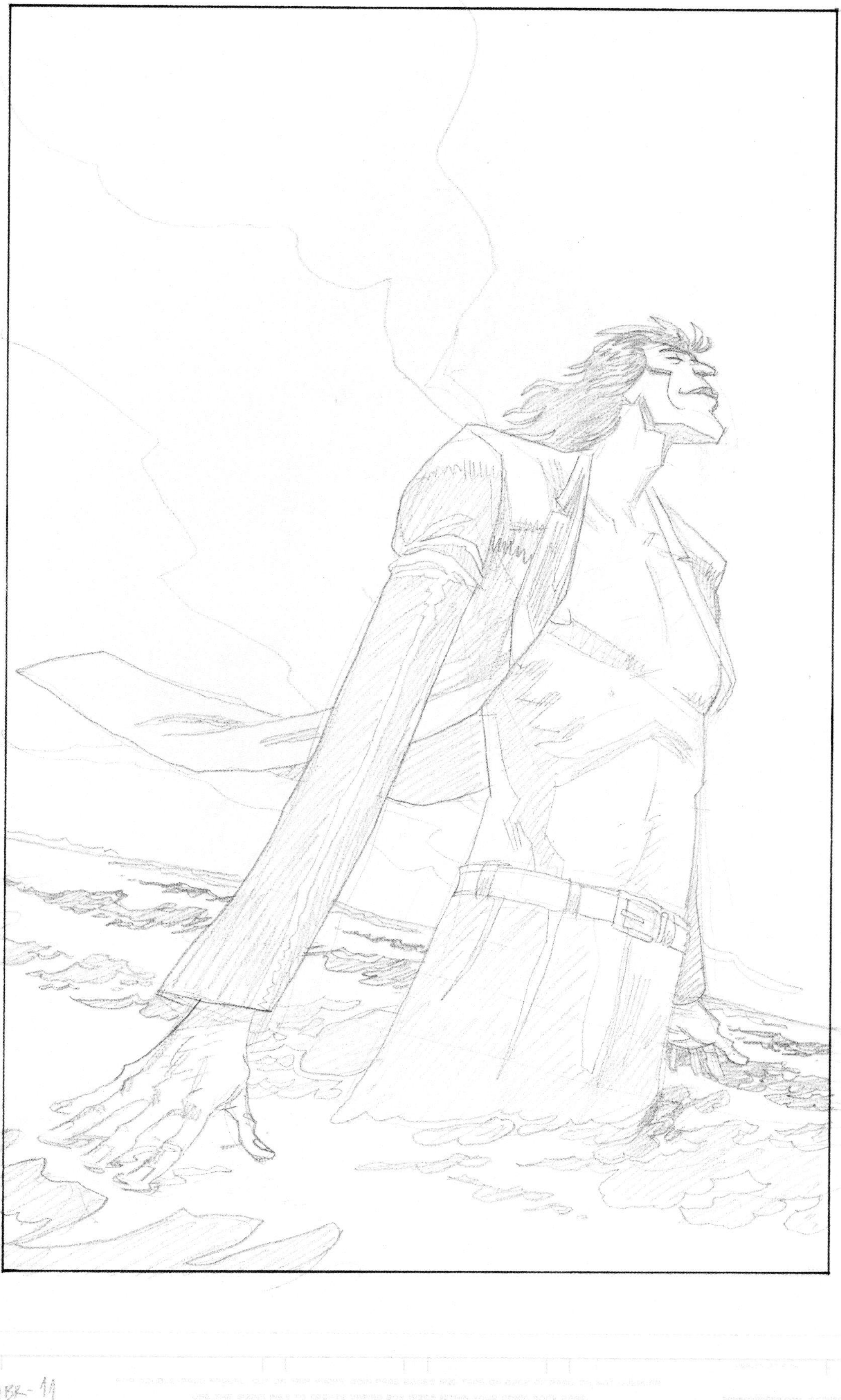

5-ABR-11

COMIC BOOK ART BOARD 2 25

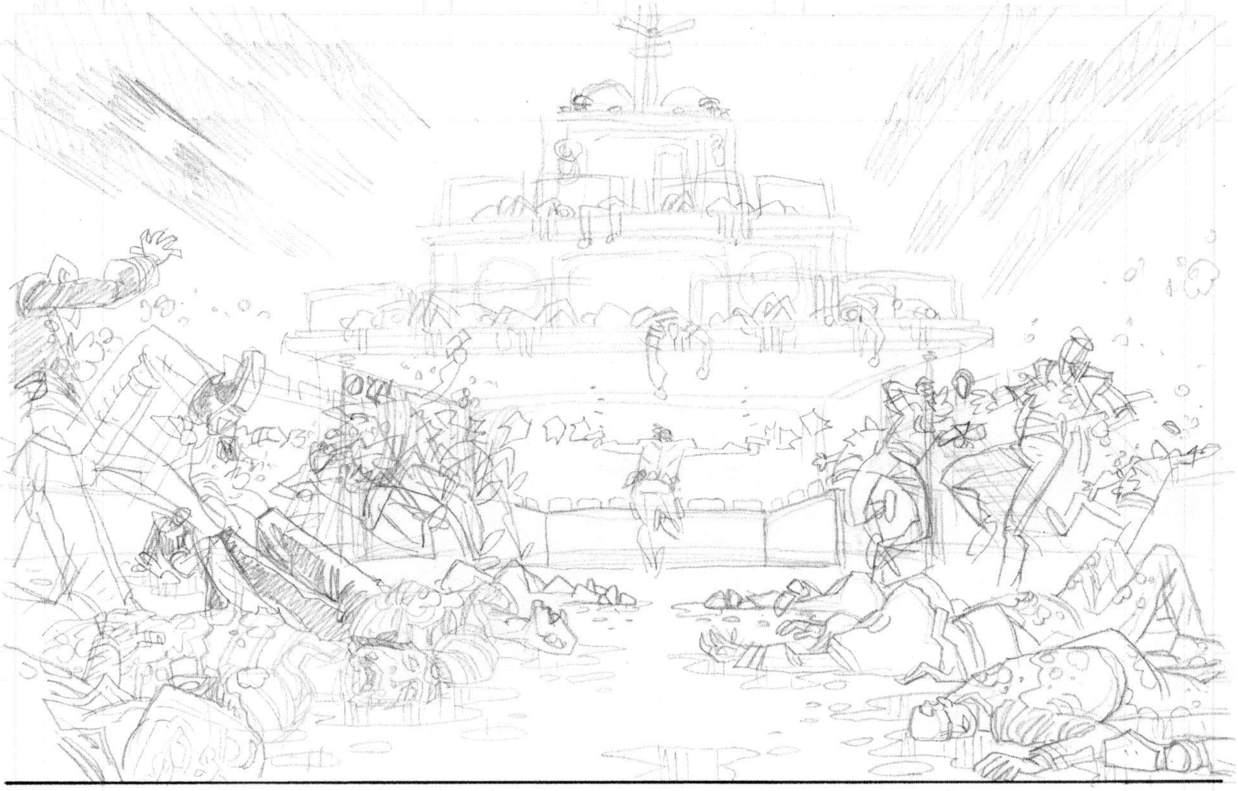

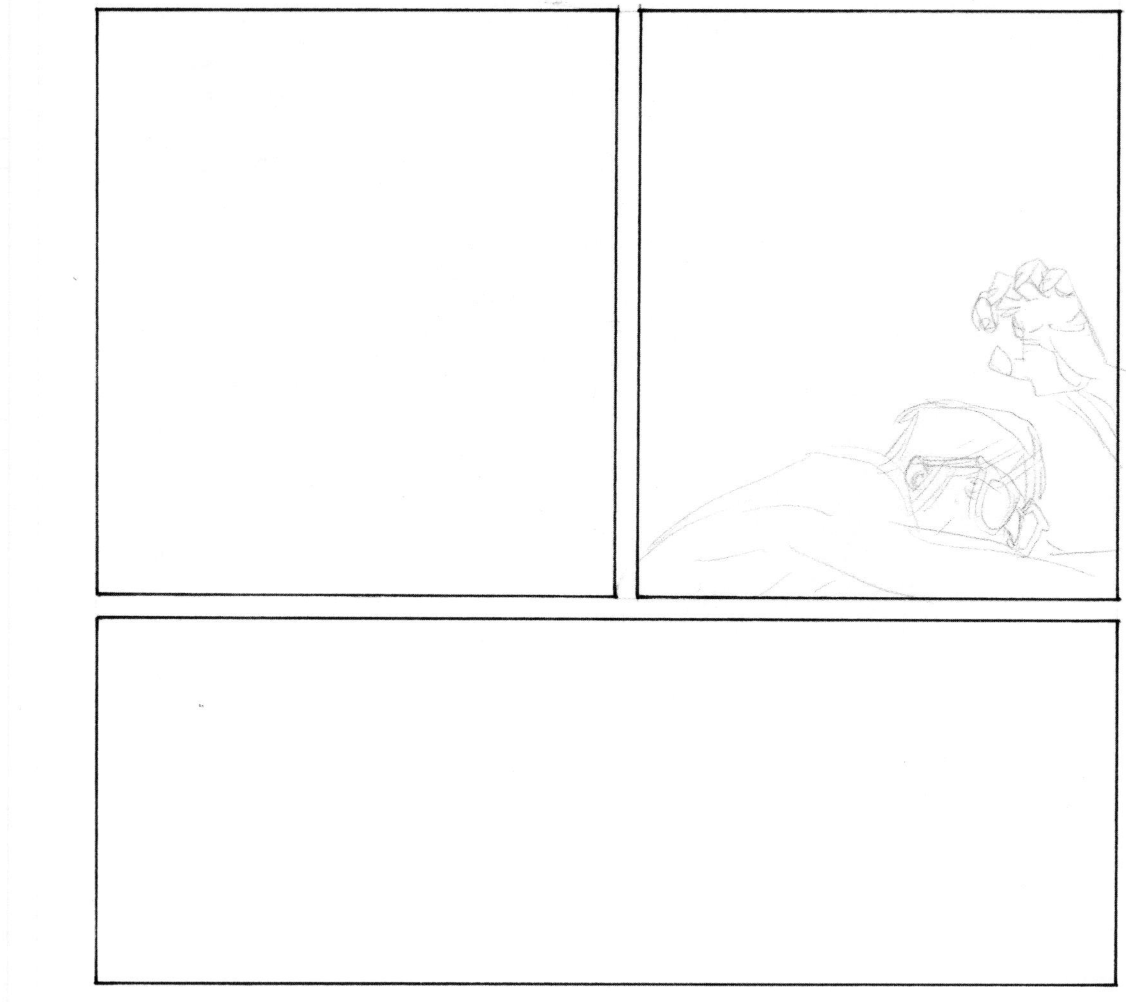

CANSON® COMIC BOOK ART BOARD TITLE ISSUE # 2 PAGE 32 DATE CREATED BY

EXTEND ALL BLEED ART TO SOLID OUTER LINE

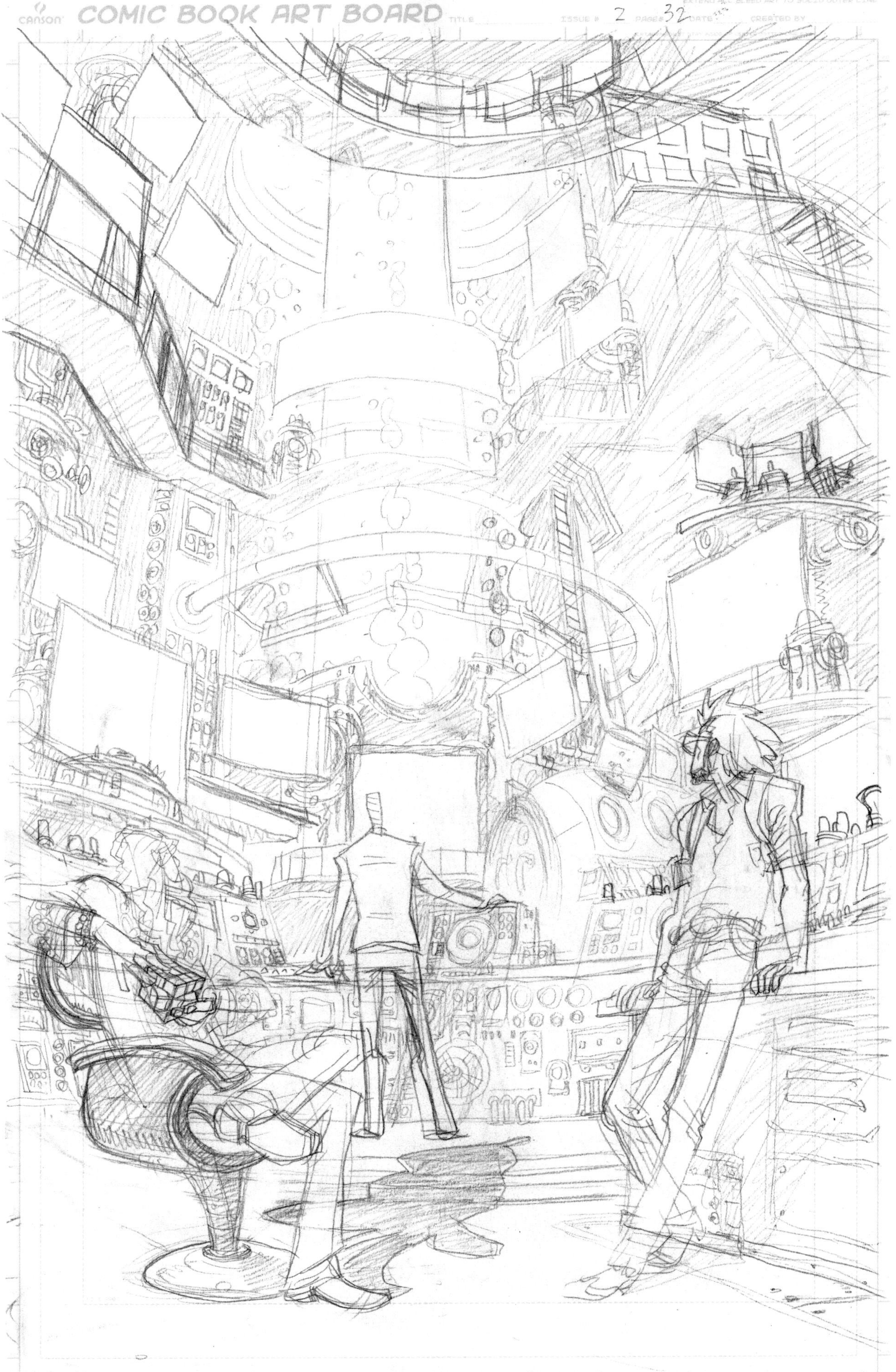

FOR DOUBLE PAGE SPREAD, CUT ON TRIM MARKS, JOIN PAGE EDGES AND TAPE ON BACK OF PAGE. DO NOT OVERLAP

USE THE GUIDELINES TO CREATE VARIED BOX SIZES WITHIN YOUR COMIC BOOK PAGE

25-6-2011

CASANOVA: AVARITIA #3 P01

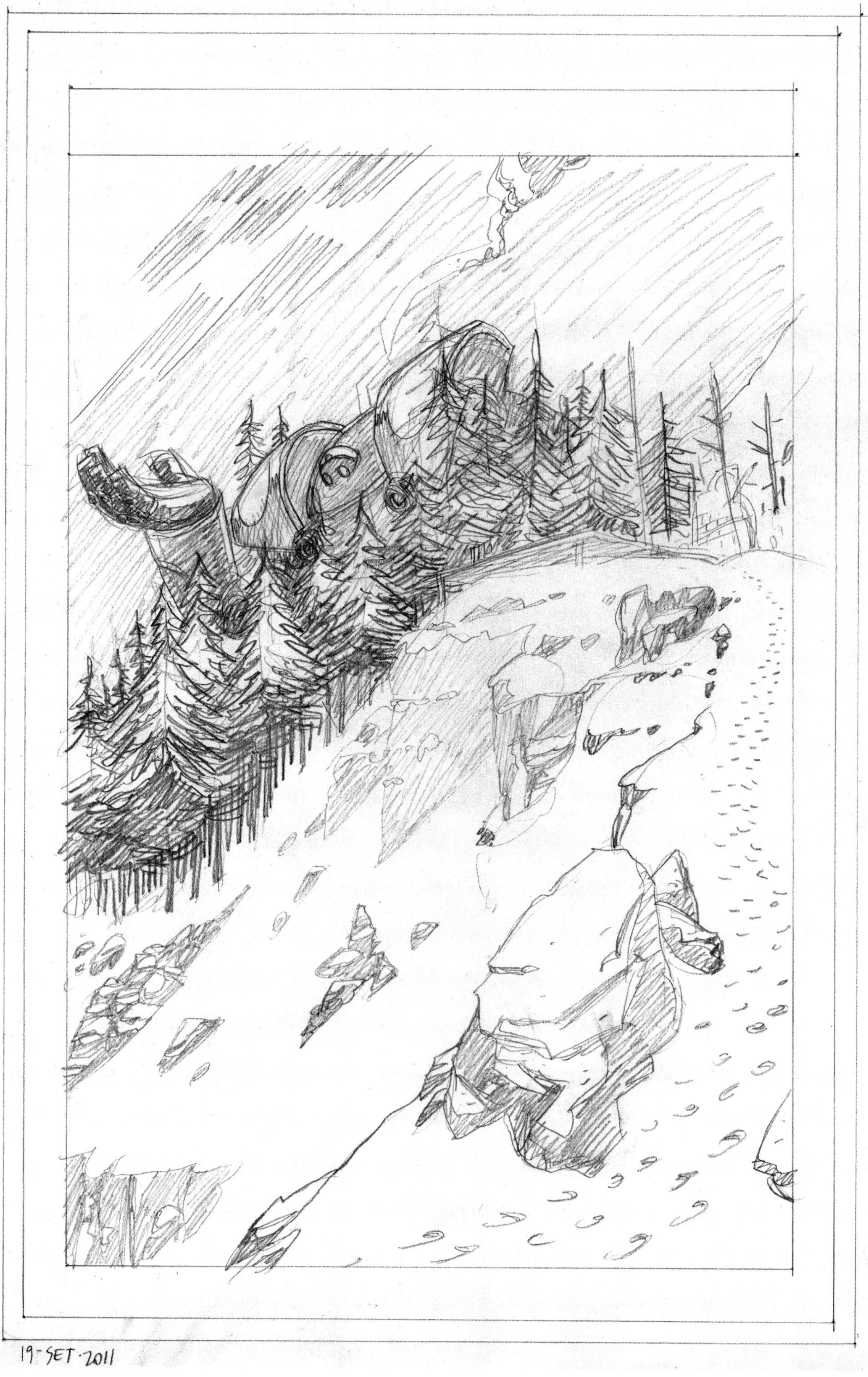

19-SET-2011

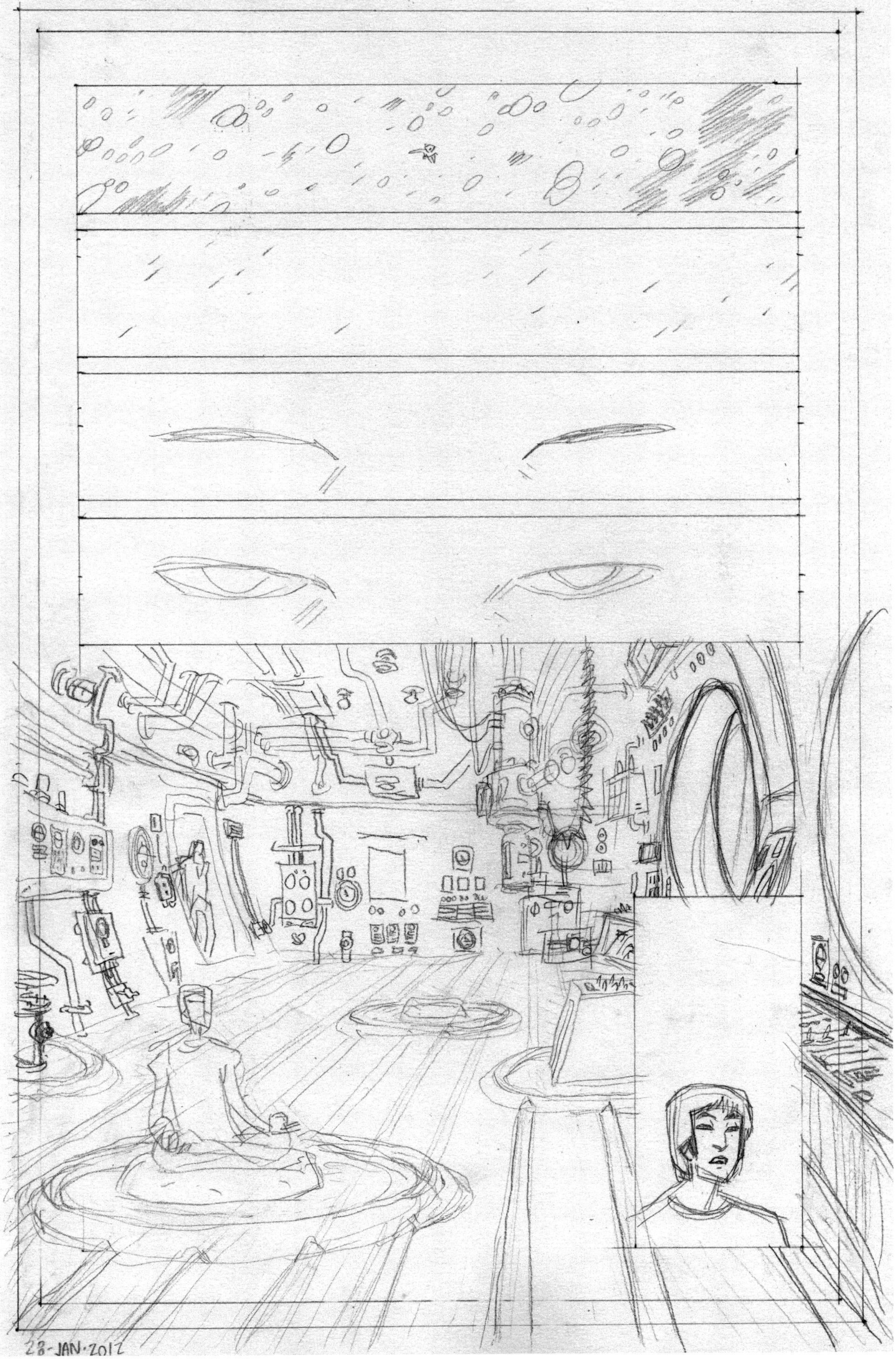

28-JAN-2012

CASANOVA: AVARITIA III P. 25

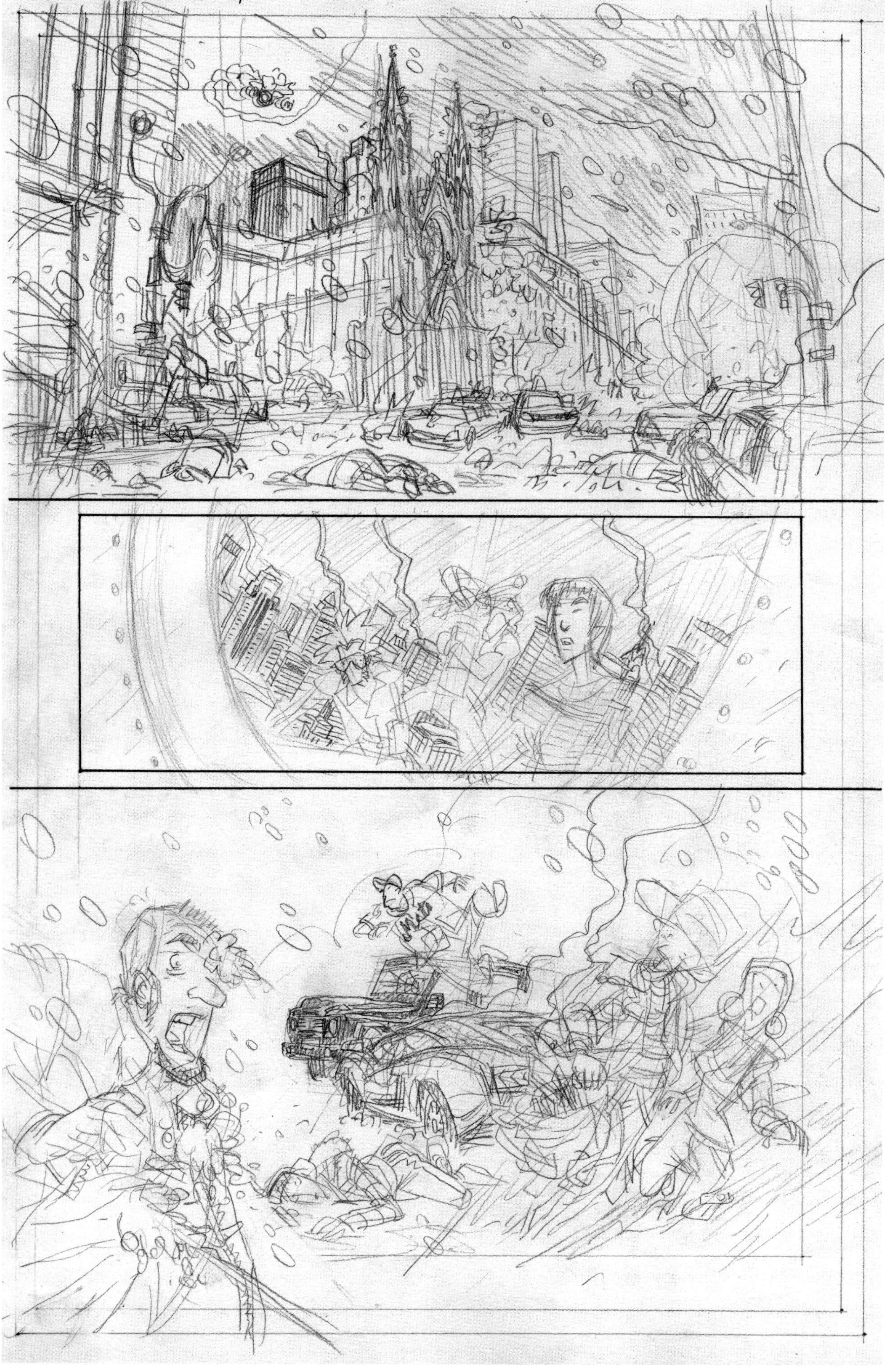

CASANOVA: AVARITIA III P. 29

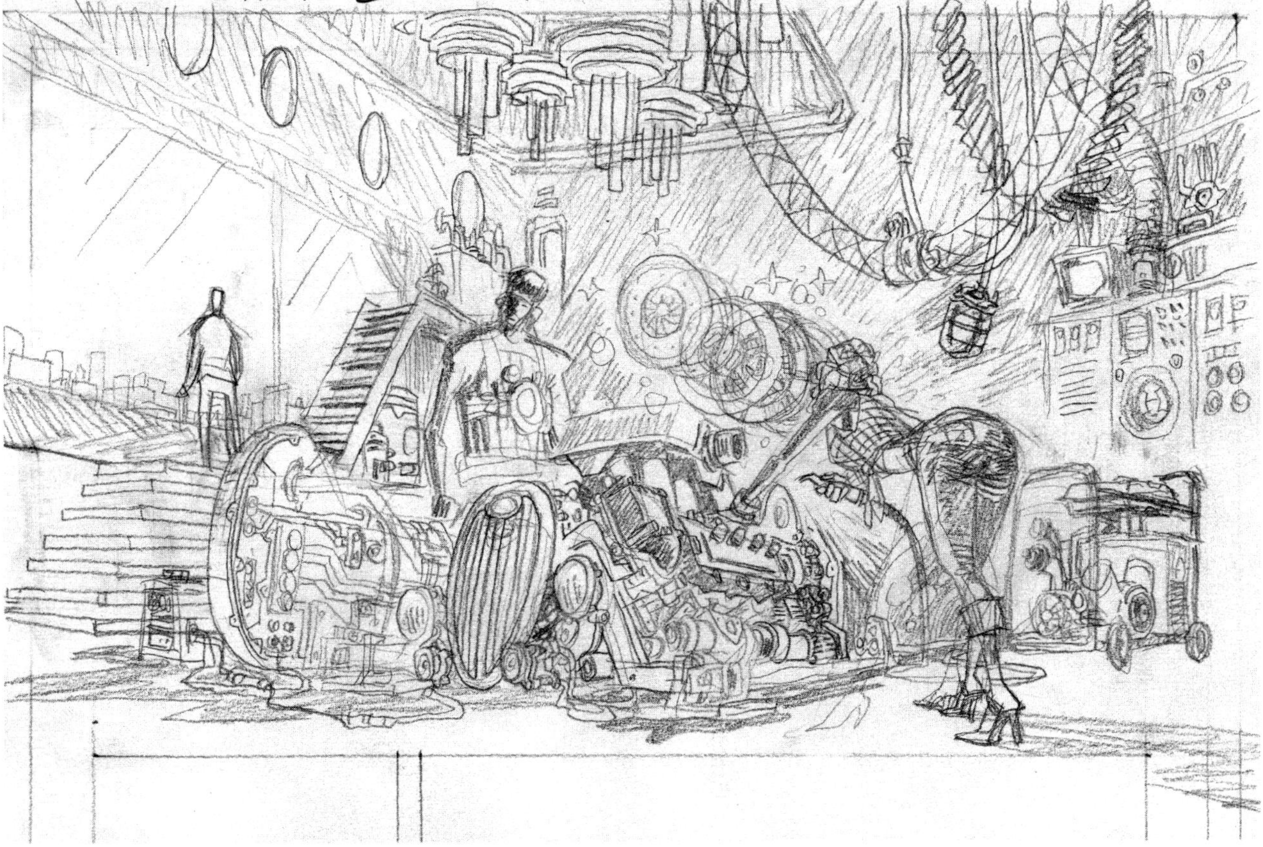

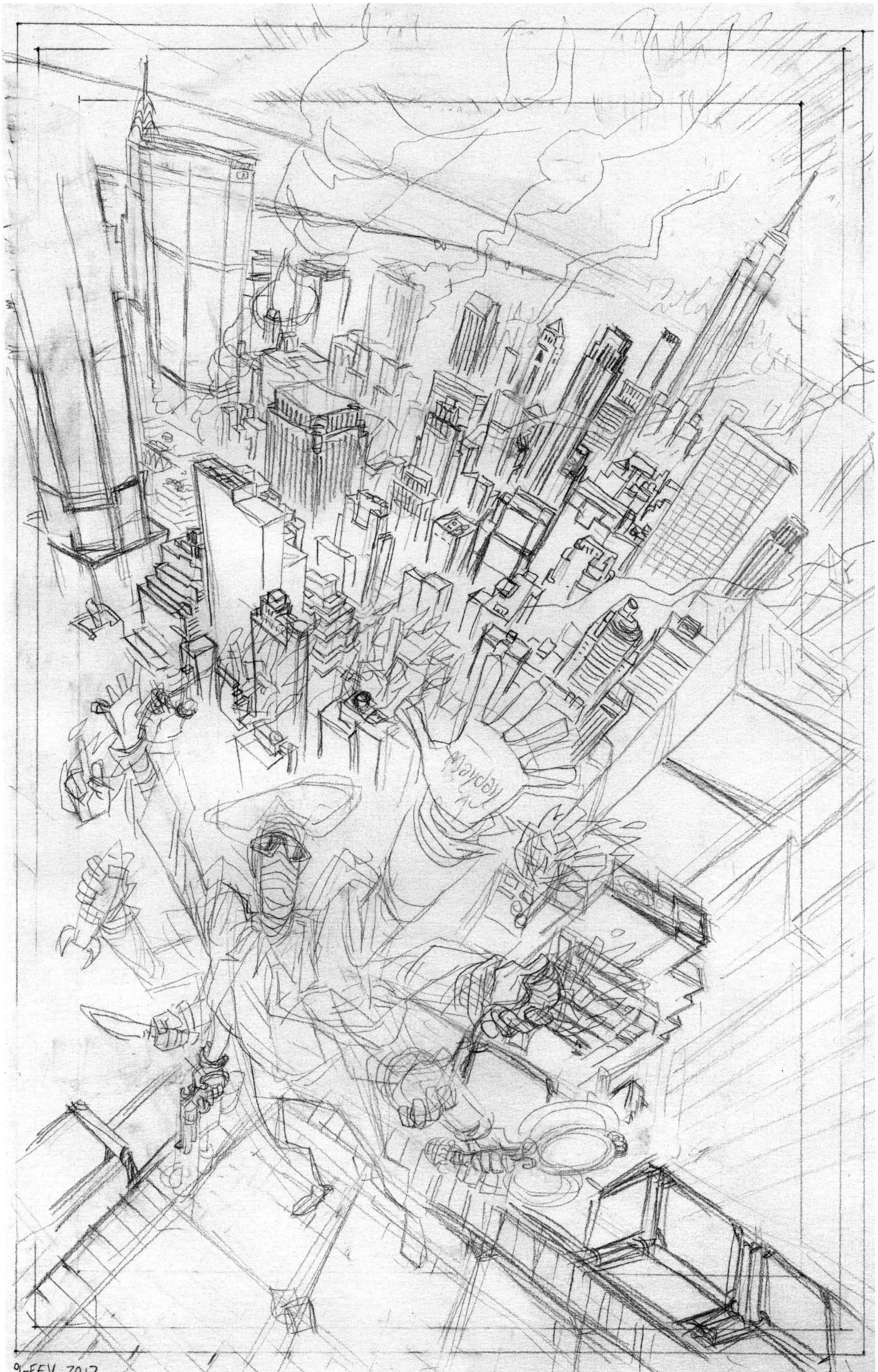
Mayday

9-FEV-2012

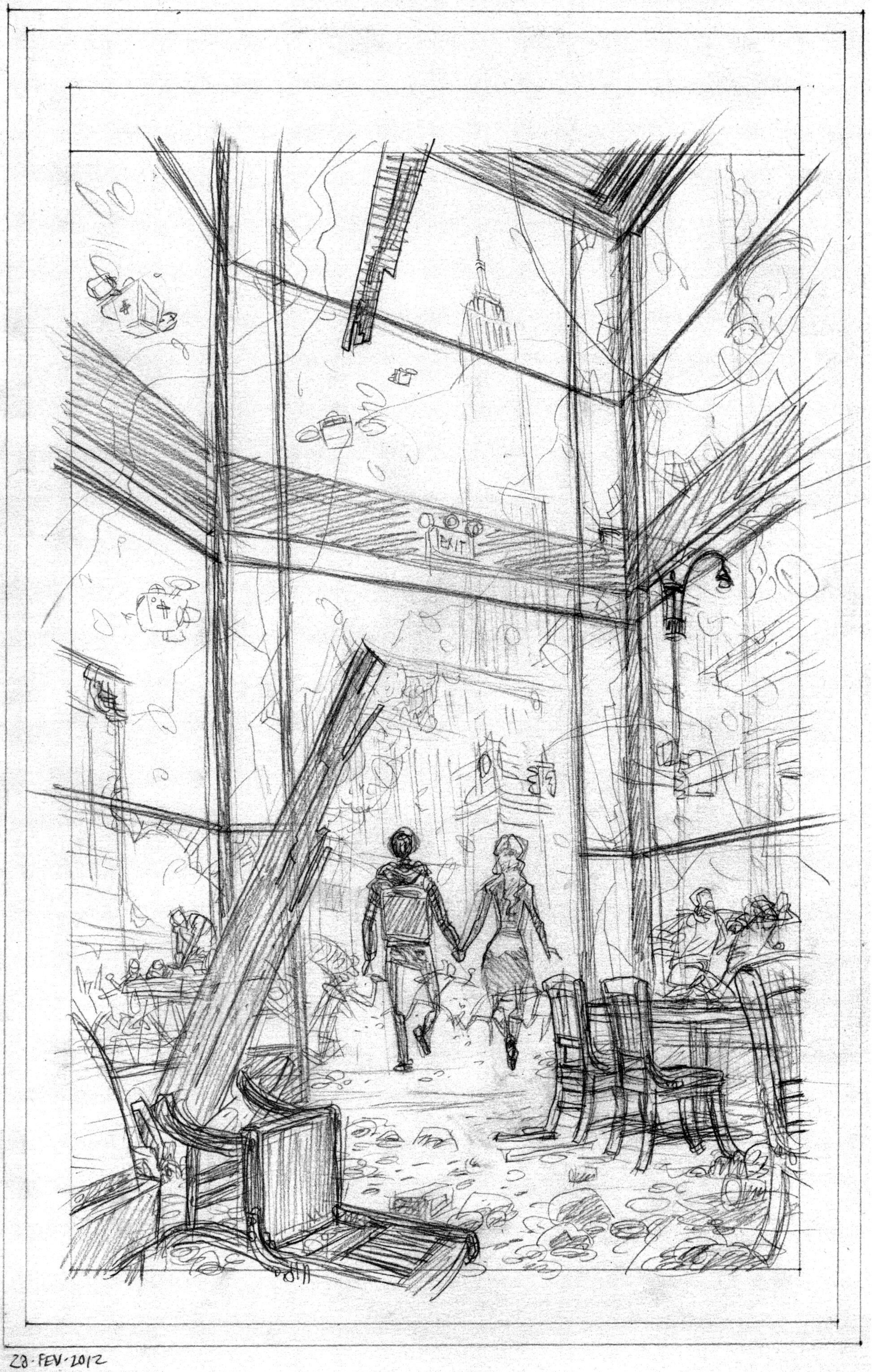
EXIT

28·FEV·2012

CASANOVA: AVARITIA IV PG. 11

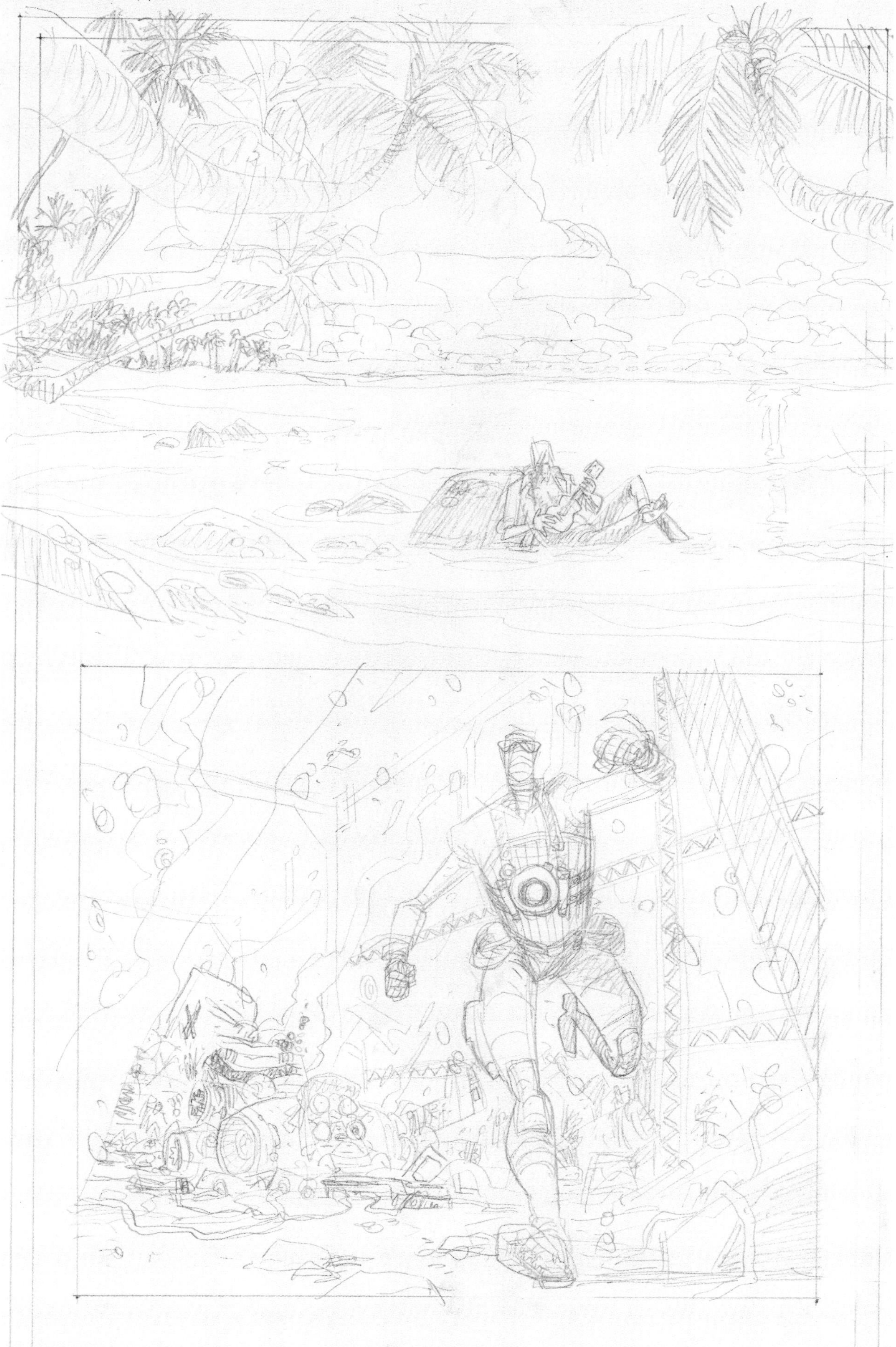

26-MAR-2012

CASANOVA: AVARITIA IV P.15

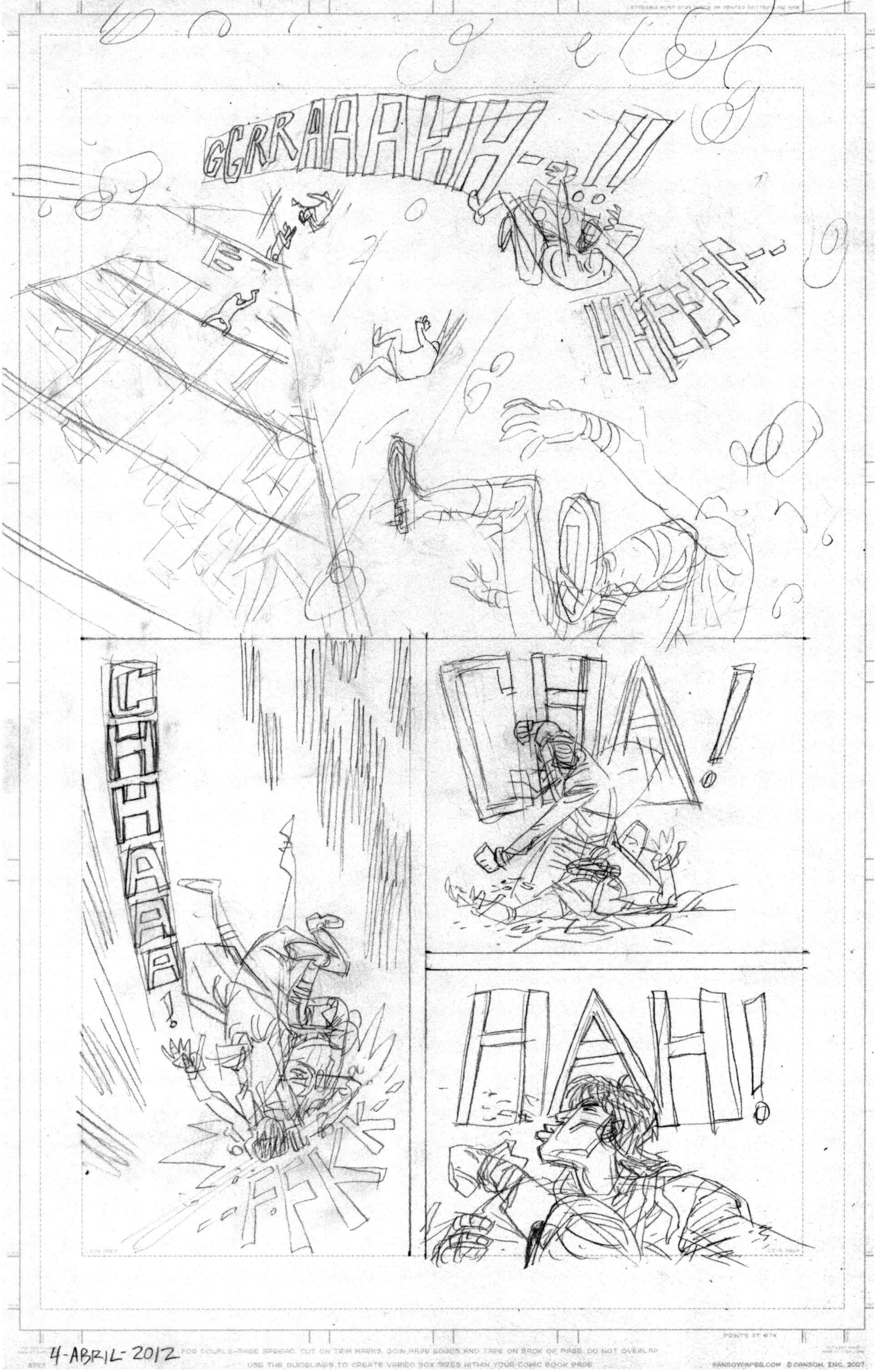
GGRRAAAHH--!!
HHEEFF--
CHHHAAAA!
CHA!
HAH!

4-ABRIL-2012

CANSON CASANOVA: AVARITIA IV COMIC BOOK ART BOARD TITLE ISSUE # PAGE # P.16 DATE CREATED BY

EXTEND ALL BLEED ART TO SOLID OUTER LINE

LETTERING MUST STAY INSIDE OF CENTER DOTTED LINE BOX

WHOOP
HAH!
YOINK!

PRINTS AT 67%

4-ABR-2012

FOR DOUBLE-PAGE SPREAD, CUT ON TRIM MARKS, JOIN PAGE EDGES AND TAPE ON BACK OF PAGE. DO NOT OVERLAP.

USE THE GUIDELINES TO CREATE VARIED BOX SIZES WITHIN YOUR COMIC BOOK PAGE.

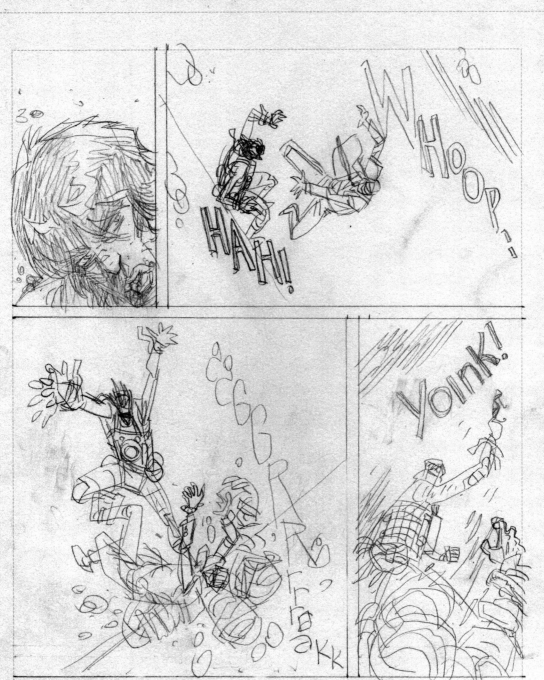

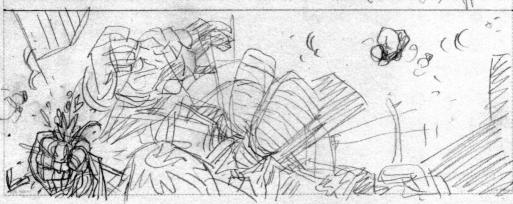

CASANOVA: AVARITIA IV ART BOARD TITLE ISSUE # P 17 DATE CREATED BY

EXTEND ALL BLEED ART TO SOLID OUTER LINE

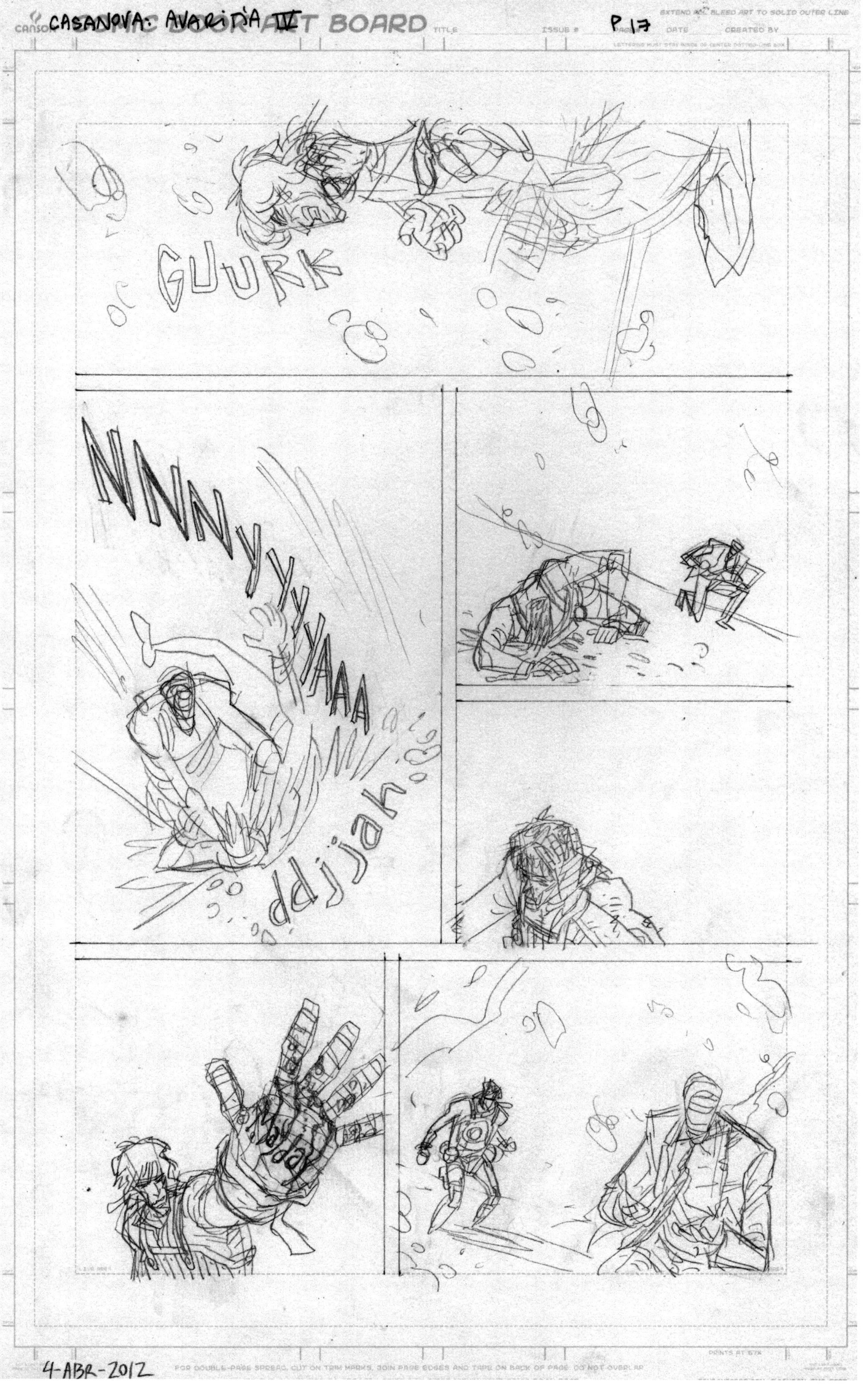
GUURK
NNNyyyYAAA
ddjak

4-ABR-2012

FOR DOUBLE-PAGE SPREAD, CUT ON TRIM MARKS, JOIN PAGE EDGES AND TAPE ON BACK OF PAGE. DO NOT OVERLAP

PRINTS AT 67%

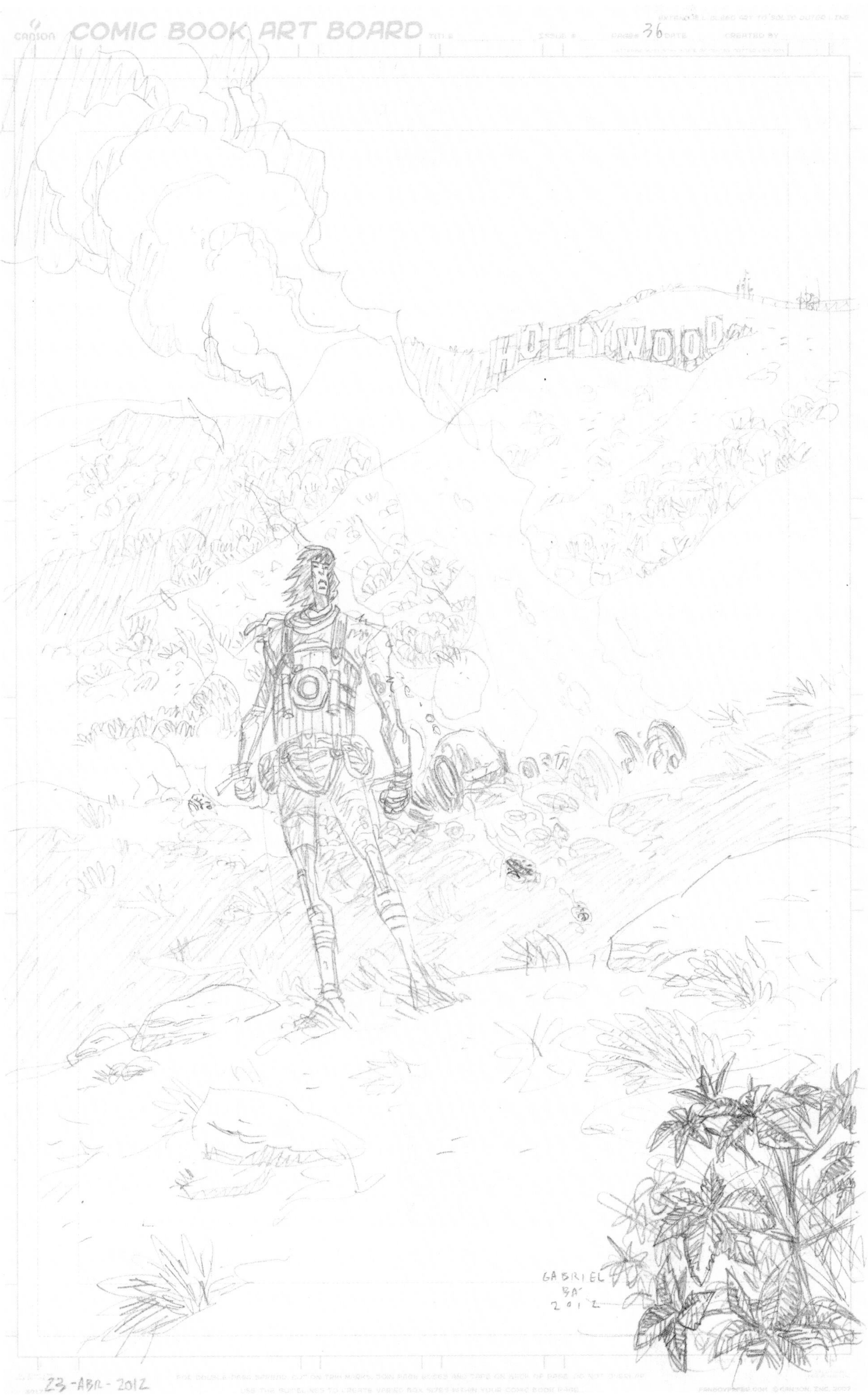
COMIC BOOK ART BOARD
36
HOLLYWOOD
GABRIEL BÁ 2012
23-ABR-2012

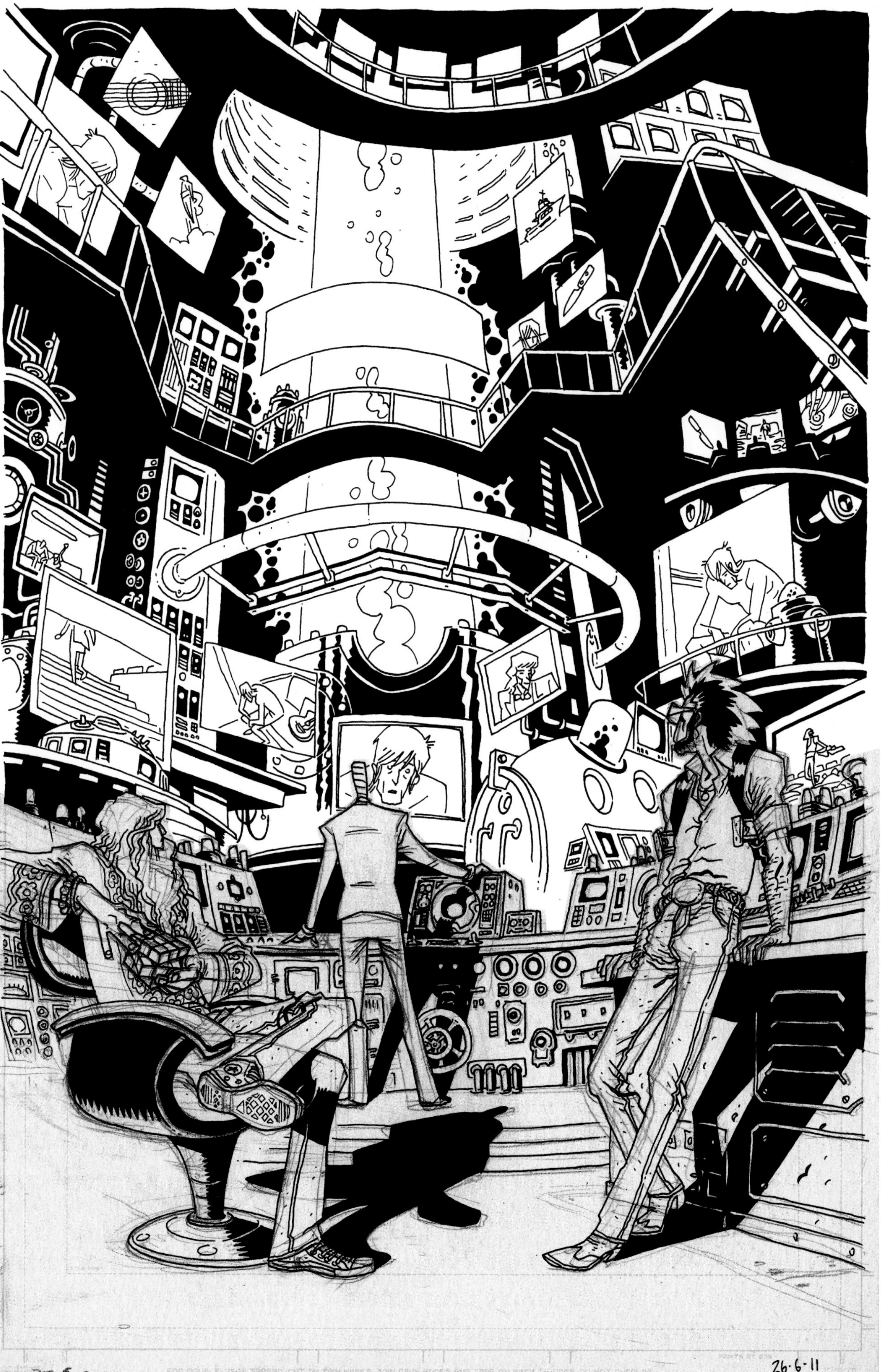

25-6-2011 26-6-11

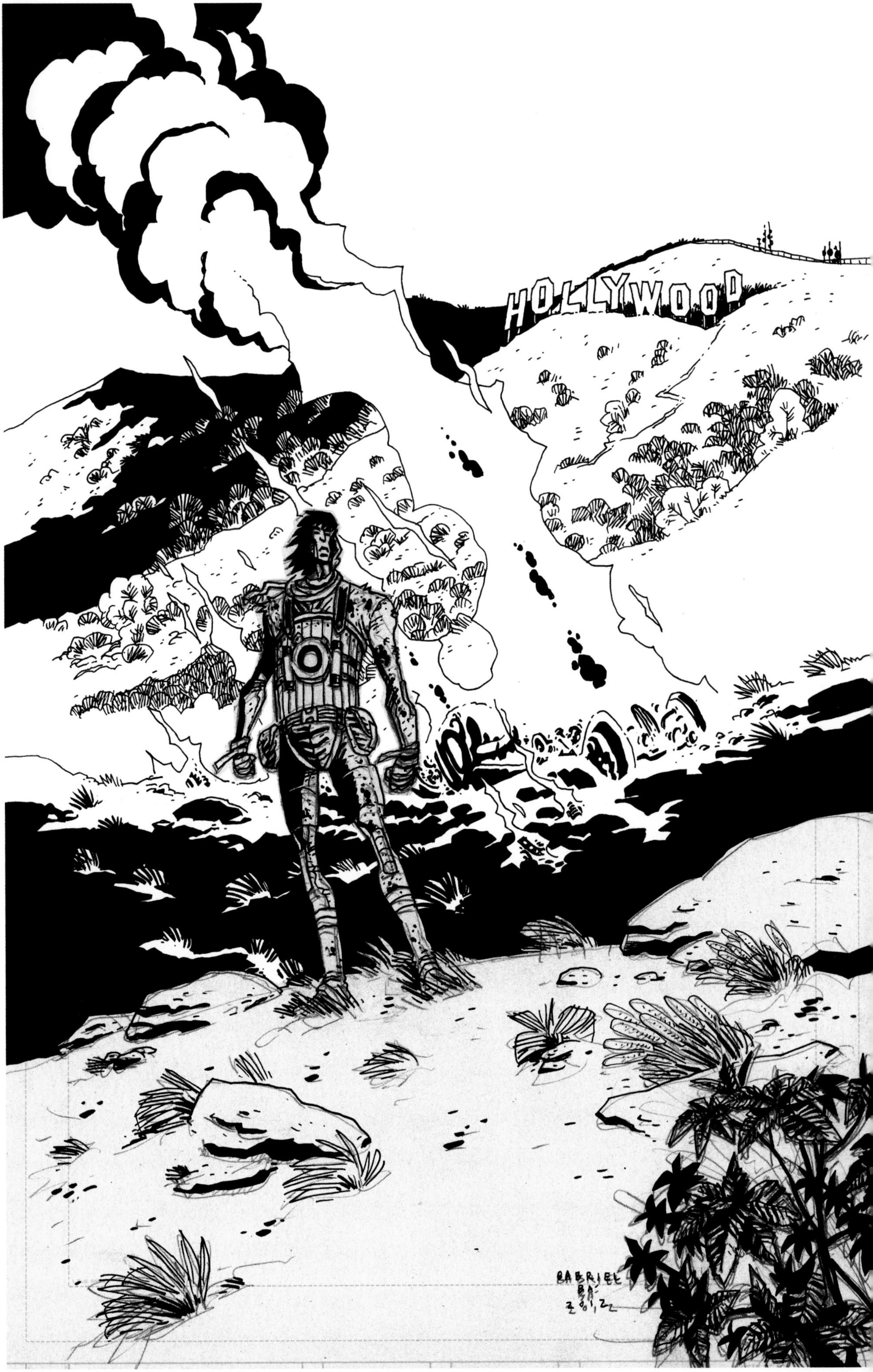
HOLLYWOOD
GABRIEL BÁ 2012

TEAM CASANOVA HONOR ROLL

Alejandro ARBONA　　Editor, CASANOVA: LUXURIA, GULA, AVARITIA (Icon Comics reprints and collections, 2010-2012)

Érico ASSIS　　Translation: CASANOVA: LUXURIA, GULA (Panini Comics, Brazil edition, 2012, 2014)

Estudio FENIX　　Design Group, CASANOVA: LUJURIA (Panini Comics Spain edition, 2011)

Drew GILL　　Designer, CASANOVA: LUXURIA (Image Comics collections, 2008, 2014)

Jennifer GRÜNWALD　　Designer, LUXURIA, GULA, AVARITIA (Icon Comics reprints and collections, 2010-2012), spare Russian bits, salvage and recovery

Gina KAUFMANN　　French bits and obscenities, CASANOVA: LUXURIA (Image Comics edition, 2006-2007)

Sean KONOT　　Letterer, CASANOVA: LUXURIA (Image Comics edition, 2006-2007)

Laurenn McCUBBIN　　Designer, CASANOVA: LUXURIA issues, hardcover & softcover (Image Comics edition)

Willem MEERLOO　　Designer, CASANOVA: LUXURIA (Urban Comics France edition, 2012)

Harris MILLER III　　Team CASANOVA representation, 2007-2013

Ben RADATZ　　E.M.P.I.R.E., W.A.S.T.E., and X.S.M. logo design (2006)

Marco RICOMPENSA　　Supervision, CASANOVA: LUXURIA, GULA, AVARITIA (Panini Comics Italy editions, 2011-2013)

Benjamin RIVIÉRE　　Translation, CASANOVA: LUXURIA (Urban Comics France edition, 2012)

Raúl SASTRE　　Translation, CASANOVA: LUJURIA (Panini Comics Spain edition, 2011)

Rosie SHARP　　Backmatter transcription, general bedlam (2014)

Andrea TOSCANI　　Translation, CASANOVA: LUXURIA, GULA, AVARITIA (Panini Comics Italy editions, 2011-2013)

Lucia TRUCCONE　　Letterer, LUXURIA, GULA, AVARITIA (Panini Comics Italy editions, 2011-2013)

Steve WACKER　　Senior Editor, LUXURIA, GULA, AVARITIA (Icon Comics reprints and collections, 2010-2012)

Eric STEPHENSON　　Patron Saint

Warren ELLIS　　Patron Sinner

Matt Fraction writes comic books out in the woods and lives with his wife, the writer Kelly Sue DeConnick, his two children, a dog, a cat, a bearded dragon, and a yard full of coyotes and stags. ***SYMBOLISM***. He won the first-ever PEN USA Literary Award for Graphic Novels; he, or comics he's a part of, have won Eisners, Harveys, and Eagles, which are like the Oscars, Emmys, and Golden Globes of comic books and all seem about as likely. He's a *New York Times*-best-selling donkus of comics like *Sex Criminals* (winner of the 2014 Will Eisner Award for Best New Series, the 2014 Harvey Award for Best New Series, and named *TIME Magazine*'s Best Comic of 2013), *Satellite Sam*, *ODY-C*, *Hawkeye* (winner of the 2014 Will Eisner Award for Best Single Issue), and, oh, lordy, so many more. He typed this while non-ironically drinking out of a coffee mug with "Cool Guy" written on it.

Gabriel Bá lives in Brazil. He loves comic books in all forms and shapes and believes everything is possible in comics. But even so, he doesn't see enough comics doing everything that's possible to be done. He truly believes there's still a lot to be done and he thinks this is an incredibly exciting challenge. He worked alongside great professionals like Gerard Way, Mike Mignola, Brian Azzarelo, Matt Fraction (yeah, you) and, most regularly, his twin brother, Fábio Moon. His comics have won awards and a lot of people love them. Well, he loves them too. His work has been published in 13 languages, although he only speaks four of them.

PA-ZOW!